Praise for *ValueWeb*

"Chris Skinner—one of the most authoritative voices on FinTech anywhere —has provided us another timely and thoughtful look into the fascinating convergence of technology, e-commerce, and finance that is changing the world. Ignore these trends and the insights here at your peril."

—*Seth Wheeler*
Brookings Guest Scholar and Former Special Assistant to
The President for Economic Policy at The White House

"Society is in the early stages of another financial revolution—one that is already changing the way we live and work. This book describes the fundamentals driving the processes at play, and will be an invaluable read for all interested in the way business works."

—*Sir Roger Gifford*
Former Lord Mayor of London and Ceo Seb Uk

"Global payments are ripe for disruptive innovation. Chris Skinner argues, persuasively, that the combined technologies of mobile connectivity and distributed ledgers could deliver just that disruption, for the benefits of billions of citizens."

—*Andrew G Haldane*
Chief Economist, Bank of England

"Financial services is up for huge disruption, most importantly from the blockchain revolution. Skinner's *ValueWeb* is a sweeping and well-researched analysis of the big technology trends that will shake the windows and rattle the walls of the industry."

—*Don Tapscott*
Best Selling Author, most recently with Alex Tapscott Blockchain Revolution

"Chris Skinner captures the maturing of FinTech in his book, *ValueWeb*. Not only does he define many of the FinTech buzz words from Blockchain to Value System Integrators, he gives real examples of practical application of the concepts. It's not surprising that he calls for innovation in traditional banking and points out the dead giveaway of anyone trying to fake it as a digital bank: First, you don't need a cross-channel organisation in a truly digital bank, and second, you never mention channel or omnichannel in a digital bank. He sums up what those enlightened in managing change have known all along, it all comes down to leadership. And that's my favourite part of this book, the leaders he profiles along the way."

—*Deanna Oppenheimer*
Former Vice Chair, Global Retail Banking, Barclays Bank

"Best insight into money in the 3rd industrial revolution, aka the digital revolution, you will read."

— Lawrence Wintermeyer
CEO, Innovate Finance

"In *ValueWeb*, Chris Skinner has brought to bear his long experience in financial services and technology to create a fascinating and comprehensive overview of the blurring of boundaries between them. The book describes how technology is disrupting traditional financial services by making transactions simpler and cheaper, and how banks must proactively leverage these trends to be future-ready."

— Chanda Kochhar
Managing Director and Chief Executive Officer, Icici Bank

"Chris has a great eye for the case studies and practical examples of innovation that help you to really reflect on where banking is going."

— David Birch
Director, Consult Hyperion

"A great follow-up to his best-seller *Digital Bank*, Chris Skinner provides an in-depth look at the exchange of value in an evolving digital universe. Through case studies, interviews and personal observations, Chris explains how the world is moving away from traditional currencies towards a ValueWeb. This is another must-read, not only for those interested in the world of FinTech, but anyone wanting to get a glimpse of a future where monetary and non-monetary transfers occur instantaneously across mobile and digital networks."

— Jim Marous
The Financial Brand/Digital Banking Report

"If I could only call one person when the FinTech apocalypse happens, Chris Skinner would be the person I would call. His huge depth of knowledge, coupled with his ability to summarise complex subjects into memorable and simple to understand chapters for this book, make it a must read for any bank wanting to know which way to dig."

— David M. Brear
Chief Thinker, Think Different Group

VALUE WEB

VALUE WEB

How Fintech firms are using mobile and blockchain
technologies to create the Internet of Value

CHRIS SKINNER
Author of the bestselling DIGITAL BANK

This book is published by Marshall Cavendish Business
Marshall Cavendish Business is an imprint of Marshall Cavendish International
1 New Industrial Road, Singapore 536196

All requests for permission should be addressed to the Publisher, Marshall Cavendish International (Asia) Private Limited, 1 New Industrial Road, Singapore 536196. Tel: (65) 6213 9300. E-mail: genrefsales@ sg.marshallcavendish.com. Website: www.marshallcavendish.com/genref

Other Marshall Cavendish Offices:
Marshall Cavendish Corporation. 99 White Plains Road, Tarrytown NY 10591-9001, USA • Marshall Cavendish International (Thailand) Co Ltd. 253 Asoke, 12th Flr, Sukhumvit 21 Road, Klongtoey Nua, Wattana, Bangkok 10110, Thailand • Marshall Cavendish (Malaysia) Sdn Bhd, Times Subang, Lot 46, Subang Hi-Tech Industrial Park, Batu Tiga, 40000 Shah Alam, Selangor Darul Ehsan, Malaysia

Marshall Cavendish is a trademark of Times Publishing Limited

National Library Board, Singapore Cataloguing-in-Publication Data

Names: Skinner, Chris.
Title: Valueweb : how Fintech firms are using mobile and blockchain technologies to create the Internet of Value / Chris Skinner.
Description: Singapore : Marshall Cavendish Business, [2016]
Identifiers: OCN 930303368 | ISBN 978-981-46-7717-2 (hardcover)
Subjects: LCSH: Electronic funds transfer. | Banks and banking--Technological innovations. | Internet banking.
Classification: LCC HG1601 | DDC 332.178--dc23

Printed in Singapore by Markono Print Media Pte Ltd

CONTENTS

INTRODUCTION

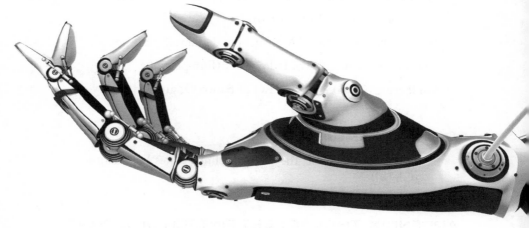

After writing *Digital Bank* in 2013, I turned to other ideas, since that book was primarily about the challenge faced by banks to adapt to new technology. For those who are unaware, the key premise of *Digital Bank* is that a bank must be built for the internet age. That means transforming the structures built in the last century for the physical distribution of paper in a localised, physical network, and reconstructing operations for the digital distribution of data in a globalised network based upon the internet. A digital bank is an internet-based bank, in other words.

In that book I first mentioned bitcoin, the new digital currency. Over the years since, bitcoin as a currency has declined in volume, but the technology that currency was based upon, a shared ledger called the blockchain, has gone mainstream. Banks, payment processors, asset managers, governments, regulators and companies in general have all been experimenting with how to use the blockchain ledger to record the exchange of value.

This led to me thinking increasingly about the exchange of value and how we value things. More and more, I began to write about value stores, value tokens, value structures and value systems. I soon found that others were talking about the Internet of Value and therefore it soon became natural to talk about the ValueWeb. The ValueWeb is all about how the internet is changing the way we value things in trade and finance, but also in life and relationships.

Value is not only exchanging money and currencies, but also *likes* and *favourites*. Pageviews, Klout and followers are a major force of value today. Companies will pay to get attention, and attention translates into views. It is for this reason that individuals are becoming important as media channels. An individual with millions of followers is a big influencer in their communities, and that is bankable. It is why someone like Felix Arvid Ulf Kjellberg, a 25-year old Swede, is one of the most important voices on the planet. Who is Felix? He's better known as PewDiePie, a vlogger who has 40 million YouTube fans and banked over US$7 million in 2014 from advertising on his homepage. It is the reason why American Matt Stopera has become an internet sensation in China (all thanks to a lost iPhone). It is how Chen Kun, Yao Chen and Guo Degang have become bigger in China than Jackie Chan, thanks to Sina Weibo, a microblogging site.

This is the new world of global connectivity and it is driven by the mobile network integrated with the smart network of the internet. Instantaneous, non-stop, global, real-time connectivity is changing the way we think and relate to each other. However, this new connectivity would be nothing if we could not trade and exchange value cheaply and easily through it. This is the focus of the book: how we can trade easily and instantly on a globalised basis through the mobile internet.

In this context, we need a cheap, global, real-time value exchange structure, and this is being built in two forms. On the one hand, we have a new form of value exchange being constructed through the blockchain; on the other, we have the old form of value exchange being replaced by the blockchain.

This is the two-stream world explored in *ValueWeb*. The pages that follow provide you with an in-depth review of what is happening in building the new world of value exchange, and the likely developments over the years to come. Unlike *Digital Bank,* this book does not focus upon banks or banking per se, but on the wider question of how the Internet of Value is being built, how it will operate and what it means.

It is for these reasons that I have consciously sought to interview the key players in the emerging world of the ValueWeb, rather than focusing upon banks and payment processors. It is why the case studies and interviews contained in this book are with many new start-up companies and observers of this new world of the Internet of Value, rather than established companies and existing players.

The first half of the book therefore explains *ValueWeb,* and points to two specific trends that are shaping this new world.

First, the mobile connectivity that is allowing every single person on the planet to be able to use an electronic network connection. Seven billion people are now connected through a network when, just ten years ago, less than a billion people were on the network. That's a massive change, because everyone on the planet can now connect and exchange value in real-time, person-to-person—if you prefer, peer-to-peer or P2P. The key here is that mobile P2P connectivity enables everyone to be able to trade and exchange value one-to-one, globally and in real-time. Most importantly, a mobile telephone not only allows you to trade, i.e., buy things, but also to create new entrepreneurial structures, i.e., sell things.

A mobile is both a payment device and a point-of-sale (POS). This is why mobile trade is rising fast and is allowing every single person on this planet to connect, trade and exchange in real-time. This is transformative, as people who could not access trade and finance ten years ago can do so today. This will lift many out of poverty and is a big focal point for investment in the mobile ValueWeb, as illustrated in an interview with Kosta Peric of the Bill & Melinda Gates Foundation.

As Kosta points out, you cannot build a mobile ValueWeb that includes everyone on the planet if you have expensive and slow-value exchange systems. The old exchange systems—the banking system—takes days to process payments and charges a high cost. The new exchange system has to be cheap—almost free—if poor farmers in emerging markets are to use it.

This, therefore, is the second big trend explored in the book: how to build an instantaneous and near free value exchange system. This second trend is clearly based upon the new technology spawned by the bitcoin currency, called the blockchain. That discussion is possibly best illustrated by my interview with Chris Larsen of Ripple Labs, a major player in the building of new structures for global value exchange between banks. However, there are many other views that are just as important, which is why half of this book is about cryptocurrencies, bitcoin and the blockchain.

So these are the key issues explored in *ValueWeb:* how mobile and blockchain technologies are building a new internet, based upon the global exchange of value in real-time and almost free. These themes are explained in depth in the first half of the book, and then illustrated through the interviews with the people building this ValueWeb in the second half.

So that's the new book. Half of the book explains the ValueWeb, and then the second half explores the people building it. I hope you like this book, and welcome feedback.

Chris Skinner, Autumn 2015

1.
WELCOME TO THE VALUEWEB

The first steam engine was patented in 1606 by Spanish inventor Jerónimo de Ayanz y Beaumont but it wasn't until 1829, some two centuries later, that George Stephenson sent *The Rocket* on its way, creating the first viable railway service. The railway created the tracks that built America and fuelled the process of getting goods from A to B fast—but it took two centuries to get there.

Rail was just one of several innovations during the 19th century that saw the Industrial Revolution transform life. Another key invention was electricity. Electricity is generally attributed as an invention to Michael Faraday in the 1820s, although again its roots go back two centuries previous, when the words *electric* and *electricity* made their first appearance in print in Thomas Browne's *Pseudodoxia Epidemica* in 1646.

In other words, the last great revolution in trade took 200 years to establish. This new one—the networked revolution of providing our planet with communication, P2P, for everyone—has taken about 70 so far. The roots of the network revolution start with the invention of the computer. Different folks have different views of which developed first but I believe it was ENIAC, the World War II weather forecasting system that was created in 1943 and was up and running in 1946.

70 years later, we have this machinery in our pockets and purses, with the average smartphone being more powerful in terms of computer processing power than NASA's Mars spacecraft of the last decade. But it takes a long time to digitise the entire planet; we began with the building blocks of networks, access, and infrastructure, and have gradually moved from information and commerce to caring and sharing, to what I see today as the most radical network transformation, focused upon value.

It is interesting, for example, that the most radical changes the internet has introduced so far has been the disintermediation of the travel and entertainment industries, with music and film revolutionised in its distribution and pricing. Yet, in banking and payments, the only real innovation until recently was PayPal. And PayPal is not really an innovation in banking and payments, but just an extra layer on top of existing banking and payments infrastructures.

But the network transformation of how we exchange value, which I call the ValueWeb, is transformational in all aspects of banking and payments.

That is why we are seeing so much investment in FinTech, with over a thousand new start-ups receiving over $12 billion in investment in just the last few years alone. According to the latest statistics, FinTech investments are doubling year-on-year, and 2015 looks set to be a new record year, as we see $20 billion being pumped into this market from venture capital funds, private equity and other sources.

This is why we are seeing so many new names becoming mainstream, and a third of all this investment is going into payments start-ups, because the time is finally ripe to reinvent banking and payments through technology. Currency Cloud, Transferwise, TraxPay, Square, iZettle, Stripe, Dwolla, Klarna and others are all changing the payments game.

The main theme of my previous book, *Digital Bank,* is that we built our financial systems in the last century for the physical distribution of paper in a localised network, and now have to rethink that system for the digital distribution of data in a globalised network. It is not just an evolution of the business model, but a fundamentally different business model.

The old structure has been cemented into place by old systems, and seeks the transfer of goods and services through a value exchange system that is hand-to-hand rather than peer-to-peer. If you take our old value exchange mechanisms, we had banks and counterparty banks and infrastructures like Visa and SWIFT that were all required for enabling monetary transactions.

We then added PayPal to overcome the challenges that created for us, as the network moved towards globalisation. As a result, we don't just have a four-pillar model in place—issuing bank, acquiring bank, card processor and merchant—but, in some cases, an eight-pillar model.

This costs, as every counterparty is taking a fee. That will not work in the age of the internet, and does not support a globalised value exchange system, which is why the open sourced network has created bitcoin.

Cryptocurrencies, of which bitcoin is one, are the manifestation of what is needed to support a ValueWeb. We cannot have global value exchange without some form of digital currency, a cryptocurrency, and the digital identity that goes alongside this. That is why cryptocurrencies are so fundamental to the transformation we are seeing today.

Now most people think when bitcoin is mentioned that we're going off on some flaky tangent. That's because bitcoin has been associated with cybercriminal activities and has had its name tarnished by suspicious exchanges like Mt. Gox and Bitstamp. These are just early day issues in an early day experiment, however, and thinking that bitcoin as a currency is suspect because of Mt. Gox and Bitstamp's issues is a bit like saying the UK Pound is flaky because of the collapse of Northern Rock and Bradford & Bingley.

However, where I do agree with many critics is that bitcoin will need some form of change as the idea of being a money without governance just doesn't wash. Money without governance is like having a society without police. It leads to terrorist funding, money laundering and drug running, as illustrated by the activities of the dark net marketplace Silk Road. However, just like the change in commerce on the internet that saw free downloads and copyright theft through Napster and Pirate Bay, you eventually see order from chaos.

Out of the anarchy of the music and entertainment revolution, we have seen iTunes, Netflix and more create a better value world that people feel, generally, is worth paying for. In a similar way, we will see the fledgling movements of the cryptocurrency world move towards mainstream adoption over time. In fact, we are already seeing it. USAA, the New York Stock Exchange and BBVA invest in firms like Coinbase; J.P. Morgan, Goldman Sachs, Barclays and others are seeing how they could use the blockchain for securities settlement (just use Colored Coins); and, in the meantime, several banks are actively working with Ripple to replace their counterparty transaction engines.

In other words, the use of cryptocurrencies and smart contracts through the blockchain is already happening. But there is more to the ValueWeb than buying and selling physical and digital goods and services. It's about creating and sharing ideas, thoughts, entertainment and more.

The ValueWeb is represented by *likes, shares, favourites* and *page views*. My blog gets around 2,000 page views per day, whilst my Twitter handle has over 11,000 followers. That means that I have a value and a presence that can influence. It is why firms want to advertise on the blog, pay me to mention them and ask for retweets. I ignore them all, as that's not my business model.

The ValueWeb allows guys like PewDiePie, the Slow Mo Guys and reformed porn stars to make millions from their cute, weird and funny YouTube sites. This is because anyone can be a voice today. Anyone can be a channel. Anyone can be a social media star.

Take a look at YY in China, where karaoke singers are making $15,000 a month from *likes* of their songs, and you'll see what I mean. In the ValueWeb, anyone can create value through digital goods and services but also from digital thoughts and ideas. That's the difference, and the currency is not just monetary but also influence and entertainment.

But there's more to the ValueWeb than this, as it's not just about currencies for buying and selling goods or sharing ideas; it's about inclusion. Take a look at the Bill & Melinda Gates Foundation newsletter for 2015. In the newsletter, a specific section talks about wiping out poverty by creating financial inclusion through the mobile network:

> "In the next 15 years, digital banking will give the poor more control over their assets and help them transform their lives. The key to this will be mobile phones. Already, in the developing countries with the right regulatory framework, people are storing money digitally on their phones and using their phones to make purchases, as if they were debit cards. By 2030, two billion people who don't have a bank account today will be storing money and making payment with their phones. And by then, mobile money providers will be offering the full range of financial services, from interest-bearing savings accounts to credit to insurance."

The mobile phone is truly transformational for the poor and financially excluded. It has allowed fragmented groups of people who had no ability to communicate over distance to suddenly access digital reach. Goat herders, fishermen, sheep farmers and cattle ranchers across Africa are now becoming merchants and businesses through the reach of their mobile. A mobile text message can pay for wool, milk, meat and more, and they are able to advertise their goods through Instagram, Facebook and Twitter. This truly is a revolution, as that means we now have seven billion people who are connected one-to-one, peer-to-peer, able to exchange digital and physical goods and services, ideas and thoughts through the ValueWeb. It is why Bill Gates goes on to say that cryptocurrencies like bitcoin will be fundamental to this shift in thinking:

> "Bitcoin is an exciting new technology. For our Foundation work we are doing digital currency to help the poor get banking services. We don't use bitcoin specifically for two reasons. One is that the poor shouldn't have a currency whose value goes up and down a lot compared to their local currency. Second is that if a mistake is made in who you pay then you need to be able to reverse it so anonymity wouldn't work. Overall financial transactions will get cheaper using the work we do and Bitcoin related approaches. Making sure that it doesn't help terrorists is a challenge for all new technology."

In summary, the ValueWeb is a new generation of the internet that is underway right now, illustrated by FinTech investments, and is geared to redesign the exchange value for the internet age. It is rethinking the structure of how we deal with buying and selling through the net, whilst digitising money and more. Through the ValueWeb and the deployment of cheap, mobile technologies, every single person on this planet can now be part of the value ecosystem. That is a fundamental shift for our planet as it means that anyone, anywhere can be a merchant; anyone, anywhere, can buy or sell anything, anytime; anyone, anywhere can be a voice, a media star, a channel; and anyone, anywhere can monetize the things they make and even the things they think, just by sharing and caring.

THE WAY VALUE IS SHARED ON THE VALUEWEB

Previously, we had a world of physical value exchange with physical tokens. The physical value tokens were cards and cash; the physical value exchanges were stores and garages and shops. The store of value was the bank. This last element was importantly different to the others, as the physical value tokens could only be used at the physical value exchanges. When they weren't being used, some folks kept them under their bed, but that's not a safe value store. So we had governments create a system to regulate the value stores to ensure they were safe, secure and could guarantee that they would not lose the value tokens.

Then the internet came along and changed the game, since now our value tokens are digital. Value tokens are the units of value used to recognise worth. Units of value can be esoteric things, such as Facebook *likes*, Twitter *favourites* or LinkedIn *shares*; to virtual and digital currencies like World of Warcraft Gold or Candy Crush Points; to loyalty tokens from air miles to retail store cards; to prepaid stores such as airtime on the mobile network; to cryptocurrencies like bitcoin; to real world currencies in a physical or digital form, from cash and cheque to card and mobile wallet.

As can be seen, a vast array of value tokens exist, some of which are a closed loop, like air miles and loyalty cards, which are hard to cash-out; whilst some are transparent and easy to trade, like cryptocurrencies. The tokenisation of value is the digitisation of money. In fact, as the industry talks about tokenisation, we should just think of airtime and cryptocurrencies as part of that kaleidoscope of value tokens that now exist. After all, these are just digital tokens of value that represent something of worth that can be traded.

They can be used anywhere, anytime, globally, on digital value exchanges through websites and digital domains. The value exchanges operate 24–7–365, and there are no geographic boundaries to where I choose to invest or spend a value token. Equally, we have a wide range and variety of value tokens, not just money. Of course, money is now digital and we have digital dollars, euros and yen, but we also have cryptocurrencies. Cryptocurrencies change the game because they operate outside centralised control through the decentralised structure of the internet. That is a game-changer and is the reason why we are seeing banks and bankers investing in bitcoin. But the internet has gone much further and deeper in digitising value, as the value tokens we use are no longer necessarily of a monetary form.

For example, as mentioned, we have value tokens generated through loyalty schemes with retailers, airlines and others trying to lock in customers through reward points. In fact, one of the greatest value tokens is airtime on mobile networks. This is illustrated well in Zimbabwe, where the national currency imploded due to hyperinflation and so only South African Rand and US Dollars were accepted as payment. The problem here is that local retailers often do not have small change when you buy something. Give them $10 for a $2 item and you'll be lucky to get any change. This has been solved by offering airtime minutes on the mobile network as change.

Equally, we are creating our own value tokens in games with World of Warcraft Gold being one of the best examples. What do you do when you spend months or years playing a game and then get bored with it? How can you monetize your valuable points? Trade them with other players and start another game, of course.

More fundamentally is that we have value being generated by just being liked for your ideas. PewDiePie creating videos for YouTube, or even people like me writing blogs and tweeting, creates a value feed that generates revenue. PewDiePie generates revenues through adverts on his video feed. In fact, the most impressive social network is YY.com in China, which takes virtual currency and streaming video to heights not yet reached by Western social networks. On YY, users can play games, talk to their friends, or use virtual coins for social deals à la Groupon. But what really makes YY standout is the fact that it has a built-in system that enables site users to earn real profit. Top karaoke singers regularly make $20,000 per month from virtual gifts. YY allows users to spend virtual roses as tickets to access live content from their favourite artists and teachers.

Here's how it works. Say you have some type of talent; perhaps you're a tech-savvy musician or passable karaoke singer. To make money on YY, you create an artist account, put up some of your songs, and hopefully develop a following. After building up a respectable fan base, you could even schedule a live concert on the site, and for the price of one "virtual rose", your followers would be able to watch the performance and interact with others attending the concert via video and chat. After the concert, you would be able to exchange your hard-earned virtual roses for real money.

So we have many new forms of value tokens being used in many new forms of value exchange, and the question is: where's the value store and how can you trust in these new forms of value exchange?

The first piece, the value store, is the bank—but banks are not stepping up to the mark. The majority of banks will only bank money, currency and related investments. You might be able to store gold and silver at the bank, but it's unlikely that you can bank World of Warcraft Gold (unless you're Fidor Bank, of course). As for banking YY *Roses*, QQ *shares,* Facebook *likes* or *favourite* Tweets, there's nothing out there right now. That's quite worrying as, in ten years' time, most of our existing memories may have become unreadable and lost. When Facebook becomes Sharedome and then Gameground, all your historical memories become incompatible with successive generations of systems.

And with the average person born today potentially living for over a century, what will today's millennials be looking at in 2115 to remember their lives? Will we be living in a digital dark age? Vint Cerf, a "father of the internet", thinks so. As Mr. Cerf puts it: "The key here is when you move those bits from one place to another, that you still know how to unpack them to correctly interpret the different parts."

This is the key reason why you need a value store—a bank—that guarantees readability, rather than compatibility, generation through generation. Equally, it needs companies that can guarantee to be around for over a century, and there are few that can offer that, other than banks. After all, most banks have been around for over three centuries, because they are licenced, and therefore this is one of the few industries that could provide a guaranteed value store for digitised memories and value tokens.

In summary, we therefore have taken physical value tokens, exchanges and stores and digitised them.

- Physical cash and cards become digitised cryptocurrencies and value tokens
- Physical shops and retailers become digital domains and websites
- Physical bank branch structures become digitised value stores

The next question is: how do you generate trust in this digitised world?

This requires digital identities to be associated with these digital value tokens, exchanges and stores.

THE VALUEWEB AND BIOMETRIC BLOCKCHAIN AUTHENTICATION

Now we need to focus on digital identities, as you cannot have digital value tokens, exchanges and stores without secure digital identities. And there are two forms of identity: you and your devices.

Your identity is embodied in a secure authentication of you, which is increasingly moving to biometric authentication. In fact, we now have multi-authentication capabilities of you: your voice, your fingerprint, your eyeball, your heartbeat and more. These are all capabilities for authentication through your devices. Your mobile can provide the biometric authentication of you. Soon, other devices will authenticate you. For example, the Royal Bank of Canada is trialling the use of Nymi, a wristband that authenticates heartbeats, as is the UK's Halifax bank.

The Nymi band records a customer's heartbeat, which is then synced with a smartphone or other device. A Bluetooth connection to the band is then all that's needed to login to the banking app, because sensors detect that the authenticated person is still wearing the band.

Other methods are improving the use of biometrics for authentication, too. Facebook has been developing DeepFace, a facial recognition system, to look at two photos and, irrespective of lighting or angle, identify who is in the picture. In 2014, they could do this with 97.25 percent accuracy compared with the human brain, which can achieve this with 97.53 percent accuracy. By now, they may have even surpassed this.

Therefore, we are adding more and more devices with more and more biometric technologies to ensure that humans can easily interact with devices without the need for PINs, passwords or tokens. In fact, by 2020 every smartphone, tablet, and wearable device will have an embedded biometric sensor, according to Acuity Market Intelligence; and half of mobile commerce and one in ten in-store payments will be authenticated with biometrics, says market researcher Goode Intelligence.

But this raises the question: who authenticates that it is your device being used for authentication? Even more importantly: who authenticates your devices when they start doing business with each other? When your fridge orders groceries; your TV orders entertainment; your car orders fuel; who authenticates it is your fridge, TV and car that are ordering, and what role do you play in the process?

These are all key questions and the answer is: the blockchain.

We've talked about the blockchain as a technology for transactions but, more importantly, it is becoming a technology for authentication, thanks to its smart contracts capability.

For those unsure of the blockchain's full potential, a simple explanation is that the blockchain is the ledger system created by the Bitcoin protocol. This is a ledger where everyone can see in a public forum the exchange of transactions, because every exchange of bitcoins is recorded on the blockchain in a public domain. Not the details of that transaction, but that a transaction took place. You can never revoke or eradicate that the exchange took place, and its time and place. In other words, you have an irrevocable record of a transaction occuring.

That irrevocable record of the transaction could be buying or selling something, or it could be transfers of ownership or recording of contracts. It is this area that is most interest in the context of authentication, as device purchases will be recorded on the blockchain in the future, as will any other purchase of goods or services.

This means the blockchain potentially becomes a global recording mechanism of transfers of ownership; a global invoice system, if you like. The key for me is that the blockchain may, over time, become our global system for recording everything of value being exchanged.

Now, let's say that happens, from a machine-to-machine commerce internet viewpoint, the blockchain becomes our fundamental method of authenticating machine-to-machine transactions. When my fridge, TV or car orders stuff, there is no biometric so my blockchain registration of these devices becomes the authentication.

In other words, the bank sees a request of payment to Tesco of £35.12 for groceries, requested by *Chris Skinner's refrigerator*. How do they know it is *Chris Skinner's refrigerator?* There's just an automated check of the last transfer of serial number XY12-FFDC-90LT-DPP1 (my fridge's serial number) on the blockchain. Yes, according to that record, the last transfer of XY12-FFDC-90LT-DPP1 was a purchase made by Chris Skinner, who owns this bank account, on 1ˢᵗ December 2014 and there has been no transfer since, so the bank authorises the payment.

So I now have no role in this process, except to authorise transactions. Then, when I do, the bank checks I'm breathing, using my heartbeat for authentication.

This is a world away from where we are today, but a world that will be with us within a few years—so we'd better get ready.

THE ORIGINS OF MONEY IS PART OF OUR DNA

In most science fiction movies, there is no money. Hollywood's vision of the future has removed the need for cash, and I've blogged before about Gene Roddenberry's views on money in "Star Trek: Money is a terrible thing". His idea is that money will disappear as we explore space and, as we send rockets out to Pluto, his vision is getting nearer. Money hasn't disappeared from society yet, however. It has just changed from a physical form and moved to a digital structure. The new digital structure of money is not just a cryptocurrency, however.

The cryptocurrencies may be the value exchange mechanisms between machines, but it's the chips inside machines that are our new wallets. As we move into Web 3.0, we move into machine-to-machine commerce—and this can only be transacted in a neatly organised value system.

My vision for this new value system is that every machine, or commercially enabled thing if you prefer, will have intelligence inside. A chip. That chip inside will be designated an owner. The owner in most cases will be you and me, and these things we own are part of our recognised digital identity structure.

So I have a number of things designated as mine on a shared, internet ledger. My car, fridge, television, front door, heating system, several watches, shoes and jackets are all registered as mine. All of these things have chips inside, and these chips give them intelligence. My heating can be controlled from my watch; my television orders my entertainment; my fridge orders a regular grocery shop; and my car drives itself to gas stations and refuels as often as needed.

In order to do this, all of these devices have been recorded as mine. They are attached to me through my digital identity and my digital identity is recorded on a trusted, shared ledger for the internet of things. If my car refuels too often or my fridge makes an exceptional order for over $1000 of groceries, I get alerts that require my biometric approval.

All of these things are transacted through the air, via a shared ledger of trusted exchange. In my case, they are recorded on some form of poundchain; Americans operate on a dollarchain; and the Chinese on a renminbichain.

These digital currency chains not only transact value exchange, but also manage identities and ownership. This is how you can achieve the science fiction vision of value exchange immediately and invisibly through the ether.

The reason why this is a likely outcome of the Internet of Value and Web 3.0, the Internet of Things, is that we are moving towards a revolution in trade, as well as a revolution of financial value exchange.

This can be seen from the earliest forms of homo sapiens and how we adapted through every generation of trade. In his brilliant book *Sapiens,* Professor Yuval Noah Harari provides a brief history of humankind. He explains how we have created a world of fiction in order to allow humankind to ascend to the top of the food chain.

Companies, money, governments, religions, law and all the things that structure our world are all fictional creations of humankind that allowed us to conquer the world. It's a complicated idea to explain here, but the gist is that no animals have companies, money, governments or legal systems. Most animals function as part of a hierarchy lead by an alpha male or queen matriarch. Man has created social structures and relationships of trade and communication that allow hundreds, thousands and millions of people to live together. By contrast, most animals have tribes of no more than a couple of dozen creatures. We have tribes of hundreds of thousands, organised in cities and all working alongside each other, thanks to our formalised structures of trade.

In the book, Harari traces homo sapiens back over 200,000 years and notes that 70,000 years ago we began to migrate from Africa across

Asia and then, 45,000 years ago, to Australia and more recently (16,000 years ago) to the Americas. The key to our expansionism was language and shared myths that enabled us to believe in gods, demons and priests, and allowed us to move from being nomads to fishermen to farmers, exchanging trade and value along the way.

> "While we can't get inside a Neanderthal mind to understand how they thought, we have indirect evidence of the limits to their cognition compared with their Sapiens rivals. Archaeologists excavating 30,000-year-old Sapiens sites in the European heartland occasionally find seashells from the Mediterranean and Atlantic coasts. In all likelihood, these shells got to the continental interior through long-distance trade between different Sapiens bands. Neanderthal sites lack any evidence of such trade. Each group manufactured its own tools from local materials …

> "The fact is that no animal other than Sapiens engages in trade, and all the Sapiens trade networks about which we have detailed evidence were based on fictions. Trade cannot exist without trust, and it is very difficult to trust strangers. The global trade network of today is based on our trust in such fiction entities as the dollar, the Federal Reserve Bank and the totemic trademarks of corporations. When two strangers in a tribal society want to trade, they will often establish trust by appealing to a common god, mythical ancestor or totem animal. If archaic Sapiens believing in such fictions traded shells, it stands to reason that they could also have traded information, thus creating a much denser and wider knowledge network than the one that served Neanderthals and other archaic humans."

Harari's book is fascinating, and this extract is partly an explanation as to why homo sapiens are the only hominid's left on this planet. 200,000 years ago, there were many other hominid species including Homo Erectus, Homo Neanderthalensis, Homo Rhodesiensis, Homo Tsaichangensis, Homo Sapiens and Homo Floresiensis. According to analysis by Harari and others, it is the very fact that we could create trade systems based upon shared fictions that exchanged forms of value through language, information and things that were useful or beautiful—shells, obsidian, stones, flint—that we ascended to become the most intelligent of species and, consequently, dominated the planet.

By contrast, most became sentient or, as Harari refers to it, underwent a Cognitive Revolution, we began to search, explore and then, some years later, farm and settle. Until just over 10,000 years ago, most humans were hunter-gatherer nomads. We would move from area to area through the seasons, exploring and gathering food. Sometimes we would starve, since we had no means of developing crops. That changed after the last Ice Age, which some scientists believe created annual plant growth. As a result, we could seed fields of grain and grow food stocks.

Farming worked well to allow humans to produce food to last throughout the year, and hence we could create settlements. Then we had too much food and produce. As a result, we had to create another form of value exchange and, being homo sapiens, we invented this new shared fiction of money.

Various stories appear about money but the first mentions date back over 12,000 years ago, when ancient tribesmen in Antonia swapped Obsidian stones to store value. What this represented is a move from basic production of goods to the trading of goods and services, and we have seen the progression of the use of currency and value stores through the ages as civilisations and societies have developed. However, our progression of these stores of value are changing and moving faster and faster, as our technologies develop.

For example, the Antonians not only traded in stones but other forms of value, from cattle to sheep. In other words, it was more of a form of bartering than currency itself. Seven thousand years of development led to a revolution in trade and commerce, however. In fact, every time we progress in technology, trade and commerce, we have a revolution in finance.

In 3,000 B.C. priests in ancient Sumer revolutionized trade and exchange when they invented money. This first form of money was a coin, a shekel, which priests offered to farmers in exchange for their excess produce. This happened because the Ancient Sumerians were one of the first civilisations to farm, and create an orderly system of food production. Mankind went through a revolution of trade and commerce as farming became commonplace in civilised communities.

Farming created money—coins that were made from precious metals, such as gold. This worked for an eon but proved difficult when distances were involved. Carrying a heavy bag of gold coinage was not ideal when you might encounter bandits or thieves, or had a horse that could only carry so much weight. Hence, the Chinese invented paper money 2,300 years later, in 740 B.C. This was predictable in value—unlike gold coinage, which had to be weighed and measured. The paper money was issued and underwritten by a government—the Tang Dynasty—and proved to be a far more reliable mechanism for trade.

So we moved from barter, then farming, to coins for a trusted value store, to cash for trade across distances.

This system worked well until the next big change in trade and commerce: the Industrial Revolution. As businesses were created that sourced goods from overseas and traded across national boundaries and over great distances, a new form of currency was needed. Hence, traditional coinage was too heavy to carry across such distances, bearing in mind that they were made from gold, and governments started to licence institutions, banks, to enable trade on their behalf. The new government-licenced institutions could therefore issue paper money—a cheque or bank note—that could be as trusted as a gold coin. This was a key move—from coins to paper—and enabled the rapid expansion of trade and commerce globally, as the industrialisation of economies developed fast in the 18th and 19th centuries.

However, it didn't work quite so well when workers moved from factories to offices. During the 1950s, the United States led the revolution in office work and professional entertainment became *en vogue*. The trouble is, when you're entertaining a client, it proves to be a real pain if you end the lunch or dinner and have to write a cheque. Writing a cheque interferes with the client engagement—you have to take your eyes off the focus of conversation—and so Frank McNamara invented the credit card.

Frank was an executive at the Hamilton Credit Corporation and had a problem. His finance company was struggling with uncollected debt, whilst Frank needed a way to make more money. McNamara came up with taking the idea of a charge card, back then being used mainly just in department stores, to the restaurant business. His innovation was to use the charge card in restaurants and then add interest to the monthly payments. That way the finance company was able to make a profit from every card that was issued.

He managed to convince many restaurants in lower Manhattan to sign up for the card, by offering customers a 10 percent discount for every purchase. Many restaurants and stores signed up, because there was no fee or charge and it made it easier to purchase meals without worrying about cash. This led to the launch of the Diner's Club in 1950, and so was born the new industry of the credit card.

This brings us nearly up-to-date. As we have seen, in 12,000 years we moved through the following progression:
* barter for nomadic societies
* cash for farming societies
* cheques for industrial societies
* cards for office-based societies

But now we live in a networked society, a globally connected world. That demands a new form of currency and some would immediately point to bitcoin or the blockchain. That's relevant, but it's only part of the answer. Just as cards needed Visa and MasterCard to succeed globally, and just as cheques and cash need to be backed by a trusted mechanism of government licencing and banks, we need an internet-age value exchange mechanism that is trusted, immediate and works through time and space, to support the chip-based economy.

In the chip-based economy, anything can exchange value with anything, anywhere, anytime. All objects will soon have intelligence inside, a chip inside, and will need a method of transmitting value and exchanging and trading. This internet-age system will therefore be based upon chips. The chip-based economy means that the Internet of Things can work.

The internet of things creates a grand vision of the not too distant future where everything communicates with everything else. We would have chips as tiny as nanodots inside every brick, pavement slab, tyre, wall, ceiling … you name it. We have more intelligent chips inside car engines, visual entertainment systems, wearable devices, from rings to necklaces to bags to shoes. Everything is communicating with everything else and our devices are all attached to us through the blockchain.

The result is that my futuristic vision of no one paying for anything becomes a reality. I drive to the big city and park. My car tells the metering system it's my car and it's parked here until I come back. When I come back it asks the system how much it owes and pays. I do nothing.

My car then drives me to the gas station—I don't drive anymore as it's self-driving—and it asks the station robot for $30 of LPG. The robot pump system delivers and I just sit, working and enjoying the entertainment and world around me. The car drives off and all of the transaction is seamlessly in the background.

I've asked my Tesla to take me downtown to a decent bar—I haven't been in this town before—and it delivers me to Joes 99er. Joe—or the guy behind the bar—gives me a large whisky and Bud. It's my usual tipple and my shoe just told his stock management system that's what I'd want. I felt a little vibration from my shoe that confirmed this would be ordered and just let it go. It was too much trouble to shake my left foot for a gin and tonic.

After three Buds and whisky combos, I jump back in the car and I'm ready to hit the casino. The car asks me three times if I really want to do this—it knows what happened last time—and I just say, "Yea". I'm cool and mellow and a little bit drunk, something I'm ultra-aware of as I'm supposed to be sober in charge of a self-driving car. (Why that law still exists, I have no idea.)

So the car drops me at Caesar's Shed, it's five steps down from the Palace, and I start shooting some blackjack. My shoe vibrates again, as I've just lost $2,000 in the first five minutes and my budgeting balance for the month for gambling has been reached. But it's only 2nd June for heaven's sake. I stamp my foot and the balance is lifted, along with a healthy top-up of $10,000 moved from my savings account in real-time.

By the end of the evening, my savings are gone and the bank's given me a loan of $15,000. I hate it when I click my shoes together and say, "There's no place like home". After all, that's the trigger for my biometric check to ensure it really is me saying that I want an extra line of credit. No one notices the heartbeat check and the touch of my finger to the side of my glasses.

Ah well, a good night was had and not a payment or authentication was visible. Just wireless credits and debits from the stamp of a shoe to the touch of an eyebrow.

The world has changed a lot in the last ten years. I remember in 2010, I used to keep lots of pocket change in my car to pay parking metres, and got frustrated with the endless stops at tollbooths to swipe my credit card. By 2015, things had improved immensely. Now I just have NFC payments, prepaid apps and one-time passwords. No longer would I jiggle around trying to find the right change.

You buy a fridge, a car, a house, a smartphone, a wearable, a whatever. All the things you buy have clear serial number identifications as well as chips inside to enable them to transact wirelessly over the web. Upon purchase, your device is recorded as being yours using your digital identity token (probably a biometric or something similar). The recording of that transaction takes place on the blockchain.

Now, you have multiple devices transacting upon your behalf. Your fridge is ordering groceries from the supermarket; your car auto refuels as it self-drives the highways; your house reorders all the things needed for the robot vacuum and other cleansing devices it uses; and so on. Each transaction is a micro-purchase around your wallet, but involving no authentication of you. The authentication is of your devices. Should a large transaction occur, or maybe just to check-in as contactless payments do with every twenty or more transactions, you are requested to agree that this is your device ordering on your behalf by providing a Touch ID or similar. And all of this is being transacted and recorded on the open blockchain ledger of your bank cheaply, easily and in real-time.

What this provides is the scenario I keep referring to, invented years ago by Gene Rodenberry, when he came up with the idea for Star Trek. Now Star Trek has lots of things that were forecasts about the future that came true, from communicators that were the predecessors of Motorola flip phones to body scanners that could be hand-held. One of the other predictions was that we wouldn't need money.

Have you ever seen anyone pay for anything on Star Trek?

The reason you don't need money in the future is that all the transactions you make take place wirelessly around you, through your internet of things. You walk into a store or mall, and all of your devices and identity are communicating your location and intention. As a result, you never pay for anything. You just authorise with the blink of an eye or the wave of a watch.

So we have now moved through the following progression:

- barter for nomadic societies
- cash for farming societies
- cheques for industrial societies
- cards for office societies
- chips for networked societies

MANUFACTURING (back office)   PROCESSING (middle office)   RETAILING (front office)

PERSONAL TRANSPORT

UBER

ACCOMMODATION

 airbnb

TRANSACTING

Products
Services

CONTRACT

The chip-based economy, enabled by the blockchain, can exchange finance, goods and services for anyone trading anything, anywhere, anytime. This is why I call the blockchain the Uber of finance, as it's creating a globally connected marketplace for trusted exchange.

Uber is a marketplace connecting buyers (people who want a ride) with sellers (drivers). The blockchain is doing the same by connecting people who need to transact (buyers) with those who have what they want (sellers) through a trusted third party (the blockchain) that is decentralised and networked.

As money is a technology communities use to trade debts across space and time, the blockchain can be used to create a shared ledger for shared economies. The reason we have a financial system is because most value exchange is based on a lack of trust, and so you need a central authority to provide this trust. The central authority provides three key things that enable the value exchange of cash, cheques or cards to occur:

- It **validates** the value token is real and not a forgery
- It **safeguards** that, once you have accepted the token in exchange for goods and services, it is irrevocable
- It **preserves** the details of what was traded, so that there is no omission or lie in the transaction

What is crucial about the blockchain is that it can provide the necessary validation and safeguards, because things cannot be spent twice, preserving the exchange through a public history of the transaction. Many in the financial industry now believe that we are developing a true system for the chip-based economy based upon some form of blockchain development that allows us to exchange value in real-time for almost free. The blockchain creates a marketplace for globalised value exchange that is trusted, secure and irrevocable.

2.

THE VALUEWEB BUILDER PART ONE: A MOBILE NETWORKED PLANET

As mentioned in the opening, the biggest driver of change is the mobile network. The mobile network is growing rapidly, with almost every country now seeing adoption by virtually their whole population. According to statistics from July 2015, more than half of the people living on earth today are using a mobile phone to connect and communicate. That is 3.73 billion individuals of the 7.36 billion living on earth. You may see other figures, such as mobile subscriptions exceed the world's population—there are over 7.5 billion mobile subscriptions—but this relates to the fact that some individuals have two or three mobile accounts for their phone and tablet computers.

This is important, as active mobile users are increasing fast. A decade ago only one in five people were on the mobile network; today, it's one in two; tomorrow, it will be nearly everyone; and, as each person joins the network, things change. This is because there's a network effect. The network effect has been known since the telephone was first invented, and it means that as each device is added to the network, the connections are multiplied. Therefore, 1 phone = 1 connection; 2 phones = 2 connections. But once you add a third, the network effect kicks in as there are now multiple communication links.

This network effect snowballs over time, so that each new connection adds greater and greater connectivity, adding greater and greater value. In other words, the network effect sees an increase in the value of goods and services as the number of users multiplies. This network effect was first cited in 1908 by Bell Telephone, but the mobile internet has amplified this effect

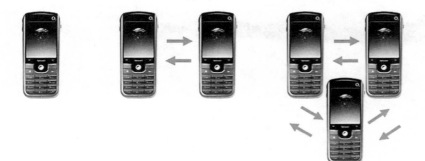

massively. In fact, it leads us to network economics. Network economics leverages the network effect to create trade and commerce, and is the reason why we see mobile social as a critical marketplace today.

Mobile social allows everyone on the planet to share everything instantaneously. Viral is the word, and allows a selfie from the Oscars to be seen by a billion people in seconds. Ellen DeGeneres's selfie was retweeted over two million times during the 2014 Oscar ceremony and has, by now, probably been seen by most people who have any awareness of the Oscars.

And this illustrates the Internet of Value well, as the mobile telephone used to take this selfie was a product placement by Samsung. So how much was that worth? A selfie that could be shared by a celebrity for free on the mobile Internet of Value? About a billion dollars, according to Maurice Levy, a marketing representative for Samsung. Maurice's team handled the product placement of the Samsung phone used to take the selfie; a month later he was presenting at a marketing conference and said that Samsung had worked out that the photograph is worth $1 billion for the company, thanks to the millions of people who viewed the tweet.

That's the network economics and the network effect in action, and clearly illustrates the Internet of Value, where a billion dollar moment takes place for free in real-time, globally. The global mobile internet where we are all connected is changing the game fast, and is the core tenet of the ValueWeb.

EXCHANGING VALUE FROM ANYWHERE, ANYTIME, ANYPLACE

We see wearable technologies, semantic web and cryptocurrencies emerging around us, and much of the time we may laugh. For example, I put forward the idea some time ago that we will soon live in a world where everyone has a chip inserted inside them. The chip will hold their identity, medical and financial records, and will authenticate them as they cross borders or exchange value. Is this really practical? It sounds laughable, but then we laughed at a lot of things in the past that we now take for granted. The mobile telephone is a great example. Some of us may be old enough to remember that when mobiles were first being used in the late 1980s, we thought they were for idiots. We had pictures of young professionals shouting "buy, buy, buy" and "sell, sell, sell" down their huge, mobile phone handsets. Many people believed they would never use a mobile phone. Why would you need one?

Ten years later, we all had one. Twenty years later, we cannot imagine life without one. For example *We are Social*, a specialist agency in social media, publish a yearly in-depth review of the onward march of the mobile social internet. In their 2015 statistics, every part of the world has a high density of mobile usage.

Fifteen years ago, many banks launched internet banking services. Many customers wouldn't use it though. It was thought to be insecure and technically complicated. Browsers weren't ready for it, and dial-up lines made it slow and awkward to use. Today, we couldn't imagine life without internet banking. Just ten years ago, payments were made in person or by telephone. Internet payments were available with PayPal but were, again, not trusted or used. Today, PayPal is the de facto payment service for online. But PayPal sits on top of the card and bank networks, is run by eBay and owned by America. It is not the internet currency of the wiki world. That is why bitcoin is taking off, as we will see in the next section.

All of this reminds me of a conversation I had with a journalist from the Financial Times in 1997. I was heading up the banking vision for NCR at the time, and said to him that we would soon be paying for anything, anytime, anywhere. He said to me: "Do you seriously expect

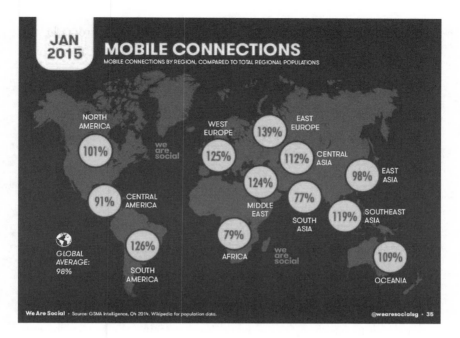

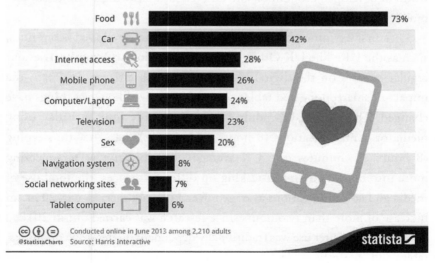

me to believe that one day we could be paying for things from the top of Mount Everest?" I said, "Yes". He didn't take me seriously and wrote a fairly negative view about our ideas for the future. Sixty years after Everest was first climbed, Standard Chartered Bank sent two mountaineers up the mountain to set another world record, by being the first to use its Breeze mobile banking apps on top of the world. In July 2013, they not only successfully used the app to check their bank balance at 8,000 metres, but also brought shares and conducted funds transfers on their way to the top.

Not everywhere is the same

Although we can transact from anywhere with mobile apps, it's worth noting that we have very different mobile adoption rates, however. Japan and Korea have 100 percent smartphone coverage; 80 percent of Europe's population are mobile subscribers; whilst, in Sub-Saharan Africa, the figure is just 39 percent. But that's changing fast, and Africa and other under-developed economies are where we are seeing the fastest changes. For example, in 2012 only 11 percent of Sub-Saharan Africa were mobile.

In other words, there is a two stream world: a rapidly moving smartphone world of developed economies, and an even faster moving world of simpler mobile devices in under-developed economies.

Let's first examine people's move to mobiles in developed economies, such as the UK. The UK Office of Communications (Ofcom) carries out regular surveys on the digital lifestyles of British citizens. In 2015, the impact of smartphone and tablet computing showed how fast things have changed. The average UK adult now spends more time each day using media or communications (8 hours, 41 minutes) than they do sleeping (8 hours, 21 minutes, the UK average); but, because we're squeezing more into our day by multi-tasking on different devices, the total use of media and communications averaged over 11 hours every day in 2014, an increase of more than two hours since research was carried out in 2010.

Where computer use was traditionally dependent on desktop computers, tablet and smartphone devices are starting to dominate how we work and play. Over four in ten UK households had a tablet computer in 2014, up from a quarter the year before.

GENERATIONAL GAPS

Unsurprisingly, young adults are particularly glued to their smartphones, using them for 3 hours, 36 minutes each day, which is almost three times the 1 hour, 22 minutes average across all adults. What are they doing? Talking. Not talking with their voices, but with their fingers.

More than 90 percent of the device time of these young adults is message based, chatting on social networks like Facebook, or sending instant messages through services like WhatsApp, or even firing off traditional mobile phone text messages. Just two percent of children's time is spent emailing—compared to 33 percent for adults. But 10 percent of children's device time is spent sending video and photo messages, sharing or commenting on photos via services like Snapchat, or circulating 15 second videos over Instagram's sister app, Vine.

In a global context, these results are stunning. According to statistics from Facebook, Twitter, Apple and more:

- 1.44 billion people use Facebook mobile every month (April 2015)
- 655 million people only use Facebook mobile (July 2015)
- 100 billion apps have been downloaded from Apple's App Store (June 2015)
- 80 percent of a user's time is spent using apps on mobile
- $10 billion is the income Apple generated from apps in 2014 (Hollywood made $10 billion =from box office receipts in 2014)
- 500 million tweets are sent every day

Among the adult population, it's the 16-24s who spend the most time on media and communications. The UK statistics from Ofcom show that they are cramming over 14 hours of media and communications activity into 9 hours 8 minutes each day by multi-tasking, using different media and devices at the same time.

The comfort with using mobile social media is shown specifically by a Digital Quotient (DQ), which Ofcom calculated for a range of age brackets. Six year olds who have grown up with YouTube, Spotify and the BBC iPlayer, have an average DQ score of 98, higher than for those aged between 45–49, who scored an average of 96. Digital understanding peaks between 14 and

15, with a DQ of 113—and then drops gradually throughout adulthood, before falling rapidly in old age.

The thing to consider here is that six year olds are growing up with smartphones and tablets, but have no idea who Steve Jobs is; 15 year olds wonder why old folks sit at desktops; 35 year olds question why everything is not as digital as they are; and 50 years olds wonder why their bank's legacy systems are celebrating the same birthday as they are.

These demographics are important when it comes to mobile value exchange. For example, 82 percent of American 18–25 year olds owned a smartphone in Q4 2013, and 61 percent of those engaged in mobile banking. That compares to around 60 percent and 30 percent respectively for their parents, according to a March 2014 report from Alix Partners.

These ageist differences are not necessarily a surprise, as the internet is barely a quarter of a century old. The first time a commercial internet transaction took place was on 11th August 1994, only a couple of decades ago. This first, secure, online purchase was for a copy of the *Ten Summoner's Tales* album by Sting. Twenty years later, over $1.5 trillion of internet-based shopping takes place via mobile, tablet and PC. Of this, about a third of all internet shopping is now made via mobile.

Today, for that exchange of value which is commercial, banks are the most trusted. According to statistics gathered by Open Mobile Media in 2014, banks are the most trusted mobile payment provider with 43 percent of consumers claiming this as their preference. This is important, as this space is growing fast. According to Gartner Group, the global market for mobile payments is forecast to be about $720 billion worth of transactions by 2017. This is up from about $235 billion in 2013. Equally, there are specific days that are ramping up this traffic from Black Friday to Cyber Monday.

Black Friday is the second biggest shopping day of the year in America, as millions of shoppers descend on stores across the country on the Friday after the Thanksgiving holiday, hoping to save on their Christmas shopping. In 2014, Black Friday online sales broke new records, with mobile traffic outpacing PC traffic for the first time. Analysing customer transaction data, IBM found that browsing on smartphones and tablets accounted for 52.1 percent of all online traffic on Thanksgiving day, fuelling record online purchases on Black Friday. Thanksgiving saw online sales topping $1 billion and Black Friday passing $1.5 billion. Mobile sales accounted for 27.9 percent of these sales, up 28.2 percent over 2013.

Cyber Monday is the biggest shopping day for Americans, and is the Monday after Thanksgiving. This is the busiest day for online shopping over the five-day period, with Cyber Monday online sales topping $2 billion for the first time ever, up 8.5 percent over 2013. IBM noted that Cyber Monday mobile traffic accounted for over 41 percent of all online traffic, up 30 percent over 2013, with Monday sales 22 percent of total Cyber Monday online sales, an increase of 27.6 percent over 2013.

MOBILE MAKES INVISIBLE BANKING VISIBLE (AGAIN)

The critical difference with mobile is that it is a fundamentally different business model to every traditional value exchange, due to a very simple thing. Visibility. Some would call it transparency and others would call it real-time, but I would call it making invisible banking visible.

Half a century ago, all bank transactions were done on paper and we all had a visible view as to how each transaction hit our balance sheet. Each debit and credit was logged visibly in front of us in a branch, and we knew our exact balances at any given moment. Then, thanks to automation, balances became invisible as they moved on to computers. This meant that banks could charge us whatever they wanted as we went overdrawn. Whether we were overdrawn on purpose or by accident, it didn't matter.

Part of the reason why banks went this way—trying to gather revenue by applying fees on unexpected overdrafts—is due to free banking. With free banking, the banks had to work on charging us more and more fees for overdrafts, and find more and more ways to get us overdrawn.

This is why American banks have traditionally processed all the withdrawals to an account, before applying any deposits. If the debits cause the customer to move into an overdraft situation, then fees are applied before the deposits are added—a practice widely scorned.

When banking is invisible, the easiest thing to do is to charge us, the customer, for making mistakes, and that is the practice of most banks over the past half century. But that practice will disappear. Slowly but surely, the punitive charging of customers will go away, because mobile is making invisible banking visible.

Customers get real-time balances and can know their purchasing behaviours and balances at the point of sale. They can use mobile apps to predict behaviour, and even have the app tell them if they can afford to buy the item they are considering. This is why the main activity on mobile today is balance checks. Soon, it will go beyond this to predictive and intelligent purchasing, where the consumer does not even have to think about the mobile and the payment service, as the two will work together in harmony to tell them what they can and cannot afford to buy.

Making invisible banking visible removes the revenue stream from charging customers for mistakes, so banks will then have to make money in different ways, such as by telling the customer how to spend, save and live smarter.

After all, banking is just bits and bytes but, until recently, it has depended on a face-to-face engagement. Now, those requirements are disappearing and this is why we have seen such a fast change to digitalise payments.

For example, we are seeing similar changes in advice and KYC (Know Your Client). Many banks are realising that customers do not want to visit branches to pay in cheques, so create the remote cheque deposit app. They don't want to visit a branch with their passport and driving licence, so send a courier. They don't need to talk to someone in a branch for advice, they can get that through a Skype call.

The major bet in this mobile space for the smartphone generation is to gain the dominance of mobile wallet usage, and this is where we are seeing massive battles taking place between the internet giants of PayPal, Apple, Samsung, Google and others.

MOBILE IS THE AUTHENTICATION TOOL

As mentioned, many wallets are developing biometrics to authenticate the device user. Most are using fingerprints, although you can also use heartbeat and eyeball recognition. As a result, the more I think about mobile as an authentication tool, the more attractive it becomes.

First, you can check the customer is who they say they are by locating if they have a second token—a mobile registered to their account—with them. Some banks in Asia use this method to ensure that if you go to an ATM, you only withdraw cash if you have both your bank card and mobile together in the same location.

That leads to a second advantage: the fact that you can geo-locate customers using mobile. A company called XYVerify does this using telecom masts, rather than your mobile device. The system establishes your location based upon where your signal can be located between different mobile transmitting masts. It can then use an independent verification mechanism to determine whether you really have your phone with you.

Third, I like mobile authentication because you can authenticate who the customer is interactively using One Time Passwords (OTP) by text messaging. Again, used by some banks, an interactive text or app-based OTP process means that the mobile can offer a great second level authentication tool.

Fourth, you can check it's really who you think it is using mobile biometrics, and this is the biggest growth area. Apple and Samsung are using fingerprints, but there are alternatives. Banca Intesa in Spain was using mobile apps for iris recognition; Voice Commerce offer voice verification by mobile; and Nymi by Biomix provides an app that links to a watchstrap in order to use your heartbeat as verification.

Locating customers and verifying and authenticating them through the Internet of Things will become the norm. It will be the case of knowing who is where, doing what, in real-time, and being able to check it is who you think it is without forcing an action—a token or PIN being activated—but by sensing the person through the network.

We are very near to this today and getting nearer, so let's stop worrying about fraud and risk with mobiles and start thinking far more about fraud and risk minimisation.

AS MOBILE CAME ALIVE, PAYPAL ALMOST DIED

PayPal should be the dominant player in mobile payments and mobile wallets, as they owned the internet payment space. Certainly they have a strong mobile presence. For example, PayPal saw a 43 percent increase in mobile shoppers in the United States over Thanksgiving, and a 51 percent increase on Black Friday 2014.

PayPal's Q2 2015 earnings showed that "total payment volume grew 28 percent to $66 billion and revenue reached $2.3 billion, an increase of 19 percent. We processed 1.1 billion transactions, a jump of 27 percent. We added 3.5 million new customer accounts to reach 169 million." The results from the same quarter, the year before: "revenue grew to $1.9 billion. PayPal gained 4 million new active registered accounts to end the quarter at 152 million, up 15 percent."

The thing is that, as 2012's figures show, PayPal's growth is not always spectacular. Back in 2012, PayPal was being threatened by the growth of Square, a mobile first POS system. Square and its siblings—iZettle, Sumup, Payleven, mPowa and more—were all focused upon mobile innovations. PayPal had been playing with mobile for years, but had not seriously committed to it. In fact, much of PayPal's operations were focused upon grinding the web machine and they had built this business model around web transactions.

That model was threatened by new, mobile-focused players and, by the time PayPal saw it, their initial reaction was derisory as, to compete with Square, they launched a Triangle.

Finally, they did react properly by introducing PayPal Here—a smartphone POS dongle for magnetic stripe and chip & PIN payments. The developments continue with PayPal Beacon, a bluetooth hands-free easy way to pay, and a partnership with Samsung on easy authentication via fingerprint. They acquired  Braintree, Venmo, Xoom and Modest. All of these relate to building their mobile business and this is reflected in PayPal's mobile numbers:

2006: under $1 million mobile payments processed

2007: $7 million

2008: $25 million

2009: $141 million

2010: $750 million

2011: $4 billion (up 525 percent)

2012: $14 billion (up 250 percent)

2013: $27 billion (up 99 percent) of $180 billion in total transaction value

2014: $46 billion (up 68 percent) of $235 billion in total transaction value

The fact is that PayPal are the leading digital wallet provider and preferred choice for mobile digital payments in America today.

This shows that having almost lost the mobile plot, PayPal have turned it around to win by creating a mobile-first strategy. The key to this has been focusing upon owning the mobile space through innovation, and no company illustrates innovation better than Venmo.

Venmo appeared as a result of a weekend among two developer millennials, because one of the two friends forgot his checkbook. According to Venmo's co-founder Andrew Kortina:

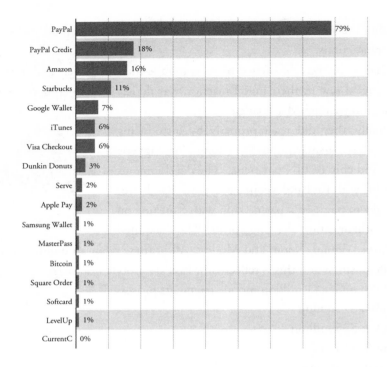

PayPal	79%
PayPal Credit	18%
Amazon	16%
Starbucks	11%
Google Wallet	7%
iTunes	6%
Visa Checkout	6%
Dunkin Donuts	3%
Serve	2%
Apple Pay	2%
Samsung Wallet	1%
MasterPass	1%
Bitcoin	1%
Square Order	1%
Softcard	1%
LevelUp	1%
CurrentC	0%

"One of the weekends we were getting together to work on this idea, Iqram [Magdon-Ismail, Venmo's other founder] was visiting me in NYC and left his wallet in Philly. I covered him for the whole weekend, and he ended up writing me a check to pay me back. It was annoying for him to have to find a checkbook to do this, and annoying for me to have to go to the bank if I wanted to cash it (I never did). We thought, why are we still doing this? We do everything else with our phones. We should definitely be using PayPal to pay each other back. But we don't, and none of our friends do. So we decided, let's just try to solve this problem, and build a way to pay each other back that feels consistent with all of the other experiences we have in apps we use with our friends."

Four years later, Venmo's processing power is doubling year-on-year ($700m processed Q3 2014 vs $1.6bn Q2 2015), because it was designed by millennials for millennials, and understands that new developments can take place in hours.

This is a critical point: things change at light speed for the mobile world. Photos, headlines, ideas and apps can go global in minutes. It is the age of real-time, almost free instantaneous change, and it's hard for the overnight batch analogue generation to keep up.

We are living in fast cycle change where many bankers—and consultants— are finding it hard to keep up. Right now, by way of example, we see a mega battle playing out between Square and PayPal. More importantly, we see a major battle between firms like Stripe and Klarna (Klarna is covered in more detail in the second half of this book), companies most executives in financial firms haven't heard of—even though they are core to every business by enabling simple, fast value exchange, peer-to-peer through the mobile network.

The challenge for incumbent firms

As mobile internet reinvents commerce and value exchange on this planet, we are seeing companies creating specialist apps like Venmo and specialist processing like Klarna, which unbundles banking to simplify the process

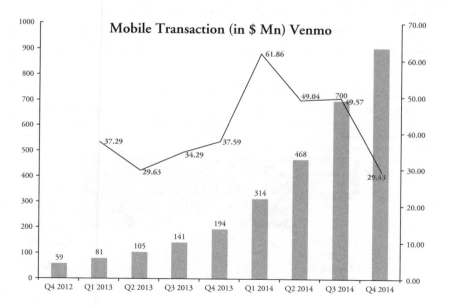

of value exchange. PayPal and Alipay simplified the activity of paying by providing a layer over the traditional complexity of payment systems. Prosper and Zopa have simplified credit markets by providing connectivity between those who have money and those who need it.

Paying and enabling credit are the narrow areas of finance being restructured through simplification, but any aspect of value exchange can be flattened by simplicity combined with network economics. In fact, via apps and mobile, we are seeing the unbundling of banking.

Any financial activity can be levelled by technology in the age of the ValueWeb. Any financial activity can be simplified. Any financial marketplace can be flattened by connectivity, peer-to-peer, person-to-person.

This is why banks have changed tack and become integrators and aggregators of components of finance. A bank cannot compete with a specialist who is simplifying a marketplace or financial activity, because an incumbent bank's systems and structures are usually too rigid, old and inflexible to change. That is why the new entrant simplifier can create P2P credit at less than 100 basis points differential (one percent difference between their lending and savings rates) compared to a bank's 400 basis points or more. A bank has to cover the costs of their premises, people and infrastructure. A start-up has none of that legacy or overhead.

This is why banks need to work with the simplifiers and incorporate their best practices into their own. This is why the likes of Venmo and

Unbundling of a Bank

Braintree were purchased by PayPal. Any incumbent player who tries to resist the onslaught of the simplifiers is going to fail, because the simplifiers are reinventing activities and markets overnight.

Could PayPal have invented Venmo? Sure. Did PayPal invent Venmo? No way. Why didn't PayPal invent Venmo? Because simplification comes from kids and complexity comes from incumbents.

The incumbents are too bogged down in their own complexity to see simplicity. That's why the ValueWeb is so hot, because it's reinventing financial activities and simplifying markets. And the main space it is shaking up is in the consumer's mobile handset via a virtual wallet.

WALLET WARS HAVEN'T REALLY STARTED YET ...

When talking about wallets, there are many variations: digital wallets, virtual wallets, mobile wallets and more. For the purposes of the ValueWeb, when we say "wallet" we mean all of these, but will refer specifically to mobile wallets for ease of terminology.

Mobile wallets have been talked about for a long time. Google Wallet was perhaps the first big launch and, since then, there have been many. For example, in 2012, I thought the wallet wars were about to begin when the UK mobile network O2 launched a wallet. At the time, there were not many available. The chart on the following page illustrates this well.

Today, the O2 wallet has been retired and the Orange system is not a wallet but just an NFC payment called Cash on Tap. Of the others, Barclays Pingit has developed fast. Since it launched in February 2012, the Pingit app has been downloaded three million times and the total amount of money sent using the service had reached £540 million by July 2014. That's about £250 million a year at the current run rate, which is not that amazing considering that the UK spends 2,000 times more on cards annually (£500 billion a year).

Google Wallet looked like the megabeast when it launched in May 2011 but it is still primarily for American users, and appears to be stagnating. Like Google Checkout, it appears to be a service that Google hopes will succeed, but never really does. In a development of 2014 for example, you can just plug money into Gmails.

O2 Wallet: product comparison table

Key features	Money messages Allows users to send cash as easily as sending a text using a mobile phone number	Digitise the contents of your wallet Enables customers to digitise existing cards to make it easy and quick to pay by mobile	Compare and go Allows consumers to compare prices and shop easily via their mobile	Offers Provides a range of offers from top brands	NFC Enables consumers to use NFC-enabled handsets for contactless payments - if the terminals are in place
O2 Wallet Send and receive money, compare prices and shop, digitise existing cards, O2 Money Account Card	✓	✓	✓	✓	✗
Barclays Pingit Send and receive money using just a mobile phone number	✓	✗	✗	✗	✗
Google Wallet Store payment cards and offers on your phone (currently only availble in US)	✗	✓	✗	✓	✓
Orange Quick Tap Pay for things with your NFC-enabled handset if terminals in place	✗	✗	✗	✓	✓
PayPal Manage your PayPal account, send money, buy things	✓	✗	✗	✓	✗

O2 Wallet is a seamless and secure digital wallet service that will deliver the benefits of mobile money to more UK consumers than any other product or service currently available.

O₂

With almost half a billion Gmail users, that could make a difference, but I don't think so. That's because people see different brands for different things:

- Amazon is for buying
- Google is for searching
- Facebook is for sharing
- Apple is for entertaining
- PayPal is for paying (as is Square)

That's why, for all of the efforts of Google, Amazon, Facebook and Apple, the most likely winner is the one that already has the breadth, depth and name in this space: PayPal. As cheque and cash usage declines and cards are displaced by wallets, every provider of payment services wants to be the next PayPal. This is why there's so much activity in this space, as everyone wants to create the next generation PayPal—and that's what the mobile wallet will deliver.

IS APPLE PAY THE WALLET TO RULE THEM ALL?

After years of indecision and procrastination, Apple finally announced their plans for the payments space in September 2014, alongside the announcement of the Apple Watch and iPhone 6. They opted to use NFC (Near Field Communications), meaning that all iPhones could now become contactless payment devices.

In addition, having rolled out Touch ID for fingerprint recognition, the introduction of Apple Pay also endorses the further erosion of banks at the front-end of banking. Banks are becoming back-end engines rather than front-end brands. As an illustration of this point, major card companies (Visa, Mastercard, AMEX) and leading US banks (Wells Fargo, Citi, J.P. Morgan, Bank of America) were a part of the announcement; but it is Apple Pay, not using your Apple device via your bank, that people noticed.

A key difference about the launch of Apple Pay—bearing in mind this was released before similar wallets appeared on Samsung and Android—is that it uses NFC chips to communicate securely and wirelessly with existing point-of-sale terminals. Another key point is that it uses the Touch ID fingerprint sensor to authenticate purchases. Using the iPhone's camera means that users can take a picture of their bank card, and the details are automatically added to the Apple Pay service. Once the mobile device is set up, users can then make payments in any compatible retailer simply by tapping their phone and pressing their finger on the Touch ID sensor. If

Pay

Your wallet.
Without the wallet.

Gone are the days of searching for your wallet.
The wasted moments finding the right card. The
swiping and waiting. Now payments happen
with a single touch.

Apple Pay will change how you pay with
breakthrough contactless payment technology
and unique security features built right into the
devices you have with you every day. So you can
use your iPhone 6 or Apple Watch to pay in an
easy, secure, and private way.

Coming in October

they have an Apple Watch, it's even easier, as you just touch the watch to
the reader.

When you use the service Apple is not aware of what you bought, how
much it cost or where you bought it from—that information passes directly
to your bank. The shop also does not get to see your payment details which,
it's claimed, makes this very secure.

Another notable aspect of the Apple Pay system is Stripe, the payment
start-up that Apple chose as it's API (Application Program Interface)
provider for getting merchants to take payments. Started in 2011, Stripe
had gained a valuation of $3.5 billion when Apple Pay launched, purely
because it offers an easy way for accepting Apple Pay in their iOS apps.

Why Apple Pay matters

Some say that Apple Pay is nothing new or original. However, it is an
important wrap around for the banking system.

First, the Apple Pay wallet includes almost a billion people who already
have an account via iTunes. There were over 885 million iTunes accounts
as of December 2014, increasing by around 100 million accounts every six
months. That's a good starting place.

Second, it's Apple. Apple have this way of taking stuff that's out there that doesn't work well and making it brilliant. That's what they did with MP3 players; and remember that when the iPhone first launched, everyone thought that Nokia was unassailable. Nokia's brand was worth more than Google's or Apple's in 2009. Today, they're dead and Apple is viewed as unassailable. They're not, of course, but they're surely in a position of strength, and Apple Pay with the iPhone and iTunes wallet could become the dominant player.

Third, Apple has the additional features of Touch ID and PIN for secure entry and access. Add to that SIM recognition and geolocation tracking, with telephone lock if lost, and you have a pretty secure device.

Fourth, it's incorporated NFC so you have a true wallet. Integrated NFC, Touch ID, geolocation and more, all wrapped up in an iTunes account that already exists. That's a great start.

Finally, and most important of all, is that we've been waiting for a mobile wallet. There have been many attempts already, but none have succeeded because they've each been missing a function. A reason and incentive to use a wallet are the key factors. Now, the reason I'd use the Apple Pay wallet is if it displaced the need for me to register my card or prepay details in other apps. Why do I have to load payment information in the Starbucks app, and then again in the Uber app, and then again in the eBay app, and then again in the Airbnb app? We need one app to unite them all, and I think Apple Pay is that app. Apple Pay aggregates the payments for all apps. That's the dream, and companies like Stripe are enabling that dream through their APIs.

These five factors are all in Apple's favour, and there have been a lot of companies gunning for mobile wallets and no one has taken that space yet. So here's the long-term vision: Apple develops the mobile wallet of choice. The mobile wallet is tied to the smartphone and soon has crossed over to a watch. The watch uses the heartbeat as the authentication factor, rather than the fingerprint. It's also factored in voice recognition biometrics and more. Therefore, as you walk around and see stuff, you just say *yes* or *no* to purchase. The wallet is live on your wrist and you continually see balances, affordability, purchase history and location. The actual purchase pattern is invisible and non-intrusive.

We then move past this, and Apple Pay is part of your life as a watch or a phone, but it's also in the cloud and around you as you connect with things. So you don't need to get out of the car to refuel. Your Apple Pay cloud just pays for you, and you confirm the amount by just breathing "yes". Your television pre-orders the movies and series you like. If you don't fancy that particular program, the order can be cancelled and funds are automatically reimbursed to you. In other words, you don't even think about it, but can see everything aggregated in one place.

But here's the real killer thing about Apple Pay downstream. If it succeeds in being the wallet of choice, and all consumers start to switch to the mobile wallet with NFC rather than the card with swipe or PIN … could Apple then launch its own payment mechanism? The Apple Pay wallet system, with its own bank partner (if it needs one); you won't need PayPal or Visa or MasterCard. You will just need Apple.

Mobile wallet wars: Apple Pay vs Samsung Pay vs Android Pay

I was surprised to hear one of my colleagues recently purchased an iMac in the Apple Store using his Apple Watch and Apple Pay. Yes, he's an Apple guy, but really? A £1,000 purchase via a fingerprint? I thought, as do most, that you could only make small transactions using contactless payments. In the UK under £20 (£30 from September 2015), and in the United States under $25. But it is not the case at all.

The key here is that it is the point-of-sale (POS) software that is making the difference, not the device or payment instrument you are using. The POS makes the difference between whether you are limited to low value or high value payments.

The low value limit is when there's no verification involved or, rather, no Cardholder Verification Mechanism (CVM). That is not the case with Apple Pay however, as Apple Pay is based upon a biometric Touch ID. In this case there is an additional layer of consumer identification based upon the device and an additional recognition layer, i.e., your fingerprint. This method is therefore based upon a Consumer Device Cardholder Verification Method (CDCVM) rather than no verification. This is the reason you can have high value payments with CDCVM but are limited to low value when you lack this device authentication.

All of this has appeared just as Samsung ramps up its entry into the wallet market—and Samsung have one big advantage over Apple, as their wallet uses a technology called "Magnetic Secure Transmission", which allows its mobile payment system to be used on standard credit card machines. Apple Pay's NFC connectivity is limited to only a small number of companies who have this sort of terminal at the checkout. With the Samsung Pay wallet, you just swipe on the screen, select the card you want to pay with and then input your PIN or fingerprint to authenticate. That's not only incredibly easy, but also capable of being used as a CDCVM for a high value payment at the checkout.

Then there's Android Pay, the Google upgrade to Google Wallet to compete with Apple and Samsung. Some claim Android Pay has advantages over Apple and Samsung by being integrated with loyalty programs, such as MyCokeRewards. Its contactless payment system doesn't require a fingerprint or other authentication (although that defeats the high value payment option) and, perhaps of most importance, Android phones offer far more choice, from the Samsung to HTC to LG to the original Moto and Nexus handsets.

Could mobile wallets kill Visa and MasterCard?

What intrigues me with Apple Pay, Samsung Pay, Android Pay, Facebook Pay and more—don't forget their overseas equivalents such as Alipay and Yandex Money—is that we now have the big internet heavyweights in the world of technology weighing in on payments. Their aim: make it easy, cheap and convenient to pay whilst engaged in entertainment, sharing and fun. It's all about removing the friction of payments (which should be what the banks do).

The good news is that these new wallets have allowed banks to remain in the online money business. The bad news is that banks are now wrapped in a stranglehold by these major players.

The evidence of what this means is that banks are going to be squeezed on margin. We've already seen this with Apple forcing lower fees per transaction from their bank wallet players, giving Apple a slice of margin off the top that equates to billions when you multiply 800+ million iTunes accounts making an average $3.2 in transactions per month (as of June 2013).

Android, Samsung, Facebook and other payment models will follow the same approach over time, as banks don't want to lose the opportunity and threat of being included or excluded from these heavyweight players' networks. But it's not the banks I feel sorry for, but Visa and MasterCard. Right now, the card companies have been very adept at pushing innovation. They've been at the heart of contactless rollout, NFC and developing the mobile wallet. But what happens if Apple or another player came out tomorrow and said that they're now going to be transaction rails to your bank? Visa and MasterCard (and the rest) wouldn't stand a chance.

I'm not saying they will do this, as it would involve too much negotiation with banks and such like, but it could happen. It may not be in their interest to do anything, but let's just say that one day they decide that all of your payments will be taken monthly from your bank account, or any other preferred source, for a charge of $1. In so doing, you get a 5 percent reduction in all your purchase costs. The reduction is because there are no fees being taken by the card companies and retailers and banks have agreed a good deal with Apple to be in the loop.

HAVE BANKS MADE A FATAL MISTAKE?

This leads into a whole dialogue about the general role of banks in this new mobile wallet world. In the good old days, for big challenges, banks would get together and create a co-operative to solve the problem. SWIFT, Visa and MasterCard were all bank created co-operatives. Admittedly, times have changed and now Visa and MasterCard are private entities, but originally they were created to solve problems that a single bank could not tackle, like making global payments and processing billions of card transactions.

Since then, I wonder if banks have taken their eye off the ball. As the internet took over, banks decided to ignore the need for online payments and let start-ups, such as Alipay, Yandex and PayPal, take over. Now the start-ups are more than upstarts, as they have taken a major chunk of online transaction processing.

Take PayPal's latest exploits. On Monday 20th July 2015, PayPal split from its mother ship eBay and rocketed rapidly to a $50 billion valuation. The last time PayPal was trading publicly, in 2002, just before eBay acquired the business, it was valued at $1.5 billion. That's some explosion of business, especially as the mother ship is worth less than its baby. At the time of the split, eBay was trading at just over $34 billion. It's no wonder as PayPal has almost 170 million active users in over 200 markets trading in 57 currencies.

Banks should have been creating a collegiate version of PayPal for global online payments. The nearest you get to that is something like the domestic Dutch payments system iDEAL, created to lock out PayPal. Meanwhile,

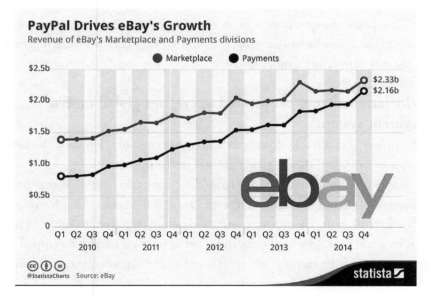

PayPal Drives eBay's Growth
Revenue of eBay's Marketplace and Payments divisions

Sweden has upstarts like Klarna solving the problem in an even better way, and one that doesn't involve using cards.

Why didn't the banks cooperate to create a global online payments system?

So now we have mobile wallets in play from the big technology firms, with banks desperate to get in on the action. Apple Pay, for example, managed to agree deals with 750 banks to operate with their wallet in the first quarter after launch, and at vastly reduced transaction fee rates. I wouldn't be surprised if, in a few years, every bank is somehow wrapped up in someone else's wallet.

Mobile wallets like Apple, Google and Samsung achieve two things for these firms at the banks expense:

(a) They own the customer relationship

(b) They have the banks completely under their control

If you don't believe the latter point, then just look at how all the US banks have reduced their fees to ensure they are part of the wallet. This means that these technology heavyweights could demand further, deep discounting in the future; if they get this from one bank, then all the other banks will have to follow.

This raises the question: why it was that banks could solve insoluble issues in the 1970s by working together, and yet they couldn't work together in the 2010s to create a mobile wallet?

Why haven't banks cooperated to create a global mobile payment system?

The answer is that banks don't trust each other anymore. However, because of this lack of trust, they're giving ground to the upstarts.

Apple Pay is not trying to disintermediate the banks, but what they have achieved is to create a front-end wrapper around the banks. That front-end wrapper reduces the friction for paying and takes over the relationship. What this means is that, like Starbucks and Uber apps, banks will be wrapped in layers of processing through APIs and apps by others, gradually reducing the visibility of banking to a pure utility status.

We have known this for years, but wave after wave of wallet announcements from technology giants should send a few shudders down the corridors of high offices in the banking world, as those banks are now paying to be included in something that diminishes their status. It's a lose-lose situation.

Does anyone actually need a mobile wallet?

No one's won the mobile wallet war yet, not even Apple, Google or PayPal, but it is there to be won. Why has no one taken this crown yet? Because no one has yet worked out what a mobile wallet is for.

For example, two surveys of iPhone 6 users in November 2014 and March 2015 found that 6 percent were using the Apple Pay service (up from 5 percent), 9 percent had tried it but weren't using it (up from 4 percent), leaving 85 percent who had never tried it (as opposed to 91 percent). The main reason those who had tried Apple Pay, but didn't use it generally, was due to forgetfulness as almost a third (32 percent) of respondents said they just forgot it was an option.

In other words, the mobile wallet has to be relevant and seen in the same way as card or cash, and it's not at the moment. This is where we can look to Asia, with probably the greatest successes in developing workable mobile wallets found with Tencent's WeChat and Alibaba's Alipay in China. These two heavyweights are in a head-to-head battle to gain consumers through their mobile online services and, as a result, both are taking mobile wallets extremely seriously. Both are investing heavily, and aiming to capture this market for mobile money before anyone else does. That is why they have now opened their own banks.

WILL BANK DEVELOPMENTS IN CHINA LEAD TO A GLOBAL MOBILE BANKING REVOLUTION?

China is leading the world of banking with the opening of digital banks WeBank and MyBank. These two potential bank titans launched in 2015 as offshoots of QQ and WeChat, owned by Tencent, and Alipay and ANT Financial, owned by Alibaba. These movements follow a number of notable achievements from both Tencent and Alibaba, from the trillions of dollars that flowed into Alibaba's money market fund to the remarkable volume of messages generated by the Red Letter Day promotion. It leads me to wonder why these developments are so far ahead of Europe and America. Why haven't Google, Amazon and Facebook succeeded in creating their own banks and payment systems? What will happen when they do?

Alibaba is the Amazon of China while Tencent is the Facebook. A third player, Baidu, would be the Google. However, the most intense rivalry exists between Alibaba and Tencent, especially when it comes to money.

For example, the first move to shake up the financial markets with new private players began in June 2013, when Alibaba launched a money market fund called Yu'ebao. At the time Alibaba's chief executive, Jack Ma, was quoted as saying: "China's finance industry, especially the banking industry, only serves 20 percent of clients. I see the 80 percent of businesses that have not been served. The financial industry needs disruption. It needs outsiders to come in and transform it." Transform it, it did, as investors flocked to the new service. Within nine months, the total number of investors in the fund topped 81 million people. Compare that with the fact that there were only 77 million active equity trading accounts in the whole country at the time. In other words, within nine months, Alibaba had attracted more people to invest in its fund than all of China's stock traders.

WeChat followed Alibaba's lead and launched Licaitong, a fund that also attracted fast take-up, helped somewhat by their promise of high returns. When Alibaba's fund Yu'ebao launched, it offered 7 percent interest rate returns. As a result, Yu'ebao accumulated $98 billion in assets and 200 million users by the end of July 2015; Licaitong has attracted just over $15 billion.

So these two internet players—Alibaba and Tencent—are setting the benchmark for innovation in China and, from a financial markets viewpoint, the world. For example, take payments. Both companies offer a payments service that is wrapped into their chatroom offers. Alibaba offers Alipay while Tencent offers Tenpay as part of WeChat and QQ, their messaging systems.

To promote the use of such payment systems, these two giants created incentives to send payment messages to celebrate the Chinese New Year. The idea began in 2014, when Tencent promoted its 400 million WeChat users to send each other virtual red envelopes, which would be deposited into their mobile payment accounts. The gimmick became a big hit, with 40 million virtual envelopes being exchanged, worth a record 400 million yuan ($64 million). Jack Ma of Alibaba called it a "Pearl Harbor moment" for his company, and ramped up the game in 2015 by announcing it would give away more than 600 million yuan ($96 million) to its 190 million users as "lucky money" gifts if they used its red letter messaging system. Tencent responded within hours by saying it would also gift 800 million yuan ($128 million) to users of its virtual red envelopes service, and blocked Alipay users from their WeChat friends. Tencent's WeChat won that battle, with over one billion virtual red envelopes send on 18 February 2015, compared with 240 million sent through the Alipay Wallet. As can be seen, the rivalry between the two firms is intense.

Then China's regulators offered private companies the opportunity to apply for banking licences last year, resulting in these two key internet players both launching banks in 2015. The two banks are rather different, however. Tencent launched WeBank first in January 2015, and focuses upon microlending due to the restrictions placed upon its bank licence by the regulators. For example, they cannot open branches and are unable to take deposits. After all, they don't want these banks competing head-to-head with the large, state-owned banks; this is why the new, private banks are focusing upon the underbanked and unbanked in China at this early stage.

For example, Tencent's WeBank has chosen micro-lending as its first major business area, lending 800 million yuan ($130 million) during June and July 2015. Loans have quite a steep interest rate of 0.05 percent per day, or 18.25 percent per annum, and Tencent has so far only offered this lending on its QQ messaging service, but everyone expects this to expand to WeChat soon.

Similar to WeBank, MyBank was launched by Alibaba in June 2015 and also focused upon the small depositors. At its launch, Eric Jing, MyBank's executive chairman, said that "answering to the needs of those who have limited access to financial services in China is our mission" and "is here to give affordable loans for small and micro enterprises". It sounds very similar in strategy to WeBank, focusing upon microlending through the internet.

In other words, although China has opened up its banking sector to the private markets, it has managed to do so in such a way as to avoid any direct threat to the traditional, state-owned banking sector. Will that change in the future, and what does all of this mean for users in Europe and America?

The answer is that we will see some emulation of the experiences in China in Europe and America, but it will be very different. Firstly, China's story is of a newer economy building itself into a powerhouse, but most of China's large companies are state-owned. Of China's 12 largest companies, all of them are state-owned, including the largest banks ICBI, the Bank of China, the Agricultural Bank of China and China Construction Bank.

This is very different to European and American banking structures, even considering the 2008 banking bailouts, and means that China's regulators are highly restrictive over what internet banks can do. For example, they've ensured that the Chinese banks do not compete in the same space as the state-owned banks by banning branch operations and limiting their operations to credit markets. However, there are some interesting nuances underlying what has happened in China that our internet giants will learn from, particularly Facebook.

For example, although WeChat was only launched four years ago, it already has over 550 million monthly active users (MAUs). That's almost three times the MAUs of Japan's Line, and ten times the MAUs of Korea's Kakao. In fact, it's only 150 million MAUs short of Facebook Messenger, the largest messaging system out there. This is why it is worth exploring what is likely to develop over the next year or two, because the cornerstone of WeChat is payments.

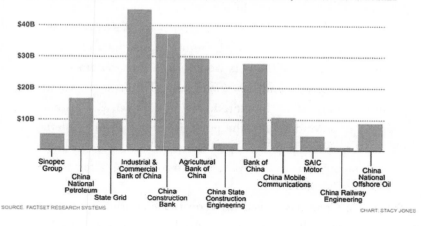

2014 PROFITS OF CHINA'S 12 LARGEST, AND GOVERNMENT-OWNED, GLOBAL 500 COMPANIES

SOURCE: FACTSET RESEARCH SYSTEMS

CHART: STACY JONES

Using the WeChat Wallet, WeChat users can order food deliveries, buy film tickets, play casual games, check in for a flight, send money to friends, access fitness tracker data, get banking statements, pay the water bill, ID music and search for a book at the local library, all via a single, integrated app. It's very similar to the example I outlined earlier, where the ideal app would allow me to order taxis, coffee, music and accommodation without having to enter my bank details in Uber, Starbucks, iTunes and Airbnb's apps as separate services. That's what WeChat's Wallet achieves, and enables the user to easily order services in any app that sits on the WeChat platform. It's more elegant than Alipay, since that service is geared towards Alibaba's commerce platforms.

Now the beauty of the WeChat Wallet is that it's a Trojan Horse for quickly getting a user's payment credentials registered, and then using that payment capability to unlock a range of new monetization opportunities for the entire ecosystem. This was noted by Connie Chan when she blogged about WeChat on the Andreessen Horowitz site recently. In the blog, Connie points to how Facebook Messenger could copy WeChat Wallet in Europe and America, and notes that it is no coincidence that the man who runs Facebook Messenger is the former CEO of PayPal, David Marcus:

"To get a sense of this in the U.S.: Just imagine how many more transactions would occur on Facebook's platform if more users linked their credit cards to Messenger, how much faster Pinterest's buy-it button would take off, how much faster Snapchat users would move from sending cash to buying goods, and how many more Twitter users would pursue options to buy products. In this sense, WeChat gives us a window into the potential evolution of Western social networks and buying behaviors if they, too, succeed in convincing users to embrace payments on their platforms."

What Ms. Chan has picked up upon is the clearly evolving model of not just Facebook Messenger but also Apple Pay, Twitter and others. The battle is for the wallet, and the way to win the wallet war is to create a single, integrated app that has a payments wallet at its core. If you become the standard core wallet, then you rule the mobile, social world. That's what China's WeChat has achieved, and it will be intriguing to see what happens as Facebook, Twitter and other mobile social systems deploy their "buy it now" buttons.

WHEN EVERYONE ON THE PLANET HAS A MOBILE, THINGS CHANGE

So far, we have focused mainly on developed economies, and how they are using mobile but, as mentioned earlier, the real action with mobile is in other economies, particularly Africa, Central and South America, and large parts of India, China and South Asia. All of these areas are creating substantially different innovations, especially where there is large-scale poverty and financial exclusion. This is because mobile provides a unique, new method of financial inclusion.

In particular, Africa is high on the agenda of many governments and charities, most notably the Bill & Melinda Gates Foundation (see the interview with Kosta Peric in the second half of this book). The Foundation has the goal "to help people in the world's poorest regions improve their lives and build sustainable futures by connecting them with digitally-based financial tools and services". In fact, it goes further than this, with Bill Gates arguing that poverty will be eradicated in his 2014 annual update: "I am optimistic enough about this that I am willing to make a prediction. By 2035, there will be almost no poor countries left in the world. Specifically, I mean that by 2035, almost no country will be as poor as any of the 35 countries that the World Bank classifies as low-income today, even after adjusting for inflation."

This is a prediction that is based upon financial inclusion, allowing the poorest nations to save for their families and insure their crops; transfer money freely and easily and have everyone capable of being a merchant —and it's all thanks to the mobile networks for financial inclusion.

According to the World Bank, absolute poverty has halved in the last 25 years, as has the number of children dying under the age of five. In a large part, that is thanks to technology and the sharing of knowledge across the world through networked systems. It means that the tracking of diseases and health issues are being managed far better, and ensures a better quality of care even in the poorest countries. But, despite all that, there has been little progress to make financial transactions work in emerging economics cheaply, easily and readily accessible. That is why most charitable, philanthropic and political interests are focused upon deploying financial inclusion to the world's poorest regions over the next quarter century.

Technologies can make digital transactions very inexpensive and easy, as the mobile telephone has become pervasive, and what poor people need in order to move out of poverty is access to financial services. Most poor people keep their cash at home, where it earns no interest and can be easily stolen. The poorest people buy livestock and seeds, but are unable to insure them. That is why they get caught in a poverty trap, because they cannot get insurance to cover bad years of crops and production.

That is why the Bill & Melinda Gates Foundation, along with the World Bank and United Nations, is focused upon how to improve the availability of financial tools for the poorest, and are focused upon accelerating the use of mobile for financial inclusion. It starts with money transfer as the way to bring everyone onto the network but, very quickly, merchants realise they can accept those digital payments, too. This means it soon becomes a digital currency. In the world's poorest regions, there is more money going through mobile transfers than in the local currency, as people are not cashing out but just transferring digital messages. Now all economies are trying to emulate these capabilities and, over the next few years, this will become totally pervasive.

The transaction system is the key element, then the people can be drawn into the economy. It is anticipated that up to two billion new customers in the world's poorest countries will be brought into the formal economy over the next decade, using services that most of us take for granted, such as building a credit record. Two billion new bank customers, who can also take out loans and mortgages, as well as saving and investing.

All of these digital records will be created, and it will make assessing an individual's credit risk far, far easier. This makes it easy for everyone to be entrepreneurs too, thanks to M-commerce. As a result, billing and credit will change completely, and the pace of change is going to be fast. I would be surprised if mobile digital transactions are not pervasive in most countries within the next ten years.

This is underpinned by mobile and digital structures. If you can't do it through a mobile telephone, then it's not worth doing. This is down to using mobile services to offer insurances for crop failure along with simple transmission of value from towns to villages. In addition, the mobile network can exchange value not just in terms of sending and receiving money, but also other forms of value. For example, after the failure of the national currency in Zimbabwe, shops accept South African rand, US dollars or airtime on the mobile network as payment. In Indonesia, after typhoons and other natural disasters hit, the World Bank issued food stamps in the form of mobile text messages. In war-torn areas of Afghanistan, the post-war rebuilding of trade and commerce is happening using mobile payment systems to allow secure and trusted transactions.

As can be seen, mobile is transformational and, in underbanked regions, is even more transformational than the use of mobile smartphone services in developed economies. By way of example, billions of people have previously been excluded from electronic networks and finance because it was too expensive to reach them. Now it is cheap and easy. Alcatel sells a mobile handset for under $2 and all of this has made mobile network services easily accessible. There are now more people on earth that have access to a mobile phone, than have access to a toothbrush or a toilet. This trend will only continue as we see a billion new mobile users in the next five years, increasing the number of active mobile users from 3.6 billion to 4.6 billion, according to the GSMA.

AFRICA SHOWS THE WAY TO THE FUTURE

A big source of inspiration in mobile financial inclusion has been the success of M-PESA in Kenya.

M-PESA is one of the first and leading implementations of mobile money transfers between people in Kenya, through the mobile network operator Safaricom, a subsidiary of Vodafone. Vodafone was asked to set up M-PESA by the Kenyan government, and launched the service in March 2007 as a joint venture, 40 percent owned by Vodafone Kenya and 60 percent by the government, which they reduced to 35 percent through a privatisation sale in June 2007.

The actual service provides a simple way to move money between people using mobile messaging, and it has revolutionised payments. This is because most people in Kenya were unbanked, so they either had cash or nothing. No credit and debit cards, cheques or other ways of paying. To move money between towns and villages was fraught with risk, as you would have to physically give the money to a bus driver or taxi driver and hope they would deliver it.

Now, with the mobile telephone as the core value exchange mechanism, it has changed everything. As one Kenyan farmer puts it: "I can just walk from my *shamba* (farm) and get money. I don't have to spend and go into town. If the agent does not have cash today, then I will come back tomorrow. It is cheaper to wait."

One key aspect that determined the success of M-PESA has been this agent network. Agents in the towns take money and text the agent in the location the money needs to be delivered. The agent in the receiving location gets the text message and then issues cash to the target recipient.

It is this agent system that has generated trust, security and safety and, therefore, its success. For example, Originally, Vodafone and the government estimated they would gain about 200,000 users in the first year. By the end of year one, they had achieved ten times that number with over 2 million users. Two years after launch, M-PESA employed 12,000 Kenyans in provision of services to 8 million customers. That's 20 percent of the population in two years. With only 4 million people with bank accounts in Kenya, this means that Vodafone have accidentally become Kenya's largest bank in Kenya. The figures for 2014 are even more phenomenal:

- 14 million Kenyans actively use M-PESA, moving Sh4.2 trillion (USD$42 billion) per annum through the network
- Over six million transactions are carried out over the service daily through M-PESA's now 80,000 strong agent network, which is more than Western Union does globally
- According to statistics provided by the Central Bank of Kenya, there were 825 million mobile transactions up to November 2014, compared to 732 million transactions in 2013
- Kenyans made an average of 75 million mobile money transactions in 2014, with October having the highest number of transactions at 82 million
- Nearly 60 percent of Kenya's GDP moves through mobile money transfers across all providers
- In 2009, only 41 percent of Kenyan adults had access to financial services, rising to over 70 percent thanks to mobile financial inclusion and mobile credit histories

Kenya's banks became angered by M-PESA's success. The whole thing spilled over into a full-scale row in late 2008 when the local papers reported that the largest banks had formed a committee to try and get the service stopped. The committee made their case to the Kenyan finance minister in December 2008, arguing that M-PESA was a Ponzi scheme that was unregulated and would lead to people losing their money. They made other accusations, such as that rogue M-PESA agents were skimming cash off the top of each payment and stealing customers' money.

The bankers' pressure on the finance minister had some effect as some newspapers began to report that M-PESA was a "disaster waiting to happen" due to the lack of an appropriate regulatory structure. Nevertheless, such lobbying failed due to the service's popularity and government ownership. In fact, two charts offer us the clearest picture.

First, the number of bank branches in Kenya has grown from a few hundred in the 1970s to almost 4,000 by 2012. Secondly, the number of bank account holders has actually quadrupled from 2.5 million in 2007 to over 10 million today. This change is wholly attributable to people building credit histories through the mobile network, and that network became incredibly easy to access as the number of agents increased.

As can be seen, a successful agent-based mobile financial network can be transformational and has led to increased competition from a variety of providers, including the banks. In particular, Equity Bank gained a mobile network licence in partnership with Airtel in 2014, and has launched services that compete with M-PESA. Equity Bank cap mobile money transfers at KSh25, whereas M-PESA customers can pay up to KSh125 for a transaction. Equity Bank will lend money for only 1–2 percent interest per month, which more than halves the interest rate fees compared to M-PESA's lending product, M-Shwari, which charges 7.5 percent. In response, M-PESA slashed transaction charges by 65 percent, and the market has heated up considerably.

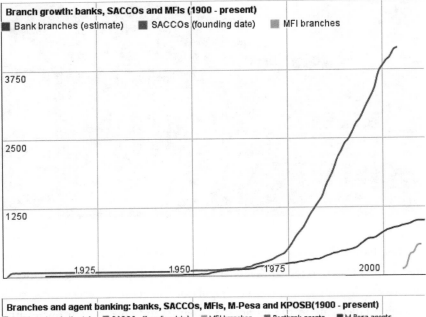

Branch growth: banks, SACCOs and MFIs (1900 - present)
■ Bank branches (estimate)   ■ SACCOs (founding date)   ■ MFI branches

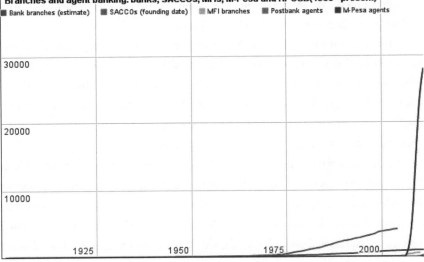

Branches and agent banking: banks, SACCOs, MFIs, M-Pesa and KPOSB(1900 - present)
■ Bank branches (estimate)   ■ SACCOs (founding date)   ■ MFI branches   ■ Postbank agents   ■ M-Pesa agents

The most interesting thing is that the market in Kenya, and across Africa for mobile money, is maturing fast. From something that trailblazed a new way of doing things, it is now a market which is a standard-bearer for mobile everything. This means that African and other emerging

MFS Experiences in Tanzania

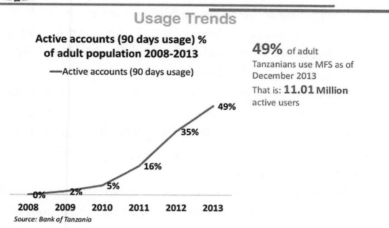

Usage Trends

Active accounts (90 days usage) %
of adult population 2008-2013

—Active accounts (90 days usage)

49% of adult Tanzanians use MFS as of December 2013

That is: **11.01** Million active users

49%

35%

16%

0%   2%   5%

2008   2009   2010   2011   2012   2013

Source: Bank of Tanzania

economies are leap-frogging developed economies as: (a) they have jumped to telecommunications without ever laying landlines; and (b) they have jumped to electronic payments without ever having cheques or cards. Much of this is because there is no legacy infrastructure involved, and the countries where there was lack of infrastructure are being reinvented overnight by mobile networks and, as a follow-on effect, mobile financial inclusion.

However, there are not that many M-PESA's out there today, which raises the question: why has M-PESA been so successful and why isn't there an example of another M-PESA elsewhere?

How do we create more M-PESAs?

There are examples of similar successes elsewhere. Tanzania, for example, saw a massive rise in mobile money usage between 2011 and 2013. By the start of 2015, there were 16 countries where mobile money accounts outnumber bank accounts, up from just nine in 2013. Cameroon, the Democratic Republic of the Congo, Gabon, Kenya, Madagascar, Tanzania, Uganda, Zambia and Zimbabwe were joined by Burundi, Guinea, Lesotho, Paraguay, Rwanda, the Republic of the Congo and Swaziland. So the

M-PESA success is being repeated across Africa, but there are key factors necessary for success, one of which is having a strong agent network.

This is why there are some people betting that the next M-PESA will happen in Latin America or, to be more specific, Brazil. Of the 200 million people who live in Brazil, 40 percent are unbanked, mainly in the northeast of the country. But Brazil already has a large agent network.

This is because Brazil has long been the leader in branchless banking through agency transfers. Brazilian banks' agency networks have a presence in every one of Brazil's almost 6,000 municipalities. This means that one of the most crucial elements of the mobile money transfer system, the agent network, is already in place in Brazil.

Equally, the regulator seems supportive of repeating the Kenyan success. The Banco Central do Brasil (BCB) introduced new regulations in 2015 that could give the necessary boost to take a full mobile money deployment to scale in a Latin American country for the first time. The regulations are an innovative mixture of "light-touch" and caution, and the BCB has clearly observed the experiences of Kenya and is trying to emulate them.

NUMBERS OF REGISTERED AND ACTIVE CUSTOMER ACCOUNTS[28] BY REGION
(DECEMBER 2014)[29]

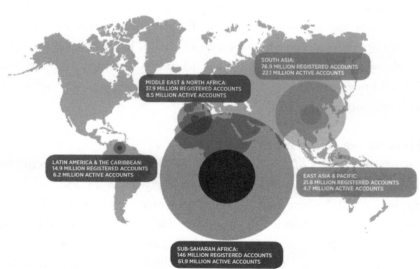

Chart taken from the GSMA's Mobile Money Adoption Survey 2014

When we see mobile inclusion break out of Africa to Latin America and Asia, then we will really know that mobile financial inclusion is changing the world. For now, it's still early days. For example, the GSMA's annual mobile money adoption survey finds that there are 255 mobile money services live across 89 countries, with 300 million users. That leaves a huge potential for future growth, as 300 million accounts represents just 8 percent of mobile connections in the markets where mobile money services are available.

ARE BANKS FAILING TO GRASP THE MOBILE OPPORTUNITY?

Having put the case for mobile as a transformational technology in both developed and emerging economies, some media and technology observers believe that banks are failing to grasp the mobile opportunity. I totally disagree. When I look at the innovations in finance today, I would say that banks are *leading* these markets, rather than failing them.

This is because banks have adapted over the last quarter century to becoming more agile, nimble and capable or responding to the mobile challenge. For example, Bank of America, one of the larger banks, has been at the forefront of internet banking adoption since the early 2000s. Today, they have 48 million customers, of which 31 million use online banking and 17 million mobile banking on a regular basis. In some ways, it is surprising that only two-thirds of customers use online and just over a third mobile, but the things that Bank of America is doing with mobile is far ahead of other industries. For example, BankAmeriDeals targets offers in real-time, based upon customer proximity to stores. When the customer is near a store they regularly use—Ping! They get a deal coupon on their mobile to use immediately. Relevant, localised, proximity-based deals are an innovation I haven't seen elsewhere in the mobile industry yet.

And that's just one of the biggest banks in the world, but many others are *getting it.* For example, the UK's struggling Royal Bank of Scotland (RBS) recently upgraded their banking app to use fingerprint recognition via Apple's Touch ID to sign-on to their banking app. That's a unique feature that is well ahead of the pack, as some banks tell me they can't do this due to local regulators, for example.

In fact, when we get excited about Apple Pay and new bank apps like Simple and Moven, we often make the mistake of thinking innovation in mobile could replace core bank services. To say banks are failing to grasp the opportunity due to these services, is not recognising that these services are just wrapping themselves around banks through the mobile ecosystem. That's fine, but banks are also innovating in that system.

For example, in the UK, Paym and Zapp are mobile structures for real-time money transfers created through the bank clearing system. iDeal and Blik in the Netherlands and Poland are similar systems. These are examples of banks working collaboratively to deliver real-time service to the mobile customer. The fact that PayPal exists because banks could not work collaboratively to create a secure internet payment service is an example of where banks have failed. Another is Apple Pay, which demonstrates the failure of banks abilities to create a mobile wallet.

In Turkey, Poland, Spain, India, Africa, China and Japan, we are seeing banks grasping the opportunity. Jibun Bank in Japan is a joint venture between the Bank of Tokyo-Mitsubishi and the telecom provider, KDDI. Jibun was one of the first banks to offer a mobile wallet, demonstrating leadership as a mobile-first bank since 2008. In fact, it was the first mobile-first bank I ever encountered.

Banks were missing a trick in the days before the smartphone, by not using the mobile network for payments and balance checks, but since 2007 most have been working in earnest to innovate and differentiate via the mobile smartphone. In fact today, banking is the industry that is ahead of the curve when it comes to developing and deploying mobile innovations.

3.
THE VALUEWEB BUILDER PART TWO: CRYPTOCURRENCIES

Once we have a system in place where we can connect electronically to transfer value person-to-person, peer-to-peer (P2P), between anyone on the planet, things get interesting. As discussed in the last chapter, not only are we able to communicate value in real-time globally, but we are able to include everyone in that network, from farmers on the plains of Africa to traders in the offices of Wall Street. Every mobile telephone can be a point of purchase and a point of sale. That means that those farmers in Africa can now sell milk, meat and leather to those traders in Wall Street, in real-time with an immediate exchange of information.

This is why the ValueWeb is such a fundamental change, as we now have no barriers of distance or exclusion due to cost. Everything is global, real-time and almost free. The problem then arises that the old system for money is not global, real-time and almost free. It is slow and unwieldy. That is because the old system was built for the physical distribution of paper in a localised network based upon buildings and people. The new system is being built for the digital distribution of data in a globalised network based upon software and servers. It is a very different system.

In this new system, moving money cannot take days and involve counterparties who network through 20th century systems. It demands moving value immediately, and needs a counterparty system built for the real-time movement of money.

This takes us into a critical discussion of money. What is money?

Some define money as a track of debt. A record of exchange. A proof of contract. A store of value.

Money is in fact all of these things, and has been established as a core part of society, as discussed earlier. What is interesting today is that the real-time exchange of value is more than just monetary exchange. It is *likes*, *shares* and *favourites* in our social networks; it is air miles, loyalty points and virtual coupons in our retail networks; it is barter, exchange and negotiation in our commercial networks. All of these networks are morphing into a new form of value exchange, as they move onto the internet. This new form of exchange therefore demands a new form of money. The ValueWeb demands its own currency. A digital currency. A currency that can be moved from Kilimanjaro to the Empire State building immediately and for almost no charge.

DIGITAL CURRENCIES—A HOT TOPIC OF DEBATE

The ValueWeb is based upon two key technologies: mobile, to allow everyone to exchange value in real time, and digital currencies, to provide a store of value to exchange. Digital currencies are a big area of contention right now, as there are hundreds of currencies being developed. You may have heard of some of them: Ripple, Litecoin, Ethereum, Dash, Dogecoin, BanxShares, Bytecoin, Stellar, BitShares, MaidSafeCoin, Nxt, Peercoin, Namecoin, Monero ... the list is lengthy and we cannot discuss all of them here. Suffice to say that most are variations of the daddy of them all: bitcoin.

bitcoin is the best-known digital currency due to its extensive media coverage, both good and bad. We are going to discuss bitcoin in this chapter, as bitcoin—and its variants—offers, for the first time, a way to exchange value online, in real-time, for almost free. It is the closest we have come to achieving a digital version of cash. In other words, it is the other half of the ValueWeb. Mobile provides the first—so we can connect the planet peer-to-peer in real-time—and digital currencies provides the second, so that we can exchange something the planet feels has value in real-time. This is the underpinning of the ValueWeb, as the ValueWeb cannot exist without a cheap and almost free system of real-time global exchange. Therefore, for the purposes of this book, we will refer to bitcoin as the digital currency.

But what is bitcoin itself? It is, in fact, many things. It is a currency, a protocol, a technology, an ecosystem, a transaction

A QUICK OVERVIEW OF BITCOIN

An explanation of bitcoin production

New bitcoins are generated by a network node, and these network nodes are created each time a solution is found to a specific mathematical problem. The people trying to solve these math problems are called miners, and each time they successfully solve the problem they create a new bitcoin. This math challenge is so difficult to solve that there are businesses dedicated to this, with data centres running thousands of computers focused upon bitcoin mining. The reason they do this is that each time a bitcoin is created, the company or person who solved the math problem receives 25 bitcoins, which were worth $250 each as of August 2015. Hence the bitcoin miners do this to earn virtual currency rewards.

A QUICK OVERVIEW OF BITCOIN

How many bitcoins are there?

The production of bitcoins is limited to 21 million, although the exchange of bitcoins is far higher than this. The first four years of the Bitcoin network saw 10.5 million bitcoins created, and the amount is halved every four years. Therefore, 5.25 million are being created from 2014 and 2018 and then 2.625 million between 2018 and 2022. This is to ensure scarcity, as the total number of bitcoins that will ever be produced is 21 million.

At that point, you will be able to buy a fraction of a bitcoin, allowing there to be quadrillions of value available through the currency. For example, each bitcoin can be divided into up to a million pieces, with the smallest unit of value being 0.00000001 bitcoin. Equally, the final one percent of bitcoin nodes created will take 128 years to complete, with bitcoin #20,790,000 produced in about 2032 and the 21 millionth in 2140!

system, a contracts system and more. It is also very confusing, so let's start at the beginning and take it from there.

bitcoin is the world's first, truly decentralised online currency. Instead of a central bank issuing the currency, bitcoins are issued by anyone with a computer or smartphone, using encryption algorithms. In other words, extremely difficult mathematical problems are incorporated into each coin and transactions are cryptographically authenticated. This makes bitcoin a combination of a commodity and a fiat currency. The creation of bitcoin dates back to 2008, when Satoshi Nakamoto published a white paper about a peer-to-peer exchange of value for the Internet age.

The advocates of this currency are libertarians, who believe that the Internet of Value should be allowed to operate without government intervention. They claim that money does not derive from government or barter systems, but is purely a record of debt. I completely disagree with this view. Their definition of money covers all forms of exchange of value, from beads and shells to digital tokens. That's not my definition of money and, in terms of banking, this is an important difference.

My definition of money is cash or, to be more exact, the central bank definition of money, which is M0. M0 is a "measure of the money supply which combines any liquid or cash assets held within a central bank and the amount of physical currency circulating in the economy (also referred to as narrow money)."

It is bank notes and coins. It is legal tender and trusted because it is backed by a government. Anything else is a commodity of value. Gold, oil, gas, air miles, beads, shells and bitcoins are all stores of value, but they are not money. Money is the government-backed currencies circulating in the economies of the world. Without that structure, the world would not work as it has for the past 5,000 years.

The first appearance of money, in the form of a nationally recognised exchange, dates way back to Ancient Sumer, when the priests discovered that the barter system had broken down. Farmers were producing an abundance of goods, and some farmers now had excess and could not exchange or trade their produce. As a result anarchy broke out, with regular fights between the farmers over their goods and produce.

The priests understood the issue and invented money. Effectively, they created a national currency called the Shekel (nothing to do with today's Shekel) and the farmers could cash in their excess or unwanted crops for Shekels, which were then tradable with the women in the temples who represented the Goddess Inanna.

In other words, money was invented at the same time as accounting (the second oldest profession) and prostitution (the oldest). So that is money—coins, notes and cash. All the other forms of value exchange before this—crops, beads and shells—were commodities that were recognised to have value, and were value stores, but these things were not money.

That is a matter of record and is the reason why I assert that money was invented by governments to control societies.

Money is controlled by government to ensure society and economies run smoothly. Libertarians believe that bitcoin represents money without government.

Here is a fundamental difference, and why I refer to bitcoin as a tradable commodity—but it's not money.

Now, there are many other forms of value exchange and recording of debt, such as an IOU, but an IOU is not money. It is not a freely tradable currency that can be exchanged for goods and services that is nationally recognised. It is purely a record of value that is a contract of trust between the counterparties involved.

Bitcoin and other digital and crypto currencies sound like money, but as soon as these currencies are traded in and out, they become subject to government scrutiny and intervention, as evidenced by the case of Ross Ulbricht and the Silk Road website (see the case study at the end of this section). This operated outside the remit of government control through the dark net, but ultimately was shut down as the US government tracked and traced this illegal online activity.

This is why you cannot have a non-government organised community of value—whether the libertarians like it or not—as we will discuss in the course of this chapter.

Banks deal with money as an exchange mechanism, and then provide secure mechanisms to store the value of those currencies, alongside related commodities and other tradable instruments. The latter are founded upon money, and are exchangeable into and out of currencies through the monetary systems of the world. That is where banks provide the exchange mechanism. The focal point here is that, gradually, new digital currencies could circumvent this exchange mechanism by taking the role of a trusted third party away from the banks.

So the key question is whether a digital currency, such as bitcoin, could become a digital exchange mechanism of value as well as a digital value store.

WHAT IS THIS THING CALLED BITCOIN?

If you'd invested $1,000 in bitcoins in summer 2011, you would have been sitting on around $500,000 by December 2013. By August 2015 your bitcoin holdings would have sunk to $125,000. So what is bitcoin?

First, there are several aspects related to the currency. It first came to light when the mysterious Satoshi Nakamoto—someone who has never been seen or identified—posted a paper entitled *Bitcoin: A Peer-to-Peer Electronic Cash System* on the Cryptography Mailing List in November 2008.

The first line of this paper begins: "A purely peer-to-peer version of electronic cash would allow online payments to be sent directly from one party to another without going through a financial institution." In other words, Mr. Nakamoto had invented a peer-to-peer payments systems for the internet age and had, as it turns out, solved the one challenge everyone else had failed to solve before: double counting. This is through a shared ledger system controlled by the internet called the blockchain. We will talk about the blockchain in depth in the next chapter, but will need to reference it here as it is part of our discussion of bitcoin.

This is because since bitcoin appeared in 2008, it has morphed into both a digital currency and a technology. (For bitcoin the currency we use lower case "b" whilst, when we talk about Bitcoin the technology, we use an upper case "B".)

So let's focus upon bitcoin, the digital currency. bitcoin claims to be the next generation currency that will dominate global trade. Some claim it will displace national currencies. Others claim it will replace Visa, MasterCard, PayPal and even the banking system. I believe it is the Wikicoin for the Wikileaks generation. A generation who Occupy and are the 99 percent, and who were disgusted at the political puppeteering of Visa, MasterCard and PayPal when the American establishment tried to shut down Wikileaks by squeezing their sources of funding in December 2010.

A QUICK OVERVIEW OF BITCOIN

Using bitcoins

Before you can buy any coins you must create a wallet to store them. You can do this by installing the bitcoin client, the software that powers the currency, or use an online wallet, where this data is stored in the cloud. This is easier to set up, but you will be trusting your money to a third party. Once you have a wallet you'll also have an address that looks something like this:

1GVA4cyUc7wXCu1nsN6Tah-VkMXE4vC1nGe.

This is safe to distribute and is what people would use to send you money. You can think of it like giving out your account number and sort code. You can then buy bitcoins from exchanges. Most exchanges allow you to just enter how many bitcoins you want to buy and the address you want them sent to, and then pay for them by transferring money from your bank account.

After Julian Assange's website leaked compromising videos and documents from US government sources, the US government asked American companies to stop funding being directed to the service. As a result, Visa, MasterCard and PayPal all stopped fund movements to Wikileaks. It resulted in a Distributed Denial of Service (DDoS) attack on their services, bringing down the Visa and MasterCard websites—and coincidentally saw

A QUICK OVERVIEW OF BITCOIN

What is the bitcoin blockchain?

A bitcoin transaction is recorded on a public ledger system called the blockchain. The blockchain is a shared ledger system that means all of our bitcoin wallets can be seen publicly. No one knows who made the transaction, but the fact there is an electronic shared ledger ensures transactions cannot be made twice. This is why the blockchain is critical, as it is what the entire Bitcoin network relies upon for trust. All confirmed transactions are included in the blockchain. This way, bitcoin wallets can calculate their spendable balance and can be verified to ensure they are spending bitcoins that are actually owned by the spender. The integrity and the chronological order of the blockchain are enforced with cryptography, and this is why this technology is spreading.

the first upsurge in bitcoin activity at the same time.

Bitcoin is all a part of that movement and is an essential force in changing the way we perceive value exchange in the internet age. It may not be bitcoin that is the long-term digital currency of choice, as we see many more digital currencies appearing today. These include Altcoin, Litecoin, Dogecoin, XRP, and even government-backed digital currencies like the Ecuadorian digital currency.

In other words, bitcoin, or something similar, is a fundamental change to the way we think about money and trading value. The challenge has been for the authorities— the regulators and government agencies—to realise that this change is taking place. What has been interesting is that change took place, as we shall see in the next section on the Bitcoin technology.

The challenge is that governments now need to find other ways to levy tax rather than income, and banks need to find other things to bank than money. Banks should be banking bitcoins and other digital currencies, to legitimise them. The trouble with bitcoin is that it's very technical.

Here are a few statistics. Bitcoin launched in 2009. In 2013, it took off in value mainly thanks to China adopting the currency, and America saying it may have some legitimacy. At the end of 2013, it was claimed that around 200,000 email addresses were linked to bitcoin accounts, but that over half of all bitcoins were linked to just a thousand email accounts. Then the currency got into trouble as the largest trading exchange, Mt. Gox, failed.

THE MT. GOX MELTDOWN

Bitcoin has gone from the leading light of the future of money to a leaky, flaky, shaky infrastructure. This is the result of the Mt. Gox meltdown, along with other exchanges since. In other words, the essence of bitcoin—the blockchain and the algorithms—are all perfectly fine and make eminent sense. The issue is that the infrastructure being built for trading bitcoins is a complete Wild West, amply demonstrated by the implosion of Mt. Gox and the problems that followed.

Mt. Gox was a bitcoin exchange based in Tokyo, Japan. Launched in July 2010, it became the largest exchange for trading the bitcoin currency within three years, processing seven out of ten bitcoin transactions. In February 2014, the Mt. Gox company suspended trading and closed its website. Soon after, the firm filed for a form of bankruptcy protection from creditors called *minji saisei*, or "civil rehabilitation". Like Chapter 11 in the United States, it means the firm is given time to sort out its issues, in this case, time to allow courts to seek a buyer.

In April 2014, the company began liquidation proceedings with the news that around 850,000 bitcoins belonging to customers were missing and likely stolen, an amount valued at more than $450 million at the time. Only 200,000 bitcoins have since been reclaimed, with the rest disappearing, and subject to various theories that they were stolen or lost due to fraud and mismanagement.

In particular, there is a discussion of the Willy Bot. It is called the Willy Bot because trading bots ran rampant through the Mt.

A QUICK OVERVIEW OF BITCOIN

Bitcoin is just for geeks

This is probably true today, as it's very difficult to use. However, firms like Circle are simplifying this and, given the state of where we are right now, many would say that bitcoin is a bit like the internet before Tim Berners-Lee. It's a great technology but needs something to simplify it before consumers will really get it. And that is happening, as demonstrated when you find bitcoin payments alongside PayPal, Visa and MasterCard at the checkout, as you do with Expedia, Dell and Air Baltic.

bitcoin trades are anonymous

No. bitcoin transactions are visible on a public ledger called the blockchain that link every transaction to your IP address and therefore can be traced. In fact, achieving total anonymity in bitcoin is pretty much impossible.

Gox system during November 2013—as the price rose from $200 to $1200—using various names, including "Willy". This trading bot placed repetitive buy-only orders that always manipulated the price upward. Another bot called "Markus" was selling, and these two bots, along with others, caused the rollercoaster ride of the bitcoin price.

The Willy Report blog makes clear that the Mt. Gox collapse was probably due to an inside job, and provides plenty of evidence to this effect.

Another issue then arose: the organisation representing bitcoin, the Bitcoin Foundation (see interviews with Brock Pierce and Jon Matonis in the second section), went bankrupt. Again, there were many claims that this was due to bad management. For example, In March 2014, a prolific blogger about all things bitcoin announced war with the Bitcoin Foundation, and specifically its leadership, for allowing the Bitcoin community to lose millions over Mt. Gox. He stated, as do many others, that they were complicit in the failure of the exchange, being friends of the Mt. Gox leadership, and should step down.

Much of this anger was directed at the Bitcoin Foundation, because the foundation has stepped up to represent the fledgling market. This is a market that wants to exist without government and without governance. That is why they resent a centralised leadership in any form, and the Bitcoin Foundation is seen as a centralised leadership.

CRIME-AS-A-SERVICE WITH BITCOIN

Crime-as-a-service is now available. Europol were one of the first to note this trend, in a report published late last year. According to the organisation's 2014 Internet Organised Crime Threat Assessment (iOCTA), the model allows cybercriminals to develop sophisticated, malicious products and services before selling them on to the less experienced to use via the "digital underground" world. As a result, it's getting easier for less technically minded criminals to engage in cybercrime, putting companies at even bigger risk.

> "In a simplified business model, a cybercriminal's toolkit may include malicious software, supporting infrastructure,

stolen personal and financial data and the means to monetise their criminal gains," the report states. "With every aspect of this toolkit available to purchase or hire as a service, it is relatively easy for cybercrime initiates—lacking experience and technical skills—to launch cyber attacks not only of a scale highly disproportionate to their ability but for a price similarly disproportionate to the potential damage."

They followed this report with an assessment that cryptocurrencies are becoming the value exchange of choice for crime-as-a-service. Apparently, digital currencies are increasingly serving as a money laundering platform for "freelance criminal entrepreneurs operating on a crime-as-a-service business model", according to the latest Europol report. The EU's law enforcement agency said that the decline of traditional, hierarchical criminal networks will be accompanied by the emergence of individual criminal entrepreneurs, who come together on a project basis. The report also argued that individuals with computer expertise are very valuable to criminal organisations and that people with such skills are expected to advertise their services in exchange for payment in cryptocurrencies.

"Virtual currencies are an ideal instrument for money laundering. In addition to traditional layering methods, cryptocurrencies use specialised laundering services to obfuscate transactions to the point where it is very resource-intensive to trace them."

In a similar vein, I attended a policy forum in the first quarter of 2015, where the UK's National Crime Unit was saying that it spent "an inordinate amount of time investigating cryptocurrencies". I asked what they meant by that, and they clarified that it was time spent understanding them. When I then asked if they saw much criminal activity in cryptocurrencies, they said, not yet. The National Crime Unit discovered that cash is used for most money laundering. The money launderers only use cryptocurrencies if the payee demands payment that way.

However, this is because cryptocurrencies are still minor league compared to cash markets, and they are being studied as some of the action in cryptocurrency exchange is for illicit activities on the dark net.

A QUICK OVERVIEW OF BITCOIN

You can use the blockchain without the currency

No you can't. In order to make the blockchain work, you must have a native currency behind it that records the value exchange using a public and private key. Therefore, you could use another cryptocurrency to use the blockchain, but bitcoin has most of the cryptocurrency market liquidity today. Therefore, it doesn't make sense to invent another one.

For example, in a further Europol study produced in February, they find that bitcoin is the preferred currency of paedophiles. bitcoin is increasingly being used to pay for live streaming of child sex broadcasted over illicit internet sites. Europol's EC3 cybercrime centre found considerable evidence that individuals with a sexual interest in children are becoming more entrepreneurial. As live streaming of abuse for payment has become an established reality, they found that there has also been a clear shift from traditional credit card payments to ones providing the most anonymity, including virtual currency.

In line with the International Centre for Missing and Exploited Children (ICMEC) findings, it is clearly evident that there is an apparent migration of commercial child sexual exploitation, along with other criminal enterprises, from the traditional payments system to a new, largely regulated digital economy made up of hosting services, anonymising internet tools and pseudonymous payment systems.

Add to the above the use of bitcoins for terrorism. The United States Central Command have been studying the alternative payment methods terrorist organisations use to raise and transfer money around the globe to support their activities. Digital currencies proved to be the most efficient mechanisms for the transfer of funds due to their decentralised nature that facilitates anonymous donations, as opposed to traditional banking transactions that use fiat currencies. An Israeli analyst has come up with concrete evidence that the terrorist organisation ISIS is raising funds in bitcoins, most likely in the United States, to fund their operations.

What is intriguing in all of this is that the libertarian cryptocurrency community believe they are unassailable. Money is decentralised by bitcoin and they believe it is therefore immune to governmental and regulatory control. Anyone who disagrees is a statist.

Conversely, for the reasons given above—terrorism, drug running, extortion and sex trafficking—this idea of a decentralised market that governments are excluded from controlling may be wrong. To be clear, however, bitcoin and cryptocurrencies are not the problem here. You have massive use of cash for terrorism, money laundering, drug running and paedophilia. It is the reason why the US dollar has more physical stores outside the United States than inside. Equally, it should be born in mind that cryptocurrencies are not anonymous, are traceable and are available in a form that can be identified, so governments do have ways to manage them.

The most likely start point will be during the cash-in and cash-out moments of cryptocurrency usage. You may be able to use cryptocurrencies in a revolving credit and debit scheme bilaterally but, as soon as you try to cash out or put cash into the scheme, the national jurisdictions will make the transaction subject to national laws.

REGULATING CRYPTOCURRENCIES

The biggest question about bitcoin is whether it's really important or just a bubble that's about to burst. Advocates would obviously claim the former and critics the latter, and both views have some substance.

On the advocate's side, the economy is in its early days and, like any new form of commerce, will have its challenges. The greatest of these is government resistance. Governments, along with media, have labelled bitcoin an economy that fuels the drug trade, terrorism, money laundering and illicit crimes. Much of this spawned from the website Silk Road, which has now been shut down, but any torrent-based web service in the dark net can see that bitcoin is of value, as it's the nearest thing to cash that's out there. As a virtually anonymous currency, it fuels illegal activities.

Nevertheless, thanks to many of the advocates, the government resistance has gradually changed, as illustrated by New York's agreement to issue BitLicenses. On 17 July 2014, New York became the first American state to regulate bitcoin, and other forms of cryptocurrency, when the New York Department of Financial Services (NYDFS) Superintendent Ben Lawsky announced the idea of a BitLicense. While some in the bitcoin community welcomed this regulation as a validation of bitcoin's right to exist, the libertarians oppose it as the first roots of centralisation. The BitLicense was finalised in June 2015, after two years of consulting with the financial and bitcoin communities.

Announcing the final ruling on 3 June 2015, Ben Lawsky noted that "We have a responsibility to regulate new financial products in order to help protect consumers and root out illicit activity. That is the bread and butter job of a financial regulator. However, by the same token, we should not react so harshly that we doom promising new technologies before they get out of the cradle. Getting that balance right is hard, but it is key."

The rules for businesses that want to apply for a BitLicense are detailed and cover everything from capital requirements to anti-money laundering. Firms have to keep data about clients for years, maintain security checks on staff, hold assets that protect deposits to a value that guarantees customer safeholdings, perform KYC and AML checks, and so on. The BitLicense requirements include:

- The BitLicense application itself costs $5,000
- Firms must keep detailed records of customer names, addresses, dates, and transaction amounts for at least seven years
- Audits will be made every two years by the NYDFS
- Firms must get written approval before changing products or services, or creating new ones
- Mandatory internal anti-money laundering programs must be implemented, including enhanced oversight of foreign customers and those who transact in amounts greater than $10,000
- Firms must have an internal cyber security program to protect personal and financial information from hackers
- Firms must show a clear disaster recovery plan in the event of attempted or successful theft

In fact, the more you read through the BitLicense details, the more it sounds like a bank license. It treats the trading and exchange of value in virtual currencies as almost the same as trading and exchanging value in fiat currencies. This is the critical point. When Mt. Gox, and other bitcoin exchanges, went bankrupt, the majority of consumers who lost money had no protection, no guarantee and no comeback. By having a license, the government can then guarantee that when you deal with virtual currencies in virtual worlds, you have the same protections as dealing with real currencies in real worlds.

This is the balance that the regulators are trying to strike worldwide, and the New York license created a precedent. The license applies to any virtual currency businesses, such as those trading in bitcoin, which will have to be licensed to engage in business with New York retail or institutional customers. Consumers using bitcoin or merchants accepting bitcoin do not have to register.

Does the BitLicense solve everything?

These BitLicense rules make cryptocurrency trading firms, for all intents and purposes, banks. Equally, it means that for every step the cryptocurrency markets innovate ahead of the curve, the lawmakers review, analyse and try to keep up. Whether they can keep up or not is a different question.

The advocates would defend their position by first saying that bitcoin transactions are not truly anonymous. They can be tracked and traced, as every bitcoin movement is logged with an IP address exchange to show who sold what to whom on the public shared ledger system.

The advocates would also say that bitcoin is similar to cash, so do you make cash illegal? No. And like anything in the world of trade and technology, there are always some people out there who will use innovation for criminal purposes. Just as cybercriminals, launderers and paedophiles use the dark net, they will use methods of exchange in that network that work for them. That may be bitcoin but, when bitcoin did not exist, it was just as easy to use barter, gold, virtual accounts and other forms of value exchange. You don't shut down the internet just because illegal activities take place on it, so why would you shut down bitcoin just because some people use it for illegal ends?

The arguments rage on and on—as evidenced in our interviews in the second half of this book—with governments accusing bitcoin of being used for many illegal activities, the worst of which in government eyes is tax avoidance. Again, that may be true, but tax avoidance is legal. Tax evasion is not. The real issue faced by governments is that bitcoin can be used to move value without government control. That's why they're worried. Maybe they should be or, maybe, they should think about taxing in other forms. Rather than directly taxing income, tax consumption. Tax everyday usage of everyday services. Tax in a different way.

In other words, according to the advocates, bitcoin is going to succeed in spite of government blocks, so live with it. That is why we are seeing governments around the world struggling so much with bitcoin. Some see it as private money to be used as a tradable instrument (Germany), others question its legitimacy and are trying to regulate it (USA) and one is starting to see it as the citizen's choice of stored value and therefore ban it (China). Intriguingly, for all of China's attempts to restrict the use of bitcoin, they have failed. According to Goldman Sachs, a year after China introduced regulations to restrict bitcoin's usage, it's as strong as ever, with 80 percent of all bitcoin activity recorded in China, as of February 2015. Whatever happens, the bottom-line is that a digital currency is here, and the obvious question is: is it here to stay?

Today, bitcoin is a virtual economy with a market capitalisation of over $3 billion in August 2015. Bearing in mind that currency trading in the global financial markets is worth over $5 trillion a day, this is peanuts. But bitcoin is still in its infancy and, if its market capitalisation increased to let's say, a trillion dollars in five years, then this is a serious marketplace.

But then the core question is whether bitcoin will be the main virtual currency? There are many others out there, from Litecoin to Peercoin to Ripple to Erethreum and more. So there will eventually be a single currency, and is bitcoin it?

That's where I'm not so sure. I know that bitcoin is a great whirlwind ride, and that people are making a quick buck out of it, but is this the real cryptocurrency for the next generation? Is it the new Visa? I don't know. I think it is more probable that an institutionalised version of bitcoin, a legitimised version, will be more likely to succeed. We are in the early days of building the ValueWeb and a digital currency is required to underpin the ValueWeb. There will be one. Which one is hard to identify as yet, but bitcoin does represent almost 80 percent of the digital currency markets. Bitcoin is leading the rise of a new generation of finance, a generation that is based upon digital value exchange that is fit for the networked age.

WHY BITCOIN NEEDS A FOUNDATION

Since the Mt. Gox implosion, confidence in bitcoin has somewhat dampened, as demonstrated by its flat-lining value (see diagram below).

You would think that when Dell, Baltic Air, Wikipedia, the German newspaper *Taz* and the Royal National Lifeboat Institution (RNLI) all announce that they will be taking bitcoin payments—as they all did in July 2014—the price would jump. It didn't.

The bitcoin price has been around $600 for the past six months, dipping down to under $400 in April (when Chinese businesses began receiving official deposit shutdown notices from banks for trading in bitcoins) after the peak of over $1,100 per bitcoin in December, just before the Mt. Gox collapse. By the end of 2014, it was flatlining at just $200.

Why is the bitcoin price flatlining? Because the most excited innovators, who brought into the bitcoin concept, were stung by the losses at Mt. Gox. Mt. Gox was destroyed by a bug, but the resulting losses were about 5 percent of the total bitcoin marketplace at that time; $500 million lost in a $10 billion economy. The market needs those propagators who got stung to return before bitcoin will start to prosper, although the movements of companies and charities like Dell and the RNLI do make a difference. As does the Bitcoin Foundation.

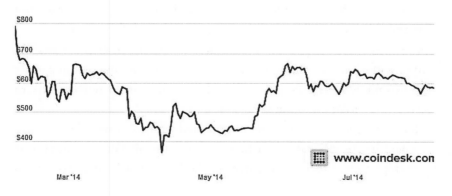

The Bitcoin Foundation was established in July 2012 with a vision "to ensure all people have the opportunity to realize Bitcoin's potential". The Bitcoin Foundation is a charitable fund that is designed to achieve three key objectives: to standardise, promote and protect the Bitcoin infrastructure.

First, in order to *standardise* the core development of the Bitcoin infrastructure, the Bitcoin Foundation funds a core development team to make bitcoin more respected, trusted, and useful. The team has three full-time developers who have led bitcoin core development through the latest versions.

The second part of the Foundation's activities focus upon cryptography. Cryptography is the key to bitcoin's success. It is the reason that no one can double spend, counterfeit or steal bitcoins. If bitcoin is to be a viable money for current users and future adopters, it needs to maintain, improve and legally *protect* the integrity of the protocol.

In order to do this, the Bitcoin Foundation provides global policy leadership, publishing various documents and acting as leading advisor to US policymakers and regulatory agencies. In other words, the Bitcoin Foundation provides funding for government lobbying, making all the rounds to Congressional offices and regulatory agencies, as well as advising and collaborating with international governments, such as the Isle of Man, Luxembourg, Brussels and Gibraltar.

Third, the Bitcoin Foundation exits to *promote* Bitcoin by hosting annual conferences that bring the community, as well as supporting and funding community resources like Bitcoin.org. In other words, they are pretty active as the central voice of the bitcoin community.

A key point here, that the Foundation underscores, is that they are not a centralised or controlling service. Bitcoin is not built for centralisation or control. That is why the Bitcoin Foundation is trying to organise but not centralise the bitcoin community. It is why the Bitcoin Foundation partner with existing web services, press, individual leaders and resources to try to create a more robust and stable ecosystem.

So why is the Bitcoin Foundation smeared with controversy?

There has been extensive criticism of the Bitcoin Foundation and its leadership, such as their involvement in the Mt. Gox failure. Former vice-chairman of the Bitcoin Foundation, Charlie Shrem, has been heavily implicated in issues, such as money laundering charges, and for his role in assisting agents of the infamous online drug marketplace Silk Road. Executive chairman Peter Vessenes' relationship to former board member Mark Karpeles, the disgraced CEO of bitcoin exchange Mt. Gox, has been highlighted as inappropriate.

The Bitcoin Foundation provides a public voice. In fact, what we're seeing is the emergence of the system from grass roots anarchy (2010) to organised chaos (2014) to a regulated and functioning economy (2018?). That is where bitcoin is going, and the Bitcoin Foundation is part of the glue to organise the chaos.

As the Bitcoin Foundation fails, banks wake up

Having said that Bitcoin needs a voice, the Bitcoin Foundation ran into big problems at the end of 2014. Part of this had been due to calculating that the bitcoin currency price would maintain its growth, which it did not. The reality around the Foundation came to light in April 2015, when a new Bitcoin Foundation board member, Olivier Janssens, posted an update on Reddit titled: *The Truth About The Bitcoin Foundation*.

It's pretty revealing.

"First of all, the Bitcoin Foundation is effectively bankrupt *and* the lesson for all of us in Bitcoin is to never put any trust in a centralised org again that wanted to represent Bitcoin."

I don't agree with that statement, as I think the lesson is, don't give your money away to something that has no regulation, no guarantees and no transparency.

The libertarians were fairly upset, especially as they funded the Bitcoin Foundation to act in their interests. The result is that the Foundation almost fell apart and had to be rebuilt, which it has been under the new chair, Brock Pierce (see his interview in the second half of this book). In fact, the libertarians believe that decentralised control solves everything, as the community will then self-regulate. It's an interesting idea. Today, the one percent control everything and the 99 percent revolt. Tomorrow, if the 99 percent control everything, then what happens to the one percent? Most likely they find a way to create a new control mechanism and retain their one percent privilege. It's an interesting battle.

But the real issue with the Bitcoin Foundation turns out to be the centralisation of focus and the application of that focus. Certainly the Bitcoin Foundation was close to Mt. Gox, and it really doesn't help when the organisation created to promote and support bitcoin's developments is accused of being corrupt. In fact, between the multiple failures of exchanges in bitcoin and the failing of the organisation created to promote their cause, it begs us to ask: what will happen to bitcoin now?

The answer: not much, as you have to bear in mind that the Bitcoin Foundation and Mt. Gox are not bitcoin, but operators around the markets of bitcoin. Meanwhile, some have pointed out that the failure of the Foundation may be more to do with being unlucky or stupid, than anything else. After all, the Bitcoin Foundation had $4.7 million of net assets at the end of 2013, but these were mainly in the form of bitcoins valued at $900 each. A year later, the value of bitcoin had tanked to $250 each, wiping almost 75 percent off the value of their asset base. Meanwhile, expenses were around $1.47 million, while revenues were less than one million. In other words, the Bitcoin Foundation was created during a rapid growth in the value of bitcoins and did not know how to handle the rapid loss of bitcoin value, while trying to sustain their operation. That created a challenge of how to keep going and is the reason why many people have stepped down or been fired (including Jon Matonis, a former Executive Director with the Bitcoin Foundation during this period, interviewed later in the book).

All in all, we are seeing the natural development of order in the cryptocurrency community, where the unregulated markets of exchange (Mt. Gox) go through a trough of disillusionment as even their leadership (the Bitcoin Foundation) cannot function effectively, while the traditional authorities (governments) wake up to see how they can make this work effectively (via the banking system).

And bitcoin has strong backing

Bitcoin is being discussed as "legal tender", "a currency" and "an alternative to banking" everywhere, when it is none of these things. As mentioned earlier, bitcoin is a multifaceted thing. It is not just a currency and technology, but a form of value store, trade and investment instrument.

Equally, bitcoin and the Bitcoin technology has some very strong backers. Here's just a few things that some famous faces have been saying:

- "I have invested in Bitcoin because I believe in its potential, the capacity it has to transform global payments is very exciting. It has been obvious to us all for quite some time that people aren't satisfied with the business as usual approach adopted by the major payment networks. There's a real desire for greater levels of control, freedom and scrutiny over what happens with our money, Bitcoin addresses these concerns and that is why so many people believe it represents the future." –Sir Richard Branson, founder of Virgin
- "Bitcoin is exciting because it shows how cheap it can be." –Bill Gates, founder of Microsoft
- "Far from a mere libertarian fairy tale or a simple Silicon Valley exercise in hype, Bitcoin offers a sweeping vista of opportunity to reimagine how the financial system can and should work in the internet era, and a catalyst to reshape that system in ways that are more powerful for individuals and businesses alike." –Marc Andreessen, founder of Netscape
- "Bitcoin offers, for the first time, a method for transferring value and making payments from anywhere to anywhere, in real-time, without any intermediary." –Larry Summers, Secretary of the US Treasury under President Bill Clinton
- "Bitcoin represents not only the future of payments but also the future of governance." –Dee Hock, founder of Visa

These statements all advocate bitcoin, both the currency and the technology, and is the reason why so much venture capital is moving into both bitcoin systems and structures. Almost $350 million was invested by venture capital firms in bitcoin start-ups in 2014, and the estimate for 2015 is that this will near $1 billion. Intriguingly, this investment movement mirrors the investment in Silicon Valley start-ups during the creation of the internet. In other words, real-time value exchange is the core of the third-generation internet, the ValueWeb, and the investment movements are mirroring that behaviour almost exactly.

A timeline of bitcoin developments

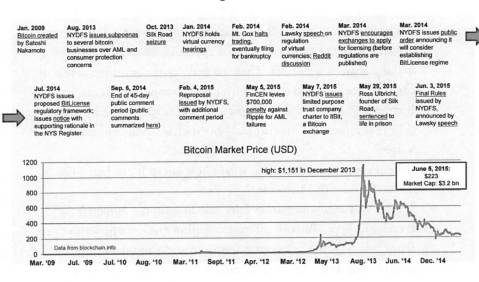

Jan. 2009	Aug. 2013	Oct. 2013	Jan. 2014	Feb. 2014	Feb. 2014	Mar. 2014	Mar. 2014
Bitcoin created by Satoshi Nakamoto	NYDFS issues subpoenas to several bitcoin businesses over AML and consumer protection concerns	Silk Road seizure	NYDFS holds virtual currency hearings	Mt. Gox halts trading, eventually filing for bankruptcy	Lawsky speech on regulation of virtual currencies; Reddit discussion	NYDFS encourages exchanges to apply for licensing (before regulations are published)	NYDFS issues public order announcing it will consider establishing BitLicense regime

Jul. 2014	Sep. 6, 2014	Feb. 4, 2015	May 5, 2015	May 7, 2015	May 29, 2015	Jun. 3, 2015
NYDFS issues proposed BitLicense regulatory framework; issues notice with supporting rationale in the NYS Register	End of 45-day public comment period (public comments summarized here)	Reproposal issued by NYDFS, with additional comment period	FinCEN levies $700,000 penalty against Ripple for AML failures	NYDFS issues limited purpose trust company charter to itBit, a Bitcoin exchange	Ross Ulbricht, founder of Silk Road, sentenced to life in prison	Final Rules issued by NYDFS, announced by Lawsky speech

Bitcoin Market Price (USD)

high: $1,151 in December 2013

June 5, 2015: $223 Market Cap: $3.2 bn

Data from blockchain.info

Mar. '09   Jul. '09   Jul. '10   Aug. '10   Mar. '11   Sept. '11   Apr. '12   Mar. '12   May '13   Aug. '13   Jun. '14   Dec. '14

WHY VALUE STORES NEED REGULATIONS

Having said that the political and economic agenda could all be for naught, if the politicians and economists can work out ways to regulate this marketplace, then maybe the two worlds could work in harmony. The development of regulations for bitcoin, and the need for it, is illustrated well by a story I recount often about *Second Life*, a virtual world that was popular in the 2000s and had its own virtual currency, the Linden Dollar. The Linden Dollar (L$) traded at L$275 to one real dollar, and created a virtual world of commerce. People were trading virtual houses, virtual clothes and virtual versions of designer labels. There were even examples of a two-stream Second Life, where some firms showed their real world goods and services in the virtual world and, if you liked them, you could order the real world versions of those goods and service.

Second Life's popularity disappeared when their banking system collapsed in summer 2007, however. The banking collapse was a reaction to Second Life being forced to close down gambling facilities in their virtual world in July 2007. Until then, the website had been a phenomenon, growing from virtually no users to over 10 million in a year. This was incredible, and everyone felt it demonstrated the new emergence of business models.

The virtual world did have some real banks, but it also had many virtual banks. For example, several banks invested in major projects in Second Life including ING, Wells Fargo, SAXO Bank and Deutsche Bank to test how this world worked, but the biggest bank being used to convert real US dollars into virtual Linden dollars was Ginko Bank.

The trouble started when internet gambling was forced to close under US law. The management of Second Life decided that they also had to close access to gambling in virtual worlds to comply with this policy, and this led to a major run on the virtual banks.

This is because unbeknownst to the management of Second Life, Linden Labs, much of the virtual trading in the virtual world was related to gambling. Therefore, the closure of gambling in the virtual world meant that people immediately started to take money out of the virtual banks—a bit like the run on UK bank Northern Rock in the same year, but worse.

Now imagine you are Andre Sanchez, the one-man band behind Ginko Bank, Second Life's largest virtual bank. You have over a million real US dollars on account, translated into around L$275 million that you are managing for the Second Life community. Suddenly, your customers demand their money be converted back into real dollars, and you drown in their demands. What Andre Sanchez did, as a 32-year old student living in Sao Paulo Brazil, is close down the virtual bank, leaving customers with real dollar losses of around $1,000,000.

This led to calls for compensation from Linden Labs, but they said it wasn't their job to regulate the banks. However, the virtual users of their virtual world did not like that answer and so spent three months demonstrating outside their virtual headquarters.

This is the reason why bitcoin and virtual currencies need to be regulated, with a market structure that will operate at three levels:

- Legitimising bitcoins
- Trading bitcoins
- Storing bitcoins

We already have a structure for generating bitcoins based upon mining, the blockchain and the protocol.

We then need a structure for trading bitcoins that is more reliable than the Mt. Gox version we saw crash and burn.

Finally, storing bitcoins will be the choice of the individual but, for the safest store, they'll probably put them in the bank, as banks have guarantees as safe stores (that's why they have licences). So from being the bad boy of the net, bitcoin moves into the mainstream model of value exchange, just like stocks, shares, money and other stores of value.

WHAT CAN YOU BUY WITH A BITCOIN?

Most interest in bitcoin arose during 2013, when the price went from $20 in January, to $266 in April, to $100 in May, to $1300 in December. This was a market that was manipulated by Mt. Gox, and the fact that bitcoin has maintained pricing between $200 and $250 consistently since Mt. Gox's collapse shows that it is a market that is small but stabilising.

Don't think that bitcoins are an investment instrument—bitcoins are for buying things. An MIT study published in 2014 shows that bitcoins are being spent, not hoarded. The hoarding idea was something that started back in 2009, when the coins first emerged. Of course, back then there wasn't much you could buy with a bitcoin so most of them were unspent for over a year. That's not the case today, as most bitcoins are spent within 24 hours of purchase, as illustrated by this chart from MIT (see opposite).

The findings from the MIT report, which analysed a variety of sources, including bitcoin wallet provider Blockchain, Bitcoin Charts and Coinmarketcap, provides evidence that bitcoin is evolving as a currency and that, whilst far from mass adoption, liquidity is on the rise in the system. Though no formal definition of "spending" was given to fully clarify the data.

This is important, as hoarding bitcoins would mean that the virtual currency would never become mainstream. Hoarding would mean that the currency would never fulfil the promise laid down by its supporters, who say it will streamline monetary transactions and free the world from the control of big government and the financial manipulations of big banks. Therefore if, as is reported in MIT, the coins are being spent rapidly, what are they being spent on?

Here are some examples. Richard Branson claims you can pay for a Virgin Galactic flight into space using bitcoins, but only one person has taken that opportunity. Air Baltic, Expedia, Dell and a few other merchants accept bitcoin payments, but it's still limited. But what if Amazon started taking bitcoins for goods and services, would eBay and Apple follow? And if they did, could this become a trillion-dollar economy? And, if it did, what would that mean?

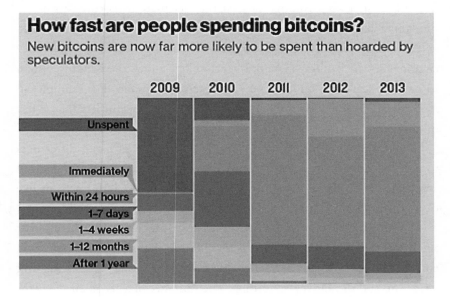

How fast are people spending bitcoins?

New bitcoins are now far more likely to be spent than hoarded by speculators.

WHAT WILL MAKE BITCOIN SUCCEED?

It's all about trust and confidence. Trust and confidence in the Bitcoin system is easily boosted or burst by the media hype and the headlines. All of China starts using bitcoins and the value increases rapidly. The value went from around $130 to $1300 in just six months last year in 2013, because Chinese consumers started buying bitcoins. Bear in mind that this just means that a $1.3 billion economy grows to a $13 billion economy and then, as users remove their gains, the economy flatlines again.

Many Chinese reclaimed their gains due to the Chinese government removing what appeared to be a tacit endorsement of the currency, saying that it's ok if you want to buy them but the People's Republic does not support the use of bitcoin.

Then exchanges like Mt. Gox go bust, and add on a few challenges like Distributed Denial of Service (DDoS) attacks and the technical nature of bitcoin itself, and this relegates the emerging currency to a techno-geek world that most dare not, or cannot, enter. These are the key factors that will make or break bitcoin and, for those who are watching its ecosystem grow, it's obvious that these are the growing pains of a rebellious child.

So what does bitcoin mean to banking, trade, finance and commerce? To be honest, I keep coming back to the fact that, at its core, it offers a fundamental disruption to banking and payments if its currency succeeds, and a fundamental solution for banks if its technology succeeds. Its currency circumvents the banking system; its technology allows the banking system to create a real-time, almost free value exchange system. For example, in November 2014, an $81 million transaction took place in less than a few minutes and for virtually no cost. We will come back to this point.

The real value of bitcoin is that it offers a number of major differences to previous cryptocurrencies by being decentralised, encrypted, exchanged anywhere for no fee or charge and being able to be used 100 percent like cash (although not completely anonymously).

Whether bitcoin survives to emerge as the cryptocurrency of the internet age is still questionable, but there is no question that a cryptocurrency will emerge. Critics will question what this means for money laundering and terrorism, and the answer is: nothing. The existence of a cryptocurrency for the internet age is not what drives money laundering and terrorism. What drives money laundering and terrorism are money launderers and terrorists. These underworld tendencies will exist whether the cryptocurrency exists or not.

This is why banks are asking: *Should banks be banking bitcoins?* More fundamental is a different question: *Do bitcoin users want to bank their bitcoins with banks?* And the answer may well be *No*. After all, why would @Anonymous, the 99 percent and the Wikileaks fans want to #Occupy the bank with their digital assets?

Maybe the more likely outcome will be that bitcoins will be banked with a new digital asset store, such as … Google? Amazon? Or a new store that has no government control called something else … Whatever emerges will be incredibly interesting and exciting and that is why banks should watch the bitcoin space.

AN $81 MILLION TRANSACTION THAT COST JUST 4 CENTS TO PROCESS

As mentioned several times already, the key to the ValueWeb is being able to transact in real-time for almost free. Transacting in real-time is no challenge when you have a global mobile internet. Everyone can connect to everyone. The challenge is that exchanging value in the current system is hard, because the current system was built for the last century. SWIFT, Visa, MasterCard, Western Union and other value exchange systems across borders take days and charge high fees. They're not real-time and almost free. However, the Bitcoin technology of shared ledgers does create a real-time and almost free system, as evidenced by a transaction that took place on the blockchain on 6 December 2014. That was an $81 million transaction that took place immediately, in real-time, and it cost just 4 cents to process.

It could even have taken place on a Sunday morning, as Bitcoin operates at near zero cost 24–7–365.

When you can process any value exchange in real-time for nearly free, what happens to our back-end infrastructures? What does it mean for clearing systems like CHAPS and VocaLink in the UK; TARGET2 and SEPA in Europe; CHIPS and Fedwire in the USA; Visa, MasterCard and China UnionPay globally? And how much are these processors considering these impacts?

What this means in reality is that there will be a decentralised service that can be used outside the banking and government system, for those who want to take advantage of that capability. There will also be a much larger community that will continue to deal with finance and banking, as they used to, but now through a cheap protocol technology to record their transactions.

In other words, the financial markets are looking at the smart contracts capability of Bitcoin to see how they can leverage this technology, as we shall see in the next chapter. The markets operate as they always have, with governments taxing the citizens who use bitcoin exchanges on their conversions of monies in and out of those exchanges. The banks offer secure storage of bitcoin and other services, but also record their messages, settlements, clearing and processing on the blockchain.

Soon, we will see banks that can securely process multimillion dollar transactions on the blockchain for near free. So what do we pay for? We pay for the trust, the guarantee, the certainty and the confidence that our bank will process those transactions securely and reliably and reimburse us for any losses if they do not. That's the beauty of this new technology protocol and it will revolutionise banking, payments and financial markets. The question is "when" rather than "if".

Ken Tindell
@kentindell

+ Follow

A $81,904,090.09 bitcoin transaction:
blockchain.info/tx/8f1d3a8ef6b... <
Transaction fee was $0.04

Case Study: The Silk Road story

Silk Road is the notorious website that exploited the dark net to sell illegal goods and services. Primarily a site for ordering drugs, the preferred payment method was bitcoin and the preferred modus operandi was the internet technologies called *torrent*.

It's a fascinating story and demonstrates the libertarian versus statist stand-off. The libertarian versus statist conflict is very live and, for those who have not encountered it, is led by many bitcoin activists. The bitcoin activists claim they have invented *money without government*, and believe that society should be free to operate as it wants. If people want to exchange drugs, paedophilia or organise terrorist activities, that is a lifestyle choice and they should be allowed to do just that. They hold that if these activities are disapproved of by the majority, then the collective will shut it down rather than the government.

Obviously, some of us would see this as an extreme standpoint, as the very fact of allowing terrorist funding, child pornography or drugs to be freely traded through the net is undesirable for most. Nevertheless, the libertarians have a viewpoint.

Ross Ulbricht was a libertarian. Therefore, Silk Road was created as a service unconstrained by statist intervention and completely impervious to interference, since it was totally anonymous. Or so he thought. So how did he get arrested, jailed and given five sentences—including two for life—to be served concurrently with no chance of parole? There were two key factors that led to Ulbricht's arrest: perseverance and arrogance.

Perseverance is best illustrated by the Drug Enforcement Agency's (DEA) Special Agent Carl Mark Force IV, who spent over a year developing access to Ulbricht through the torrent chat rooms.

The second aspect is the arrogance of Ulbricht. For example, a year before his arrest he was warned that Silk Road's IP address was leaked, and visible to other computers—which gave the DEA their big break. From that IP address, they found the server and from that server, all the communications across the Silk Road community.

And there's the rub: if Ulbricht had been a more professional programmer and less arrogant, Silk Road would probably still be running today. Torrent or, in short form, Tor technologies, are completely anonymous and bitcoin payments cannot be traced easily through Tor.

Just to clarify on these two points.

Tor—The Onion Router—was a software infrastructure developed by the US Navy in the 1990s, with the aim of protecting US intelligence communications online. After its release and subsequent enhancements since 2002, it's become the preferred network for drugs, fraud and other illicit activities, as it allows users to browse the web almost completely anonymously. Tor achieves this by directing internet traffic through a free, worldwide, volunteer network consisting of more than 6,000 relays to conceal a user's location and usage from anyone conducting network surveillance or traffic analysis. This is the basis of the Silk Road, and was the reason why Ulbricht believed his anonymity was bulletproof.

Equally, Tor may be near anonymous, but bitcoins are not. All bitcoin transactions are public, traceable, and permanently stored in the Bitcoin network. Bitcoin addresses are the only information used to define where bitcoins are allocated and where they are sent. These addresses are created privately by each user's wallet. However, once addresses are used, they are then linked with the history of all of the transactions they are involved with. Anyone can see the balance and all of the transactions of any address—as users usually have to reveal their identity in order to receive goods and services, bitcoin addresses cannot remain fully anonymous. For these reasons, bitcoin addresses should only be used once and users must be careful not to disclose their addresses by, for example, using multiple wallets for different purposes.

Doing so allows the user to isolate each of their transactions in such a way that it is not possible to link them. People who send you money cannot see what other bitcoin addresses you own and what you do with them.

Nevertheless, what should concern the authorities is that if someone copied the example of Silk Road and employed professional programmers, then the dark net libertarian dream of money without government, and exchange without controls, could be realised.

4.

THE VALUEWEB: FUELLED BY FINTECH

During the past few years, the term FinTech has become commonly used, but why? My contention is that the ValueWeb is the key development. As mentioned, the ValueWeb is based upon two technologies: mobile, to allow everyone to exchange value in real time; and digital currencies, to provide a store of value to exchange. As these technologies have risen, so has the focus upon digitalisation in banking and now FinTech.

FinTech is the new market that integrates finance and technology. This new market is a hybrid of the traditional processes of finance—working capital, supply chain, payments processing, deposit accounts, life assurance and so on—but replaces their traditional structures with a new technology-based process.

In other words, the term FinTech describes a whole new industry. It's a little like talking about retailers, and saying that Amazon is a retailer. Are they a retailer or an e-commerce company or both? I would claim that they are a digital service provider of fulfilment, but that's purely because they fulfil consumer orders as well as cloud-based service delivery through AWS. In other words, they're not a retailer at all, but a company in a whole new marketplace.

In the same way, FinTech is not an R&D function of finance, but is a new emergent market of digital finance that will, over time, displace the traditional financial markets. This is because the ValueWeb is building the Internet of Value, and the Internet of Value replaces the old world of physical banks dealing in physical currencies. Just as I argue in my previous book, *Digital Bank,* banks have historically dealt with the physical distribution of paper through a localised network of the branch, whilst the ValueWeb deals with the digital distribution of data through the globalised network of the internet. The digital network replaces the physical network, and the FinTech community is building the new system. Eventually, the new system becomes what I call the ValueWeb.

The ValueWeb, like FinTech, is a new, fresh and vibrant marketplace. It is a market filled with youth and new blood. A market that rejects wearing ties and the tradition that goes with the suits of banking. A market that wants to rock the world of finance with technology. That is the market that I think of as the ValueWeb, built upon FinTech.

For example, if you examine the investment, from venture capital firms in FinTech, a third of their investments are aimed at firms dealing with payments, and another third on peer-to-peer (P2P) finance platforms and P2P lenders. And that investment cycle has ramped up massively in the past few years. Estimates vary, but the numbers are: under a billion invested in FinTech in 2012; $4 billion in 2013; $12 billion in 2014; and $25 billion in 2015. This is a huge investment swathe into a new industry, because this new industry is building the Internet 3.0, the Internet of Value, the ValueWeb.

That new world is supporting, displacing and disintermediating the old-world finance with technology. It is creating a 21st century world of finance based upon technology. That to me is FinTech.

FinTech builds a new world of finance using a digital core that is IP-enabled. It sits hand-in-hand with the digital bank, as the new definition of finance and banking.

So the ValueWeb is a new market and FinTech is 21st century finance. It is the new form of banking. Some of the old form players will metamorphose into these new digital FinTech players, and some of the new players will take over the markets of the old incumbents.

The result is a hybrid new market of IP-enabled financial firms, including digital banks and digital insurers, who have technology at the core of their business. That is the FinTech world I want to work with.

WHY WOULD VCS INVEST SO MUCH IN FINTECH?

Venture capitalists (VCs) are investing billions in FinTech because it is building the ValueWeb. It is creating the Internet 3.0. This is therefore as big as the first and second generations of the internet, and somewhere out there are the next Facebooks, Twitters, Googles and Amazons. That is what the VCs are trying to find and, in their industry parlance, they are called "Unicorns".

Unicorns are new technology start-ups that achieve a valuation of over $1 billion. There are quite a few of them out there, including Uber, Airbnb, Twitter, WhatsApp, Snapchat, Pinterest and more. To put this in perspective, Microsoft's market value at IPO was $500 million, whilst Cisco's was $300 million. Alternatively, the market capitalisation of Barclays Bank is just over $60 billion today … about the same as ten Lending Clubs. The difference being that Barclays is over 300 years old, whilst the latter is less than 10 years old.

This is the reason why everyone is interested in FinTech and the ValueWeb, as there are quite a few FinTech Unicorns out there and growing fast. Eighty-three FinTechs were contending to be Unicorns by the end of July 2015, up from 70 in May and just 17 the year before. The biggest of these include peer-to-peer lending firms like Lufax, Lending Club, Prosper, SoFi and Zopa; and many new payment firms, like Square, Stripe, Klarna and TransferWise (see the Top 25 Unicorns list for 2015 at the back of this book).

Market valuations are not necessarily an indication of real value, as the exit value of some of these privately funded firms may be very different to their paper value, but it does show the hype around FinTech, which is why bank CEOs are concerned. This was clearly shown in the annual shareholder letter of J.P. Morgan Chase bank in February 2015. The letter, from CEO Jamie Dimon, included the following key words:

"Silicon Valley is coming. There are hundreds of start-ups with a lot of brains and money working on various alternatives to traditional banking. The ones you read about most are in the lending business, whereby the firms can lend to individuals and small businesses very quickly and—these entities believe—effectively by using Big Data to enhance credit underwriting. They are very good at reducing the 'pain points' in that they can make loans in minutes, which might take banks weeks. We are going to work hard to make our services as seamless and competitive as theirs. And we also are completely comfortable with partnering where it makes sense.

"Competitors are coming in the payments area. You all have read about Bitcoin, merchants building their own networks, PayPal and PayPal look-alikes. Payments are a critical business for us—and we are quite good at it. But there is much for us to learn in terms of real-time systems, better encryption techniques, and reduction of costs and 'pain points' for

customers. Some payments systems, particularly the ACH system controlled by NACHA, cannot function in real time and, worse, are continuously misused by free riders on the system. There is a true cost to allowing people to move money. For example, it costs retailers 50–70 basis points to use cash (due to preventing fraud and providing security, etc.). And retailers often will pay one percent to an intermediary to guarantee that a check is good. A guaranteed check essentially is the same as a debit card transaction, for which they want to pay 0 percent. For some competitors, free riding is the only thing that makes their competition possible. Having said that, we need to acknowledge our own flaws. We need to build a real-time system that properly charges participants for usage, allows for good customer service, and minimizes fraud and bad behavior."

Jamie Dimon's 2015 shareholder letter illustrates well the challenge for incumbent firms dealing with the ValueWeb. J.P. Morgan Chase is suffering the pain of seeing their credit markets attacked by P2P lenders and their payment markets attacked by cheap, real-time alternatives. The ValueWeb, remember, is driven by mobile for real-time, peer-to-peer connectivity and digital currencies to exchange value cheaply. These are the two technologies driving the attack on traditional, incumbent banks like J.P. Morgan Chase.

These new players concern bank CEOs because they take away the pain of dealing with old processes in old banks. Banks take weeks to process lending decisions, whilst P2P lenders take seconds. Why does it take banks weeks? Jamie Dimon doesn't say, but I suspect the answer is because banks are laden with sedentary processes built in the last century for the physical distribution of paper in a localised network. The branch network was filled with human automatons who could manage transactions but not assess risk. Risk is a head office function managed by specialists, who are trusted not to lend to people who are not creditworthy (hence the reason why we avoided a credit crisis!). The process needed to work out whether the applicant was suitable or not would take weeks. Now, self-service forms online have replaced the automatons, and automated systems have replaced the specialists. That's why the new P2P providers can replace banks with instantaneous decision-making services at a fraction of the

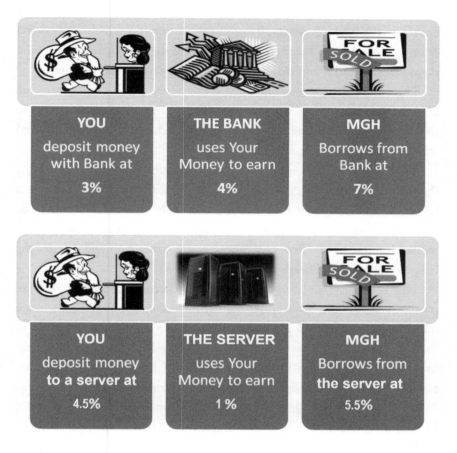

cost. After all, a server for $1,000 is far cheaper than a specialist head office credit risk manager costing tens of thousands.

That is the real core challenge of the ValueWeb, as it is built by FinTech, which replaces buildings and humans with software and servers.

Wrappers, replacers and reformers are all targeting banks

FinTech start-ups generally fall into one of three categories: *wrappers*, *replacers* and *reformers*.

The *wrappers* are ones that incumbent financial firms do not need to worry about so much, as they are wrapping themselves around the old financial marketplace. These are the Movens, Simples and Apple Pays of this world. Or PayPal, Google and Facebook. They are not trying to replace or reform the banking system. They just want to remove the friction—the "pain points" as Jamie Dimon refers to it—from the old system by wrapping themselves around it and making money easy to save, spend and use.

Then there are the *replacers*. Their focus is 100 percent to replace core bank services with software and servers. These firms are more worrying, as they've grasped one basic idea: you don't need a third party organisation to transfer finance; you just need a server.

It's what Zopa, the world's first P2P lender, realised very early on (see the interview with Giles Andrews, CEO of Zopa, in the second half of this book). What Zopa realised is that you can easily take money from those who have it and transfer to those who need it, using the processor as the trusted intermediary. The server processes the transaction and assesses the risk. No human hand needs to be involved.

This is why the replacers need to be more keenly watched, as they are trying to replace the bank rather than remove the friction. And there are many replacers. For example, Zopa's P2P lending model has caught on to such an extent that it has been copied globally with a Zopa-style start-up in almost every country: Prosper and Lending Club in the US; Bondora, Lendico, Trustbuddy, Ratesetter, Smava and more in Europe; Harmony, PPDai, Lufax, Society One, Dianrong, ANT Financial and more in Asia. In fact, in China alone, there were more than 2,000 peer-to-peer lenders by 2015.

You know something is hot when it's copied around the world. Add on to this a sprinkle of crowdfunding and you have a market expected to be worth over $1 trillion by 2025, according to Foundation Capital. That market is across all credit products, from personal loans to small business lending to mortgages and realty.

That's a serious displacement of a core banking product, i.e., credit. In fact, Goldman Sachs produced a report about the new lending marketplace in February 2015 and concluded that the new P2P players would disintermediate traditional financial companies in six key sectors: consumer lending; small business lending; leveraged lending (i.e. loans to non-investment grade businesses); mortgage banking (both origination and servicing); commercial real estate; and student lending. What that means

Slide courtesy of *Foundation Capital*

in real terms is that US banks earned around $150 billion in the credit markets of 2014, and Goldman Sachs "estimate $11 billion+ (7 percent) of annual profit could be at risk from non-bank disintermediation over the next 5+ years".

And it's not just happening in credit markets, since remittances, foreign exchange, trading and more are being attacked by neat and nimble new players from Currency Cloud (global money transfers) to eToro (social trading).

Then there are *reformers*. These are using the key technologies of mobile and digital currencies to transform financial services.

Mobile is transformational because access to financial services for everyone on this planet will mean that no one needs to be excluded. Digital currencies are transformational because the creation of a value exchange without banks is a totally new concept and marketplace.

So there we have it: wrappers, replacers and reformers. If I were a bank, I'd be watching all of them and be just a little bit worried. It is the reason why Jamie Dimon fears these start-up companies. He not only underscores that the bank is "going to work hard to make our services as seamless and competitive as theirs" but, in a step further towards banks as value systems integrators, he states that J.P. Morgan "are completely comfortable with partnering where it makes sense."

Will J.P. Morgan integrate Lending Club and Prosper into their credit risk operations and structures, and what will this do to their margins, processes and operations? These are questions that the banks are trying to assess, as they have to face it: the day of stand-alone, vertically-integrated banking is over.

AS ROBO-ADVISORS TAKE OVER

A big part of Jamie Dimon's concerns in the shareholder newsletter discusses the challenge of P2P and payments companies, but the threat to traditional firms is far wider than just lending and payments. It is all aspects of finance and value exchange, as FinTech builds the ValueWeb.

The ValueWeb affects everything from retail and commercial banking, to investment banking and asset management, to transaction banking and insurance, to private banking and wealth management.

According to a poll of 400 senior executives by State Street Bank released in July 2015, four-fifths of senior asset management staff expect the fund market to be disrupted by an outside participant in the same way Apple upended the music industry with the introduction of iTunes. Yu'ebao take just one click.

Meanwhile, Google commissioned research last year on how it could enter the asset management industry, as has Facebook, so there is serious interest in emulating these money market funds in Europe and America. That is why a number of key executives have publicly spoken out about their concerns for this new ValueWeb marketplace, and the fact that it makes it easy for the strong technology players to become strong financial technology players.

> "Google and Amazon entering the market is a real possibility. The trouble is, we as an industry always seem to be behind the curve on these things, but it is good that people are worried, as it will sharpen up our act."
>
> —Helena Morrissey,
> Chief Executive of Newton Investment Management

"I am the CEO and am paid to be paranoid, and I am paranoid about this. The big danger for companies like ours is we become complacent and believe our business is safe forever. It's not. Having said that, it costs us £500 million a year to run our business and that is a big commitment, even for Google. I do not see them manufacturing funds but I can see them coming in and distributing funds."

—Martin Gilbert,
Chief Executive and Co-Founder of Aberdeen Asset Management

"The next generation of investors will be totally different to the ones we have now. It is not the behaviour of Google we need to worry about but the behaviour of our clients."

—Alexander Schindler,
Member of the Executive Board at Union Asset Management and
President of the European Fund and Asset Management Association

The investment management industry is broken, and we can see more and more proof that this industry is more challenged than the retail and commercial banking markets as robo-advisors take over. The robo-advisor is an internet robot that automates our wealth management. There are now many examples of such firms: Betterment, Wealthfront, Motif Investing, FutureAdvisor, Personal Capital, Hedgeable (USA); Nutmeg, Wealth Horizon, Rockfox, Swanest (UK); MoneyFarm (Italy); Vaamo, OwlHub (Germany); Moneyvane.com (Switzerland); and InvestYourWay (Europe). However, we should not assume that these robo-advisors will wipe out the traditional industry that quickly. For example, by the end of 2014, the US asset management start-ups had raised just over $420 million in funding (Wealthfront had raised $130 million, Motif Investing $126 million, Personal Capital $104 million, Betterment $45 million and FutureAdvisor $22 million).

The two industry giants are BlackRock and Charles Schwab. BlackRock spends $400 million a year, or 4 percent of its net revenues, just on marketing. Charles Schwab spends $300 million a year, or 5 percent of its net revenue. Both are doing well, and growing, but the disruptive innovators are definitely out there and gaining pace. For example, Wealthfront achieved over $1.5 billion assets under management by the end of 2014. It took them just two-and-half years to get to $1 billion of assets, whilst it took Charles Schwab six years. $1.5 billion may be virtually nothing compared to the $2 trillion that Charles Schwab manages, but the threat has been noted.

So how will the incumbents respond? Perhaps the best example is what Charles Schwab and others are now doing: offering asset management for free. You pay nothing for the robo-advisor but make money through cross-pollinating the portfolio with other services, generating advertorial income and more. It's a different game but if you're not playing it, you're not in the game.

THE FINTECH MARCH INTO INVESTMENT BANKING

It's more difficult to see the FinTech stars and Unicorns in the investment space, as it's more opaque, having been disrupted by technology fundamentally over the past twenty years. The rise of program, then algorithmic, and now high-frequency trading created a strong move to low latency, server farms, co-located along with the exchanges. The exchanges themselves were attacked by new FinTech firms like BATS, Chi-X, NASDAQ and others, and these companies are now dominating much of the equities trading areas. Trading on BATS in the USA now represents 20 percent of all equities, doubling their market share in just two years by acquiring Direct Edge. Pretty good for a ten-year old garage start-up based in Kansas. Similarly, in Europe, BATS Chi-X trading now exceeds the London Stock Exchange and Euronext (not bad for an eight year old start-up).

Admittedly these guys are owned by institutions—BATS lists GETCO as its largest shareholder. Other owners include Morgan Stanley, Credit Suisse Group AG, Nomura Holdings and Citigroup. In other words, the low latency high frequency markets are pretty much dominated by players that are owned by the market makers.

But then you do have a large volume of day traders, spread betting,

Exchange Traded Funds (ETFs) and Direct Market Access (DMA), that wasn't there before. That's also a FinTech change. It isn't what I'd call FinTech itself, however, as these are all offshoots of trading structures rather than companies that are creating new business models in the way we see with Betterment and Wealthfront.

In this area, there are three emerging markets of real FinTech change: social trading strategies, market funding platforms and market data services. In the area of trading strategies, we saw early innovators like ZuluTrade, eToro and StockTwits became accepted very quickly as new forms of social trading.

ZuluTrade is probably the largest global social trading network at the moment, both in terms of numbers of traders and investors. Offers full trade copying (supporting multiple brokers) and social interaction capabilities with free, fully functioning demo.

eToro is very much focused at the novice investors with eToro acting as both broker and social trading network. Much focus is given on education for novice investors with an easy to use interface.

StockTwits is a social communications platform for the financial and investing community that takes tweets and uses them for trading.

There are many other social trading systems out there for everything from commodities to equities, although the most popular space appears to be in Foreign Exchange (FX) markets, with firms like BelforFx, CopyFX, FxPro, FxStat and more.

There are also a lot companies emerging in the market data area, with names like Contix, Finalta, Kensho, Quovo and SumZero high on my list. These companies are all major providers of insight for trading that adds to the social trading network.

Finally, there are market funding platforms where the crowdfunders firmly sit. These include Kabbage and Funding Circle, which are the top small business funders in the US and UK respectively, but there are lots of other interesting financial platforms out there, including: AngelList, BankToTheFuture, CircleUp, CrowdCube, EquityNet, Fundable, FunderHut, Fundly, Healthfundr, IndieGogo, Innovestment, Invesdor, Microryza, MicroVentures, Seedrs and Seedups.

It is an interesting space, as it is creating narrow-finance focused, seed funding investments and financing for innovation, creativity and new business start-ups. As mentioned, this market is also getting funding from the large institutional investors, too, so it's more a way of de-risking early round funding than necessarily creating an alternative market to the core equities markets.

All in all, trading strategies, trading analytics and alternative finance are the three big FinTech categories in the investment and capital markets space, on top of the low-latency, high-frequency changes we have seen in the last decade. It also means that the investment markets are being just as radically changed by FinTech as the retail and commercial bank space, and asset and wealth management space. We just don't see it so often because there isn't yet a big new beast in this space that hasn't been acquired, funded or integrated by an existing player.

Bank FinTech worries are obvious ... solutions are not as clear

When I talk about the ValueWeb and rise of FinTech with banks, I am typically asked a whole raft of questions:

- How do we transform our legacy structures?
- What is the biggest obstacle to becoming a digital bank?
- You mention partnerships, but all cooperative structures failed in the past, how can we succeed in the future?
- Can you show us someone who is doing this right and making it work?
- What should a bank do when we have millions of customers who trust us?

This shows that the incumbent financial institutions are worried about the future and not complacent. The problem is that they all know they need to do something, they just don't know what to do or, rather, their bank CEO doesn't know what to do.

The frustration is that the bank is worried about FinTech, has woken up to digital and is thinking about what to do. They've invested in apps and APIs, restructured services, trying to get off legacy and doing the things that should be done. But the problem is the CEO doesn't get it. The CEO has grown up in the bank, understands the bank, loves the bank, but has no idea what this digital stuff is all about. If you are in a bank that needs to wake up to digital and FinTech, then make sure that the CEO is awake first.

THE REPORTS OF MY BANK'S DEATH ARE GREATLY EXAGGERATED

Jamie Dimon referred to the arrival of FinTech in his 2015 shareholder newsletter as "Silicon Valley is coming". What is interesting is that, in response, J.P. Morgan has been hiring a whole host of Silicon Valley talent. They have to do this to compete with the new wrappers, replacers and reformers. As Jamie Dimon puts it: "We move $10 trillion a day. We're one of the largest payments systems in the world. We're going to have competition from Google and Facebook and somebody else … when I go to Silicon Valley… they all want to eat our lunch."

But, for all of the rise of the ValueWeb and the threat of FinTech, banks have one natural advantage that protects them. It's called a bank licence, and history dictates that the death of banking isn't going to happen soon. Most banks have been around for a century or more—can you name any other industry dominated by players that have been around for a century or more?

Airlines? Maybe. Most airlines have their roots back into the mid 1900s and have grown through acquisition and merger, just like banks. There are new players out there—SouthWest, Easyjet, Ryanair—but most airlines have been around a long time.

Grocery stores? Probably. Most have high barriers to entry—the store network and margin squeeze through volume—and have players who have been around for a long time—Walmart started business in 1962, Tesco in 1919—but that doesn't mean new players like Aldi and Lidl cannot make an impact.

Pharmaceuticals? Ah, now that's a business based upon product innovation and patents, who then control the supply chain through copyright. Sounds a bit like music, but drugs are harder to copy. GlaxoSmithKline's roots date back to 1715 and Pfizer to 1849.

And this is where the argument of the new entrants falls down for me, as they continually compare banking to music, entertainment, film, photography and similarly digitally disrupted industries. But these are not like-for-like industries, as they don't have strict regulations, high barriers to entry and strong capital requirements. The only area of similarity is that banking can be a purely digital activity, like music, entertainment and photography.

Banking is therefore similar to these firms but, unlike these industries, it also has many commonalities with pharma, groceries and airlines. These are markets with a strong store distribution footprint, tight controls and high costs of capital—just like traditional banking. So the real dialogue is between the new entrant who think that banking is a pure digital play versus the incumbent who feels that the distribution, controls and costs of banking makes it far more like pharma.

Banks are too regulated to be disrupted

Equally, taking this a step further, banks are not just protected by their licenses and, because regulations determine licenses, are too regulated to be disrupted easily. In fact, I would claim that banking is not being disrupted, but evolved. What is happening is that FinTech is merging with banking to create the new platforms and architectures for the ValueWeb.

As we build the ValueWeb, the banking evolution is in replacing the architecture of banking to be a core digital activity rather than a physical one. Like books, music, entertainment, travel agents and more, banking is something that can be done through devices with no physical need for service. You cannot have that with airlines (you need to physically travel) or gas stations (you need to physically put gas in your car), but you can have some services, like banking and music and travel orders, made through a pure digital play.

However, unlike music, books and travel agents, banking will not be wiped out by a new player creating a new way of doing things. There will be no iTunes, Uber, Amazon or Expedia revolutionising banking. The reason for this is that, unlike all those other lines of business, banking is regulated. Banking is integrated with government policy; it is a political instrument; it is used as the government's control mechanism for social order; and it is key to a country's economic success or failure. For this reason, it is in a government's interest to licence value stores and value exchanges. This controls monetary supply and economic stability. Consequently, banks are given the luxury of time to adapt that book stores, travel agents and music shops didn't have.

Equally, we get a lot of folks saying that a new giant will emerge from the FinTech community to displace banks. There will be a new J.P. Morgan or HSBC. I don't think so. First, the P2P community are being given securitised funds from the banking community, so banks win whether they do the lending or the crowdfunders do it for them. In fact, it cuts costs and displaces risk to the P2P platform, so it's more efficient in many ways. A win–win for the banks, in other words.

Cryptocurrencies have proven they can't be trusted—Mt. Gox, Bitstamp, the Bitcoin Foundation—and so the technology is moving from the Wild West of the Web to the Ripples of the banking fraternity. Again, from chaos comes control, and banks keep their status of being transactors and stores of value. Mobile will take banking to the masses and the millions of unbanked. What's interesting is that the unbanked become banked because they build mobile money credit histories that can be trusted. As previously mentioned, when M-PESA launched in Kenya in 2007, there were only 2.5 million adults with bank accounts; eight years later, over 15 million Kenyans have bank accounts, thanks to mobile credit histories. The banks win again.

Meanwhile, as all this so called disruption is happening, the banks can live with the threats and opportunities therein because they know they have time to evolve due to their regulatory requirements. As Transferwise and Holvi bathe in the misguided belief that the regulator doesn't care about them, there will come a day when it does. When that happens, Transferwise and Holvi will either be acquired, merged, moved into the banking control ecosystem, or shut down.

Meantime, I am not saying that banks will not need to change. They must adapt to survive. Their survival will be determined by how quickly they can step up to the challenge of being digital and not physical. The ones who work out their digital core architecture, infrastructure and organisational evolution strategy first (along with a branch closure and staff redeployment strategy), will be the ones that will lead the rapid change from physical to digital. The ones who wait will either be beaten by competitive forces or decline. Meantime, the ones who create new models through FinTech, will be the ones funded and also acquired by the early digital leaders of the traditional system. Either way, they will all become evolved into the ValueWeb—and in ten years, the biggest banks today will still be the biggest banks in the world. However, the banks ten years from now will be value systems integrators of best-in-class apps, APIs and analytics that enable them to offer the ultimate delivery of value aggregation for their clients.

What would it take to cause a disruption?

Finally, to conclude my contention that banking is not being disrupted, but, instead evolved or adapted, it's worth considering what it would take to cause a disruption.

First, I don't think of disruption according to the conventional, dictionary definition, but in the sense that Clayton Christensen meant it in the book *The Innovator's Dilemma*:

"Disruptive innovation, a term of art coined by Clayton Christensen, describes a process by which a product or service takes root initially in simple applications at the bottom of a market and then relentlessly moves up market, eventually displacing established competitors."

And the question today is whether Klarna, Holvi, Zopa, Lending Club and brethren are doing the above or not? To a certain extent, it seems clear that they are. According to Foundation Capital, P2P lending and crowdfunding will be worth over $1 trillion by 2025, and companies like Apple are taking over the customer wallet. The counter-argument is that there are banks that underpin all of these movements, with wholesale markets moving heavily to support of the likes of Lending Club. Equally, others see markets expanding.

For example, many banks won't lend to high-risk projects and companies. A new start-up small business will always find it hard to get unsecured lending from a bank, unless they have a robust business plan. But companies like Kabbage and Funding Circle have stepped into this space and are helping to widen markets. Small businesses gained access to over £2 billion of new funding through alternative lenders between 2010 and 2015. But then, Funding Circle does partner with banks like Santander to do this, so they're basically picking up business that banks don't want. Is that disruption?

Possibly. Today, banks don't want this business. Tomorrow, it's their core business. Equally, banks are not helping themselves. For example, it was reported that in 2014 UK banks charged businesses £425 million in hidden fees.

IS FINTECH SO SPECIAL?

Although everyone's excited about FinTech, FinTech is nothing new. FinTech is actually pretty old. I could claim that if FinTech is about providing technology platforms to exchange finance, then that's been around since banks first implemented technology platforms in the 1960s. In fact, I do claim that banks are FinTech companies.

The reason why we're all excited about FinTech is because there are so many new start-up firms attacking the flawed business model of the incumbents. The start-ups aren't using technology from the last century, which is based upon products and branch distribution networks. The new firms are built around customers using internet services on their mobile and wearable devices.

This is why we're excited about FinTech, as it replaces buildings and humans with software and servers. That's the new world of FinTech.

It goes further and deeper than this, as it means that FinTech firms can target narrow finance—the unbundling of banking—and just offer component pieces as either peer-to-peer connections, such as lending, credit and payments; or as new ways of connecting, such as buy now and pay later (Klarna), or matching payments data (TransferWise), or creating new digital exchanges on shared ledgers (Ripple).

That is why we are excited about new FinTech, since it destroys the fat overhead of old FinTech. That doesn't mean that the old FinTech is not aware of the change. Most incumbent banks are investing in, developing with, acquiring from or doing something with new FinTech. The real question is, how can an old FinTech bank become a new FinTech bank? How can a bank move from a product-centric structure based upon physical distribution to a new customer-centric structure optimised for digital distribution?

This is the fundamental question for a bank, and I argue that to be fit for new FinTech structures, banks have to turn their operations on their head. The core of the new FinTech is digital distribution, so old FinTech must get rid of their foundation based upon physical distribution. Once committed to doing this, then the bank can begin the change of architecture and organisation to become a customer-centred digital platform, rather than a product-focused physical structure.

For many bank leaders, this is too radical. It's too hard. For the bank leaders that feel this way, they add to the existing structure a head of digital and give them the job of change. A far better approach would be to launch a new bank, as delegating digital to a separate department is the road to ruin. Digital should be at the core.

Launch the new bank and let it grow. Let the new bank destroy the old bank. Let new FinTech eat the old FinTech dinosaur.

THE SPECIAL RELATIONSHIP

Equally, some people talk about FinTech and banking as being a bit like the American Revolutionary War (1775–83), fought between the Americans and the British. Although the American colonists eventually beat the British, it all ended up in a "special relationship"—and that's what many think will happen between the banks and FinTech.

I liken the Brits to the banks and the Rebels to the start-ups. The start-ups may win the battle, but there won't be a war. Just a symbiotic special relationship. Just as America and Britain became strong allies over time, the banking ecosystem will develop a special relationship with FinTech.

In fact, there already is a special relationship. Many banks are investing in and mentoring start-ups, helping them to flourish and grow. Many banks are engaged in the blockchain and cryptocurrencies. Many banks are offering joint ventures with crowdfunders or investing in P2P lenders. Santander announced over twenty use cases for the blockchain in banking in July 2015, Barclays are nurturing blockchain start-ups, whilst UBS opened a London-based blockchain research lab.

On the P2P lending side, American P2P lending platforms have been dominated by institutional money since 2008 when, under pressure from regulators, the peer-to-peer lenders relaunched as bank-to-peer lenders. Around 80 percent of the American lenders' loans are funded by institutional investors and hence, in America, they have dropped the "peer-to-peer" label.

In the UK, Santander and RBS have partnered with Funding Circle to offer a service that, if your credit history, as a small business, is not good enough to get a loan with them, you can go to Funding Circle. Equally, Goldman Sachs and Société Générale are backing Aztec Money, an emerging peer-to-peer financing platform where people can bid for company invoices.

There are more and more of these partnerships developing, which means that these new markets are growing with bank support. Some believe that these markets will eventually bite the hand that feeds them and take over—but do they need to? Not necessarily. Much of FinTech is serving the underserved markets, such as small business loans, lending to higher risk consumers and enabling payments in easier form over the old bank rail network. This is why many banks refer to the FinTech community as *alternative finance*—although, interestingly, many FinTech companies refer to themselves as *narrow finance*.

Narrow finance focuses upon a piece of the financial system and democratises it or, in other words, connects that system by replacing the trusted third party institution with a trusted third party processor. FinTech focuses upon replacing buildings with servers and, in so doing, wipes out a ton of overhead costs. There's nothing *alternative* about this—it's core.

However, even if FinTech does grow into a larger monster, there's plenty of time for banks to respond by either acquiring or launching competitive services, such as Goldman Sachs' P2P lender. Just to put it in perspective, crowdfunding websites managed to source €1.5 billion ($2 billion) in equity and debt to European small- and medium-sized enterprises (SMEs) in 2014, compared with €926 billion of new investments by Europe's banks to SMEs in 2013. Similarly, the P2P lending sector has grown rapidly, with the five biggest platforms (Lending Club, Prosper and SoFi, all based in San Francisco, and Zopa and RateSetter in London) enabling a million loans between them and at a rate of well over $10 billion a year by 2015; but those loans are still tiny compared with the $3 trillion of consumer debt outstanding in America alone.

In other words, there's a long way to go before FinTech becomes mainstream, and it's going to be a long time before the world really takes notice. By the time it does, most banks will own this sector—or a large part of it—so don't write off the banking system too soon.

WHAT FINTECH MEANS FOR BANKS

Many commentators criticise banks for being slow, clueless or stupid. Many talk about how banks don't do this or don't do that, fail at this or fail at that, have no idea and cannot change, are stuck in the past or have their heads in the sand. In reality, every bank executive I meet is concerned about the future of their business. They recognize that the traditional structures of banking are changing, and that their margins (therefore profits) are disappearing and that they need to move from physical to digital. They understand that FinTech is changing the market for good, and that peer-to-peer, mobile and blockchain are important.

Their problem is that they don't know what to do about it, and consultants cannot tell them. It reminds me of the moment in 2006 when I heard that YouTube had been bought by Google for $1.65bn. In a presentation made a year later, the story was told of how the CEO of McKinsey called in his global team and asked them: what's YouTube? None of them knew or had even heard of it, because they were firewalled out.

In other words, we're living in fast cycle change, where many bankers (and consultants) are finding it hard to keep up. Right now, by way of example, we see a mega-battle playing out between Stripe and Klarna, yet most bank executives haven't heard of either company, even though they are core to their business. For example, a survey of 110 C-suite, UK bank executives was released in July 2015 by Adaptive Labs, showing that most of these C-level decision makers have no idea what's happening in the world of FinTech change or, at the very least, have no idea who their new competitors are. This lack of focus is because of the very nature

Awareness of start-ups by executives at banks

Entrants	I'm aware of the company and what they do.	I'm aware of them but don't know what they do.	I've never heard of them.
nutmeg	23%	35%	43%
Betterment	8%	19%	73%
Square	15%	27%	57%
venmo	6%	15%	78%
azimo	6%	26%	67%
TransferWise	15%	35%	51%
LendingClub	18%	36%	45%
RateSetter	17%	26%	56%
PayPal	92%	8%	0%

* 110 senior execs ranging from director to C-suite were asked about the startups they were aware of.

Source: Bye Bye Banks? © July 2015 The Financial Brand

of Unicorns. Unicorns can appear within months and suddenly eke out a critical position in a key market space.

Uber is a great example of this. Uber is the highest valued Unicorn. Launched in 2010, the fledgling company was worth over $50 billion by July 2015. It's not surprising, when you look at their volume of business. Uber bookings were worth $687.8 million in 2013, rising to $2.91 billion in 2014. For 2015, their bookings are estimated to be worth $10.84 billion and anticipated to be more than $26 billion in 2016.

A great example in finance is Venmo. As discussed earlier, the idea came during a weekend break, where two young guys in their 20s needed to settle their bills at the end of the weekend, and wrote an app to do that. The app sits on top of PayPal, and four years later was processing over $1 billion in payments between friends.

Venmo illustrates well that this is the age of real-time, almost-free, instantaneous change, driven by the mobile internet, which offers global peer-to-peer connectivity. This age is hard to grasp for the overnight, analogue generation. That's why bankers don't need to hire consultants or millennials. They just need to inhabit the living, breathing culture of digital innovation.

This is best illustrated by a bank CEO who asked me, what would be the first three things he should do? I replied that he first needed to build a vision based on the premise that they will never see the customer face-to-face—only deal through screens—and make no margin on their loans. I said that this vision needed to assume that the consumer can get everything his bank offers now for free elsewhere. Based on this supposition, how is he going to make money?

You make money by delivering value in new forms, such as the Brazilian bank Banco Original (see Guga Stucco's interview), which is crowdfunding the bulk-buying of new cars in order to secure major discounts for their customers, and giving them competitive loans in the process. Or like the Ukrainian bank, Privatbank, that's overcoming concerns about buying goods online by creating its own version of Amazon/Alibaba, where you buy goods online in the bank branch or at home and the goods are delivered to a secure locker in the bank branch. You only pay when you're happy with the product and, as this happens to be when you're in the bank branch, you can get a loan, too.

These are the new models of banking, where value is created through ancillary services to financial products, not by the financial product itself. In a world where everything is free, banks have to be much cleverer at value generation, and not rely on old-world products with fat margins that won't exist in 10 years.

Once you have a vision of how to make money when everything is free, go build that vision. Communicate that vision. Make everyone excited and be passionate about what you believe. Finally, deliver the vision.

WHAT DO NARROW BANKS MEAN FOR WIDE BANKS?

In this world of choice that emerges from the integration of new technology and old financial models, we see hybrid systems emerging that bring together the best-of-the-best. A great example is Metro Bank and Zopa joining forces to work together in the UK. The deal allows deposits from Metro Bank retail customers to use P2P lending as an asset class for their deposits, with the expectation that this will provide higher returns on their savings. It's an innovative deal in that P2P lending surely cannibalises that other asset class: credit. But it's all about choice, and if customers know that they can place money in Zopa, then why not allow them to do so through the intermediation of the bank to assure its viability?

This is where it gets interesting, as innovative deals have appeared like this before. Fidor Bank (Germany) has been offering Smava's P2P lending for some time through its operations, whilst Caja Navarro (Spain), a non-profitable foundation, offered its own version of P2P some years ago. They called this "Civic Banking" and gave every customer the right to know the profit they made from each transaction and account. Through Civic Banking you could also invest in friends and family businesses and loan requests, with the bank ensuring the loan was repaid.

This is the key point about aggregating the customer experience. If a customer has so much choice, do they really want to be opening numerous accounts with eToro, Circle, PayPal, Zopa, Friendsurance, etc., or do they want to have an aggregator on top? I think the new emergent form of retail bank will be that aggregator. Like a TripAdvisor for travel, we will see front-end services that integrate many back end providers for finance. Some may say that this is just what the comparison websites do, but the comparison websites are not integrating and aggregating. They are just providing a rate choice—after that, you have to go to the provider's own website to complete the transaction.

The new component-based bank will find the best providers of alternative finance and offer these services through their own portfolio of access. A one-time, sign-on to get access to choice, all in one window. That's what Fidor are offering and, through the deal between Metro and Zopa, it's another step in the right direction.

Meanwhile, I was surprised to see that SMEs (Small to Medium Enterprises) are being commonly rejected for credit by banks, because they don't meet their risk criteria. They are too small, too new, too untested, too risky to lend to. So banks are recommending they go to Funding Circle and similar alternative finance houses. These alternative finance houses opened a lifeline for businesses in the UK in the last year. For example, see Funding Circle's homepage from August 2015 on the following page.

Followed by the same 16 months earlier (yes, this was 20 April 2014).

Note the statistics: £225 million of lending enabled by Funding Circle a year ago climbing to £781 million just over a year later, more than tripling the enabled funding in just over a year. Meanwhile, the number of businesses borrowing through Funding Circle has almost doubled in that time, as has the awareness of this alternative financing marketplace. A lot of the funding of Lending Club comes from the UK Government, and it's interesting to note that almost 98 percent of P2P lending funds in the United States come from institutional investors.

So you have two key things happening. First, the large banks are turning small businesses away to alternative finance, whilst de-risking their own portfolios by funding the AFHs. So the alternative finance firms become the risk managers. That's all well and good, but then take the other headline: *SMEs stung by £425 million in hidden fees.* This is where the Christensen disruptive innovation does start to hit as the alternative finance market looks like nothing today.

Here, in lending, it is a narrow bank focus on SME and consumer credit. A Funding Circle or Zopa squeeze the process of getting funds to those who need them to the max. And their customers love it: 77 percent of Funding Circle users say that after their first loan, they would return to Funding Circle first next time, rather than a bank.

So, on the one hand, banks are de-risking their credit portfolios by both funding narrow banks and encouraging their higher-risk customers to use them. On the other, they are stinging their higher risk customers—small business customers—with higher hidden fees. Furthermore, their customers now love their narrow bank and would not return to their old bank in the future.

In my view that's a broken model. Broke for the bank, that is, unless it really does not want any SME or consumer credit market operations in the future. The Metro, Fidor and Caja Navarra approach of integrating the narrow bank offers into their customer aggregated experience. Instead, what RBS and Santander, who partner with Funding Circle, appear to be doing is saying that we would rather offload you to the narrow bank, than keep you with our bank.

WHEN PAYING IS FREE, WHAT THEN?

What happens when the cost of payments reaches zero, the speed of payments is instant, and everyone globally can make and take a payment? I keep returning to this question, as it's the infrastructure that has to be changed. I recently spoke to Klarna, for example (read the interview with Niklas Adalberth in the second half of this book), and they said that they don't worry about PayPal, Stripe, Square or others, as they're all built on Visa and MasterCard foundations, which is a system that is out-of-date. That was an intriguing conversation, and the key is to look at how things need to work today.

Things need to work today where we exchange everything, everywhere, for virtually free. Blogging, emailing, entertaining, creating, sharing, transacting, are all free. How do you make money when everything is free? By creating additional value on the basic exchange. Add value to blogs by writing good blogs. Add value to entertaining by being more creative and entertain better. Add value to payments by providing information enrichment around the payment. The payment itself will be free.

I remember some years ago a Japanese banker saying to me that his greatest concern was when a bank opened offering payments for free, funded by Google adverts. Well, it's here now. Everything is free. How do you make money when services are free? Ads, information, value added services and more. These are the key things.

But a bank, payments processor or institution cannot provide money for nothing and payments for free if their systems are built for the old way of doing things. The old way being through counterparty systems that take days to process, involve a lot of human handling and run on systems that update overnight.

This is why the shared distributed ledger technology created by the bitcoin white paper of Satoshi Nakamoto is so important. It's not bitcoin, or even the blockchain, that is important, but the fact that he created a trusted, shared ledger system through the internet that can record any exchange of value between anyone in real-time for virtually free. That is the key reason why this is being debated so actively by banks. So as we rapidly turn our archaic batch, back-end systems into real-time distributed ledger systems, we will see a move from payments in days with high fees, to value exchange in real-time to almost free. That solves problem one.

Another problem is the disruption caused by FinTech. Some believe FinTech will destroy the existing archaic financial system. Some believe banks will just win out and be central in the FinTech reform. I believe we're seeing something else. We're seeing a hybrid system emerge, where banks are nurturing and investing in FinTech and FinTech is trying to destroy the things in banking that don't make sense.

It doesn't make sense to exchange value in days through a network that creaks. We can change that to a system that works in real-time for almost free, and that's the shared ledger. It goes further, though. Klarna, Stripe, Square, Holvi and more are not built on the shared ledger. Instead, they are all FinTech firms that are trying to get rid of legacy bank structures constrained by old world technologies, and enable them to work better in this new world.

Similarly, the P2P lenders and crowdfunders are trying to get rid of outdated banking operations, and replace them with new world structures. It's happening, but slowly. In a recent *Economist* article, they noted that "individuals and funds provided over €1.5 billion in equity and debt to European SMEs in 2014 … a pittance compared with the €926 billion of funding made available by banks but the amount is more than doubling each year."

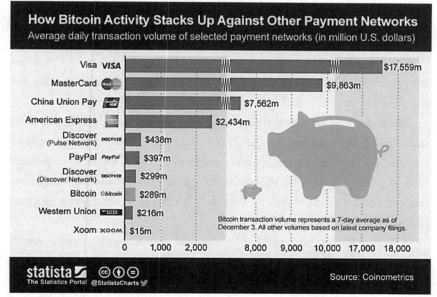

Source: Coinometrics, May 2015

Similarly with SWIFT, Visa and MasterCard. If you look at the stats, they speak for themselves:

In other words, the incumbent system can probably give itself years before it has to change. But this doesn't indicate complacency among the banks. They are changing before they have to change, by investing and embracing the innovation culture.

What you end up with is an old banking system radically transformed by the mobile internet into a new value exchange system that integrates technology with finance. A new world order, but one that is rooted firmly in old world wisdom. And one of those wisdoms is that you don't trust storing money in a system that leaks; and you don't trust trading with someone you don't know, unless there's a system that ensures you get what you are promised.

That is why banking and blockchain are coming together, and why the old system is embracing the new.

IF SERVICES ARE FREE, HOW DO WE MAKE MONEY?

I have this mantra in my presentations about payments. Payments is being attacked by FinTech start-ups like Klarna, Square, Stripe, Alipay, PayPal (Venmo, Braintree) and more. It's the second most active area for investors after lending (P2P and crowdfunding) and the most mature sector for new competition to traditional bank processors.

My mantra is not about payments as a sector though, but the failed structure of how we pay in the 21st Century. If I send a payment from London to Sao Paulo today, it takes seven to ten working days to process. How ridiculous is that? If I telephone my friend in Sao Paulo, it's immediate, real-time and free via Skype. So why does it take so many days to process a payment from UK to Brazil?

The problem is how to change that old counterparty transfer system between sending and receiving banks via SWIFT networks and low and high value clearing systems. Now that's slowly being solved by companies like Ripple. The idea is to create a banking shared ledger that would allow counterparties to share a trusted exchange system in real-time on the internet, for almost free.

And that is my mantra: that everything in banking should be real-time and almost free. You cannot run a 21st century financial system using old technologies that are slow and expensive when everything else around us is fast and free.

Now here's the central question: if everything is almost free, how do we make money?

Most service providers haven't answered this question. That's why Square, Stripe, PayPal and co add an extra little fee for usage on top of the card scheme fees. That's one way to make money. I prefer another way, though. We make money by informing, augmenting, supporting and managing money.

In what ways can we inform, augment, support and manage? There are few examples as yet, but two stand out.

One is a bank that has created a restaurant app—Shinhan Bank in Korea. The restaurant app provides reviews and ratings of all the restaurants in the country. Like a TripAdvisor, you can find restaurants near you, book a table, write a review and, most importantly, pay through the app. The way you pay is using a QR code on the bill or, even easier, just create your wallet in the app and payments are taken automatically with bills provided electronically.

The thing I like about this bank's app is that it's succeeding in becoming the country's main app for foodies and cuts out the other banks. The other banks are not part of the app, so you can only pay for your meal through the wallet or QR code if you are a customer of this bank. As a result, their competitors are now asking to be part of the app and the bank is charging a fee to the other banks to include them in the wallet.

Another great example is a bank that is looking to social media to create loyalty. You've probably heard the crowdfunders idea of gathering enough people who want a particular product to get a discount on that product. If you can find a hundred mates who all want to buy the new BMW 5-series, then BMW will give you a discount if you order a hundred BMW 5-series this week. Well, there's another bank that is taking this idea to leverage value for their customers.

The idea is that the bank will monitor their customers' Facebook *likes*. If they find a large group of customers who have all *liked* the announcement of the new BMW 5-series, for example, then they would approach BMW to negotiate a deal. The bank might then commit to buy a hundred cars in the first week of release and, by doing so, would contact all the customers who *like* the new BMW 5-series and let them know that if they want one, not only would they get a whopping discount, but a competitive loan from the bank, too.

In other words, the bank is seeking increased loyalty from their customers by giving them value. The bank cross-sells a loan to the customer at a discount rate and, most importantly, gains a hundred loans in a week for a three- to five-year period. The customers are locked in and the bank is happy. The customer is happy too, as they have a new BMW 5-series ordered at a 20 percent discount *and* a discounted loan.

This is a win–win for both sides, and that's how future banks will have to behave to differentiate in the Internet of Value. The future bank will make money by creating and unlocking new ways to deliver value through data.

So, when asking the question, *If everything is free, how do we make money?* The real answer is, *By thinking differently and creating additional value through design*. A tough ask for an old bank, but not an impossible one, as illustrated by the two examples above.

HOW WILL BANKS DIFFERENTIATE IN THE FUTURE?

This is a common question, based upon the massive changes taking place in finance, where everything is becoming real-time and free thanks to the ValueWeb. We can expect banks to move towards being lifestyle choices rather than payments processors.

Historically, customers chose a bank because it was physically local to their home. It didn't matter what the bank charged, as all banks were much the same. Over the years, as banks retrenched and customers moved online, banks became even less differentiated. Now, most people are picking their banks for the same reason, as in its physically local (over 60 percent of new accounts still make the decision based on the branch being near); but once the account is opened, they never want to go there again.

Soon, as the dynamics of the role of the branch shifts and becomes less important, customers will stop opening accounts due to the proximity of the branch and will move towards lifestyle-based choices. How does the bank reflect my personality, needs and goals? Do they share common ethics and values with me? Do they fit my lifestyle and outlook?

These questions rarely impact today. After all, when the headlines about Barclays fixing LIBOR hit, everyone said they would close their accounts, but the proportion of customers who actually did was miniscule; but they will become more important in the future, particularly as customers become digitally competent.

This is when banks will see a new relationship. One that is screen-to-screen rather than face-to-face. A screen-to-screen relationship is very different and will see customers demanding a contextual relationship. A contextual relationship relates to you through your devices, chips and lifestyle, not just through data analytics and push marketing. A contextual relationship will use the internet of things to sense when to make you that credit or loan offer, but extends further and deeper than this. A contextual relationship will be customer intimate by using deep data analytics to track our digital footprints, but will only relate to us on a permissions basis and will focus upon the context of the relationships, not just the permissions.

It would be easy to push a credit offer at me ten times a day, but the contextual relationship will know just when that offer is good to be made. A contextual relationship will recognise when it is a good time to talk. A contextual relationship will drill down to understand the kind of things I buy, connect me with people who buy like me and will support me in purchasing more of the things I buy. But the real lifestyle choice bank goes one step further than all of this, by connecting to my lifestyle.

These banks will recognise that the new bank, the lifestyle choice bank, shares common views and is relevant in the context of the relationship.

What is a relevant bank?

A relevant bank is one that informs, educates and empathises with me through communications in the place I'm at ... namely my social space.

That is where the really differentiated banks of tomorrow will sit: providing relevance in the context of where the customer sees the relationship, and relationships are in the social space, not in the branch.

We can already see banks developing social context to be relevant as a lifestyle choice, with the leading name in this space being Fidor. I often talk about Fidor's experiments with Facebook to gain *likes* for example, and the reason I do this is because they were the first bank using the social space as their main place to build customer relationships.

It is this thinking that will become the differentiated lifestyle choice for customers selecting banks. It won't be brand or size or branch, but whether they fit in with the way I think. That's what Fidor does—it talks to customers in an adult way about money; it's what ICICI Bank is doing in India with their social outreach program; and it's what many banks will be doing downstream.

Banks will become social beasts, providing social outreach to gain social relationships in social spaces. Customers will choose their banks based upon their social outreach and relevance and synchronisation with their lifestyle. It's just a matter of time.

It's a brave new world

There are three slides I use in my presentations that illustrate this big change. This is the change in banks becoming social, and moving from being trade focused to community focused. The first illustrates that banks must be in the social network, because that's where their customers are.

If the customer is building their relationships through digital social networks, then banks have to be in those networks and relevant.

The second thing I focus on is the sharing economy, and the fact that within these online social communities there is a lot of value shared. This value is not necessarily in monetary form, but in a social form. *Gifting, shares, likes, favourites* are all forms of caring and supporting in these communities and can lead to real value exchanges that do translate into monetary value. For example, in the largest social network you've probably never heard of, called YY in China, top karaoke singers regularly make $20,000 per month from virtual gifts, with one college student reportedly earning an astonishing $188,000 per month by using the site to give Photoshop lessons.

This creates an easy way to generate income from ideas through *likes* and *shares*. In fact, through the social network, there are many alternative ways of building value other than, or even instead of, trading pure products or traditional services. We see this with crowdfunding and crowdsourcing through sites like Kickstarter and Indiegogo, but it goes further. For example, any individual can be a media station. A great example is PewDiePie, who makes about $7 million a year through YouTube videos of his reactions to popular game releases thanks to his near 40 million subscribers. That subscriber base is bigger than most TV channels.

Money	Worth
Commerce	Community
Trade	Talk
Profit	Profile
Selfish	Caring
Global	Global

So banks need to make the cross-over between the traditional financial world of trade and the new inclusive world of sharing and caring. This is the key: digital banks are making a transition from being pure cold profit machines to warm and fuzzy relationship providers.

Finally, when we reach that level of understanding, we can see why cryptocurrencies are so important, as we have moved from a card-and-cash physical value exchange to a chip-based digital value exchange. In this new world, tokens are just as important as gifts and likes and shares as money. Hence, in the new community-based model, banks focus upon the digital exchange of value through tokenisation rather than the physical exchange of currencies to provide products and services.

CUSTOMER ENGAGEMENT IN A DIGITAL WORLD

So what do we mean by a community focused, social bank? It is clear that a community focused social bank operates in a different way, creating relationships through digital media. Here's the way it will work.

In the new world, the customer will first engage with the bank digitally. It will come from some point of contact through their social media. A friend *likes* the bank on Facebook or tweets about them. It's something complementary like "just got a loan with digibank", and so you decide to have a look at digibank. You find that digibank has good interest rates, a nice mobile look and feel, so you register with them an interest. The digibank asks you to download the app or *like* them on Facebook to get relevant deals and offers, so you do both. The app asks if you will accept push notifications, which you accept.

At this point, if the bank is any good, you are hooked. You are an acquired customer, as there's no way you're going to tell the bank to go away when you see what happens next.

First, the bank starts to send you interesting things based upon your digital footprint. It knows that you like Coldplay from your Facebook *likes*, so you get a push to buy Coldplay tickets for this Friday at 9 p.m. … or would you like digibank to do it for you? You get a push saying that, as you're walking into town today, would you like a cappuccino at Starbucks? Half price if you say *yes* (and by the way, you've just signed up to Starbucks' loyalty program, and of course you don't have to pay for the coffee, it's all done through your account automatically). And hey, you know that BMW you were lusting over online last night on Google—yes, you were searching and looking—well, you can afford it, based upon this financing plan.

The KYC (Know Your Client) process is immediate—the bank just asks me to send a photo of my utility bill and passport or drivers' licence—and they ask if I want to switch or just try us out? I say try you out, and they ask for $100 deposit, just to show what they can do. OK. Wow! Digibank immediately credits my account with $125—$25 is my try-out welcome gift (they'll give me another $250 if I switch)—and off we go.

I start getting more and more relevant push notifications:

- Use Uber now, and your taxi is 25 percent discounted (they know I'm going to a meeting and don't want to be late)
- Cheap tickets for United tonight (they know I like them from my Facebook *likes*)
- Take out a digiloan of up to $2500 and we'll credit your account with the cash within five minutes (they can tell I'm about to go overdrawn with my main bank account)

After a week of this, I think they're pretty cool, amazingly perceptive and a little scary, so I decide to check them out properly. I want to see how they behave in real-life. Do they have a branch? They don't have many, but there are two near where I work. I go to both.

In the first one, the concierge says, "Hello, this is your first visit to digibank, I believe. Welcome. What can we do for you?" I ask him how he knows this is my first visit, and he lets me into the secret: "Your app told me." I tell him that this is a bit scary, and he says: "Well, Chris, may I call you Chris? Let me show you the privacy settings on your app and let's change them to suit your preferences."

I am then shown how the app works. Fantastic. I change the privacy settings to *only personalise push notifications* and switch off the general *always greet personally everywhere* option.

I go to the other branch to see if it works and, sure enough, the concierge here says: "Welcome to digibank. What can we do for you today?" I like these guys.

The scenario would build and build until my mortgage, pension, loans, investments and everything else is with digibank ... but the main thing here, and the reason for writing about it, is that I've just turned the bank relationship on its head.

My start point is through my social community via social media, so digibank has to reach me through the social community. Digibank is then leveraging big data consistently across all touch points to be relevant to me. They are accessing and using my complete digital footprint to gain a relationship with me. It is how they know about Coldplay, United, my meeting and location-based habits. Finally, digibank's human interactions are fully supported by information from my digital footprint, which is why these interactions are exceptional.

Now, the only way to deliver that capability is by having everything built upon, and sitting on top of, a digital infrastructure designed for the internet age. Hence, when a bank says that digital as a channel to add to their existing infrastructure, they've got it a thousand percent wrong. After all, digibank starts with digital community relationships and ends with branch-based relationships. Most existing banks start with the branch and end with digital. Digibank is designed for the digital distribution of data in a global network; most banks are built for the physical distribution of paper in a local network. And digibank is focused upon leveraging every point of the network to maximise the relationship 24–7.

Most banks are focused upon just having a relationship. That's why the ones that are true digital banks, rather than just banks with digital channels, will win.

5.

THE IMPACT OF THE VALUEWEB ON EXISTING FINANCIAL INSTITUTIONS

A brainstorming session with a group of banks raised this question: are we going through a Kodak moment in banking? Are we seeing a Nokia-type change? Will banks miss the tipping point and die from the reformation of the internet, or will we respond and change in time?

Kodak and Nokia were market leaders in their respective areas, but were deniers of change. Kodak didn't believe digital cameras would replace their business; Nokia didn't see that the smartphone would wipe out their mobile leadership. Are banks going through the same blindspot moment? By not adapting to the ValueWeb fast enough, will many banks disappear?

There are a few things we know:

- We have seen other industries decimated by digital—books, music, photography—and know that the same is happening to banking
- We know that the greatest asset to a bank is data, but banks do not leverage their data assets: according to Forrester, only 3 percent of data is tagged and less than 0.5 percent analysed
- We know that banks are structured inefficiently in product silos that lack customer focus
- We know that we have legacy systems that are inefficient and need refreshment
- We know that cryptocurrencies are redefining the digitisation of money and currency
- We know that thousands of companies are launching new innovative models of managing money and value
- We know that billions of dollars is being ploughed into these new companies to force change in the banking system

We know banks have to change, but they are not the same as technology firms, like Kodak and Nokia. The regulatory, compliance, audit and governance requirements, combined with capital reserves that are massively onerous, means that few outside can get into the banking game.

This has certainly proven true. During the past quarter century, everyone forecast that banks were dead and would be disintermediated. It hasn't happened. It's why there are only a few big banks in most countries, and little competition.

However, bearing in mind the list of challenges the banks face, is that a good reason to sit back and be complacent today? And what about all of these new FinTech start-ups—will they change the business?

Most bankers I talk to today say *yes*. Or at least most bankers who understand the FinTech change in our world. These bankers believe that cryptocurrencies are designed to wipe out the banks middle office processing structures; that P2P will wipe out their credit product offers and more; and that the front-end relationship is being taken over by the likes of Apple Pay. These bankers believe Apple Pay will wipe out Visa and MasterCard over the next decade; that Bitcoin will replace SWIFT; and that they have to enable peer-to-peer connectivity for value exchange, rather than act as the control freaks the banks have been for the past quarter century.

MAJOR PARTS OF BANKING ARE STUCK IN THE LAST CENTURY

During my lifetime, two things have fundamentally changed the world: travel and technology.

As a boy, my life was connected locally. We had a local newsagent, pub, shops and garage (gas station), and my friends all lived within a 15-mile radius. My father worked in a city 12 miles from where we lived, and all of his friends were pretty local, too. The furthest point of our network was my grandparents, who lived 200 miles away in Devon. We visited them once a year, and the journey would take almost eight hours, as the road network was limited to minor roads. The fastest roads—motorways (interstates)—were just being built.

It is amazing that these memories sound like they are from the 19th century, and yet I'm talking of a life less than half a century ago. Back then, my father once visited Boston, America. I thought he had gone to the moon, as no one travelled that far. My first overseas holiday was in Spain, and my first flight happened in 1973. I thought I was an astronaut.

Now I travel non-stop. Areas of the world that were discovered just a century ago by great explorers, are now as easy to get to as my grandparents was 50 years ago.

Then you add to this mix technology, and everything changes further as everyone is now connected one-to-one across the planet. My friends are global, not local, and seven billion people (there were just three billion when I was born) can relate to each other directly via the social mobile web.

So it amazes me in this globally connected world that has been transformed by travel and technology that banking has not kept up with such changes. By way of example, I received a cheque the other day. That annoyed me to begin with, as paper is so last century. The cheque was in Canadian dollars. I paid it into my account and a week later I got a letter from the bank. The letter stated: "We received you deposit of a Canadian dollar cheque which we have sent to be processed by the issuing bank. We cannot be sure how long this will take to process, and advise that it may be up to six weeks. Equally, any charges incurred in such processing will be deducted from the deposit amount."

No argument, a *fait accompli*. Six weeks later, I get a note saying that the payment has been processed but the receiving bank charged me CAD$127 and my bank £50 for processing. In other words, we live in a world transformed by technology that is globalised through travel, and yet the banking network cannot even process a cheque without having to do this by moving paper across land-based mail networks involving lots of manual processing. Now that really does sound like something from the 19th century.

Thinking about how a cheque from Canada takes six weeks to process and has significant processing charges reminds me of Heidi Miller's speech in 2004. It was delivered at the largest banking conference called SIBOS, run by SWIFT, their global processor, and it is still talked about today.

What did Heidi say that was so compelling?

She asked a variety of questions, including:

- Why do banks make everything so complicated for their clients?
- How can banks help customers become more efficient and productive, when their own back offices are so expensive, fragmented, outdated and "non-interoperable"?
- If banks truly aspire to be leaders in the payments and securities industries, why is it that so many innovations in their business are pioneered by non-banks?

- If banks can send a secure message to any company over the internet, why should they pay SWIFT to do it for them?

The last question was the most controversial, bearing in mind it was SWIFT's conference, and is the reason why banks still talk about her speech. She also gave this specific challenge:

> "Let me tell you a story about a friend who lives in Europe and bought a boat in the United Kingdom. This gentleman is a very well-known former executive of a large global financial services company. He is eminently creditworthy. He had enough money sitting in his U.S. bank account to buy many boats. When the boat was ready, he called his bank to arrange payment. And his bank told him it would take about six weeks to transfer the funds. My friend could have sailed to New York, withdrawn the cash from his bank account, had a leisurely dinner, sailed back to the United Kingdom, paid for the boat, and still had time left over for a Mediterranean cruise before that funds transfer would have been completed."

That situation has not changed in ten years—in fact with FATCA, AML and KYC, it's getting even harder. And here's the rub: because it's so darned difficult, people are inventing ways to get around it. PayPal may be a pimple on the banking systems' backside today, but its volume of payments processing is exploding, thanks to the ease with which it enables cross-border trade. And bitcoin has been invented precisely to overcome the deficiencies in the banking system.

Bitcoin only exists, as does PayPal, because exchanging money through the new net is not being supported by the banking system. If the banking system works in the old world of pre-global travel and technology, then the new world has to create something to fill the gap. That creation is bitcoin.

Bitcoin fills the gap of global connectivity and, unlike my Canadian cheque, it's free to exchange globally via the net. No charges, no waiting and no issue. That's the power of the Bitcoin exchange and the reason why we need banks to focus upon change, fast.

We are not Borg, we are Human and dancing to a different tune

Building on the theme of the divide between the old world of finance and the new, and why (some) banks aren't fit for the 21st century, brings a few more points to mind, in particular about control and centralisation. Banks were built to be control freaks. They need to own the complete end-to-end cycle of everything. This is why they are reluctant to outsource, and build their own data centres rather than using Amazon's or others. They have to develop their own software, systems and services, which is why they have more developers than Microsoft. They don't trust shared services or other ventures, and so everything becomes point-to-point, counterparty-to-counterparty.

That's all well and good for a world of physicality, but in this age of cloud-based distributed services, it doesn't work. In fact, the whole vertical end-to-end processing of finance is fundamentally flawed.

Equally, the structure of banking is fundamentally flawed for today's world because it was built in a structure of physicality. Local banks served local people through local branches, reporting centrally to a central body that is typically the country's central bank.

It is precisely this old arrangement that has caused all of the struggles with changing payments structures, such as the 15-year old change program

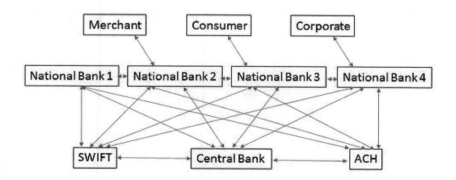

for the Eurozone called SEPA. Payment structures used central clearing houses that were operated by the country's banking collegiate and regulated by the central bank. Now there is no country or central bank, just a world and a World Wide Web. Hence the point-to-point counterparty model of the last century, built for national operations, is fatally flawed in a world of decentralisation, and makes the need for bitcoin even more compelling.

Let's examine it in another context: broadcasting. In the past age of control and centralisation, entertainment was provided by just a few national channels and programmed for the masses. The programming was all local language and focused upon local and national content. The channels had a central base, usually in the country's capital city, and could command high earnings from advertising.

Now, we can broadcast from our bedrooms to the world. People share whilst sitting in cafes and are their own media. They both create and consume, and the media they consume is global. Language and borders are no longer barriers.

Banks have tried to maintain this structure, doing so as a viable alternative has proven too elusive. And yet an alternative business model is emerging: cryptocurrencies and virtual value stores. As they emerge, banks will find customers creating their own financial ecosystem that suits their lifestyles, and all that centralised control will crumble overnight.

It will be particularly interesting to see how this destroys the structure of the local bank serving local needs via point-to-point, counterparty structures.

In 2010s, the network is finally hitting the banking system hard. The power and wealth of the network is all about interactivity. Interactivity

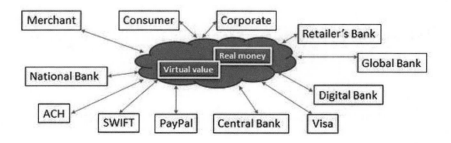

disrupts and decentralises, as everyone has a voice. This is what we are seeing with social media, and what we are seeing with entertainment and value: the decentralisation of control.

Banks may be stuck in the past, but the past cannot be ignored

Banking is different, yes, but there is a clear friction between the old value exchange systems—the financial services markets—and the new ValueWeb systems that are being created by the FinTech community. The friction is caused by the old system needing to work with the new system. You have to migrate the old with minimum risk to the new, and the new needs to be built in such a way as to allow the old to catch up.

The more I think about that friction, the more I can see it in every aspect of banking. Incumbent banks need to migrate to digital, but it's really hard when you have 42 deposit systems, 57 transaction systems and several dozen others that have all been built at various times, and are now in place due to mergers and acquisitions and over-inflated CIOs of the past. Attempts to consolidate systems have been made, but the cost of replacement versus the cost of maintenance is always a major factor.

Now new customers, the mobile internet, digital transformation, cloud and blockchain technologies and more, are demanding migration, and yet the risk and cost is too great. This is a known factor and known risk within the bank, but all banks deal with it.

Meanwhile, the innovators and developers are frustrated by the fact that the old bank is sitting there and not incorporating, enhancing, renewing and leading with the latest technologies. They wonder why there's no clean data structures, easy data analytics capabilities and leverage of bank knowledge of the customer. They wonder why the new world cannot be embraced and just dump the old world.

But you cannot have a new world without the old world and vice versa. The old world runs things right now. Visa, MasterCard, SWIFT, EBA, ECB, CHIPS, Fedwire, RTGS and ACH systems make banking work. Card networks, money transmissions and counterparty connectivity enable banks, merchants, corporates and institutions to interoperate with trust and security. You cannot dismantle and remove that overnight. Meanwhile, the old systems have to keep running alongside the new. This is why banks spend so much on maintaining legacy and why, regardless of the demand for change, the only new things that make a difference are those that wrap around the old bank networks (like Apple Pay, PayPal, Moven, Simple, etc.).

This is why there were two items I recently spotted that show this frustration between old and new. The first was research that found European banks spent £40 billion on IT in 2014, but only £7 billion of that investment went into new systems (17.5 percent); the remaining £33 billion (82.5 percent) was spent patching and maintaining legacy systems. It is that legacy that frustrates but must be migrated, and it's not just legacy systems, but legacy everything.

The second item was a slide presented by Anthony Thomson (co-founder of Metro Bank and Atom Bank) shown at a recent conference. The slide showed that *half* of banks' operational costs are wrapped up in legacy. Legacy buildings, legacy processes, legacy systems and some legacy people, too. It's that legacy that bank CEOs and boards are all aware of, but it cannot be exterminated overnight. It has to be migrated.

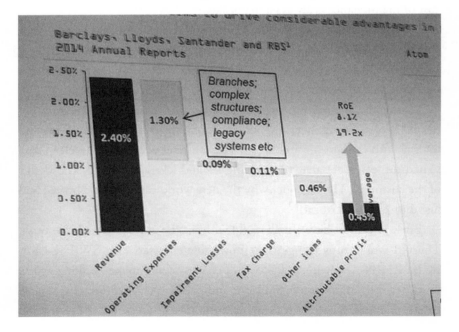

The real question is: can it be migrated fast enough to keep up with new business models and new innovators?

The answer to that question is *yes*, because banks also have legacy customers. That is why half of banks' costs are wrapped up in legacy, as customers want branches to stay, to keep using cheque books, to have access to tellers and more. This is why banks never close down old things, but just add new to the old. That is also where incumbent banks have the advantage, in that they have customers. Many have millions of customers, and customers are unlikely to change easily.

For example, the UK's Metro Bank claim to be gaining new account openings at the rate of around 15,000 a month through 40 branches, but how many are switching their main account to Metro Bank? Getting numbers in this area is difficult, but the Payments Council published figures in January that show who is using the account switching service, and the winner by far is Santander.

The winners and the losers

Brand	Gains	Losses	Net gains
Santander	78,734	18,812	59,922
Halifax	40,794	25,669	15,125
Nationwide	25,243	10,383	14,860
Low volume participants (C Hoare & Co, Virgin Money, Cumberland Building Society, Reliance Bank and Tesco Bank)	689	499	190
Bank of Scotland	3,790	4,093	-303
Danske Bank	541	910	-369
Bank of Ireland (UK) (includes Post Office)	333	820	-487
AIB Group (UK) plc (includes First Trust Bank and Allied Irish Bank)	159	956	-797
Ulster Bank	180	1,515	-1,335
Lloyds Bank	53,019	59,335	-6,316
Clydesdale Bank (includes Yorkshire Bank)	1,117	8,955	-7,838
RBS	2,735	11,258	-8,523
HSBC (includes First Direct and Marks & Spencer)	18,949	30,082	-11,133
NatWest	12,674	27,542	-14,868
Co-operative Bank (includes Smile)	4,508	23,611	-19,103
Barclays	9,455	31,574	-22,119

Source: paymentscouncil.org.uk. The figures only include the customers who used the switching guarantee service.

Why is Santander doing so well? By buying customers. Their 123 account is a loss leader, but it is proving very effective in gaining short-term market share.

So how are the new banks going to compete? Offering a loss leader product to get the rate switchers to switch? Or hoping that being the new, cool, sexy kid on the block will make things happen.

I can tell you now that the latter will fail, and customer acquisition and change is the biggest challenge for any new start-up. It's why mBank often said that their challenge was getting 4.3 million customers to follow them in their path to digitise, getting them off the old bank platforms and onto the new. They point out that the fresh start-ups are minnows by comparison. As a digital-only player in Germany, Fidor Bank has gained less than 100,000 customers; Che Banca in Italy, backed by a bigger bank (Mediobanca), has gained just half a million, even with distribution through bank branches.

So the core question is: can the new banks sustain themselves when they are going to face years of losses as they build their new bank and have to attract customers?

In code we trust

Regarding how software and servers are replacing buildings and humans, the aim of the FinTech start-ups is to replace the bank-in-the-middle with the processor-in-the-middle. This lowers margins considerably, as the processor is doing the work of what would previously have been hands-on desks. Zopa gets rid of

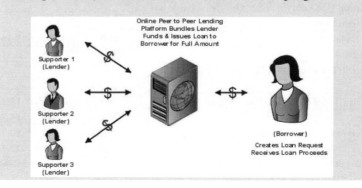

the costly organisational structure that takes deposits and spreads them across borrowers by placing the processors in the middle.

Bitcoin's intention from the start was to replace the banking system. The first line of Satoshi Nakamoto's white paper makes it clear that this *"purely peer-to-peer version of electronic cash would allow online payments to be sent directly from one party to another without going through a financial institution."*

All of these things have one thing in common: get rid of the fat and costly physical infrastructure and replace it with digital.

Now banks are not asleep. They have woken up to this challenge and many are developing and offering APIs to ensure their processing is in the middle, rather than someone else's. Interestingly, governments are also aware of the challenge. Many may not have noticed, for example, that snuck into the UK Chancellor's Autumn 2014 budget statement was the line: *"The UK Government is to launch a 'Call for Evidence' on how APIs could be used in banking to improve transparency and help customers compare financial services providers."*

Governments are moving to component-based regulation as banks move to component-based competition. The world is changing fast as processors replace people and digital replaces physical. Are you keeping up?

THE FRICTION OF THE OLD VERSUS NEW MODELS OF FINANCE

Everything is moving to P2P. The core of this change is articulated best by the bitcoin community, who believe we do not need a trusted third party to exchange value. The technology *is* that trusted third party—in code we trust—but it goes further than this, and it hits at the core of why digitalisation is disruptive in banking.

The truth is, all financial services are now being transacted direct, person-to-person, person-to-business, business-to-business through a networked connection. Or it can be.

- Loans are easily made one-to-one through peer-to-peer lending.
- Small business funding can be conducted easily through crowdsourcing.
- Payments can be made via mobile or net direct.
- Global transactions can be processed through code, without banks or SWIFT involved.

Now there is a downside to all this, as the real role of banks as *trusted* intermediaries is that they ensure these movements of value will be made securely and are guaranteed.

Where are the guarantees with these other technomediaries? Well, they do cover the bases. Default rates at Zopa and RateSetter have been 0.69 percent since launch, and 1.5 percent at the higher-risk SME lender, Funding Circle. From the websites of these firms, you can see their guarantees:

Zopa (P2P lending):
Reducing lending risk
At Zopa, if a borrower misses a repayment, a collections team chases on your behalf. But if a borrower reaches a point where they are behind on their loan repayments by at least 4 months, we've created the Safeguard fund to step in and give you back your money, including interest owed. It's funded by a contribution from the fee a borrower pays when their loan is approved. As you can see, there's a buffer on top of what it expects to pay out. The Safeguard fund has covered all bad loans since it launched. This means not a single lender has lost money on loans covered by the fund.

Funding Circle (SME lending):
Lending to businesses: what's the risk?
Every business on Funding Circle has been assessed by our experienced credit team. They are established and creditworthy and have typically been trading for

around 10 years. However, it's still important to remember that with lending to businesses, there's an element of risk that some may not be able to fully repay their loan. If this happens, the loan becomes what's known as a bad debt. The bad debt rate is currently: 1.4 percent.

M-PESA (P2P payments):

You thought the funds held in M-PESA were held (and used) by Safaricom
The funds are deposited in several commercial banks, which are prudentially regulated in Kenya. In addition, the funds are held by a Trust and are therefore out of reach from Safaricom, which cannot access or use them. In the unfortunate event of Safaricom going bankrupt, the creditors of Safaricom would not have access to the M-PESA funds.

In other words, all of these new models are protected and secured against risk, as far as prudentially possible, as these new models would not work if they weren't. That's the problem with bitcoin right now. It's not secure or protected, and that's why the banks are getting interested in how to work with it. However, that removes one of the main reasons for creating these new models: removing the high cost, third party intermediary.

And this is where it gets most interesting, in that banks have traditionally been a high cost, trusted intermediary because:

1. They built a model of organisation of the physical distribution of paper in a localised world
2. The model is predicated upon manual processing and human services
3. The company is focused upon achieving the highest shareholder return, and hence purely profit motivated

In the new P2P world:

1. The model is one based upon the digital distribution of data in a networked world
2. The model is predicated upon digital processing and automated services
3. The business, as a result, is focused upon achieving the lowest cost processing and hence cost motivated

This is where the old and new models collide, and where we are seeing the greatest innovations amongst the FinTech start-up community. The challenge is how the traditional banking community step up to this new model.

What is the new model?

The core of the banking model is represented in various ways, but I encapsulate it as three companies in one:

- a retailer that has customer intimacy
- a processor that has operational excellence
- a manufacturer of products

This is simplicity itself and is represented in many management books from Michael Treacy and Fred Wiersema's *The Disciplines of Market Leaders*, where he proposes that firms can only be good at one of the above three, to James Champy and Michael Hammer's *Reengineering the Corporation,* where companies are boiled down to people, processes and technology.

My own banking model is customers, channels and products:

- a retailer = customers and people
- a processor = process and channel
- a manufacturer = product

I believe that a bank will only excel in one of these discipline areas.

Traditionally, banks have owned all three spaces and tightly coupled them, but this is where the traditional bank model is being attacked. New entrants are trying to come up with better front-end user experiences through apps; they are trying to create easy to plug-and-play APIs (Application Program Interfaces) to allow anything to be processed anywhere, by anyone; and they are re-inventing products by offering cloud-based delivery of services. Across these services, I can then bind my own offers. I can integrate FX, mobile and payments cloud products through APIs into a great customer app. In other words, my skill now becomes that of the integrator and identifier of the components that offer the best structure for my financial lifestyle. Now I can try and do that, or I can buy the service and have someone else do it.

This is what banking is becoming: an assembler of financial management tools, delivered in the way that works best for their clients. No longer do banks need to build and control the components. They can just source them.

This is already happening. Fidor allows customers to access loans through P2P social lending service Smava on their bank platform; Barclays is inviting Credit Unions to offer payday loans through their branches to stop the payday firms charging high interest; ICICI Bank use SmartyPig to offer iWishes to their millions of customers as social savings; and the list goes on. What is actually happening is that we are finally seeing that componentisation of banking to which I referred in my last book as Banking-as-a-Service. Like the car industry, banks are being broken apart to provide assemblage of service rather than creating it all.

Banks will become showrooms of assembled pieces, delivered as an integrated whole to the customer who cannot be bothered going out and doing it all by themselves. This new component structure, internet-based organisation for assemblage, is growing every day.

OLD BANKS NEED TO RECONSTRUCT THEMSELVES

How incumbent banks reconstruct themselves for this new business model is a question that comes up often. As mentioned, the basic business model is focused upon three things:

- **Manufacturing**, which runs the product and services innovation and administration centres in the back office
- **Processing**, which focuses upon operational excellence in processing orders from front office through back office
- **Retailing**, where the challenge is to be customer intimate and provide the best service experience

Banks in the 1990s decided to run these three operations across multiple lines of business as they moved into a bancassurance model. The bancassurance model meant that many banks began to create universal banking structures that offered everything in finance: retail, private, commercial, investment and transaction banking, along with wealth and asset management and insurance.

A few banks then thought they could leverage this model globally and build universal, global banking structures. The chart below is the result:

RETAIL BANKING

COMMERCIAL BANKING

PAYMENTS

WEALTH MANAGEMENT

INVESTMENT BANKING

INSURANCE

The weakness in this thinking is that no one can be good at everything, everywhere, for everyone. You're going to be poor at something. The second weakness in this thinking is that you can only do this if you control everything. Until recently, these banks did control everything. Banks controlled the end-to-end processing of finance, from product through distribution, and felt impervious to change, apart from change within, as in competing with other banks for more business. Hence, banks battled on interest rates and grew through acquisition.

The weakness in both schools of thought are now clear to see, as banks' structures crack and fade with the challenges. The crack in the structure comes from two directions: one is regulatory and the other is innovation.

The regulatory onslaught has focused upon changing the universal banking model by trying to prise apart investment markets from retail and commercial systems. This has occured in two forms: the American model of stopping banks engaging in casino capitalism through the Volcker Rule (which bans proprietary trading) and the UK model of splitting investment operations from retail and commercial operations through the Banking Reform Act (the bank can still engage in both, but must be under two separate company structures).

Neither necessarily stops investment markets from being risky or banks being too big to fail. For example, the top four American banks were 40 percent larger in 2014 than they were in 2009 and, in 2009, they were already far too big. Nevertheless, the regulators' attack has been notable, with the likes of Citibank and HSBC pulling out of "non-strategic" markets, selling "non-strategic" assets, focusing upon core competencies and restructuring operations. They have had to do this, not only because of the regulatory onslaught, but because of the sanctions and fines hitting their bottom-line after market fixing and tax dodging.

But the challenge that intrigues me more comes from technology, where apps and mobile are changing the retail experience; APIs are shifting the operations to real-time processing; and cloud, combined with data analytics, are changing the product and service.

This technology shift is creating a wealth of new companies that offer narrow finance. Narrow finance examines a piece of the business model and asks: can I do that better? It's what TransferWise have done for matching people who need to move money overseas with people overseas; it's what Zopa, Prosper and Lending Club have done for connecting people who have money with people who need money; and it's what Friendsurance, Bought By Many and insPeer are doing for insurance.

The new model of finance that takes a narrow focus and replaces buildings and humans with servers and software will win out. That's why the FinTech markets saw over $12 billion invested in 2014, up from $4 billion in 2013, and why 36 of those start-up companies are now valued at more than $1 billion each.

It is also why we are seeing the FinTech bubble, where thousands of new firms can attack the old firms' business model. The old firms' business model is based upon end-to-end control in a physical structure; the new firms' business model is based upon narrow focus using open platforms in a digital structure. The combination of the new firms with narrow focus and the regulators with a broad focus is creating a new world. The new world is one where no one controls anything, certainly not banks, as the user has the choice. Users with choice will focus upon bundling their own bank rather than having a bundled bank. Regulators will aim to break up the too-big-to-fail, oversized banks and increase competition by creating a killer marketplace for incumbents.

The new world demands that the old world banks must move to a new world model of component-based integration. The traditional, vertically-integrated bank will migrate to this new, component-based form over time. There are three clear steps to getting there:

1. Move the back office to the cloud
2. Open source the middle office
3. Deliver amazing user experience in the front office

THE BACK OFFICE IN THE CLOUD

In response to the rise of FinTech and development of the ValueWeb, there is a sea change taking place in finance, the economy and the world, thanks to digitalisation and technology. This sea change is enabled by seven key technology components within existing institutions: cloud and big data in the back office; APIs (Application Program Interfaces) and real-time connectivity in the middle office; and social media, mobile and apps in the front office.

This can be represented in a chart on the opposite page:

The two big tech changes in the back office are related to cloud and big data. Cloud offers the ability to provide a product anywhere through centralised services on the net. Big data allows a bank to leverage those services anywhere on the net with highly targeted one-to-one offers.

Imagine proactively targeting an individual with services through the net. The idea is that as I am walking down the street, you will know where I am, what I am doing and what I might need. I might be walking past a store and your front end nudges me that I qualify for a discount coupon in this store: "$25 off a 1 terabyte UBS stick if you walk in now." I'll buy it, but how did the bank know to make that offer at that time?

Obviously at the front-end they are geolocating my proximity to the store but, at the back end, they are leveraging the data about me—my digital footprint—to find the relevant offers for my needs.

This analytical capability amongst banks will be a huge battleground in the future, as it represents a core value. If my friends are getting great services

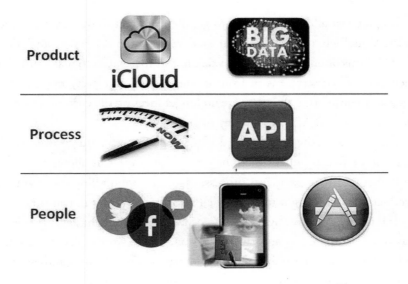

from their bank thanks to their bank knowing their needs by analysing their data more effectively than my bank, then I will defect. It's all about mass personalisation—and mass personalisation today is based upon data analytics. Big data analytics. But there's no point in having great analytics if you don't have great products, which is where cloud comes in.

In the back office, cloud will be the product. Banks and other providers will be building capabilities of financial processing that can be integrated, off-the-shelf, into the front-end. So your bank might generate a great loan product but, in the digital bank future, your loan product needs to be a plug-and-play component. It needs to be a piece of product code that I can download into my app and share and use with data to leverage customer share-of-wallet.

THE MIDDLE OFFICE, OPEN-SOURCED BANK
If the first building block is cloud and big data, then the second building block is APIs and real-time processing.

This second building block is all about the middle office that connects the front and back office, through operational excellence in processing. It is this part that allows companies to get their product to the customer and, in the ValueWeb, the product is far more relevant thanks to data analytics.

The firms offering finance and value in this space need to make sure that their product or service is in front of the customer at every opportunity, especially considering that they are no longer meeting the customer face-to-face anymore—so APIs are the way to go.

An API takes the banks' cloud-based functionality and allows anyone to integrate that product functionality into their offer. It allows Starbucks and Uber to offer a payments process, thanks to unbundling the payments products and allowing it to be stitched into anyone's offer in real-time.

It is the reason why PayPal has succeeded. If you thought PayPal's success was down to their coding or eBay's vision, you're wrong. PayPal's success today is down to their unbundling of the payments processing into an API. This can be easily seen from the charts on the facing page:

What these charts show is PayPal's cost-income ratio through the years. In Q2 2011 and Q3 2013 there is a marked spike. These are two key milestones. The first was the launch of PayPal's API in October 2011. PayPal announced that anyone could plug PayPal payments processing into their systems, and there was a spike in revenue and reduction in cost. The reason for the spike is that the global development community picked up PayPal and started to use their electronic functionality in their apps and products (front-end and back-end). In other words, PayPal is enabling the middleware through real-time APIs.

In fact, it became even smarter when PayPal simplified the whole thing for the mobile world in March 2013, as demonstrated by this second spike in revenues and reduction in costs.

What this clearly demonstrates is that those who open up their processing for plug-and-play will win. It is why Citibank opened up their Global Transaction Banking (GTB) platforms to APIs, as have several other banks. The days of playing cards close to the chest have gone. Only those who open up to the mainstream will survive. You can only be mainstream by being real-time and open sourced. Taking the back-end cloud products and making them relevant through data analytics, then delivering them through real-time APIs to the end-user is the way to go.

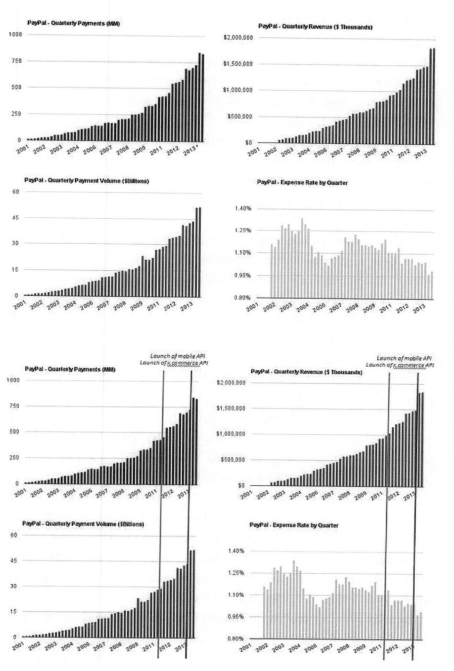

THE FRONT OFFICE, CUSTOMER-FOCUSED BANK

The new business models in the ValueWeb build products based upon cloud-shared services that leverage data and process in real-time via open-sourced APIs. Now, we arrive in the front office and the customer layer, which is mobile and social.

Many people see this as the most important layer, because this is where the relationship between provider and their client comes together, but it is not. Often people misinterpret the value of the end-user relationship. *Who owns the customer,* they ask? But the more important question should be: *who is the customer?*

Right now, some banks should be targeting the likes of GoBank, Simple and Moven as their customer, as these are the companies trying to deliver a great customer experience through mobile social media and gamification. That is not all they are doing, but a GoBank, Simple or Moven as a client of a bank processor or product provider is just as important as a bank or provider delivering direct to the user.

The mass volume processing of finance at a personalised level via the device of choice is where the real battle for the consumer will take place, while connecting people to the network is where the business battle takes place. Last century, the battle was over electricity and connecting products to the grid. This century, the world has moved from products to connecting humans to the net. Some firms will focus upon the human interface, whilst others will focus upon the content and process.

Amazon could not be the retailing giant it is today without the product providers (publishers, manufacturers and stores) and processors (post offices and delivery firms) that it partners with. In Amazon's retail business it creates no product and processes no fulfilment; but what it does amazingly well is leverage the client relationship by innovating with a complete focus upon the customer experience. That is why I love Amazon.

Equally, when we look at the likes of Uber, they are well loved because they take away the friction of the process. With Uber, my need is to get from point A to point B. In the old world, I had to find the product (the taxi) at point A to get to point B and, when I arrived at point B, would have to manage the process (the payment). What Uber does brilliantly is to take away the friction of consuming the product (taxi) and process (payment), so that all I have to do is focus on getting to B as fast as possible from A.

Meanwhile, there will be banks that I will love in the future. Banks that recognise they do not have to create any financial products, they just need to deliver them in the most customer-intimate way. One traditional bank that is adapting is Deutsche Bank. Deutsche Bank has taken all of the components of corporate financing—supply chain management, account receivables, foreign exchange, cash management, etc—and broken them into over 150 component pieces deployed in the Deutsche Bank Autobahn app store. The Autobahn app offers many sub-apps that can be tailored to the needs of the corporate client as they see fit. These pieces are all apps that make the process of finance easy to track, trace and manage. Corporate clients can then go to their Autobahn store and assemble their own pieces of treasury operations management into the dashboard of tools that best suit their business. In this case, the client builds the front-end experience from the smorgasbord of components offered at the back end by their financial partner.

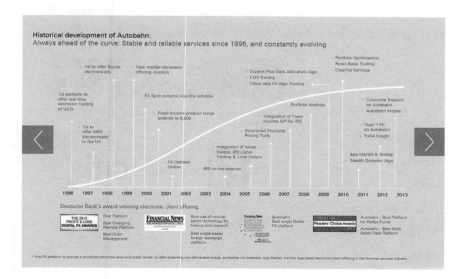

This is the nature of the new business model, where everything becomes a component piece of the value exchange ecosystem. All of these things—the data, the APIs, the apps—are component pieces of value exchange that the bank aggregates and integrates. This is the map for the future of banking.

THE COMPONENT-BASED BANK

I have tried to convey how the old world of products, processes and people—or manufacturing, operations and distribution, if you prefer—is being re-engineered by technologies. Cloud-based products and services can deliver the bank products anywhere, anytime; open source processing via APIs allow those cloud-based products to be integrated into anyone's front-end delivery; and the front-end distribution is now through the best app. We can now see that the whole end-to-end production, processing and distribution of finance is being changed by this new technology capability.

Old world business model

This old-world view is a tightly integrated model of end-to-end finance. The banks could control all the products, processing and distribution on a globalised basis by locking clients into their proprietary services. Banks developed, controlled and managed everything internally. This old world view

Back Office   Middle Office   Front Office
[Manufacturing]   [Processing]   [Retailing]

RETAIL BANKING

COMMERCIAL BANKING

PAYMENTS

WEALTH MANAGEMENT

INVESTMENT BANKING

INSURANCE

HSBC

was made possible as the exchange of value was managed through the physical distribution of goods and services, supported by paper documentation in a face-to-face relationship that was buildings and humans focused.

New world business model

In the new world business model, banks no longer need to produce, process and distribute financial capabilities end-to-end. Instead, they can just take pieces of the product, process and distribution map, and leverage that map to suit their needs. A bank can take a Zopa and Funding Circle back-end, and a Simple front-end, and offer the payment process to link the two (this is actually what PayPal does). A retailer can take their product (coffee) and distribution (stores) and link them through a payment process (payments) to make their service better. That is what Starbucks did when it partnered with Square.

It's a different world that banks have not worked out yet. Most big banks believe they have to be responsible for everything across all parts of the map. They have to manufacture, process and deliver all financial products and services in all markets: retail, commercial and investment banking. That model was broken years ago and is haemorrhaging today, as more and more players nibble at the pieces of the map.

The new players specialise in each area and do it better. As a result, they gain traction through specialisation.

- Can a Deutsche Bank or Citigroup really manage FX better than Currency Cloud?
- Can a wealth management firm really deliver the allocation of funds better than Nutmeg?
- Can a trader really outperform the best traders on eToro?
- Can a bank truly develop financial management apps that outperform specialists like Simple?

These are the questions the banks need to ask themselves as, if the answer is no, they will need to partner and cooperate with the specialists nibbling at their margins before their margins disappear. It is very similar to what has happened to physical product manufacturing.

	Back Office [Manufacturing]	Middle Office [Processing]	Front Office [Retailing]

RETAIL BANKING

COMMERCIAL BANKING

PAYMENTS

WEALTH MANAGEMENT

INVESTMENT BANKING

INSURANCE

Car manufacturers had to manufacture all the components of their cars, then integrate those components to assemble the car itself, and finally distribute their vehicles through showrooms that only bought and sold their cars, and provided all the service and maintenance, too. Then specialists appeared and these specialists could be based anywhere, as container ships allowed any components to be manufactured anywhere,

and prices dropped dramatically.

A BMW or Mercedes no longer has unique components manufactured by them, but have common parts sourced globally from specialists who can produce engine manifolds and leather seats far more easily and cheaply.

Similarly, BMW and Mercedes may assemble the components and sell them through licensed dealers, but most of the service and maintenance is performed by specialists, like Autoglass, Kwik-Fit and dedicated garage shops.

In other words, the structure of the industry changed fundamentally due to the re-engineering of the physical supply chain, allowing specialists to focus and prosper.

That is what is happening in banking today. Specialists are starting to change the financial map through the re-engineering of the financial supply chain.

The financial markets have not quite worked this one out, but there are some visionary banks that are becoming fast-moving integrators, aggregators, assemblers and generators of components and capabilities. A good example is PrivatBank in Ukraine.

Case study: PrivatBank, Ukraine

In 2014, I ran a workshop for PrivatBank, the largest retail and commercial bank in Ukraine. Bearing in mind the political issues at the time, with Russia annexing Crimea, this was quite a special visit. I had been invited to present a keynote speech that would be broadcast live at the bank's headquarters in Dnipropetrovsk, the fourth largest city in Ukraine, with around one million people. They also wanted to show me how innovative the bank could be, and they certainly appeared to be that way, by rolling out open-source architectures, APIs and more in a completely transparent way. In fact, the bank tries to be first at everything in innovation, and clearly demonstrated these characteristics in a variety of ways.

They were one of the first banks to offer API-based services, and today offer hundreds of them as a truly component-based bank service. They are taking this one step further, with innovations such as Sender, which won "best in show" at Finovate Fall, New York, in autumn 2014. Sender enables businesses to chat and exchange value with customers without the overhead of application development. It promises to save the bank's customers hours of time by making communication and payments as easy as a Google Search.

Another interesting nuance with PrivatBank is what they are doing with their branch network. Whilst recognising that digital innovations are critical to the bank's future, they are also nurturing branch innovations. For example, most Ukrainians don't trust shopping online, so the bank has opened its own online shop. In any PrivatBank branch, one side is dedicated to the online shopping service, along with a staff member to help the customer.

Like a Ukrainian Amazon, the bank offers services for customers to shop online in branch and pick up their orders in branch via a click-and-collect service. This is all automated using kiosks, so the customer just enters the branch and enters their pickup code. The machine then opens the compartment with their goods waiting to be collected.

Even more amazing is that PrivatBank is also the largest used car dealer in the country. They are a car dealership in both new and used cars. Customers arrive at the branch and can see the cars outside. If they want to buy one, they can just go into the branch and do a deal there and then, including negotiating a loan.

WHEN WE HAVE COMPONENT-BASED BANKING, WHAT HAPPENS TO THE REGULATOR?

It is fairly obvious that, as value exchange becomes component based and the traditionally integrated markets become separated, that regulations would follow. As we move to component-based finance, we will also create a component-based regulatory regime. It's already happening.

In Europe, Third Party Account Access under the Payment Services Directive 2 will allow non-banks access to all the bank's data to enrich transactions with knowledge. Banks may want to hold back some of the data, as these are just non-bank payments institutions, but they can't. Everyone will have access and, when they do, they will leverage that access. In other words, we have non-bank payment institutions that will have open access to all the bank data about customer transactions—and because they are new and different, they will leverage that capability. Just look at Holvi or ipagoo as examples.

The regulatory regime in the UK also separates payments from banking. Traditionally, to organise payments, you need a banking licence. That's why Google and PayPal obtained banking licences. Now you just need an e-money licence, hence Facebook recently got an e-money licence. In fact, you need not even have a licence, as the UK has separated payments from banking. It is creating a new regulator—the Payment Systems Regulator (formerly the Payments Council)—and forcing banks to sell their stake in their processor, VocaLink, to ensure the whole system becomes detached and independent from the banking system.

There are also new start-up markets, like the crowdfunding and peer-to-peer lending markets, which have their own regulations, too. The UK has also introduced regulatory controls on the payday loans market, yet another independent component in the ever-growing sphere of bank competition.

In other words, as we move to component based finance and deconstruct banks into the pieces that relate to the new world of digital, the regulator will follow our movements and do the same.

BANKS AS VALUE SYSTEMS INTEGRATORS

As discussed, and as we move into the ValueWeb, banks will become Value Systems Integrators and Value Stores, or rather, there will be companies that create Value Stores and act as Value Systems Integrators. They may or may not be banks, but there will be big, new firms that act as our trusted value stores. Banks have historically controlled the value chain of finance from deposits to credit. Because of this, banks have become control freaks, believing they have to build and manage everything. Some banks even have more developers than the largest software houses, such as Microsoft, but this is last-century thinking.

Banks should not control and build everything, as they've proven they're not very good at it. A bank may be great at some things, but they're not going to be great at everything. They're going to be bad at something.

And this is where the value systems integration starts to impact. In order to be relevant in the new digital age of FinTech, banks need to start focusing on their core competencies. Those competencies may be with customer engagement and fulfilment, operational excellence in their transaction processes, innovation in product and services; but it will not be competent in all of these things.

So the bank must first work out its internal map of core competency.

Once this is completed, there needs to be some external horizon-scanning to find out if the assumption that these are core competencies is correct. Do your credit products compete profitability with the peer-to-peer lenders? Can your FX service provide the same rates as TransferWise? Are you enabling customers to meet their expectations of real-time everything in the same way as Circle? Is your offering as engaging as Moven or as flexible as Fidor?

This is important, because many banks think of Funding Circle, Lending Club, TransferWise and Circle as *alternative finance;* and yet, when you talk with these start-ups, they refer to themselves as *narrow finance.* The target of all new start-ups is to take just one piece of banking and do it better than a bank, based upon today's technologies. I would argue that most banks will fail at competing with this model, as banks try to be all things to all people, rather than one, good thing for some people.

But banks do have a great pedigree, a great history, millions of customers onboard in many instances, and a clear culture of understanding regulation and risk. Therefore, what a bank needs to do is take their map of core competencies, check if they are real and then create a new map of competency shortfall. This new map will identify where the bank is failing to live up to customer and competitive expectations.

The trick, then, is to rebuild the bank model to provide the plug-and-play capabilities that allow a hundred percent flexibility for the customer to meet their needs through the bank's services. This is what I mean by Value Systems Integration.

The Value Systems Integrator is where a bank leverages technologies to deliver the total end-to-end value chain for their clients, but through partnerships and integration rather than internal developments and management. A Value Systems Integrator knows that their customer needs a hundred different things to manage their value store and exchange, but buys and partners with a hundred different companies to deliver those stores and exchanges, rather than developing them all themselves. A Value Systems Integrator is a bit like a systems integrator such as IBM, Accenture or SAP. Do IBM, Accenture and SAP do all of the things their clients need themselves? No way. Instead, they partner, acquire and integrate to deliver.

This is the future bank. It's not a software house and it shouldn't have more developers than Microsoft. Instead, it's an integrator of many components and delivers those components to their customers in the best, and lowest, cost form possible.

MOVING FROM BANKS AS MONEY STORES TO VALUE STORES

One of the most intriguing things about the ValueWeb is its ability to create value out of nothing but a relationship. We all value our relationships. Our friends and family are probably more important to us than our work and salary. It's a bit like how we used to talk about the work–life balance, where our work was during the day and life was in the evenings and at weekends; but that's gone with the networked economy. Now we have work and life, intermingled, 24–7. When we wake we check our email, Facebook and Twitter notes to see who's talking and, before we go to bed, we do the same.

Our relationships are now being formed on the network. That doesn't necessarily mean love, but certainly our lives are becoming digitised. We stare at our devices 24–7 looking for meaning, sharing and understanding. We want to be entertained by our friends and celebrity *likes*, and we want to find knowledge and interest from sources as diverse as the Economist and PewDiePie.

Some time ago, I noted that free is the business model, because free can be monetized. My blog is free; PewDiePie's videos are free; most media is free … so how do we make money? We make money be being relevant. Relevance and attention are the new value mechanisms that attract investment, not just goods and services. Relevance and attention demand support and, just like traditional media, will get that support in the form of sponsorship, dialogue and engagement.

My blog is free because I monetize the blog through producing books, speaking at conferences, advising technology firms and banks and generally being an all-round pain. PewDiePie makes over $4 million a year from online advertising that aligns with his media channel. Free makes money. Ideas make money. Content makes money. It's all about the value of relevance and attention. If you get the eyeballs, you get the money.

This is where it gets intriguing, as this aspect of the ValueWeb is untapped by banks, and untapped by many others. Banks focus upon currency exchange and being a store of money, when they should focus upon value exchange and being a store of value. A store of value will store everything, from your cash and money to your investments and savings, to your memories and mementos.

Who stores your memories?

The average baby born in 2015 is forecast to have a lifespan of 150 years. What will these people be doing in 2165 as they reach their final years? Will they still have access to their memories? Will Facebook still be around? Will the USB sticks, the teradata hard drives and the dongles be accessible?

Many commentators are concerned about our digital graveyard, where all of our digital assets become useless a century from now, when technology has moved forward at such a pace that your valued things today become irrelevant. The problem is, that the things become irrelevant but their value to you does not. Those photographs of baby growing up are just as important to you today as they will be to your children tomorrow and their grandchildren a century from now; but who will store those memories?

So what is a value store?

A value store is what a digital bank will become: a store of all the things you value. Traditionally, banks have offered value stores in the form of lock boxes in the branch; in the future, the value store might be your dropbox on the internet. But do you trust your dropbox, your social media or your other stores to be accessible a century from now? Can a bank provide a value store that can guarantee such a thing?

Currently, banks acts as a store of your money and promise not to lose it; if they fail, you are guaranteed to get at least €100,000 returned (by European rules). What if banks promise to store my memories—what guarantee do I get, then? What about a guarantee to store my memories, which will be accessible forever? If you fail, then you guarantee to provide reimbursement to the value I insure my memories for. If I say my memories are worth €1 million, then you can charge me an annual premium to store my memories with a guarantee they will be retrievable for 100 years. Should there be an impact where you fail, I get compensated.

This is a tricky course, but there is a far wider role for a bank as a value store than as a monetary store, particularly as we move to a world of digital rather than physical assets.

DATA PERSONALISATION STRIKES AT THE HEART OF BANK DISRUPTION

There's a lot of talk about big data. Much of the conversation is about the move from mass markets and customer segmentation to the market of one and peer-to-peer personalisation. In other words, the deep data mining demanded by Don Peppers and Martha Rogers in one-to-one marketing in the 1990s is finally here. It took 20 years, but here it is, and this is at the heart of the debate about the ValueWeb, digital disruption, FinTech start-ups and bank responses.

The reason why banks are being accused of being old and stale and slow, is that they are finding it very hard to adapt from product selling to mass markets through traditional media engaged via channels, to offering contextual services to individuals via social media through digital access. This is all part of the ValueWeb revolution and, at the heart of this, is that the FinTech start-ups are putting control in the hands of the individual.

At a recent US conference, there was a lot of talk about Venmo. Venmo is a social payments app that acts as both a way of ensuring bills are paid between mates and also being a social share. We all go out at the weekend and Dave pays so Chris, John and Erin send money via Venmo a few minutes/ hours later. The next time we go into Venmo, where's Brett's payment?

What's big data got to do with that? Not much. What's that got to do with the new market of one? A lot. The market of one is all about making the individual the centre of control and supporting them in controlling their lives. The market of one can only be served by apps that leverage data and personalise it. So Venmo's success is not deep data mining, but allowing deep data sharing.

It's also interesting that Venmo came through Braintree into PayPal, and PayPal now have one of the hottest apps out there. For example, Venmo processed $141 in payments in Q3 2013, increasing four-fold to $700 million in Q3 2014, to $1.6 billion in Q2 2015. Could PayPal have created Venmo? Not really. PayPal are already being called an incumbent legacy, as they're over a decade old. Ten-year-old firms find it hard to stay fresh. That's why the new tech firms are acquiring and investing fast to keep up. It is why Braintree acquired Venmo and PayPal acquired Braintree in a similar way to Facebook acquiring WhatsApp and Instagram.

And this is where we do see the banks struggle, as they cannot create these new apps, because they don't have the structure, capability or organisation to do so. But what they can do is seed fund these apps, buy their companies, partner with the founders and more. The new landscape demands that banks work one-to-one with relevance to the individual's needs, if necessary by rebuilding using new systems and structures.

Case study: Klarna

Klarna is a great example of a company using data analytics to compete in the new ValueWeb ecosystem (read my interview with Niklas Adalberth in the second half of this book).

I decided to take a closer look at Klarna and, sure enough, they've created an interesting business based upon conversion of online interest into sales—what merchants need—rather than dealing with the regulatory risk concerns. In fact, they've been created through regulation as a business that competes with PayPal, iDEAL and the payments system, thanks to the opportunities created by the PSD (Payment Services Directive).

The model is a simple one. Customers get the goods without having to pay upfront. They pay upon invoice. Founded in Sweden in 2005, they expanded across the Nordic region in 2008. In 2010, the company moved into German and the Netherlands, then Austria, France and Italy and, more recently, the UK. The company is now active in 18 markets across Europe.

The model is incredibly effective by allowing users to make purchases online without providing their payment details to the merchants.

It originally worked by asking for the customer's national identification number at checkout (Social Security Number, SSN, in US terminology). Klarna's technologies then make a micro-credit check in real-time using the ID number and, if clear, pays the merchant for the goods. The process has now evolved to asking only for a zip code and email address.

This means the purchaser need make no complex registration or provide any sensitive data when ordering. They just pay the Klarna invoice within fourteen days using a credit card, cheque or bank transfer. In other words, Klarna has removed the online payment piece from online buying.

This is why Klarna has the strapline, *simplifying buying*, as their whole focus is to encourage sales conversions online, which merchants love, and make buying easy, which customers love. According to their deputy CEO and co-founder Niklas Adalberth, the company has "increased the sales conversion rate to 50 percent on mobile devices, from an average of 3 percent when the company's services were not used."

This is because the system makes it easy to buy. For example, like Amazon checkout, by using the zip code, Klarna can pre-fill the user's address for checkout purposes and make the checkout experience even easier. This also reduces fraud, as the goods can only be shipped to the registered address with any defaults reported to the credit bureau.

Klarna then makes money by owning the entire payment experience, end-to-end. Klarna issues the credit to the buyer and can encourage reduced payment costs by getting the payee to use a bank transfer rather than a credit card. In other words, Klarna's revenues are made from merchant fees, user fees and interest charged to users.

As mentioned, Klarna was founded in 2005 and is valued at over $1.4 billion today—a Unicorn in FinTech start-up terminology—increasing its employee numbers by a third last year to 1,200 staff, and has its foundations in behavioural data. Two of the three founders researched a Masters dissertation on how to use behavioural data for risk. Their findings were that behavioural data is four times more powerful than financial data, and this is why Klarna are happy to accept all of the risk of default payments because they use information from 250,000 transactions every day in their data models. It is also why Klarna does not sell its customer analyses to other companies.

In summary, Klarna simplified the buying process and has massively changed the northern European online landscape. You know something works when it is copied, e.g., Qliro has now launched in Sweden, a Klarna-style lookalike.

6.
REINVENTING VALUE
EXCHANGE WITH
THE BLOCKCHAIN

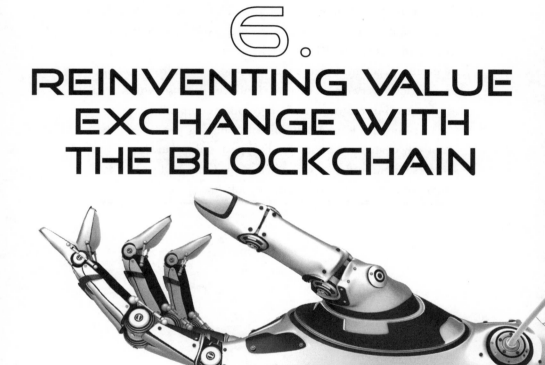

I've been hearing for a while bankers repeating the mantra *Bitcoin Bad, Blockchain Good.* This rallying cry is now so strong that if you challenge it—*Is bitcoin really that bad?*—everyone squashes the discussion. I'm now of a mind that the majority squash such discussion because they really don't know what bitcoin is about.

Reid Hoffman—the co-founder of LinkedIn and early investor in PayPal and Facebook—talks about this, and says that he only got interested in bitcoin two years ago after meeting Wences Casares, whose interview features in the second half of this book. Reid says a few interesting things in this space.

> "There are three aspects to Bitcoin that are interwoven ... One, it's an asset, like digital gold 2.0. Two, it's a currency in as much as currency is like the digital app that allows you to begin to transact and trade. And, three, it's also a platform where you can build financial and other products on top of it. These attributes all bound together are what convinced me that there's a certainty that there will be at least one global cryptocurrency and that there's a good argument that it's bitcoin, or that bitcoin is one of them, if not THE one."

He goes on to talk about how other VCs and protagonists are talking about how the bitcoin currency is a good thing. It pleases him, as he's investing for the long-term, and the long-term says that bitcoin is likely to win. So why would someone as intelligent and informed as Reid Hoffman—alongside Marc Andreessen, Richard Branson, Wences Casares and others—be so pro-bitcoin when the banks are not? My answer is that most of the people that say bitcoin is bad, haven't looked under the hood.

And here's why bitcoin is integral to the blockchain: because the blockchain does not work without a native cryptocurrency. Why would you create an alternative to bitcoin when over 90 percent of all cryptocurrency transactions are based upon bitcoins?

THE IMPORTANCE OF CRYPTOCURRENCIES AND THE BLOCKCHAIN TO BANKS

The blockchain is going to change things. What is the blockchain? Basically, it's a general ledger system that records transactions. You have a recorded and accessible electronic record of every exchange made by everyone. This can be used for any contractual exchange electronically. For example, you could record a lettings deal and the rental agreement along with the dates and frequency of payments due, which will then be taken automatically until the contract is terminated.

Today, most of these transactions are recorded on paper through government agencies, legal networks and financial systems. The reason for this is that there is no way to record such transactions electronically, as the digital services are insecure and untrusted. The blockchain has changed all of this by creating an internet general ledger that is secure and trustworthy. That is because the blockchain provides a method of recording value exchange that can never be transacted twice without the permission of the contracting parties. This is based upon a public record of the transaction, combined with a secure, private key that is held by the contracting parties. Therefore, when I transfer value through the blockchain, the person

First Blockchain marriage will take place at Disney World Bitcoin Conference

by William Suberg @ 2014-09-23 04:33 PM

Latest Transactions		
cd766096834d59b8fe007d0c6...	< 1 minute	0.61084846 BTC
5d4f7bc134cdf51f709f68ec5...	< 1 minute	9.44814786 BTC
8ff3ebc2913af520ed522ddad...	< 1 minute	0.16250487 BTC
8c99c5b51dd2b2638bd4ce6df...	< 1 minute	0.10994126 BTC
175ae25847e6eefdc2f85795a...	< 1 minute	0.10945704 BTC
cb686521f1... (eXch.cc instant exchange 🔗)	< 1 minute	40.36657527 BTC
143cb0026db89bb3de6347eda...	< 1 minute	0.7295 BTC
7cb246e794a3417a7dbcc15e0...	< 1 minute	0.4053 BTC
d6c38b01a8f89f70a3b9cd24e...	< 1 minute	2.30218103 BTC
cd8333a64ecd6f2a35ef5c517...	< 1 minute	0.0100893 BTC

receiving the contract holds a private key that cannot be broken until they give up that key to the next contracting party.

By way of example, if I recorded my marriage vows on the blockchain, as one couple did in 2014 in America, my wife and I would now have a key to that marriage contract. We share that key, and the government and legal system recognises the marriage's viability because it is on the blockchain as public record. The marriage can only be legally terminated when our divorce is recorded on the blockchain and we give up our private key recognising the validity of the marriage.

This technology enables digital value to be exchanged and recorded in a global open system that ensures, once the transaction takes place, it cannot be revoked. That is the key.

In other words, the blockchain protocol is something that can be used as a proof of record for any digital value exchange for anything. That is why banks are interested in this, as it could become a global record of value exchange in the banking system. It is why firms such as Ripple are becoming interesting, as they can displace some of the old infrastructure built for the last-century value exchange called SWIFT. SWIFT was built in the 1970s to provide an electronic system to replace telex machines in banking. Ripple is now creating a counterparty banking system that replaces this and other infrastructures in between banks and corporate clients, with a real-time, shared ledger system that can be trusted. It is not based upon bitcoin, but

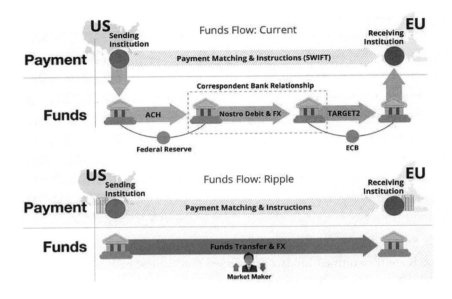

the Bitcoin technologies of the blockchain shared ledgers. It also has its own currency, called XRP, although it can transact anywhere, anytime.

Therefore, the bitcoin currency is not the important factor. The important factor is the cryptographically secure blockchain protocol, as this gives the protocol the ability to record and transfer value without needing trusted third parties, such as banks. That technology may just transform everything, including banking.

THE UBER OF THE VALUEWEB IS THE BLOCKCHAIN

FinTech start-ups are attacking narrow finance and trying to replace core bank functions like credit and payments with new capabilities. The TransferWise and Lending Club business models should worry banks. But where is the Uber of banking? This a question regularly asked in the innovators' world of finance, as Uber is the ultimate new technology Unicorn.

The key to answering this question is thinking about the business model of Uber, Airbnb, Facebook and company. All of these firms are engaged in what I call infomediation: taking a marketplace of people who have something and, through software and servers, connecting them with the people who need something. The software and server becomes the intermediary for information which, in the world of the ValueWeb, is shortened to an infomediary.

If you take the business model chart of banking that I outlined earlier, then Uber, Airbnb, Facebook, Amazon and others are all focused upon being operationally excellent processing houses. They have no product or services themselves: Uber owns no taxis, Airbnb have no beds and Facebook publishes nothing. They just have a great ability to connect people in real-time.

In other words, all of these great new companies are infomediating the content—cars, beds, photos and updates, products, information—with the context—the app in my hand or the page that I'm browsing. If I therefore redraw my chart for the new world of infomediation with the infomediaries we admire it would look like this:

Here's the question for financial firms: where is the infomediator for the ValueWeb? What is the processing machine for value exchange, and what is the role of banks and incumbent financial institutions around that machine?

It's a great question as, historically, the processing engine for the financial system has been SWIFT, VISA, MasterCard, FedWire, CHIPS, BACS and others. Now these are not going to disappear fast, if at all, but there is a new marketplace structure appearing. Originally, I would have said it was PayPal, as they've removed the friction of paying digitally, but it's not PayPal. PayPal are good but … they haven't changed anything. Then I realised that the reason we're so excited about the Internet of Value is that the blockchain is our new processing engine.

Banks have recently become far more vocal and articulate about the blockchain technology. In January 2015, USAA, NYSE and BBVA invested in these technologies ($75m in Coinbase). These two quotes of the announcement caught my eye:

> "At its core, Bitcoin is a decentralized protocol that enables exchange of value among parties around the world, giving it the potential to alter the financial services landscape."
>
> —Jay Reinemann,
> BBVA Ventures executive director

> The Bitcoin blockchain "is an opportunity for Wall Street to streamline some operations that are pretty antiquated."
>
> —Duncan Niederauer,
> former CEO of NYSE Euronext

Many other banks have woken up to the blockchain's potential:

> "Money at its core is simply a ledger for keeping track of debts and Bitcoin is truly the best iteration of a universal ledger we've ever seen."
>
> —John Reed,
> former Chairman and CEO of Citibank

> "Blockchain is a really disruptive development and banks have a lot of fear concerning this technology because, in the pure theory of blockchain, a lot of processes within a traditional bank would be obsolete."
>
> —Thomas F Dapp,
> Research Analyst, Deutsche Bank

In fact, there have been increasingly dynamic efforts to use the blockchain in financial value exchange, which gathered significant pace in 2015:

Fidor Bank were the first to experiment with virtual currencies and the blockchain. They partnered with Kraken (in October 2013) to create a digital currency exchange in Europe, working with bitcoin Deutschland GmbH in Germany. This was followed by a partnership with Ripple Labs to use its payment protocol to provide customers with money transfer services in multiple currencies at a lower cost (May 2014). In February 2015, they partnered with bitcoin.de, a P2P bitcoin trading platform.

LHV Bank are working on a new project with blockchain technology (June 2014) and developed Cuber Wallet, an app based on "Colored Coins" blockchain technology (June 2015). They also partnered with Coinbase (September 2014) and CoinFloor (July 2015).

CBW Bank and **Cross River Bank** announced partnerships with Ripple Labs to work on building a risk management system, and to provide low-cost, cross-border payments transaction (September 2014).

USAA, Nasdaq, BBVA invested in Coinbase (January 2015).

Goldman Sachs participated as a lead investor in $50 million funding for Bitcoin start-up Circle Internet Financial Ltd. (April 2015).

UBS created a research lab in London focused on blockchain technology (April 2015).

BNY Mellon have created their own currency called "BK Coins" as a corporate recognition program which can be redeemed for gifts and other rewards (April 2015).

DBS Bank ran a blockchain hackathon in Singapore in partnership with StartupBootcamp FinTech and CoinRepublic (May 2015).

Nasdaq launched an enterprise-wide blockchain technology initiative (May 2015).

CBA partnered with Ripple Labs to implement a blockchain ledger system for payment settlements between its subsidiaries (May 2015).

ANZ Bank partnered with Ripple to explore potential use cases of blockchain (June 2015).

Westpac partnered with Ripple and tested a proof-of-concept with its staff for making low-value, cross-border payments (June 2015).

Barclays Bank announced that they were working with a range of start-up companies, including Safello, to explore how blockchain technologies could be harnessed in the financial services sector (June 2015).

Santander announced 20–25 use cases that would save £12 billion ($19 billion) in bank infrastructure costs by switching to the blockchain (June 2015).

BNP Paribas experimented at making transactions faster by using blockchain (July 2015).

Société Générale ran a training program to give employees' bitcoin, blockchain and cryptocurrency expertise (July 2015).

Citibank set up three separate systems within Citi that deploy blockchain-based distributed technologies. They developed an equivalent to bitcoin called "Citicoin", which is being used internally to understand the digital currency trading system better (July 2015).

Deutsche Bank released a white paper stating that "it is entirely conceivable that banks could, for instance, set up a new digital booking and clearing system amongst themselves, enabling them to offer client transactions featuring the benefits of the blockchain, such as speed, efficiency, internationality and cost savings" (July 2015).

The Bank of England announced that central banks are looking at ways to implement "hybrid systems" involving distributed ledger technology of the type currently used to record bitcoin transactions (July 2015).

US Ripple users are now able to make deposits to their Ripple accounts from banks **Wells Fargo, Bank of America, Capital One, Capital One 360, USAA, TD Bank, US Bank, PNC** or **Chase** since August 2015.

The blockchain allows the financial system to deliver the processing engine for value exchange: *I want to exchange value—connect me with the right value tokens and value stores to exchange.*

The blockchain is not the engine. It is the technology. It is the Uber of the ValueWeb or, rather, the infomediation tool between those who have value and those who need it.

A timeline of announcements by banks involved with blockchain

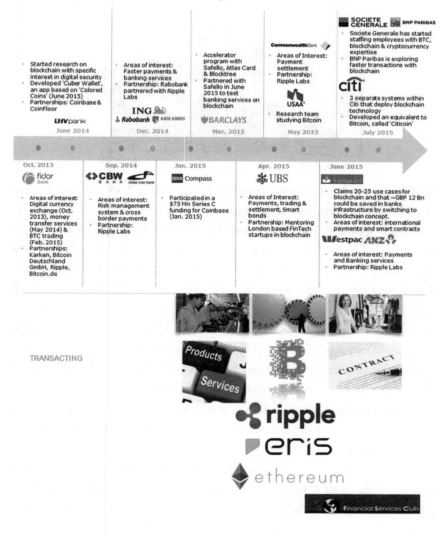

DIGITAL IDENTITIES DEMAND A DIGITAL INFRASTRUCTURE

In fact, a key attribute of the blockchain, combined with the mobile authentication just described, is that it could solve the identity issue for trading globally, peer-to-peer for almost free. This is a big issue, as no one

By Frits Ahlefeldt

knows you're a dog on the internet, but banks need to know, as they can get fined heavily for getting this wrong.

This is why the banking community spend days talking about KYC—Know Your Client. There is a strong argument that, for a digital age, we need digital identities, and the most likely outcome for this is that the digital identity for you and me, ten years from now, will be on some form of shared ledger system.

This is a way off if you look at the state of KYC now. Today, there are anti-money laundering (AML) rules that demand proof of identity by showing a passport and utility bills to check address and personage in most countries. Northern Europe is the exception, as the Nordic markets have seen governments and banks working together to promote digital identities (as far as I know, the only place apart from some parts of Asia that has done this).

Routing payments through multiple nested accounts via counterparties that are difficult to trust is complex. But surely all of this dialogue about passports and utility bills, declarations and signatories and KYC and AML, is pushing a demand for a new digital infrastructure to clear up this mess? The mess has been built up over the years by our punch card and magnetic tape based infrastructure, restricting the sharing and routing of information. In an age of big data, the fact that we don't have this data is appalling.

Meanwhile, we have a hundred different solutions companies trying to solve the digital identity infrastructure challenge and not a single, co-ordinated global initiative to solve it effectively.

Sidechains

The blockchain allows you to create a public ledger system that is accessible for all and secure. This is achieved by having a public recording of transactions that are secured by private keys. As a result, any exchange on the blockchain is secured until the private key is passed along. At that point, the ledger records the exchange of the key and the movement of a digital asset, and that asset can be anything from a currency transaction to a securities settlement to a mortgage deed to a marriage contract.

In fact, in order to allow different markets to create different blockchains to record these different styles of transaction, there are now these things called *sidechains*. Sidechains are just spin-offs of a blockchain used to record a specific market transaction, such as house deed sales, and sit alongside the main blockchain.

This is the technology that all the banks are excited about, as it allows the exchange of digital assets to be recorded digitally for near free. The interviews in the second half of this book illustrate the great debate around this technology. The core of this debate is whether blockchain technology needs to reside on the bitcoin currency. For some, such as Jon Matonis, this is a given. Why would you create another currency? For others, such as Jeffrey Robinson, as soon as blockchains are endorsed and operated using dollars, euros or yen, then why would you need bitcoin? You can make your own mind up.

WILL THE BLOCKCHAIN REPLACE SWIFT?

I made a slightly provocative comment, as it turned out, during my keynote speech at a recent conference. It was picked up in a press article, which reported that I "said the coding behind virtual currency bitcoin could also prove to be enormously transformational, potentially even replacing th SWIFT network for inter-bank payments".

This created a lot of debate, as SWIFT is the backbone of the banking industry worldwide. Built in the 1970s to replace telex machines with electronic transfers, SWIFT is a co-operatively funded network by the global banking system that allows funds to be transferred with confidence. Its very name shows its co-operative nature, SWIFT: the Society for Worldwide Interbank Financial Telecommunication.

SWIFT provides a network that enables financial institutions to send and receive information about financial transactions in a secure, standardised and reliable environment. The majority of banks use the SWIFT network to send money with, as of September 2010, SWIFT linked to over 9,000 financial institutions in 209 countries, who were sending and receiving an average of over 15 million messages per day, compared to just 2.4 million a day in 1995. In a broader context, banks trade something like $5 trillion a day in currencies alone, and most of that is handled by message exchanges to and from the SWIFT network.

Therefore, to say that a new technology, the blockchain, could eradicate a 50-year-old, bank-owned network overnight is proactive. But then there are many views expressed that show a complete lack of understanding of what bitcoin is, but it is changing. Banks are waking up to bitcoin and, more importantly, the blockchain and its ability to transform banking. Here is a technology that is being developed in the open, that has more compute power than any open source project in history, and that could fundamentally reinvent the banking system … and yet few bankers understand it, as evidenced by a recent debate with a number of banks.

First, there was the view that Bitcoin is purely for payments. No. Bitcoin, the protocol, and other cryptocurrencies, are for the recording of digital value exchanges that can take any form, from a payment to a marriage vow.

Second, that it cannot threaten something like SWIFT, as SWIFT is more than just payments. Half of SWIFT's activities are in securities settlements, for example. But the blockchain technology can record securities settlements as easily as a marriage contract or payment. This is evidenced by the newly launched investment markets service, Colored Coins, a company that records investment activity on the blockchain.

Third, that the upstart cryptocurrencies could not threaten SWIFT, as SWIFT has the scalability, security, resilience and history that provide trust in the network. Again, wrong: Bitcoin is now using more scalable and capable networking compute power than SETI, the Search for Extra-terrestrial Intelligence, which was the world's previously largest networked system.

Fourth, that the Bitcoin blockchain is of interest, but not the currency. Some people believe this is wrong, too. They state that you cannot have a blockchain in banking without a native currency—and why would you replace bitcoin as the native currency when it's had five years and thousands of man hours of development effort invested? It's an interesting discussion, and one I disagree with personally as you can have a dollarchain or eurochain, rather than a bitcoin blockchain, but only time will tell on this one.

Fifth, that Mt. Gox's collapse has destroyed all trust in bitcoins and its ecosystem. No. Just because a flaky trading system collapsed does not remove the robustness of the Bitcoin protocol.

Sixth, that it is difficult to use. Yes, but that's changing fast, thanks to the Bitcoin ecosystem. Companies such as Circle and Ripple are changing the game and Bitcoin is like the internet before Tim Berners-Lee gave us the World Wide Web. It's changing fast and becoming easier to use.

Finally, that it's not relevant because it's just a cryptocurrency. Wrong. It's a protocol, a commodity, a technology, a smart contracts system, a general ledger, a secure exchange … a many splendored thing.

Now, I write about Bitcoin all the time, not because I'm promoting it but because it has the potential to reinvent banking, money and regulation as we know it. The blockchain technology is the core technology of the ValueWeb.

WHAT DOES THE VALUEWEB MEAN FOR BANK BRANCHES?

Most observers of the banking industry believe that banks do not need branches. Most bankers say that banks need branches. Who's right? I would bet on the banker, as they're in the business. However, it is clear that we don't need as many branches.

A report by the European Central Bank (ECB) in 2013 found that there has been a significant number of branch closures over the last decade. European banks closed around 20,000 branches across Europe between 2009 and 2013, including 5,500 in 2012 and 7,200 in 2011. That represents the closure of about 8 percent of all of Europe's bank branches since the global financial crisis began in 2008, and the cull is expected to continue for many years to come, thanks to FinTech and digitalisation.

The cuts have been most severe in Spain, unravelling years of expansion by regional savings banks that had given the country the biggest bank branch network in Europe. Its branch numbers were down 17 percent by the end of 2012 from four years earlier but, at just over 38,200 branches, Spain still has more branches per head than any country in Europe—one bank branch for every 1,210 people. France has the greatest number of branches—38,450, or one bank branch for every 1,709 people. France did shrink its bank branch network by 3 percent in the four years to the end of 2012, while 5 percent of UK branches and more than 8 percent of German ones shut down. The number of branch closures is even

Dutch banking landscape: 50% of branches closed over past 10 years

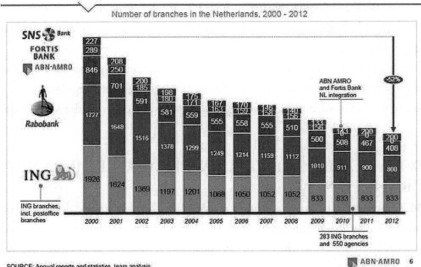

Number of branches in the Netherlands, 2000 - 2012

SOURCE: Annual reports and statistics, team analysis

ABN-AMRO 6

more dramatic in countries that are already heavily digitalised, such as Denmark, where numbers were down by a third and the Netherlands, which had closed a quarter.

The United States is the one country that has consistently refuted the need to close branches, expanding the branch footprint from around 80,000 in 2000 to over 95,000 in 2012. In fact, the number of bank branches in America doubled between 1980 and 2010, and the industry has only reduced their branch numbers three times in the 77 years since the FDIC started keeping track. However, even there, we are now seeing branch closures. Bank branches in the US fell to 97,337 in 2013, reflecting 867 branch closures in 2012, compared to just 315 closures in 2011. Bank of America has cut the number of its branches to 5,243 in the Q3 2013, a 6 percent decline. Citigroup had reduced its branches aggressively by the end of 2013, to 3,777, from 4,069 in 2012.

A British Bankers' Association (BBA) report released in Spring 2015, called the *Way We Bank Now*, noted that:

- The use of UK bank branches fell by 6 percent in 2014, as customers channelled more transactions over phone and the internet
- The number of branches in the UK fell from 13,349 twenty years ago to just under 9,702 in 2013
- In 2009, UK customers called banks nearly 50 million times to transfer money between their accounts. By the end of 2013, the figure had fallen to just over 16 million
- Between 2008 and 2013, telephone transactions fell 43 percent
- Banking apps were used 10.5 million times a day across the country in March 2015, eclipsing the 9.6 million daily log-ins to internet banking services, and both services are still growing rapidly
- More than 8 million people downloaded banking apps in the past year
- In a typical week, Brits are transferring £2.9 billion through apps
- Bank branches carried out 427 million transactions last year, the equivalent of 1.17 million per day (assuming they are open seven days a week)

- The shift to online leaves the 6.4 million people in the UK who have never used the internet increasingly out of step with their banks

British banks halved branch numbers between 1990 and 2015, and senior bankers openly agree that a network of 700–800 outlets would be an optimal size for a bank covering all of Britain. None of the big five have so few. At the end of 2014, Lloyds had 2,260 and the Royal Bank of Scotland 1,750. British banks had closed 557 branches between 2008 and 2012, resulting in 11,713 branches remaining at the end of 2012.

Some people would use this information to claim that the bank branch is dying; the bank is no longer relevant; mobile digital is all; and the customers will move to alternative media, even if the bank doesn't. Now I disagree with this view for a whole variety of reasons, but the core comes down to this.

First, even digital firms find the need for a physical presence if, for no other reason, they need to reassure customers they are real, can be trusted and are backed by humans.

Second, a digital-only play narrows the focus to only those customers who want digital-only service. Those customers are often mature, confident and competent with money. It's different to the youth millennial or iGeneration, who are confident and competent with technology, but not with paper money. The latter demographic only want human contact when it comes to big, scary things, like buying their first house or investing in a pension.

Third, and probably the most important factor, is that the digital-only bank has two forms: a digital form based upon apps for the best user experience, where the client is sophisticated in approach; and a mobile form based upon text messaging for the simplest user experience, where the client is basic. These two factors are critical to future bank services. In fact, the mobile-only play for financial inclusion is transformational, as it enables five billion people previously excluded from the financial network to be included. However, where I fundamentally disagree is that banks can exist in a digital form only. The reason I disagree with this is that there are very few digital-only behemoths—Google, Facebook, Amazon, Uber—but all of these have a physical form.

In other words, the provocative view that money is just data and can all be digitalised with no bank involved is an interesting theory, possible in our dreams, but unworkable in reality, as society wants to deal with real people in real places when it comes to real money.

> While most banks have been reducing the size of their high street presence since the 1980s, the death of the bank branch has been much overstated. More than a quarter of the UK's bank branches have been refurbished in the past three years, clearly demonstrating the commitment to bricks and mortar.
>
> BBA Report on the Way We Bank Now, 2015

The Chief Executive of the British Banker's Association, Anthony Browne, announced that the traditional bank branch is dead. Writing in *The Sunday Telegraph* in July 2014, Browne stated that the halcyon days of banking are over. It was far more difficult to deal with banks before the digital era, as you were restricted to times and appointments, and were forced to physically visit the branch and your manager.

> *The way we bank now is far easier and faster. In the pre cash machine age, branches would not even open every day of the week, let alone at weekends. Counters would close at 3.30pm sharp. You could only find out your balance by visiting your branch and getting a cashier to write it down on a slip of paper. Now we can get access to our money 24 hours a day, 365 days a year.*
>
> *Today millions of us can check our balances, make payments and apply for credit with the help of mobile phone apps whenever and wherever we please. We can talk to our bank whenever we want, by phone, email or social media.*
>
> *Digital banking has transformed speed of service. In the Seventies even arranging an appointment to discuss a mortgage could take*

months. HSBC recently had a home loan application completed online in 24 minutes. Most of our major banks are seeing a 10pc fall in branch transactions each year.

Browne's comments are reinforced by various banking statistics. For example, the UK's Barclays Bank announced a whole set of interesting stats in September 2014:

- Barclays smartphone banking apps accessed 32 times every second
- **£4.7 billion in transactions are processed using smartphone apps every month;** that's over £1,800 every second or £109,000 every minute
- Barclays Mobile Banking now accounts for 75 percent of all digital logins
- An average Barclays customer visits a branch less than twice a month but uses Mobile Banking 26 times a month
- Barclays mobile banking apps have been downloaded more than 9 million times since their launch two years ago, and are being accessed 19 million times each week

This raises another debate about the digital versus non-digital future. As we digitise everything, are we going to lose something? Does the removal of face-to-face eradicate a critical element in banking?

I think it might and, as a result, we will see a two-tier banking system. The tier one banking system will be all digital. All transactions will be remote, and most financial needs will be satisfied by a screen-based process. This is well illustrated by mBank in Poland, who wanted to compete with payday lenders (Wonga has recently entered the Polish market), and so they created a loan feature using their app that could be completed in less than a minute. mBank's loans allow customers to get funds in their accounts within 30 seconds of making the request. How is that achieved?

It is made possible by analysing every mBank customer in real-time and giving them a maximum loan setting. That means that when a customer wants a loan, they are pre-approved. Hence, you load the app and request a loan. The app shows you the maximum loan you are being offered. You then choose the actual amount you want to borrow and over what period of time, and the app shows you the total monthly payments, including all interest and charges. Once you agree, that's it. The money will be in your account within 30 seconds.

That beats payday lenders at their own game—Wonga's secret ingredient is all about the real-time analytics—and shows how banks can leverage their digital assets. But then what we've lost is that human element. The human element is the ability to see the relationship between real risk and real need. The old branch manager relationship was an important one in working out whether the customer was *good for the money*. The old branch relationship is still an important one for complex dialogue too, where corporate clients need to go for in-depth discussions of trade finance needs. And the old branch structure is critical in bringing humanity to the digital experience.

mBank and others would claim this is not so—you can service customers easily through a screen with a Skype connection—but I'm not convinced. That is why there will be a two-tier system. Those customers who are a hundred percent comfortable with screen-to-screen will be dedicated to branchless banks who offer amazingly intuitive, friction-free digital services. Banks such as mBank. Those who are looking for less self-service, more dialogue and greater decision-making based upon circumstances and needs, rather than profile and credit score, will continue to rely upon banks with physical contact through a branch or, more likely, through a representative visiting their office or home. And that is where I see the future: not a branch-based model, but one where there is humanity.

That is where the battleground lies: connecting humans to the net and humanizing the digital relationship. It's not a clear-cut branch or no-branch, all digital versus some digital future, but a multi-layered structure of competition, with some getting it more right than others.

WILL THIS LEAD TO A DIGITAL DIVIDE?

I hate the use of demographics as, when it comes to digital, I prefer psychographics. As a baby boomer, I feel more like a digital native, having developed my career in the technology industry, but according to my demographic profile, I'm an immigrant. In truth, it doesn't matter so much because there are some clear demographic differences when it comes to use of branch and paper. Older people prefer branches and cheques, whilst the young prefer mobile and apps.

Now this approach seems ageist, but the research supports such a conclusion. For example, the Social Market Foundation performed research into preferences for access amongst UK consumers last year and found:

> Face to face service in a branch is still the preferred mode of accessing bank services for 62 percent of people. While we might be comparing prices and ordering goods online, and certainly that is where we are checking real estate listings, eight out of ten people would prefer to go to a branch to seek financial advice; almost seven out of ten to open or upgrade a current account; and it's only when we ask about simpler

Chart 1: Preferred channel to access bank services

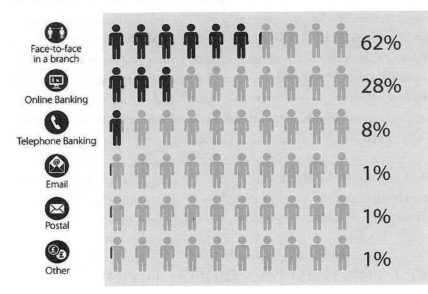

Source: Social Market Foundation/ComRes, Future of branch banking survey, January 24-26 2014

payments transactions, that other channels—primarily online banking—become a common preference ... the affluent (AB social class) and the young (25–34 year olds) have a weaker preference for the branch than others, with more than half of these groups preferring other channels. This trend in their attitudes is significant because the affluent, by way of their higher deposits, contribute the most to banks' net interest income; and the young acquire the highest number of financial products and services in these years, contributing the most to banks' fee-based income.

In other words, the financially competent and confident and the digital natives dislike branches, which means the financially less well-off and digital immigrants are the branch users. The charts below shows the preference for using online banking, which declines the older or less well-off you are.

	A/B (n=359)	C1 (n=221)	C2 (n=161)	D/E (n=267)
Account Opening	26%	20%	11%	11%
Transactions	58%	50%	36%	25%
Managing Savings	46%	39%	29%	19%

Source: SMF/ComRes, Future of Branch Banking survey, January 2014

	18–24 (n=117)	25–34 (n=156)	35–44 (n=179)	45–54 (n=182)	55–64 (n=173)	65+ (n=201)
Account Opening	15%	28%	20%	20%	13%	8%
Transactions	54%	61%	54%	45%	32%	19%
Managing Savings	37%	51%	45%	35%	28%	13%

Now the point I'm making is actually not about age and demographics. It's a completely different, but important, point: as an industry, we are too accommodating of too many choices for too many people.

Each time we introduce a new access service to the bank—mobile and apps—we don't close down an old one—the branch—because some of the people use some of the services some of the time. As long as some of the people use some of the service, we keep it available.

It is similar to the idea the Payments Council had a few years ago to get rid of cheques. There was a huge outcry because the elderly use cheques, so the action was revoked. How many old people use cheques? There's not a great deal of up-to-date information on this. For example, in a paper prepared for the UK government in 2013, only two paragraphs talk about the demographics of cheque usage:

> Women are more likely to carry a cheque book than men (47 percent of women said they always carry a cheque book when they go shopping compared to only 19 percent of men). Cheques are most popular with people aged 50 and over ... A survey on payments to retailers undertaken by the Payments Council (formerly known as APACS) in 2005 found that 46 percent of cheque use was by users aged 55 and over, despite this age group accounting for only 34 percent of the adult population.

However, this point reinforces the branch access issue: we are purely continuing these outmoded services from the last century because a small group of citizens want to use it.

Meanwhile, we introduce new services that are absorbed rapidly by digital natives and immigrants, and find ourselves stretched. The British Bankers' Association (BBA) report *The Way We Bank Now* shows how rapidly things are changing. Key statistics from June 2014 include:

- Apps offered by banks have been downloaded **more than 14 million times.** Some of these services have already achieved well over one billion uses in just a few years.
- Mobile phone banking is popular, but many customers still prefer internet banking for larger transactions. Nearly **£1 billion a day** is being transferred using the internet.
- Internet and mobile banking is now used for transactions worth **£6.4 billion a week**—up from £5.8 billion last year.

- Banking apps for mobiles and tablets have now been downloaded more than **14.7 million times**—a 2.3 million at a rate of around 15,000 per day in 2014.
- Internet banking services typically receive **7 million log-ins a day.**

The demographics here are the flipside of the data gathered for branches and cheques. For example, Barclays Pingit launched in 2012 and, after three months, offered some interesting findings:

- 29 percent of users are 18-25 years old
- 37 percent are 26-35
- 26 percent are 35-50
- 7 percent are over 50

The United States shows similar numbers, with Pew Research producing a report on online banking users in August 2013. Their findings show that under 49 year olds are far higher users of online banking than those 50 and over.

	Percent who use desktop-based online banking
18-29	67 percent
30-49	65 percent
50-64	55 percent
65+	47 percent
All internet users	61 percent

Similarly, higher educated and higher income customers are more likely to be online than lower educated, lower income ones.

Education	
No high school diploma	30 percent
High school grad	47 percent
Some college	66 percent
College+	75 percent

Household Income	
Less than $30,000 per year	48 percent
$30,000 to $49,999	57 percent
$50,000 to $74,999	71 percent
$75,000+	75 percent

So what we really have is banks offering services and trying to be all things to all people. Banks try to please all of the people all of the time, and it just doesn't wash. There's a cost overhead that the digital natives and immigrants are paying to cross-subsidise the costs of the branch and paper users. Will we see a digital divide open in banking? Will the digital crowd migrate to cost-efficient, pure digital plays, leaving the oldies and poor using the physical networks?

What is more likely to happen is that the old will have to get their kids and grandchildren to do their banking for them, whilst the poor will use mobile financial services for inclusion in the network. However, during this transition, there will be some blood on the floor, with the most likely change being the pure-play digital companies gaining the most affluent and savvy customers, leaving the incumbent banks with an even bigger dilemma on their hands.

Close down too many branches, too quickly, and they get called foul; don't close branches fast enough and they can't compete.

THE ROLE OF THE BANK BRANCH IN THE DIGITAL AGE

At J.P. Morgan's 2015 investor day, they announced three things that grabbed the FinTech headlines. First, that Apple Pay has been activated by over a million cardholders since its launch in the US in October 2014:

- Card activation is on a steady increase since October, with 1 million cards activated since Apple Pay's launch
- 69 percent of the cards registered to Apple Pay are credit cards

- 58 percent of the activity is concentrated in the top five merchants (Chase does not list the merchants)
- The users, not surprisingly, are younger and more affluent

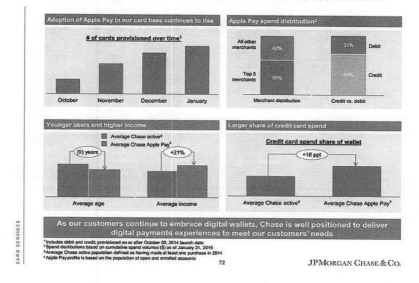

Early adopters of Apple Pay™ are attractive customers and engaged with Chase

The second announcement was a closure of branches as customers moved to digital:

> J.P. Morgan Chase & Co. plans to cut roughly 300 branches by the end of 2016 ... J.P. Morgan's anticipated branch cuts amount to roughly 5 percent of its overall footprint. It's a shift from 2012 and 2013 when the bank added 106 and 28 net branches respectively. In 2014, J.P. Morgan cut 28 banks from its footprint. Between 2013 and 2014, the bank cut roughly 6,500 or 11 percent of its branch employees.

The third thing noted came from Javelin's analysis of the investor call:

> Many of the headlines in the wake of J.P. Morgan's investor day fixate on the news that the banking giant plans to close

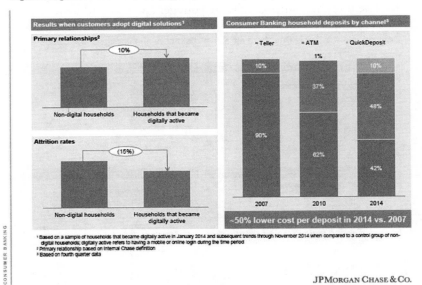

hundreds of bank branches. On the face of it, that is factual. But this is akin to focusing on layoffs without accounting for hiring in other parts of a company that can drive future growth and employment. The reality is Chase's news is an example of getting leaner, not lopping ... to be sure, Chase does forecast reducing its 5,602 branches, but only by about 300 over the next two years ... citing year-over-year numbers, Chase reported hefty increases in mobile app users (20 percent), mobile QuickDeposit transactions (25 percent), mobile QuickPay transactions (80 percent), mobile bill payments (30 percent), and ATM deposits (10 percent). And here's an important milestone for Chase's branches and ATMs: 2014 marked the first year its customers made more deposits through digital channels than at teller windows (ATMs 48 percent, mobile deposit 10 percent, and tellers 42 percent) ... Chase concludes that digital usage leads to more engaged, more satisfied consumers who are less likely to switch banks. They do more transactions, and they conduct them in cost-effective, self-service digital channels. And when they do head to a branch, there will still be plenty of them—with an increasing focus on face-to-face interactions that matter both to the customer and Chase's bottom line.

This reminded me of TSB's announcement that they had achieved significant numbers of account switchers. TSB is a 700-strong branch-based UK bank, spun out of Lloyds under European competition rules that forced the IPO of the new/old bank. They made it clear that they're getting good customer acquisition—half a million new accounts in 2014—but that this is because they have the right mix of customer access, particularly including branches.

In their first year results, they also released a report, *Why branches matter in a digital age*. In the introduction, Paul Pester, former CEO of digital bank Virgin Money, makes clear why branches matter:

> Some argue that because technology and innovation is revolutionising the way in which customers interact with their bank and money that's the only way to compete, and that emerging digital-only providers—be they from the banking industry or elsewhere—will make branches redundant. The steady flow of bank branch closures by the major established banks over recent years has given that theory an air of credibility.
>
> TSB thinks differently.
>
> TSB believes the future of banking lies in branches and technology—enabling customers to bank where they want, how they want and when they want. Yes, customers are adopting mobile and digital banking at a pace we've never seen before. But the importance of having a branch in a convenient location is as important as ever for consumers.

The report also points to research that substantiates this point:

> Although online banking is growing, branches remain
> important to customers. New data from ComRes shows that
> 69 percent of people believe that it is important to have bank
> branch close to where they live.

In fact, most banks claim that account openings are most influenced by having access to a local branch. That may change but, today, that is still the case.

Finally, there are some other factors in play. For example, Atom Bank—the UK's first digital-only bank—make clear that the customers who are most satisfied are those who don't come into branches ... but they are also the most financially confident and competent. If you are confident with money, you want to control it yourself. You don't want someone talking to you about it and, in this case, the most satisfied customers are those who you never see.

However, most first account openings will be with people who are not confident with money. They are young, have never had a mortgage or deposit account, are probably getting their first salary cheques paid and, in many cases, struggle with debt. For these young market account targets, as well as those nervous with money, the branch plays a critical role.

That's borne out by research from many banks, and these are not the targets for digital-only banks. In other words, the targets are people who are account switchers, over 30 and confident with money. For the rest, they want serious banking in real bank stores.

Why would a digital bank have branches? Meet CheBanca!

I visited Roberto Ferrari at CheBanca! in Italy in summer 2015 (see the interview with Roberto in the second half of the book). For those who don't know CheBanca!, it is a digital bank launched in 2008 by Mediobanca. Mediobanca provides merchant bank services in Italy and had never had a retail bank before. Therefore, it made sense in the post-meltdown digital age to implement a FinTech bank fit for Italy, and CheBanca! claims to be that bank. Being a digital-first bank does not mean being a digital-only bank, and Roberto took great pride in showing me his branch.

A digital bank with a branch? Yep. CheBanca! has launched almost 50 branches so far, with more to follow. This has proven critical in gaining trust and deposits, with the main aim of achieving three things that digital-only banks struggle to realise:

1. Trust
2. Brand
3. Service

These three things are harder to achieve when you are unseen, unproven and unknown. However, Roberto and his team gave me some interesting statistics that may back up this claim.

First and foremost, asset holdings in areas with a branch are 2.5 times greater than those areas that are unbranched. This reinforces item #1: Trust. When you can see where the money goes in and out, this builds more trust than the unseen bank.

Second, CheBanca! is gaining 4,000 new customers per month with 45 percent from branches and 37 percent from remote contact (the bulk, 30 percent of that 37 percent, is generated by the internet). The remaining balance of 18 percent is generated by third-party, physical channels. That means a whopping 63 percent today is coming from direct physical contact, and demonstrates the increased trust in the branch services, as well as the strength of the branch in building a brand.

Third, customer behaviours demonstrate that, for service, they prefer digital, with 37 percent of customers handling all of their transactions just through digital access. Then there are a second group of customers, 26 percent of the total, who deal with CheBanca! purely through remote servicing via the web and call centre. A third group that represent around 28 percent of all customers use all the access points (web, call centre, branch). Finally, only 9 percent deal with just the branch and nowhere else.

However, consider the first two groups—would they trust a pure digital firm with zero branches? And the latter two—for over a third of customers (37 percent), the branch is still important, even in a digital-first bank.

Interestingly, the figures continue to bear this out when you examine how customers interact with the bank versus performing transactions. A huge 89 percent of all contact is via digital access, three times the volume of contact that takes place in a branch. Just 9 percent of customers visit a branch every month, versus 7 percent contacting the call centre and 42 percent interacting via digital channels.

So there are a few things about a digital first bank branch that are different. For example, once you get inside, it looks a bit empty.

All you can see is a concierge with an iPad, a machine that looks like a teller (but isn't) and something at the back that might be a *Star Trek* transport station (and is).

Looking in the other direction across the branch (which is L-shaped), you see a few teller stations. These are stations to chat with people about account opening, service and advice, and the typical staff member here is a customer agent without a specialised banking background.

Finally, at the back of the L-shape are a few rooms with frosted windows. These are the serious advice stations. Here, customers have to make appointments to see wealth managers, mortgage advisors or similar. However, you don't need to wait if you simply need advice, as you can go to the transporter room. The transporter room is this weird funky station at the back.

Once you sit at the station, it's got all sorts of cool features, like biometric recognition using digital signature and shared screens with video operators.

This particular branch serves around 259 customers a month at these videostations, and it has proven successful at broadening and deepening customer relationships using those old bank metrics of cross-sell and up-sell. According to the bank, the service videostation has a 15 percent cross- and up-selling success rate.

Finally, if you just want to deposit a check or cash, you use the funky self-service machine. CheBanca! boasts over half a million customers overall, since the bank opened for business in 2008, and is now rolling out its digital branch formats. Today, there are four branches based on the new format. By the end of September 2015 there will be eight in a selected sample of medium and large towns. Equally, the bank intends to roll-out the videostation experience via Skype from September 2015.

All in all, there's lots of things I liked about the digital branch concept. I know folks will throw rocks, and say that digital customers don't need branches, but today's statistics and customers don't support that view.

The only thing I didn't like is having retailers for customer service and talking about up-sell and cross-sell. I'm sure that CheBanca! and Roberto will do their utmost to treat this with care, as they want to be the coolest bank in Italy and, based upon this experience, they probably are. As he points out, CheBanca! has been awarded the Best Bank for Customer Satisfaction in Italy for the past three years and has a Net Promoter Score (NPS) of 47. He claims that "sales is a result of true customer satisfaction".

7.
THE DIGITAL BANK FOR THE VALUEWEB

Having discussed CheBanca! as a digital bank with branches, we will now examine the characteristics of a digital bank. Digital banks are being created in response to the development of the ValueWeb through FinTech. As a result of these pressures, incumbent banks are being forced to become digital banks. Banks cannot compete with new FinTech start-ups if they do not become digitalised. Equally, banks cannot deal with global peer-to-peer connectivity through the mobile network if they are not digital. They cannot support the exchange of value for free, if they are not digital. But what exactly is a digital bank?

I am asked this question often. A digital bank is designed for the digital distribution of data through the globalised network of the internet; a traditional bank is designed for the physical distribution of paper in a localised network of branches. In other words, digital turns traditional banks on their head.

There's more to a digital bank than just implementing internet technologies, however.

- First and foremost, it is a bank built with a vision to reach out to customers through digital augmentation. It is built specifically to offer the customer the service of their choice through their access point of choice. The bank, therefore, has to be designed and created upon a digital core infrastructure. The digital core is a consistent enterprise-wide, cleansed data store that is accessible internally and externally through a strata of access layers. In other words, the start point of a digital bank is to be IP-enabled at its core. No legacy. No barriers, except those that avoid fraud and cyber attacks.
- Second, the digital bank then creates outreach through access. That access can be both physical and digital, but it's outreach to the digital core on the basis of providing customer choice. In other words, the customer may visit a branch, call the contact centre, make a comment on Twitter or Facebook, or touch the bank's mortgage offers via a Google search. Because the bank has a digital core, it will be aware of all these access points and touches, and will respond accordingly and consistently. For example, if the customer has researched mortgage deals online the previous night, checked

the latest interest rates on the app in the morning and walks into the branch at lunchtime, the bank will be ready with their mortgage specialists at hand—possibly through a videolink to a small branch—to provide the advice needed for the customer to make the decision over the mortgage deal.

- Third, the digital bank has an organisation that is geared to digital. The main form of customer outreach is through social media on the network, via video to advisors, and focused upon being at the point of relevance to the customer in their daily life. It focuses upon augmenting the customers' life through digital outreach, but recognises the importance of the customer engaging directly face-to-face. The human contact through the network is the magical touchpoint. All other functions are geared towards removing friction through digital enhancement.

- Fourth, the digital bank will have an innate knowledge of the customer. They will leverage data as a competitive differentiation, and see a single view of the customer as the ultimate view. They will know that data association and predictive, proactive, proximity-based service is the place they will win.

- Finally, the digital bank will have a boardroom that sees digital as their culture, rather than a project. The bank does not have a digital team or a budget for digital. They have integrated digital into their core, and see it as the duty of everyone in the bank to identify how to use digital series to touch the customer better, at lower cost and with an intimacy and data differentiation far more fit for the digital age. In other words, an Amazon-style processor of finance, rather than a Barnes & Noble.

DIGITAL BANKS DO NOT HAVE CHANNELS

So do banks need to start all over again? Is that really feasible? There are many reasons why I believe financial institutions need rebuilding.

First, we originally built systems in the 1960s based on automating transactions in the back office on a mainframe. The transactions were the debit and credit accounting ledgers, and the information derived from branch-based operations. In the 1970s, we implemented 3270 green screens in branches to feed those mainframes with data for the transaction ledgers. This was a cost-cutting, administrative and efficiency play. It worked. In the 1980s, we introduced ATMs to the network. The ATM was designed to get rid of tellers, and have become the main physical, electronic outreach point for most banks.

In the 1990s, the next major electronic movement was to remote customer support through the telephone call centre. Already, by this time, banks had multiple legacy systems created through M&A, expansion of offers and disparate IT strategies. Most banks had multiple head office systems on multiple provider platforms, because they built their deposit account administration on IBM, for example, but then introduced insurance, mortgages, cards and other product lines from other specialists, from Unisys to Fujitsu to Amdahl. This is why most call centre customer service representatives were already struggling by 1999, because they had to access multiple systems across multiple platforms to get a comprehensive customer view.

The result was that the central, head office based focus was securely cemented by 2000, thanks to the previous quarter-century developments of systems, and much of this focus was upon transaction processing for internal branch and call centre support.

Then things changed. Things changed fundamentally. The focus of support moved from internal to external.

It was at this point that we started talking about multichannel support, as we had to make what was previously only visible internally, external. We had to give customers online banking, and so we had to rethink the internal machine. Most banks didn't. They just took the internal machine, and stuck a front-end, internet bank access on it through a username and password. That is why most banks' internet banking looks just like a bank statement, because that's just what it is—an online access to the bank statement.

We got away with offering an online access to a bank statement for a decade, but then the smartphone appeared with apps and real-time, and the emperor's lack of clothing became visible. Most banks tried to move their head office focused internal systems from big screens onto small screens, but it just didn't work. It didn't work because it's not real-time, it's batch. It didn't work because it's focused upon internal cost cutting, not customer experience. It didn't work because it supported staffers, not users.

The trouble is that the back end is still a half-a-century old layer of mess that needs sorting out. In fact, banks are cemented in legacy mess, which is why they talk about channels. Branch was layered on the mainframe; ATM another layer; call centre the next one; internet banking the last one; and mobile the latest. Each layer we call a channel, and now we talk about "omnichannel integration". What complete rubbish.

There is no such thing as a digital channel. The reason there is no such thing as a digital channel is that a channel is just a layer on a legacy. It is growing the legacy. So when I hear banks talking about omnichannel or digital channel, I know that they are just adding layers to legacy. And it will not work. It will not work because the legacy is based upon a physical infrastructure view, i.e., a structure built in the last century for the physical distribution of paper in a localised network. We now need to rebuild this for the digital distribution of data in a globalised network. And the problem is that you cannot rebuild this from the front-end. You have to start rebuilding this from the core.

In other words, we have to look at that half-century old structure we've built for head office transaction recording and rethink it for a 21st century structure of augmented, non-stop real-time access.

We have to do this for both the user and their user experience, but also to ensure we can monitor in real-time. Real-time monitoring will give us knowledge of opportunities (cross-sell, increased share of wallet, loyalty offers, etc.) and threats (cyberattack, unusual activity, accessibility issues, etc.).

This is why I keep talking about transforming to a *digital core,* because I truly believe that no bank can evolve their legacy systems to support a 24–7, real-time world. Those systems just weren't built that way. That is why, when I hear the use of the word *channel,* I feel revulsion. I feel revulsion because it immediately says that you are thinking from an analogue, 20th century viewpoint.

Digital banks talk about "access" rather than "channel"

If I am against using the word *channel, multichannel* and *omnichannel*, what should we call it? We should call it *Access. Augmented Access, Proximate Access, Intelligent Access* or whatever phrase you want, but it's purely about access to services, information and support in a digital form.

Access to the banks' digital platforms via any form factor I choose—my mobile, watch, desktop, tablet, car, television. Access via Skype to a human, via phone to a human or via branch to a human; humans who are also being provided access to digital services through the banks' platforms. In other words, the whole bank sits upon a digital foundation, a digital core, a digital ecosystem.

In this world, no one thinks about segregated systems, silo structures or channels. The bank does not think about deploying layers of separated systems and then try to work out how to stitch them all together. The bank just adds new services and access for new form factors to their digital foundation.

But access is key—consistent access to a reliable, resilient, real-time digital service.

It is for this reason that I've persisted with the call to replace core systems, because then you can build a reliable structure with data in the cloud and processors for provision of access to the digital core, from the ground up. What we should be doing is replacing the old infrastructure to provide access to reliable, resilient, real-time digital services. Then the future will be adding further access and leveraged service to that digital core. Adding digital to digital rather than legacy to legacy, if you prefer.

I mentioned *Augmented, Proximate* and *Intelligent Access* because when you have a digital core platform, the information that derives from that platform can be fed to all access points and all form factors offering differentiated service and support.

Many banks talk about the likes of Apple, Amazon, Facebook and Google as their aspirational models. What is it about these big internet giants? Do they have channels? Do they have segregated structures? Not at all. They have a single, digital approach to service. They do not consider mobile, tablet, internet and telephone as separated systems and channels.

They just see access through form factors to their digital services.

That is the transition banks will undergo in the next five years. They will move from adding legacy to legacy, cementing their back end systems through front-end systems lock-in, to building a clean, core digital foundation for the bank that can then feed service to any digital or physical form factor where service is needed.

It will not be an easy transition, but it is a necessary transition if banks are going to be fit for purpose in the digital age.

DIGITAL BANKS THINK DIFFERENTLY

Some years ago, I pitched an idea. The idea is that banks can now use crowds to analyse risks through social networks. They can create a "trust score" that adds multi-dimensional analysis of all the financial and social data out there into something that makes sense. Why is this important? Because financial information is too stark and lacks completeness in its profile of what someone behaves like and whether they can be truly trusted.

- Is there a risk of being involved in moral hazard?
- What are the attitudes to risk and finance of the person or firm being invested in?
- If a firm has no record in this constituency, are there other proofs that could be provided?
- If a firm is trying to do something brand new, is there anything that could increase confidence with those individuals/firms?

In this sense, just as you vet employees with social media by checking their profiles, in future we will check customer and client profiles for risk. The core of the idea was to create a "trust passport" that has a variety of critical applications:

- For P2P transactions where the history of one party is too poor to create trust; in the current climate, there is no proof of dependability
- In cross-border transactions where the old way would be to provide a letter of credit—but many firms do not understand such

letters, particularly small firms and microenterprises working in a globalised world where they need to operate with no track record in a new environment

- In governmental and bank transactions, where governments and banks want proof of track record when no financial track record is available, e.g. trying to get hold of a visa

This passport and trust score would become critical for not only banked individuals and firms, but also for those who are unbanked or who have no credit history, as it offers an ability to use this understanding in other environments where a credit history is missing, such as mobile and gaming, where you: (a) can pick up behavioural details of transacting in these environments; as well as (b) offering a transaction support service by enabling "trust" in these non-financial environments.

As a result, banks could pick up a lot more previously unbanked business due to the depth of this risk information. More importantly, the user could now immediately secure trust with strangers to do business. For example, the small business in India that wants to trade with the multinational corporation based in the States; the landlord who wants to ensure the prospective tenant is trustworthy; the microcredit farmer who now wants a bank account; the migrant worker who is a new country and needs financial services ... anyone in fact who has no way to prove their standing. And just like eBay buyer and seller ratings, the more you work on your trust score, the easier it becomes to do business.

The problem is that very few banks can use this idea. Most banks have difficulty in getting data together within the bank, let alone integrating data from outside. Most banks are not tagging their data, let alone analysing it.

Nevertheless, I have seen a few FinTech start-ups using social media to augment financial data. One bank I know focuses upon the customer experience, and believes that you can only deliver a great experience if you develop a holistic view of the customer from their entire digital footprint, and automate context around that footprint.

This bank talks about using LinkedIn and Facebook to check that if you say you are a director at ACME Inc. since 2009, that your profile matches

this statement. If your profile is a year old, with two links and no friends, you're not approved. If you're LinkedIn with lots of ACME execs and show that you've been there since 2010, you're in.

This is the new world of digital banking from a digital-first bank. No constraints, no ties and no legacy. And this new bank is called Banco Original in Brazil (read my interview with Guga Stucco, the bank's head of innovation, later in the book).

It's about behaviours, not technology

What Banco Original, Fidor Bank and some other new, start-up banks understand, is how to use human behaviours in the digital world. Too many people in discussions about the ValueWeb are focused upon short-term technology change, rather than creating human processes in digital environments. For example, many banks I meet talk about the latest technologies from mobile, tablet, bitcoin, contactless and all that good stuff, but that is not what the future is about. The future is about humanity. The future is about designing great and engaging human experiences, enabled by technology but not focused upon the technology.

That sounds a bit wacky: how can you design a great human experience with technology if you're not focused upon the technology? It was illustrated well by one speaker who said that their rollout of contactless mobile was a waste of money. No one used it. The reason: it was not easier than using a contactless card, so they used the card instead. Customers could not see the added benefit of touching a payment point with their mobile over using a card.

There have been a lot of rollouts of new technology in banking which have not been successful, because they haven't been thought through. Bitcoin is unfortunately stuck in the challenging mode today. In a few years it will be as intuitive to use as a smartphone, both pervasive and persuasive. But it won't take off with the general mass of people in its current form.

Which brings me back to the form factors of consumer behaviour in the future. Today it is smartphones and apps; tomorrow it will be chips in everything and a connected economy through the internet of things. In the future, will you be talking about a payment, or an exchange of value? That final question is really fundamental, as we focus today on mobile payments—but tomorrow we should consider connected value, as that's what bitcoin really represents.

This will be a virtual store that represents a unitised amount for the digital exchange of value. What I mean by value exchange is designing systems for tomorrow that focus upon the connected economy, where value can be exchanged in many forms—money, bitcoins, World of Warcraft gold, iTunes, a gift of an Amazon book, an idea—that will change the whole of the banks' thinking.

We would not think about payments and devices at all, but instead, the behaviours of humans who are enabled by the digital world to connect with anything to exchange anything that represents a value to the receiver.

TAKE THE TEST: DOES YOUR BANK THINK LIKE A TRADITIONAL BANK OR A DIGITAL BANK?

One of the things that becomes quite clear, as we move into a sharing economy, is that the role of banks are changing. Banks historically focused upon profit and trade, but they now need to also focus upon community and dialogue. It is no longer good enough to purely focus upon commerce at the expense of community.

This will be a difficult transition for banks, as their raison d'être has always been on profit and trade. Now they have to show their relevance to the community through conversation. What I mean by this is that banks need to demonstrate relevance in relationships through the social network, because that is where the customers are, rather than just pushing products through channels.

So now we get to the critical question: how do you become a social bank? The answer is, you have to be a FinTech bank or incumbent banks must transform into being digital banks. The best way to illustrate the difference in thinking is to try the following test.

- Traditional bankers think about pushing products upon customers through channels. Digital banks think of building value with communities through access.
- The traditional bank uses expensive media to shout at customers: come open an account. Digital banks get engaged in the social world, and build relevance by showing that their services are cool.
- Traditional banks are product focused, and worry about their customer attrition rates. Digital banks are community focused and know that, if they build relevance to that community, then the audience will be engaged with the bank.
- Traditional banks look at digital as a channel, alongside mobile and internet and telephone and branch. Digital banks think that there are no channels—just access points internally and externally to their digital architecture, which sits at their core.

I could continue, but you get the idea. Perhaps my best illustration of the difference is Fidor Bank. Fidor Bank was launched as a pure digital bank in Germany in 2008. They are a proper bank with a bank license, and their starting point is being part of the social network. They focus upon their social network community first. Their community is in the social media world of Facebook, and they become relevant to that community by firstly offering preferential interest rates based upon the number of Facebook *likes* they receive.

By way of example, their interest rate is currently 6.8 percent on loans, and they have just over 20,000 Facebook *likes*. When they get to 22,000 *likes*, the loan interest rate will go down 10 basis points to 6.7 percent per annum.

At 24,000 *likes*, it will reduce 0.1 percent again and so on until year end, when it resets to 6.9 percent.

So why would Fidor do this? Because it builds a community. They get 2,000 Facebook *likes* and that translates into 670,000 friends and family influencing the Facebook community to also *like* Fidor. That is because, according to Pew Research, the average Facebook user has 338 friends. So every *like* makes 338 people aware of Fidor, and those influencers are friends and family.

The result is that Fidor is being exposed to thousands of people every day, and what they see is that Fidor is a cool bank, engaged with their community in a social conversation about money and finance. It is the reason why Fidor spends just $20 to gain a fully KYC (Know Your Client) onboarded customer, compared to $1,500 for the average traditional bank.

In other words, traditional banks spend a fortune pushing products through channels by shouting at them via the media; digital banks spend a minimal amount talking to people about money through their communities of interest. It is the reason Fidor spends just $125,000 per annum on marketing.

Creating conversations of relevance that build trust

In talking with relatively young banks about their digital strategies, it's intriguing to debate and dialogue with them how they want to work. By young bank, I mean banks in markets that typically did not have banks operating in the 1980s; or, if they did, they were state-run banks rather than consumer-focused banks. These would be in places like China, India, Turkey, and Poland. These banks illustrate well my core argument that *digital is not a function but a culture.*

For example, take ICICI Bank in India. ICICI was invented with digital in mind, and I have always been impressed by their focus to keep costs to the minimum and service to the maximum through digital enablement. This is why ICICI Bank can operate transaction processes at a tenth of the cost of a traditional bank and, like banks in Turkey, Poland, Ukraine and elsewhere, are starting to demonstrate innovations you just don't see in traditional banks.

Here's an example/idea, and it's one that I think is developing in these young banks, much to the chagrin of the old banks.

Let's develop the idea of a fully digital bank concept for today's world. Our bank is under 35 years old, it is cool, it is relatively unconstrained by legacy systems and it is small enough to be able to move fast and be agile. This bank is led by a technology visionary who sees the future of banking through millennial eyes and realises it has to be digital in its culture.

This bank has branches, but they are there to leverage digital enablement and support. There is a call centre, ATMs, online and mobile banking, but they are all the same: there to provide leverage to the customers' digital lifestyle and support them in their financial needs. The bank has integrated payments as an API, so that most of the cool apps have their payment service embedded. Forget setting up cards on Uber and Starbucks; you just Touch ID Bankpay and it's done.

The coolest thing the millennial bank has done, however, is moved fast to become embedded in Facebook and Skype. The bank took many of the best customer contact agents from call centre and branch, and retrained them in responding rapidly to customer needs through Facebook and Skype. The bank placed their full service banking into a Facebook app, and made it available to any customer to use. Full Service Facebook Banking (FSFB) gives you all the functionality of payments, billing, balance checks, money transfers and more, but all in a Facebook gateway to the bank.

Similarly, the bank made their Facebook page their service channel. Forget calling the bank to ask questions, just leave a comment or question on Facebook and the bank will reply within seconds. A dedicated FSFB Team has been created, from their contact and branch agents, who create conversations and relationships through Facebook.

You can connect with these agents as individuals on Facebook or via the bank's Facebook page, and you can just talk about money. The bank even holds a monthly town hall meeting on Facebook to explain complex financial matters. How does APR work? How do banks make money? Why do banks need a licence from the government? What caused the banking crisis? These are all themes the bank develops in conversations during the pre- and post-town hall meeting, and the aim is to ensure that agents are having conversations. This is because the bank sees the new world as one where they gain relationships through conversations on the network, rather than by pushing products through channels via traditional media.

It's a fundamental difference in thinking. For example, these banks measure staff effectiveness by the number, quality and depth of conversations they engage in social and digital spaces, rather than by their product sales. The aim is to encourage the conversation, knowing that the sales will come. Therefore, the annual bonus is based upon shared rewards for success, whilst the individual incentives are to engage in quality social dialogue to build relationships and trust.

So the bank deploys FSFB and then backs it up with the ability to contact any of your bank friends via video. Just Skype me and we'll talk more.

Amazingly, the bank finds that these friendly social financial networking structures encourage people to actually visit their branches to meet their Facebook bank friend in person. It becomes a community around the bank. A relationship that is social and trusted.

This is the future of banking: creating conversations of relevance through a trusted network. And if you want to see it in action just visit India (ICICI Bank), Turkey (Akbank, Deniz Bank), Poland (PKO Bank, mBank, Alior

Bank), Ukraine (PrivatBank), and other young bank markets. They are millennial banks, and they think like millennials.

BANKS WITH PRE-INTERNET AGE CORE SYSTEMS HAVE A HEART THAT IS NO LONGER BEATING

The reason why most banks talk about the next technology rather than designing for great human experiences with technology, is that they were not designed for the internet age. Their core systems were implemented in the last century, before the internet existed and yet, in order to become a digital bank, traditional banks have to rethink their ideas around core systems.

Right now, banks develop pretty much everything themselves. I can think of hardly any Tier 1 banks that have not developed their own core systems. Most banks are proud of this fact.

But banks need to replace their core systems for the digital age. How they do this is to separate the content of their systems—the data—from their processors—the engines. The question is how to replace the foundations without causing the building to fall down. It is not easy, but the interconnected, global world of technology demands that banks become far more agile and flexible. Therefore, any system that is old and inflexible should be ripped out and replaced if it relates to real-time processing.

So the banks are replacing such systems, but even as they do this, things change. Just as banks consolidate and rationalise core processing on megaplatforms, the megaplatforms become redundant because you can do it all in the cloud today. I urge financial institutions to move mission critical processing into private cloud and shared services into public cloud, as that's the best way to improve resilience and ensure business continuity.

Add to this non-stop cyberattacks and Distributed Denial of Service (DDoS) and a bank that has not bullet-proofed its current systems, let alone the legacy, is going to be hammered. IBM estimates that banks get 111 million cyberattacks a year. That's over 300,000 a day! Of these, around 87—or 1.67 a week—are really malicious and would cause mission critical damage. There's the issue right there. How can any legacy system in core processes withstand such demands?

Consolidation and rationalisation is all well and good, but systems must then evolve and focus upon continuous improvement rather than cryogenic freezing. Review every five years (or more often) and renew every ten (or more often). That's the only way that a bank, as a technology business, is going to survive.

Anecdotal research suggests that few banks have actually replaced their core system. Instead, many have commissioned consultancy and vendor white papers that talk about core systems replacement and how it can be done. But the reality is that no bank is doing it.

During the summer 2014, IBM published a research paper on *Attitudes to Core Banking Transformation in Europe.* The report is based upon interviews with 27 European IT leaders in the major banks, including nine in the UK. What they discovered is that not one is committed to core systems replacement.

In the United States the situation is similar, with only BBVA cited as a bank that's modernised its core. According to most analysts, this is the first bank to venture into such a major transformation in the last 15 years. Whilst PayPal struggles to keep up with Stripe with systems that are only 15 years old, banks sit happily with thousands of developers maintaining systems that pre-date PayPal and the internet in most cases.

That's the real reason why banks employ all of those developers. It is not for competitive purposes, not for innovation purposes, not even for cost purposes. All of those developers are there because the creaky old core systems need to be maintained, whatever the cost. In the IBM report, two-thirds of the IT leaders said that maintaining core banking systems takes up an unusually high proportion of IT budgets.

I suggest they get rid of them. Banks are not fit for the digital age if they have systems at their heart that pre-date the internet. Banks that have systems that pre-date the internet do not have a digital core. Banks that have a pre-internet core have a heart that is no longer beating.

This is the opportunity for the new FinTech crowd. The FinTech age will replace the banking age with a new core—a digital one. That is why so much money is going into FinTech.

BANKS WITHOUT A DIGITAL CORE WILL FAIL

I often use the phrase *digital core* in this context. Therefore, I was intrigued when someone asked for a definition of a digital core, and one of the replies was, *there isn't a core anymore.*

I wondered what they meant and, in explanation, they referred to the idea of a central point of systems—a mainframe—is no longer the way the markets operate. Systems should instead be spread across server farms in the cloud so there is no single point of failure. I totally agree, and therefore felt *digital core* should be explained in more detail, as so many misinterpret what this means.

A digital core is, in essence, the removal of all bank data into a single, structured system in the cloud. The data is cleansed, integrated and provides a single, consistent view of the customer as a result.

That's a big ask, and most banks tell me it's not achievable. Silo structures and line of business empires protect data sharing and lock client information in their product-focused empires; creating a single, cleansed store of cloud-based data is too insecure, creating the opportunity for any cyberattacker to bring down the bank; a single data store would not be good for risk management purposes.

I understand all these concerns, but don't agree with them. The product-focused empires are the problem. You cannot have customer-centric operations if your organisation is product aligned.

Cyberattackers also find it far easier to steal from fragmented systems than one that can track digital entries in real-time across the enterprise. Equally, banks are poor at risk management in their fragmented, product-focused structures, as evidenced by two meetings with my bank recently. The first meeting was with my business relationship manager, who explained to me all the intricacies of the banks' SME operations. I then, for the first time in living memory, allowed my new personal relationship manager to visit me. He had printed and read very carefully all my information and wanted to complete an up-to-date fact find for KYC and sales purposes.

Halfway through the conversation he asked, "What do you do for a living?" I said that I thought he would know as I talk to my relationship manager often. "Oh," he said, "that doesn't show on our records. Who did you talk to?" I explained that it was Paul, my SME manager, as I have my business account with the bank. "Oh," he responded, "I didn't know that."

This is fairly typical of all banks I talk to—their corporate, commercial and retail bank systems are separated, and never the twain meet—but it's not the way a digital bank would work.

A digital bank with a digital core would immediately create the inter-relationship profiles of the digital footprints of all individuals who touch the bank. That is the way you can drive contextual relationships and offers. It is also the only way you can drive a consistent, augmented and informed approach to clients.

Equally, a digital bank has a single digital core of data in the cloud that can then be accessed by any form. The digital core is independent of the processors, and hence you can take out a server or a system at any point and replace it with a new processor, because you are not reliant on the engines. Your reliance is on the data being clean and consistent.

For me, it is a critical factor in developing the digital bank, and yet whenever I get into a conversation about this with a bank, I'm told it is too difficult. It may be too difficult, but I suspect that if banks don't bite this bullet, the FinTech specialists who do get the data structures right will eat their lunch…

Do banks really need to change?

Some bankers do not believe that FinTech, the ValueWeb and digital is a major change program. In fact, some bankers are not even sure they have to change. Their logic goes like this:

> First, banks could quite happily do nothing, and their balance sheet and results would look the same or maybe even better because banks don't make money from retail consumers. Banks make their profits from corporate and investment banking. That drives their balance sheet and shareholder returns far more than retail bank profits.

Second, banks could do nothing on the consumer side and they wouldn't lose many customers. Most banks are operating at the same level. They move slowly and aren't innovating greatly, and are all about the same. Even if a new bank was created with a truly compelling offer, most consumers wouldn't switch.

Third, a lot of the reporting of bank revenues and profits is based upon ifs and buts. Banks make a lot of guesses and suppositions in their results based upon future contracts and returns, along with risk analytics that can change year on year. As a result, they can create accounts that look far more attractive year on year, by using these different factors to improve or decrease the attractiveness of their returns. As a result, a bank could ignore action and, if they started to lose market share, could hide their trailing position until they catch up.

Fourth, most banks are driven by cost-income ratio and shareholder return. Therefore, investing in retail bank infrastructure to improve customer service doesn't cut the ice. In fact, most of this would be overhead investment rather than balance sheet improvement. It would increase cost, not necessarily improve income, and decrease shareholder return. As a result, banks only change if they have to.

Fifth, banks are protected by their license, and the regulations and compliance requirements that go with that license. I liken it to an army camp. You have free movement of people outside the Ministry of Defence camp but, inside, it's a lockdown situation. That's pretty much how money and banking is. Outside the industry your can have free movement, so people can create pretty apps around money. But the money movement itself is ring-fenced by regulation to be secure,

resilient and reliable. It's a financial encampment that has to
be police forced. As a result, banks can just sit in that camp
for a year and not move, and nothing is lost.

The problem with all of the above is that, although it has been true
historically, can a bank really sustain itself by doing nothing? I am not aware
of any bank executive who would sit back and tell their leadership team to
do nothing. Doing something is easier. But often doing something means
doing something incremental. The challenge of the ValueWeb is that it
requires something transformational. It demands banks transform, because
there are a lot of new companies that are eating into their core markets.
P2P lenders are taking market share from the credit markets—14 percent
of that market by 2025 according to Goldman Sachs' March 2015 equity
research report; new payments firms are replacing banks in the payment
process; and many new Unicorn FinTech start-ups are appearing across all
of the financial market spaces, as evidenced by the listing in the appendix
of this book.

In fact, if you want to see how fundamentally banks are going to change,
you only need to heed the words of BBVA chairman and CEO Francisco
Gonzalez. At the bank's investor meeting in February 2015, Mr. Gonzalez
forecast that half of the world's banks will disappear due to the impact of
FinTech on the industry. Mr. Gonzalez has been leading the bank through
a fundamental change process to become a software house. That journey
started in 2007, and his leadership in this space is second-to-none. That
might be because Mr. Gonzalez began his career as a programmer, and it
is rare to find a bank CEO who has a background in IT, as most have a
background in financial management.

THE BIGGEST BANKING CHALLENGE IS LEADERSHIP

There are many barriers in responding to the challenge of FinTech,
particularly regulations, legacy and culture. These three barriers are
intertwined. Regulations stop banks from innovating; legacy systems stop

banks from innovating; a risk averse culture stops banks from innovating. All three things work together to wrap the bank in ropes of stagnation. Management are unwilling to change systems because it is too risky. Management are unwilling to place systems in the cloud because it is too risky. Management are so focused upon regulation, that innovation takes a back seat.

That's one view of the world. The other view is that these are interconnected reasons for doing nothing. These are excuses put into play by some banks and bankers to ignore innovation and change, and focus upon the status quo and shareholder value. That is the key question: how do you create shareholder value?

One bank executive recently said to me: "What makes you think we can focus upon customers and innovation and moving into digital, when our critical focus is shareholder value? We cannot innovate unless it delivers shareholder value. That is why you need to show me the ROI before we'll invest in digital. We need to see the numbers."

I responded by saying that shareholder value and stakeholder value are mutually inclusive, not exclusive. You can deliver greater shareholder value by investing in people and process and innovation and change, than by stagnation and constraints.

These constraints are false. The legacy, shareholder value, regulatory and cultural constraints are false. I do not know one bank that has not been transformed if the leader has the courage, capacity and competency to make the change work. Take the example of Michael Harte, Chief of Operations and Technology at Barclays Bank and former CIO of Commonwealth Bank of Australia (CBA). I loved his story of presenting a strategy to the Board of CBA to move their infrastructure into the cloud and the bank's executive team responding negatively. Unperturbed, Michael went to the regulator and talked through the plan. Come the next Board meeting, he represented the plan to the Executive Team, but this time had the regulator in the room supporting him. Now that's the way to make change happen, and change they did. In so doing, the bank saved 35 percent of their cost of operations per annum by moving into the cloud and became the most agile bank in Australia, from a technological point of view.

Or take the example of mBank in Poland. A bank that was doing well—it was the fourth largest bank in the country—but could see it had fallen behind in both brand perception and capability, so it transformed. Now it's the third largest bank in Poland and has won every award out there for innovation. But they weren't that innovative, they were just courageous. They had a CEO who could see the problem and had the guts to change it.

So these three barriers—regulation, legacy and culture—are false barriers and are caused by poor leadership. A bank CEO could sit there, as one told me, and just do nothing. Just oil the machine, and you'll deliver all that's needed from a shareholder's return point of view. In fact, by investing in nothing, most banks would make greater shareholder returns than by investing in something.

But if you don't invest in anything, that's a process that will keep you going for a year or two and then, before too long, all that deferred investment will have to be spent in one year to catch up with the stagnation it has caused.

So you have to invest in something. A risk averse leader will invest only in the things that have to be done. That creates a risk-averse culture and one that focuses upon just doing what the regulations require. That requires no legacy renewal. It just demands a lot of tinkering. These banks get incremental improvements and maintain parity within the industry, but they don't achieve anything special.

And there's the real rub. A differentiated bank is one that has a vision, strong leadership and the guts to make something happen. That's what I've seen in CBA, mBank and a few others—ICICI Bank, Akbank and, to a lesser extent, Wells Fargo and Barclays—but it's rare. It's rare because most banks and bank leaderships only want to do enough. They're not interested in doing their best.

Bank leaders need to be courageous and give the industry the culture to innovate to overcome the false constraints of legacy, and use regulation to create innovation.

BECOMING A DIGITAL BANK: EVOLUTION OR REVOLUTION?

Nevertheless, if the bank cannot change or does not have the leadership to change core systems, then there is an alternative approach. For example, a question that comes up regularly is: *Should the bank evolve to a new digital model, or does it need to bite the bullet and transform?* Evolution or revolution? That's a question that only the bank's CEO and management team can answer, and needs to consider the following:

- The current state of the bank
- Its ability to serve customers effectively
- The agility to maintain parity and competitiveness with other banks
- The capability to adopt and adapt to new customer demands and new technologies

Actually, this is complete nonsense. That's the way to escape making a decision. These are just excuses for not changing, because a company that wants to truly compete as an effective provider of service to customers should start from a different point. Where should they start? At the beginning. Start with the customer.

Start with the customer today. Start with how you want to relate to that customer. Start with the question: *How do we reach that customer today?* Start with a map of how and when you think you will *touch* the customer. Map out every customer interaction touchpoint. Create a heat map of the most important touchpoints where you can excel, differentiate and compete. THEN BUILD YOUR BANK.

Now the bank you build will either evolve from where you are today, or it might require a revolution. The answer will be based upon how radically different that bank vision is of customer interaction tomorrow:

- How costly and how difficult will it be to transition to the new vision?
- Is it going to be worth it in terms of upheaval and change?
- Is the organisation structure capable of the move?
- Will you impact customers through this change?

- Will those impacts create potential systems or systemic risks to the customer relationship?
- Will customers relate to the new bank?
- Does it require a different brand and presentation to be relevant or will the current bank be just as appropriate?

So there is no simple answer as to whether becoming a digital bank requires an evolution or a revolution, as it will be different for each bank, but I would start with the vision first. It all comes back to the customer— the customer is key.

How to wake up the bank

I recently had a great conversation with the head of innovation at a bank. In the middle of the conversation, we got into a discussion about how to get rid of complacency in the management team. The fact is that this bank is doing well. It's growing its customer footprint, cross-sell ratio, account holdings, deposits and credit markets. Everything on the charts is heading up, including profits. Why would a bank like this decide to decimate branches, invest in digital and reorganise around customers (rather than products)?

This is a challenge I encounter quite often, as my message is that you do need to reduce branches, invest all in digital and reorganise around customers. So here is the way to create the burning platform to change the bank.

Everyone is talking finance on technology and technology in finance. There is a difference between these two camps, however. The former camp talking finance on technology is the FinTech community. This community believes they can rebuild banking and finance for the 21st century by internet-enabling money. This community believes that the old model of banking and finance from the 20th century is too difficult to internet-enable, and needs to be rebuilt. The second group, talking technology in finance, are the financial community. This community believes that banking and finance needs to adapt to the demands of 21st century technologies, but are firmly grounded in their existing incumbent views. That incumbent view is that they can keep up by partnering with innovators, investing in front-end developments and maintaining interest in, but not necessarily adapting to, the new models of FinTech.

The reason why I distinguish between the two groups is that they are two distinct tribes.

So imagine that we're in a large city in medieval times. There's a Village one hundred kilometres away. The Village is insignificant, and the City is not aware of the Village. That's unfortunate, as the City has seriously annoyed the Village. That's because the Village sent a group to the City a few years ago to ask for help, and the guards of the City told the Village to get lost.

As a result, the Village went somewhere else for help and, luckily, they found it in the Lords of Anarchy. The Lords of Anarchy lives in a town far away. They had also heard of the City as being a law unto themselves and offered the Village men, money and weapons.

The Village recruited more and more capability thanks to this support, and gathered other villages and towns against the City. Eventually, they became a serious threat as they overthrew the City and took over their lands.

Is that how FinTech (the Village) is going to play out in finance (the City)?

It will be if the financial community or, rather, your financial institution seriously believes that digitalisation and FinTech is no threat.

This financial institution, like many others I meet, sees the Village as no threat. They have growth, profits and happy bonuses, just as Nokia and Kodak executives did a few years ago. There is no burning platform in their view, so why should they do anything radical, especially as most of them will have retired by the time any of this happens?

So, finally, here's how the burning platform emerges. Banks and insurers are technology companies. They are not seeing technology in finance, but need to rethink to be finance on technology (FinTech). The key difference is that the latter is subject to the network effect and the network effect is a core tenet of the ValueWeb, as discussed earlier.

> "Network effects is the term given to systems in which the value of each user is increased as the number of users goes

up. Such network effects are common on the internet; for example, eBay and Facebook. The value of some such systems is roughly in proportion to the number of connections between users, meaning that if the user base doubles, the value of the system quadruples. This also acts as a barrier to new competitors, since new users are much more likely to join your system than a smaller one that doesn't offer the same value. If your company believes it will able to leverage such network effects, it often makes sense to treat the first users as a loss leader and get big as fast as you can."

— Tom Murcko

Back to banking. If banks believe they can continue with products sold through channels using traditional media and haven't woken up to the network economics of FinTech, then they will surely die. A long, slow, cruel death, but they will die. That is what happened to Nokia and Kodak, and will happen to your financial institution if the executive team are not taking digital seriously, not streamlining branch operations and not organising for customer-centricity.

The reason is that network effect competition can decimate markets. It won't overnight, but it will over time. For Kodak and Nokia it was over a decade. For banks, it may be two decades, but it will happen if the banks do not change, as the network economics are obvious.

You can see it in peer-to-peer lending in the UK where, last year, the total value of P2P lending and crowdfunding amounted to £1.2 billion, taking total lending by the industry to £2.18 billion, more than double the figure at the end of 2013. It looks likely to double again in 2015 and, based on Zopa's forecasts, will continue for the foreseeable future. Zopa themselves have seen year-on-year doubling of cumulative lending for the past five years.

That sounds like a burning platform as network economics hits the lending industry. It is the same with Venmo. Venmo's processing power is doubling year-on-year ($700 million processed Q3 2014 vs $1.6 billion Q2 2015). In fact, through FinTech attacking payments and credit markets, there's a strong likelihood that, in ten years, a significant part of bank profits and margins will have moved to new start-up companies. So the bank has to adapt within ten years to be more like a FinTech firm. Maybe sooner.

A final thought on complacency, which I've heard from a few bankers. They have this view that they already have millions of customers who are unlikely to switch to alternative providers that are untrusted, unproven and unlicensed. OK. That is the luxury of today that will give you the ten years to change and adapt without losing overnight. That is the cushion of today.

People do switch allegiances over time, especially if there is a better offer that is cheaper, more transparent, more convenient and easier to use. Think how fast things change. Ten years ago, taxi drivers felt secure, Nokia and Blackberry ruled the world, Washington Mutual and Royal Bank of Scotland were the most respected banks in the world and China was irrelevant. It's a little bit different today.

So, if you're building your financial institutions strategy, there is a burning platform out there, no matter how secure you feel.

THE VALUEWEB IS LIKE MARMITE

Recently, I presented at a conference in Italy. It was a small crowd of CMOs from the Italian banks, who listened dutifully to my messages. The feedback forms were mainly 8, 9 and 10 out of 10s, but there were two or three that gave me 1–3 out of 10 mark. Now I don't mind that, because I reckon I'm a bit like Marmite.

First of all, I say that banks are being turned upside down by digitisation. Instead of being built for the digital distribution of data in a networked world, they were established for the physical distribution of paper in a localised world.

Marmite point #1: The banks now need everything to sit on a digital platform.

I then point out the technologies that are creating this new world:
- chips inside everything
- everything connected
- apps making it easy to consume using digital technologies

- the consumerization of technology
- social media fuelling a new world of everyone relating to everyone
- social finance creating new business models
- everything real-time, where data represents value
- banks as big data value stores
- the cloud delivering all of the banks' products via APIs to the end users' apps

Marmite point #2: Technology is driving the banking industry to change.

Then I go on to recommend that the banks cannibalise themselves. Rip yourselves apart and rebuild. Look at everything, from product to process to people, and work out how fit you are for this digital age. Are there others doing it better? Should you manufacture the cloud services, APIs and apps for the product, process and people; or should you assemble and integrate them? Do you recognise that you've been vertically disintegrated and that customers can build their own banks? Can you compete?

Marmite point #3: Technologies are ripping banks apart; the banks should proactively do this to see if they are fit for purpose.

Finally, I finish with a view that you cannot be complacent because your target customers and employees hate you. I show them the Millennial Disruption Index, which clearly shows that the under 35s hate banks. They would rather go to the dentist than visit the bank (71 percent) and are desperate for a Google or Amazon to take over (73 percent).

Marmite point #4: Banks have not behaved in the customers' best interests.

8.
WHAT COMES AFTER THE VALUEWEB?

What comes after the ValueWeb is like asking what comes after the internet. It's a hugely tricky question, as the internet morphs every 15–20 years and the ValueWeb is just the start of this generation of change. As mentioned in the opening chapter, the ValueWeb is the building block of the third generation internet, Web 3.0, the Internet of Value. I call it the ValueWeb, as this generation changes everything when it comes to money and trade, as well as the things we value in life and relationships. It is a clear shift from the first and second web generations.

Digital Timeline

- The first email was sent by Ray Tomlinson, to himself in late 1971.
- The first spam email was sent by ARPANET to 393 people on 3 May 1978.
- The first domain name registered was Symbolics.com on 15 March 1985.
- The first website was dedicated to information about the World Wide Web and went live on 6 August 1991.
- The first picture uploaded to the web was posted by Tim Burners-Lee (inventor of the World Wide Web) in July 1992, on behalf of a comedy band called Les Horrible Cernettes.
- The first Instant Message was sent by AOL Vice Chairman Ted Leonis on 6 January 1993.
- The first banner ad went live in October 1994 on HotWired.com.
- The first item sold on eBay (back then it was AuctionWeb) was a laser printer for $14.83 in 1995.
- The first book purchased on Amazon was Douglas Hofstadter's *Fluid Concepts and Creative Analogies: Computer Models of the Fundamental Mechanisms of Thought* in 1995.
- The first sentence spoken on Skype was in April 2003.
- Mark Zuckerberg was the first person on Facebook with

> ID number 4 (the first three Facebook accounts were used for testing) in February 2004.
> - The first YouTube video posted was uploaded on 23 April 2005.
> - The first tweet was written by co-founder Jack Dorsey on 21 March 2006.
> - The first working cryptocurrency was launched when Satoshi Nakamoto's bitcoin paper went live in 2009.

The first generation was the Internet of Business and the second generation the Internet of Society. Web 1.0 was all about building the World Wide Web, whilst Web 2.0 was focused upon social networking. Web 3.0 is the Internet of Value, and will take at least the next decade to build, create and deploy. That is why I often say that traditional banks have a decade to change—but they had better start now, because if they wait until they can see the change occurring, it will be too late. Eventually, after the ValueWeb has been created, we will move on to what I call the Internet of Life, where we won't even think of the internet as something separate. We won't think about digital or mobile or being online; we will just be immersed in the network, which will have become some sort of sixth sense.

Obviously the timings of these generations of internet can be challenged, but I place them as the first internet-based email was sent on ARPANET in 1971; the first instant message was sent in 1992; and the first cryptocurrency that worked, Satoshi Nakamoto's bitcoin, went live in 2009. What you see in these generational developments are years of building the capability that then seems to appear overnight. Twenty years or more of building the internet's plumbing took place before the first website appeared but, once it did, it took only four more years for Amazon and eBay to start selling books and organising auctions. The first instant message was sent in 1992 by AOL's vice-chairman Ted Leonsis, but it took 12 more years before Mark Zuckerberg began working on Facebook, and almost five more before they reached 100 million users.

As I say, we could debate years and details, but the point I am trying to make is that each generation of the internet's key stages—Internet, Web 2.0, ValueWeb, Life—takes around 10–20 years of gestation technologies before it hits Main Street—and the ValueWeb is in its early days. We have 5–10 years before it delivers and, during that time, other components of the ValueWeb have to come together. For example, we are talking about machine-to-machine commerce (M2M). M2M commerce is the trade that takes place in the Internet of Things, with many people believing the Internet of Things is Web 3.0, although I claim that space is the ValueWeb.

You cannot have an M2M Internet of Things trading goods and services without a cheap, real-time infrastructure that supports such things. You cannot have an Internet of Things if these *things* have identities that cannot be traced. You cannot have an Internet of Things, if the *things* cannot be associated with their masters in a cheap and easy, real-time way. This is why the shared ledger underpinning the Internet of Things, driven by the ValueWeb, is going to be key. This is the reason why the ValueWeb is critical, as you cannot develop next phase services without it.

In fact, as we look at the ValueWeb 3.0 developments, the world will work something like this. The ValueWeb develops alongside the Internet of Things, enabling machines to trade with machines. This will allow the refrigerator to exchange value with the grocery store through a registration of the refrigerator on the owner's identity, which will be on someone's shared ledger of trusted identities that might be blockchain based. This identity profile attaches that device's billing account to the wallet of its owner. The owner will get cloud-based updates in real-time of the refrigerator's purchases. They will also see what their car, television and other devices are ordering in real-time. This will all run on a shared infrastructure, which will be a cloud-based, shared ledger of trust.

As machines trade with machines, the internet on-demand for printing anything will develop. This development is hinged upon secure designs and patents, as it means the supply chain collapses from goods being imported from overseas to goods being printed at home or in the local workshop. Right now, 3D printers can easily print anything, from jewellery to clothing to guns, to even printing houses and body parts.

As people can print products at home that they used to purchase in stores, there will be a war on copyright crime and illegal printing of products. This war will be the same battle we have seen with the illegal downloading of digital goods and services, like film and music, but now in the physical world of products, from fashion to furniture. After all, if you can just get a design and source the materials, you can start producing anything in your home. That's the on-demand future.

Shortly after this, we will have things looking after us. Robots will appear, to manage healthcare in particular. After all, if we can print body parts, we can replace the parts that no longer function quickly and easily. Scientists are already solving many of the most insoluble challenges, thanks to crowdsourcing ideas through gamification. A great example is the story of Foldit.

Foldit is a revolutionary crowdsourcing computer game enabling anyone to contribute to important scientific research. The game analyses how proteins are generated and how they work, with the aim of finding solutions to diseases such as HIV/AIDS, various cancers, Alzheimer's and more. The gaming system first came to light in 2011 when the players solved an AIDS puzzle in weeks that had baffled scientists for more than a decade. People playing Foldit solved how an enzyme structure that causes an AIDS-like disease in monkeys worked in just three weeks. There are other games that are trying to solve global challenges and health issues, from finding new planets (*Planet Hunters*) to solving genetic diseases through DNA analysis (*Phylo*) to figuring out how the brain works (*Eyewire*).

The development of life sciences, further fuelled by crowdsourcing solutions, will lead to greater and greater longevity for all. Already scientists are predicting that the average child born in 2015 will live to be 150 years old; that will only be made possible by leap-frogging our health challenges, combined with assisting our healthcare.

This is where we expect to see robots appearing in the home at first: dispensing medicines at the right time through the day, every day, along with serving meals and managing the home. We already have some examples of robots in the home—vacuum cleaners—but robots generally assisting around the home of less able and aging citizens will make sense, as do robo-parts. Doctors will be able to replace arms and legs with robotic replacement parts that work well.

Bionic arms, legs and eyes are now a realistic vision, as is replacing lungs, kidneys and other internal organs. Breakthroughs in managing cancers, strokes, heart attacks and other life-threatening illnesses are also being solved at a pace.

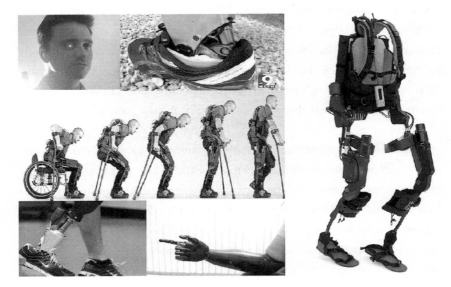

However, during the final phase of ValueWeb 3.0, the third generation Internet of Things, on-demand and robots, will not function without the underlying real-time and free value exchange mechanisms. How can my homecare robot order my drugs, medicines and food if they are unable to pay? How can my refrigerator, car and home entertainment system manage my life for me if they cannot order goods and services on my behalf?

All of these developments of M2M commerce can only be created and delivered if you have a real-time, almost free ValueWeb underpinning it all. That is why this is so fundamental.

THE INTERNET OF LIFE

No one yet knows what comes after Web 3.0, as it's too far out. You're talking 15 years or more, but there are some clues. Perhaps the best clue is from Ray Kurzweil, the renowned American author, computer scientist, inventor and futurist. Kurzweil has made some startling predictions, many of which are coming true.

In 1990, he predicted that a computer would defeat a world chess champion by 1998. In 1997, IBM's Deep Blue defeated Garry Kasparov. In 1999, he predicted that people would be able talk to their computers, and to give then commands just by using their voice by 2009. In 2011, Apple launched the iPhone with Siri and was soon followed by Google launching Google Now. These systems have been developing since 2009. In 2005, Kurzweil predicted that real-time language translation would be available to all, where words spoken in a foreign language would be translated into text in our native language. Kurzweil expected this to be available by the 2010s. Microsoft Skype Translate and Google Translate have achieved this.

People take Kurzweil's predictions seriously. Bill Gates calls him "the best person I know at predicting the future of artificial intelligence"; he's received 19 honorary doctorates; has been hired as Google's Head of Engineering; and is widely recognised as a genius.

For example, if you take his last prediction—real-time translation—there are banks in Japan implementing branch concierge robots, which can speak any customer's language as they walk into the branch. Mitsubishi UFJ Financial

Group, Japan's biggest bank, unveiled robot employees to work in their branches in April 2015. The robot is called Nao, a 58 centimetre (1' 11") tall humanoid equipped with a camera on the forehead and programmed to speak 19 languages. He  analyses customers' emotions from their facial expressions and tone of voice, which allows the robot to greet customers and ask which services they need.

Ray Kurzweil has been pretty much spot-on so far. So here are a few of his future predictions:

By the 2020s, most diseases will have disappeared as nanobots become smarter than current medical technologies. Self-driving cars will begin to take over the roads, and people won't be allowed to drive on highways. By the 2030s, virtual reality will feel a hundred percent real. Just like the Holodeck in *Star Trek*, we will enter alternative worlds that are created where we can touch, feel and smell the reality. By the 2040s, non-biological intelligence will be a billion times more capable than biological intelligence (i.e., you and I) and we will multiply our intelligence a billion-fold by linking wirelessly from our neocortex to a synthetic neocortex in the cloud.

It sounds wild, but then so many futuristic things do, and reminds me of the three laws created by science fiction writer Arthur C. Clarke:

1. When a distinguished but elderly scientist states that something is possible, he is almost certainly right. When he states that something is impossible, he is very probably wrong.
2. The only way of discovering the limits of the possible is to venture a little way past them into the impossible.
3. Any sufficiently advanced technology is indistinguishable from magic.

The third law is most true. Over a century, we have moved from flying across the English Channel (Louis Bleriot, 1909) to reaching the outermost points of space (*New Horizons* interplanetary space probe was launched in

January 2006 and targeted to reach Pluto, succeeding in 2015). The next few years as we move towards Web 4.0 will be equally amazing, and I call Web 4.0 the Internet of Life. It is when we become one with technology, living in harmony. This will come true by around 2030, and that is based upon one of Ray Kurzweil's predictions: that computers will be better than humans at performing most tasks by 2029.

In less than two decades, you won't just use your computers, you will have relationships with them through artificial intelligence (AI). AI will enable computers to read at human levels by 2029, and to even have human characteristics. According to Ray Kurzweil, speaking at the Exponential Finance conference in New York in June 2014:

"My timeline is computers will be at human levels, such as you can have a human relationship with them, 15 years from now. When I say about human levels, I'm talking about emotional intelligence. The ability to tell a joke, to be funny, to be romantic, to be loving, to be sexy, that is the cutting edge of human intelligence, that is not a sideshow."

In other words, within 15 years, we will be unable to tell the difference between a robot and a human, or between a computer and a friend. It is already happening in the social network, but we are moving towards realising the visions of films like *Ex Machina* and *Her*. In the film *Her*, Joachim Phoenix falls in love with his operating system, but "it's not an operating system. It's a consciousness." In *Ex Machina* the robots become human, and indistinguishable from humans in normal society.

This is the reality in just 15 years: we will no longer talk about computers, the internet, digital, mobile or suchlike, as it's now just part of life. You won't think about Googling something, you will just think the question and the answer will materialise in your head. You won't consciously separate life and technology, as the technology will have now become a part of you. That's why I call this the Internet of Life.

What does this have to do with banking, trade, finance and money? Well, by 2030, money will be invisible, stitched into the fabric of the third generation internet's ValueWeb. We will no longer think about value transfer to pay for things. Things just get paid through credits and debits logged by machines on our personal ledgers.

Concluding remarks

I started writing this book with the title *ValueWeb*, but I wasn't sure about the strap line. I began with *How the internet is changing the things we value in trade, finance, life and relationships*. Then I realised it was more about *How the mobile internet is changing the things we value in trade, finance, life and relationships*. Then I realised it was not catching the essence of what is really happening, which is why it became *How FinTech, bitcoin, blockchain and the mobile internet are changing everything we value*. In the end, I saw that this is far more about how FinTech is replacing traditional finance, which is why it is now *How FinTech firms are using bitcoin blockchain and mobile technologies to create the Internet of Value*.

The detail here is quite important, as the learning is around the key developments that are changing our world. It is not just the internet, or mobile, or bitcoin, or blockchain, or FinTech developments that are building the ValueWeb and changing our world—it is all of them combined. That is the key. It is the combination of all these developments that is shifting our thinking, relationships, structures and exchanges, and making us think differently about value and value stores. For example, as mentioned earlier in this book, where will we store our memories? If the typical child born today is going to live to 150 years old, what future technologies will be capable of retrieving them?

This is where I think banks will evolve from financial institutions to digital value stores. They will morph into a place we can trust to keep our data. It may not be the existing banks that serve that space, it may be new firms, such as those growing in the FinTech space right now. Either way, some companies will be the store of value for the future, and my excitement is for how we store and exchange value when the system is our partner.

In conclusion, the future is bright if you're heading there with optimism; it is dark if you are frightened by change. For me, I cannot wait to meet you there. Thanks for reading *ValueWeb*, and I look forward to your feedback.

CASE STUDIES
THE BITCOIN DEBATE

WENCES CASARES, Serial Entrepreneur

Serial entrepreneur Wences Casares created Argentina's first internet provider and later sold his online brokerage firm to Banco Santander for $750 million in 2000, when he was only 25 years old. Now 40, Casares is a star of the Silicon Valley bitcoin scene, but his Argentinian roots inform much about him.

Could you give us your view on bitcoin and its place in the market today?

I think bitcoin may very well be the best form of money we've ever seen in the history of civilization. That's a super-bold statement, I understand. We were all taught that early civilizations first bartered and later invented money, because bartering was too hard. Well, that's not true.

The way we did commerce before there was money was that everybody in our tribe would know that you killed a big buffalo and I would come and say, "Hey, can I have a little bit of your buffalo?" And you would say, "Sure, here's a bit of buffalo." And that was the end of the transaction. I had to remember I owed you. You had to remember everybody you gave buffalo to.

You had to carry a ledger in your brain for each counterparty. It was unreliable. But it worked for 25,000 years. And then, someone intelligent came up with an idea, a new technology. This person came to you and said, "Can I have a bit of buffalo?" And you said, "Sure, here's your buffalo meat." And this person said, "You know what? Here are some beets." You replied, "I don't want or need beets." He said, "No, no. It's not about that. We're going to use beets as the objective ledger in our tribe."

Instead of having to remember, you just let the beet keep track, right? It was brilliant. It was such a good technology that it took off. In some tribes it was beets; in others, salt. In other places, different things.

That worked from 25,000 years ago to 5,000 years ago. It just spread like fire—really successful technology. And then, 5,000 years ago, when tribes began to trade with each other, they needed to use the same ledger.

Gold emerged as the universal ledger. Anthropologists say that they can predict what's going to emerge as money in any tribe because it always has six characteristics. Most of all, it has to be scarce. If it's not scarce, you cannot trust it. People will create a fake. It also has to be divisible, transportable, durable, recognizable and fungible.

Those are the six things that characterize money. So gold emerged as the universal ledger and it was the best form of money we've seen for 5,000 years. Nothing has kept value the way gold has. Not the British pound, not the US dollar, not land, nothing. Not even close. Simply because of its scarcity. And some people believe—wrongly—that gold has some form of intrinsic value. And the truth is, the only value is that it's scarce and it makes a good ledger. Bitcoin, like gold, doesn't have intrinsic value. But in all but one of those six qualities, it is much, much better than gold.

In terms of scarcity, gold is scarce, but we still mine areas. Let's say you buy 0.01 percent of the gold that there is today. Next year, it will be a smaller percentage, because we've mined some more. Right? We have never seen something so perfect.

Same thing if you have some cash. With bitcoin, you buy something today, and it will be the exact same percentage of the 21 million coins that there can ever be. It's perfect. We have never seen something so perfect from that point of view. In terms of the divisibility, each bitcoin is made up of 100 million Satoshis. It's incredibly easy to divide. And in terms of the transportability, it's also something we've never seen before. Whereas with gold, it's a stupid transaction; you're dealing with coins and exact change. And we have to trust a third party. In the past, we'd go to the

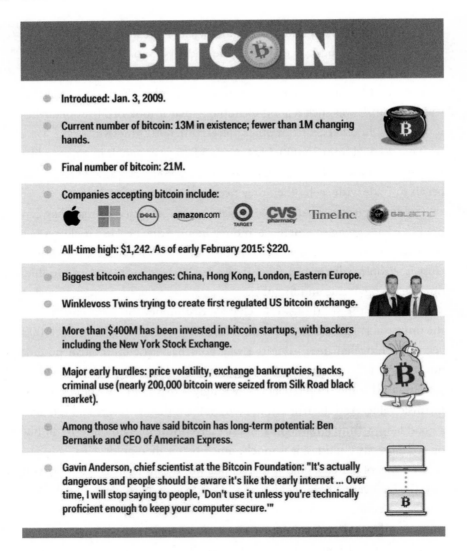

BITCOIN

- Introduced: Jan. 3, 2009.

- Current number of bitcoin: 13M in existence; fewer than 1M changing hands.

- Final number of bitcoin: 21M.

- Companies accepting bitcoin include:
  (Apple) (Microsoft) (Dell) amazon.com (Target) CVS pharmacy Time Inc. Galactic

- All-time high: $1,242. As of early February 2015: $220.

- Biggest bitcoin exchanges: China, Hong Kong, London, Eastern Europe.

- Winklevoss Twins trying to create first regulated US bitcoin exchange.

- More than $400M has been invested in bitcoin startups, with backers including the New York Stock Exchange.

- Major early hurdles: price volatility, exchange bankruptcies, hacks, criminal use (nearly 200,000 bitcoin were seized from Silk Road black market).

- Among those who have said bitcoin has long-term potential: Ben Bernanke and CEO of American Express.

- Gavin Anderson, chief scientist at the Bitcoin Foundation: "It's actually dangerous and people should be aware it's like the early internet ... Over time, I will stop saying to people, 'Don't use it unless you're technically proficient enough to keep your computer secure.'"

Medicis or the Rothschilds, and they would write letters of credit and you would trust that that the gold was there.

Since then, every time we do a payment when we're not physically together, we have to trust a third party—whether it's a bank, Visa, MasterCard, PayPal, there's always a third party, I have to trust them.

Bitcoin. It's remarkable in that it allows me to send money to you anywhere in the world, in real time, free, without any third party. So in terms of the transferability, it's revolutionary. But it's better than gold in every way except in terms of fungibility. If someone offers you two identical gold coins, you truly shouldn't care which one they give you. It's exactly the same. Truly fungible. In the case of bitcoin, each bitcoin contains its entire history within, right?

So if someone offers you a choice of bitcoins, you should choose the one that has never been attached to Silk Road or that has some dubious history. It could be that it is eventually worth less. But in every other aspect, bitcoin is superior.

So, you know, we live in a world in which there are five billion people who have a phone but do not have a bank account or a credit card. So these banks that do so well have managed to bank barely one billion people. There are five billion people who get abused for not having a bank account or a credit card. They cannot participate in the global economy. This is the first time that we see a true, realistic hope that this could change.

That's why I think bitcoin is important: it's relevant, and I think it will take time, just like the internet took time. But it may have more impact than the internet. If you go to Africa or Latin America, parts of Asia, and you ask the average person, "Look, what would you prefer: free access to information [which they're getting now with their phones], or a secure place to store the fruits of your labour and to receive and make payment?"

If they didn't have either, which was true until recently, they would choose the second because it is more relevant to them. So for five billion people, I think that bitcoin will be more relevant than the internet.

That's amazing. How long until that happens?
A long time. I am maybe the most bullish person you can find on bitcoin. I think it will be much more powerful than people think, but it will also take more time.

Decades?
Yes. If it takes one decade, it will be incredibly fast. More likely, I think it will be two decades.

What are the big applications that need to be invented between now and then?

I think the applications will emerge organically once you have consensus around the legitimacy of bitcoin. I don't think bitcoin will or should ever replace money. I think the pound should be the pound, the euro the euro, the dollar the dollar, and so on.

But I do think we need a global type of currency, like a metacurrency. If Argentina is buying oil from Iran today, for example, there's no point in their using the dollar, right? I think it will make a lot of sense for all individuals to have some bitcoin.

Right.

So more than the applications, I think what has to happen is for people to take bitcoin for granted the way they take the internet for granted.

Let me tell you a story. When I was a teenager, my mom was worried that I was spending too much time on the internet. And back then, you know, there was no browser—it was just a UNIX screen. So I remember trying to show her how this thing, the internet, would change the world. I showed her the CPU board, I explained the whole stack, the protocol, why it was free. You know, it was a total failure. She limited my computer hours anyway. And the funny thing is, if today I ask her, "What do you think of the internet?" She says, "Oh, my god. It's great! It changed my life!"

She just takes it for granted. It works. The same thing with credit cards. It's quite complicated how they work. Most people trust them, but don't have a clue how they work. To get to this point with bitcoin will take much more time than it took with the internet, because the internet was not challenging any existing assumptions. Whereas, bitcoin challenges a lot of assumptions we have about money. Once you change that, all the rest will follow.

Basically the analogy is you need the World Wide Web to be developed on top of the internet.

It's exactly like that. And look, if bitcoin continues to grow at the same rate as it has for the last five years, we can expect to finish 2015 with 50 million users. That's a five-fold increase in one year. And we'll probably have more bitcoin users and owners than PayPal accounts sometime next year. Then you can start doing something different, right?

Does the massive spike and plummet that bitcoin experienced over the last year limit the potential?

That's basically because of the volatility. The volatility is a constant reminder: Don't use money you cannot afford to lose. That's why I hope the whole ride from here to where I see bitcoin going is as volatile as possible, to keep it honest and to keep it safe.

Is bitcoin a better universal language?

Look, we live in the 21st century, and the fact that it's easier for me to call Jakarta, see someone on the screen, and talk to them for free—given all that has to happen to make that true, and yet I can't send them 1 cent? That's incredible.

What will be the first common application of bitcoin?

You know, I think it's dangerous to think that you are genius enough to do so. But if I had to brainstorm, I would say I see two very different uses: one for the developed world, and one for the developing world. In the developed world, to me, there is a clear need for internet money. The internet is super powerful, but it doesn't have its own form of money. So whenever you're going to transact on the internet, you have to use dollars, euros, pounds, and it's messy. It interrupts you for at least 35 seconds. It costs a lot of money. It's just a mess. Right?

What if you could really move money the way you would move an icon? Put it there. Put it here. Send it. Especially micro transactions. Imagine how it could work for some of the columns you're writing. Readers like me could see a summary. But if I want to read more, I have to pay a few cents. And some of your stories get enough thousands of readers to make that meaningful, right?

Or, when YouTube is telling me that I have to wait 5 seconds to skip that ad, let me just pay a few cents. And that would be a lot more relevant to the producer of that content. Right?

Let's just dig into this. So I have an iPhone that has Apple Pay rigged into it. How is it better than me just hitting Apple Pay, just hitting this button? And it clears through my credit card.

Because this is a closed ecosystem. In a closed ecosystem, it only processes when they have enough to make the transaction fees justified. They will still take a few days to receive it, and you still pay 3.5 percent to Visa. It creates that sense that it's paying immediately, but it takes three days to clear. It costs a fortune.

It's not as efficient as it could be.

It's not as efficient, and it's a fiction. But it's not really that things are happening in real time. It's like saying, "Why do I need the internet?" I can go to CompuServe, or Delphi, or AOL, and I have all of that here, but it's a closed system. The beauty of the internet is that anybody can do anything.

I imagine a totally different case for the developing world, where I think it's more interesting. You know what's the maximum number of fixed telephone lines ever sold? It's a little over a billion now.

And you know how many cell phones there are today? A little over six billion. And you know what made us go from one billion fixed lines to six billion cell phones? The real leap has nothing to do with form factor or technology. The real leap was financial. Every time you issued a fixed telephone line it was like writing a blank check. I install your phone. Use it, and I'll charge you at the end of the month. So I've got to trust your credit. So the billion people who have credit—good credit—got it. And no one else.

And with the cell phone, we got to a billion cell phones, postpaid. The other 5 billion are prepaid. It is a financial fact that people come with cash and pay you in advance and then they go use it. That's what creates the extra 5 billion. They can't participate in conferences like these. They're not part of this economy. But, man, they have a phone just like yours. They have money. They have cash. But they just cannot be part of the global economy, because cash doesn't travel here.

Yes.

There are a number of problems with today's currency system. It's expensive. It's unsafe. It carries huge transaction costs. And I think that bitcoin can be the way in which these people can participate. They love their phones and can use them to do things that you and I take for granted.

It's cash that's digital.

It's digital cash for them. You and I don't need it. They do.

(This article was originally published by *Business Insider,* February 2015. Reproduced in full with permissions.)

BROCK PIERCE, Chairman, The Bitcoin Foundation

Brock Pierce is an American entrepreneur and former child actor. As a child actor, he was in Disney films The Mighty Ducks *(1992),* D2: The Mighty Ducks *(1994) and* First Kid *(1996). Brock has been involved in the establishment of digital currencies for some time, having founded Internet Gaming Entertainment (IGE) in 2001 and Zam in 2003. In May 2014, he was elected as a director of the Bitcoin Foundation and, in April 2015, its chairman.*

About The Bitcoin Foundation

The Bitcoin Foundation is an American non-profit corporation. It was founded in September 2012 with the stated mission to "standardise, protect and promote the use of Bitcoin cryptographic money for the benefit of users worldwide". The organisation was modelled on the Linux Foundation and is funded mainly through grants made by for-profit companies that depend on the Bitcoin technology.

How did you get involved with the Bitcoin Foundation?

I was elected by the industry members. The Bitcoin Foundation board of directors is elected from the community. We have an entirely elected board and there's two different constituents that make up the Foundation today. We have individual members that pay an annual fee or a lifetime fee to be a member of the Foundation, and then we also have industry members that are companies that pay an annual fee. The board of directors is half elected by industry members and half elected by individual members—I was elected last spring by the industry members, so essentially the CEOs of bitcoin companies voted me onto the board. Then, more recently, I was elected by the board of directors as chairman, which is in reality just a glorified title for a board member with some additional responsibilities, but I'm not running the Foundation day-to-day.

The current executive director, which would be the equivalent of the CEO of the Foundation, is a wonderful guy by the name of Bruce Fenton, so he's got the day-to-day responsibilities of running the Foundation. I just have slightly more responsibilities than the other board members.

What's the current state of the Bitcoin Foundation? Where is it going?
When the Foundation was first started, it was performing many functions on behalf of the industry, so best not thought of as a Foundation, as it was more like a trade association. The original sort of things that it was attempting to do were advocacy and education; communicating what is bitcoin; why it is important; what is it used for; how is it helpful; those type of things—and educating people and making them aware of what bitcoin is able to do for them. Then there's also Bitcoin Core for the Open Source Software Project and Gavin Andersen was the lead developer for a long time. He's now stepped out of the role of lead developer, but the Foundation was financing the salaries of a few key people to support the development of the Open Source Protocol. Then the last piece was policy, which is paying attention to how governments are looking to regulate this, and trying to influence those regulations in a way that will proceed positively.

As the industry has matured, additional groups of people have come together to step in and try to fill some of those roles. The one role that we stepped out of is policy, which I'm very happy with, because the bitcoin community has got a very broad array of people and uses. When you're supporting policy there's no possible way to make everyone happy, and so you've got some very different organisations. But if some of those organisations merge to support those activities, such as Coin Center, which is run by Jerry Brito, and the Digital Chamber of Commerce, which is run by Perianne Boring, then you have progress.

They're doing most of the policy work in the capital here in the US, and that's something that we're no longer active in, because other organisations have stepped up and volunteered to do that work.

In terms of core development, we continue to support that. One of the things that we discovered throughout this process—after having talked to all of the large parties that could support us with substantial funding—is that we need to get really big cheques that will allow the industry to have the capital it needs to support the underlying development of the protocol. We would like to see that residing within an academic institution. After we did a long tour of talking to everyone that would be a large cheque writer, they liked the governance structure and fortunately Gavin and the team were able to join MIT's media lab—which is a perfect solution that should open up additional capital to support those efforts, but we continue to support core development. Gavin continues to be the chief scientist of the Bitcoin Foundation. It's an area where the industry needs all the help it can get and I hope other academic institutions get onboard. I hope that other companies operating in this space support a developer on the payroll like Bitpaidit with Jeff Garzik. You want as many people working on this as possible, preferably people that are capable and dedicated, they're not doing it in a moonlighting fashion. Hopefully, the resources to support core development continue to increase and more and more industry participants contribute in that way. And the main function, at this point, is continuing to do advocacy and education work.

A lot of people I've talked to in banking now say, "bitcoin bad, blockchain good". What is the current state of the cryptocurrency marketplace and bitcoin itself? Is it healthy?

I think it's continuing to be healthy. If you look at the capital that's coming into the industry over the last 12 to 18 months, you're seeing roughly a billion dollars in capital that's been invested. That shows that the underlying infrastructure that's being developed by the companies is working, because you've got the Open Source Protocol, and then you've got all the companies that are building up the infrastructure to make it easy to use. Think of it as the bridges, the roads, the tunnels in the TCP/IP analog. To being with, it was all about building the browsers and e-mail clients, and the sort of things that you needed to make the internet usable by ordinary people. That's what that capital is doing for bitcoin, but it takes time for that capital to be deployed and turned into products and services that make this safe and easy for a broader array of consumers.

Meanwhile, the bitcoin price is down, which is quite negative. The largest contributor to that was Mt. Gox; unfortunately, it did create a lot of negative, fallacious headlines, which the media likes. I don't think in the long run it will have a negative impact but, in the short run, I think this is going to set the industry back by a couple of years.

Let's turn to the positive view of financial inclusion. What's happening there?
That's the main benefit of this technology, and the main point I try to make, is that there are five billion people on the planet that don't have access to basic quality financial services. This technology is going to democratize the global financial system in a way that every human being on the planet has equal access to fast, secure and cheap financial services.

When I'm talking to people in the developed world and they say, "I don't understand. Why would I need this bitcoin thing?" I explain to them, "Well, you've probably never left the United States where you have a bank account, you have a credit card, you've got rule of law that's guaranteed to protect you, you've got faith in the system."

This isn't a product that you need and, to see mass adoption of a technology like this, it needs to be improving the lives of the people that use it. That is why we're seeing major growth in markets like Latin America—in Venezuela and Argentina in particular—or places like Africa, where they have very little infrastructure. These emerging economies are leapfrogging telecommunications infrastructures and skipping straight to wireless. For these reasons, I think the developing world could actually surpass the developed world in a matter of years, in terms of financial infrastructure. They won't have to spend hundreds of billions of dollars implementing it either, whether using something like bitcoin or blockchain technology.

The Philippines is looking at putting mobile payments on the blockchain, which would create broad financial inclusion of everyone in that country. You've got roughly 100 million people there and only five million credit and debit cards. So just 3–4 percent of the population have financial services like we have. This is why bitcoin has the ability to have a substantial impact on a country.

If you look at the GDP of the Philippines, something like 28 percent comes from remittances. If more of that remittance money ends up in the hands of the people, that could have a very positive impact on the Philippines as a country. This is why I think people are definitely waking up to the idea of fast, cheap, secure settlements.

How do you see blockchain technologies developing, and is it going to be the Bitcoin blockchain or something else eventually playing out as the central payments' infrastructure of the world?
I believe the answer to that is "Yes". I don't know if it will be Bitcoin's blockchain or something else. I run a small venture fund called Blockchain Capital. We've just closed 36 investments and we look a lot like an index fund because, from my perspective, we are investing in the equivalent of the internet in 1994. I don't know who the winners are going to be, but if I bet on all the best companies I'll end up with eBay and Amazon and Google and PayPal in my portfolio. I don't know how to pick the winners yet. I also don't know how the industry is going to develop, but I do have a strong view that, yes, we're going to end up with this type of infrastructure becoming the underlying backbone of the financial system for the world.

Talking about Blockchain Capital, I'm interested to know how you personally got involved in bitcoin and all this change of technology? It's not really in your space, as you came from TV and film, so how did this excite you?
Yes, so I started out in the entertainment industry. I was an actor from the ages of 3 to 16 and then I was dabbling, because I was really an entrepreneur that happened to be an actor. I was building every lemonade

stand imaginable—every business imaginable—as a kid. In the world I'd grown up in, I was on set and spending most of my time with adults, because there weren't often other kids on set, so most of my friends were directors or screenwriters or other actors. The people that I was working with for months at a time meant I wanted to be an entrepreneur. From that perspective, I wanted to go be the executive producer. I wanted to pull projects together and create films.

When the internet boom of the 1990s started, I was watching people starting these businesses and I'm like, "I'm entrepreneurial, I'm tech savvy, I'm an actor, I can do this", and so I started my first company when I was 17. This was a company in the digital media space, which was a nice combination of skills. I did that throughout the 1990s.

In 1999, I identified another developing and interesting insight and this was the beginning of what you call "persistent worlds" or "online games", such as World of Warcraft or Second Life. I recognized that these games needed digital assets, and that the digital currency that existed inside of these worlds had value. There were people that wanted to buy and sell them. This is before any game company in the world was selling these digital goods or currencies as a business.

I recognized there was a market for it, however, and so I started a business in 2001 called IGE, which became the primary market maker for the digital assets that existed in these persistent worlds. At the time, I had more demands for products than I had products. I couldn't find enough sellers, so I went and encouraged the Chinese to play games professionally and to mine digital currency. Between 2001 and 2006, I ended up building a supply chain of 400,000 people that were playing video games professionally and that mined digital currency. I would then go on and sell products—so I've been in the digital currency business almost as long as anyone.

This is how bitcoin ended up on my radar, because almost anyone throughout the 2000s that wanted to experiment with digital currency would often come to me. I've done many, many billions of dollars of business in that space. I still do over a billion dollars a year today, and so someone pings me this bitcoin was coming out and said, "Hey, what do you think of this?"

I started playing around with bitcoin in 2009 as it emerged, not because I believed in it but because people would ask me, and it was my job to know what I'm talking about. So I spent a little time kicking tires of bitcoin, and one of the things I've learned throughout the 1990s is a market timing lesson. This was because the first business I built was an internet television play before there was broadband, and I learned a lesson the hard way with that. For this reason, I said, "OK, bitcoin looks very interesting, or something like it in the future", and I waited for the market to develop enough to the point where I believed there was critical mass and momentum.

When that happened I said, "OK the future's now. I'd better drop what I'm doing and go spend all of my time working in this space", and that started in 2011.

I then got concerned about regulation and, by 2012, made a decision to get into the business. I started a number of companies in this space in 2013, acting like an incubator. An incubator doesn't scale however, and so the better approach to get broad coverage was to start a fund, and that's how I ended up running this fund.

Looking to the future, how do you see this ecosystem playing out?
Well, you're seeing a lot of different digital currencies. On the bitcoin side, over the next 12 to 24 months, I see most of the growth in the sector occurring where the users of the products don't even realize they're using bitcoin. Companies like ABRA, which is a bill payments company. Their approach to building a new method for paying and sending remittances, where the users don't even realize that it's bitcoin that's powering those transactions, is the future I see. Bitcoin as a value proposition is very fast, low cost, cross border method of sending remittances, whether for businesses or individuals. That's where I see most of the growth over the next 12 to 24 months. It's in companies providing consumers and businesses with value transfers, where they don't even realize they're using bitcoin. It's just a mechanism by which the business is able to move money across borders faster and cheaper, and that's where I see most of the growth occurring.

Then you've got other consensus mechanisms and protocols like Ripple, which has most of the growth in their business from banks as a tool for interbank settlement. Ripple allows banks to work in real-time, rather than running at T+3. Three days financial settlement is moving to something that's near instant, and that's a big push. Either way, I think everybody agrees that the idea that financial transactions in this day and age should be settled a lot faster than three days. Ripple is starting to see a lot of traction around banks, integrating that as a tool to accelerate settlement.

There are a bunch of different trends but then, just as you start to see a particular model working, things change. Some things work and some things don't work so well. For example, think about bitcoin's exchanges. Mt. Gox was the biggest exchange two years ago; Bitstamp was the biggest exchange last year; and Bitfinex is the biggest exchange this year. Even when you see a category where value is clearly being created, it's hard to pick the winners, because the industry is still very new.

There are a few companies that have emerged to become what I would call category winners. This would be Coinbase as a consumer wallet, which is an easy way to buy bitcoin in the USA. That is why I'm happy to be an investor in that company. This is because it's clear that if this industry does succeed, then they are clearly going to be one of the largest players in the ecosystem.

I like other interesting trends as well. For example, I don't know if you're familiar with ChangeTip, but they're focused on micro transactions, which, because most of the developing world cannot use the current payment systems, is going to be a key. Most of the developing world cannot use credit cards. If you have a credit card in Africa and you go online to purchase something, the merchant and the payment infrastructure and fraud detecting services have to trust you. The problem is that they more or less systematically deny anyone from Africa from being able to buy anything with a credit card. It's a trustless payment system. In this context, I think it is very compelling for allowing those excluded to be included. Bitcoin, or something like it, will allow the other 70 percent of the planet to participate in the internet economy, which is a great thing for anyone doing business online.

The total addressable market of customers expands in a pretty substantial way for buying small products and services online. Currently, with credit cards, you can't really process a transaction for less than 70 or 80 cents. That's assuming that you've got zero cost of goods sold. This is why I like ChangeTip, allowing people to buy contents for a penny, a nickel, a dime, and offering people low transactions' fees. These companies will enable the entire planet to participate in the internet economy, and ChangeTip are well along the path to becoming a category winner in that space. But, again, it's still early.

As mentioned, everyone's saying "bitcoin bad, blockchain good" these days. What they really mean is that Satoshi Nakamoto came up with a great technology, but they don't like the currency. Is that actually feasible?

It probably is. What Satoshi Nakomoto achieved is that he aggregated a number of technology innovations to create a protocol that's creating the Internet of Value or the Internet of Trust. If you think about the internet we use today, it is the Internet of Information. It's made possible because of the communications' protocol TCP/IP. The problem is that you cannot transact value over TCP/IP without a trusted counterparty or intermediary. What Satoshi solved was the issue of a double-spend. If I sent you an email with a picture attached to it, how do you know when you receive it that I didn't keep a copy for myself or sent it to four other people at the same time? TCP/IP is a protocol designed for that. What Satoshi Nakamoto has achieved is that he's created a protocol that permits the transmission of value, in any form. That is a revolutionary event. Now, does bitcoin's blockchain end up being the successful platform for all of that activity? I don't know, but do I think that it's interesting and dependable? I think bitcoin, as a non-sovereign, math-based currency, is very interesting. It's interesting from so many views. For example, from the developing world, in places like Russia and Ukraine today, or if you look at Zimbabwe and the crazy inflation they've had. It just gives people options in these places, where it is a better store of value than some of the other things that are available to them.

This is why I find bitcoin to be very fascinating and I think it's got incredible potential. I continue to be bullish on bitcoin's future, but the blockchain is obviously the larger innovation. I don't know what shape or form that's ultimately going to take. *Bitcoin is huge, but the blockchain is clearly going to change the world.*

That leads to my final question. If you're betting on the future, where do you see the sweet spot?
Ultimately you're trying to end up with investments that have market caps along the lines of Uber or Facebook. The financial system is clearly a large enough ocean that there should be the ability to create businesses with that kind of value, and so that's what we're looking at. Where are the huge markets that can be re-architected or disrupted utilizing this new technology?

Things like insurance, money remittance, interbank settlement systems, payment processing. You really just need to take a look at the world today because we're not creating new industries. We're disrupting industries with new technology to do things better, faster, cheaper.

JON MATONIS, Crypto-economist

Jon Matonis is an e-money crypto researcher and economist focused on expanding the circulation of non-political, digital currencies. His career includes senior influential posts at Sumitomo Bank, Visa, VeriSign, and Hushmail. He was an Executive Director of the Bitcoin Foundation until the end of 2014, and is a Contributing Editor of the digital currency news website CoinDesk.

Tell me about yourself and your background, Jon.

I was involved with the Bitcoin Foundation since its inception, starting in 2012, as one of the founding board directors. At the end of last year I decided to retire from the Foundation board and give other people the opportunity to step forward and work on the board.

It was never meant to be a lifetime gig for any person. Prior to that, I was working in the payment space at Visa and VeriSign, working on the public key cryptography for online banking; and prior to that I was an FX and derivatives trader for commercial banks. I have been blending all these skills into this brand new amazing field of financial cryptography.

What's the future of the Bitcoin Foundation?

In terms of the Bitcoin Foundation going forward, it still is an excellent institution. People should be encouraged to join it, as it does pay for some of the core developers' compensation. It doesn't pay for all the compensation, as no one entity controls bitcoin development. It is an open source project so it's not a centralised power struggle, but does provide some compensation. The main focus of the Foundation today, which is slightly different from when it was first founded, is to develop a standards body for Bitcoin Core, along the same type of protocol standards as the IETF (Internet Engineering Task Force). It is premature to just automatically throw that over the fence with the IETF standards process, as it would be lost. It has to mature, has to have more participation, more advocates to allow it to thrive in an IEFT structure. That is what the Foundation is preparing the protocol for, so that eventually it will go into a larger, more rigorous standards body process.

You mentioned you've been a trader and involved with the payments industry, so why did you get interested in bitcoin?

I had always been studying and focusing a lot of my research work on digital currencies and alternative monies. Even prior to bitcoin, going back to Digitcash and E-Gold days. In late 2009, I got introduced to bitcoin by a random email from Satoshi Nakamoto. I didn't give it much thought at the time, and then 3–4 months later I started to focus upon it. It seemed to solve a lot of problems encountered by the first-generation digital currencies, primarily around the centralisation issue for preventing double spends. That's the real breakthrough, and it is what got me excited both as a trader and as a digital currency monetary theorist. Bitcoin came up with a way to solve the double-spend problem, without having to go back to a centralised mint for reissuance or confirmation that the units weren't double spent. The cryptographic principles for bitcoin have been around prior to the launch of bitcoin. There was nothing uniquely new about any of the individual components, but it was unique in how it was assembled as a peer-to-peer distributed environment. That was the real breakthrough.

You say it's decentralised, which often raises the question: is this money without government?

Well, the decentralised and peer-to-peer computing capabilities are the wave of the future. So that is definitely going to last. I see that growing, in fact, rather than going in the other direction.

Regarding "money without government", we actually have always had money without government, going back to the evolution of money, even gold and pre-gold barter days. Gold was the form of money without government before the kings and monarchs started stamping their image on them. So I don't see the concept of money without government as being something impossible to achieve. Instead, we are regaining something that was lost.

But regulators and government officials, when it comes to a value exchange that is unregulated, worry about drug runners and terrorists. Do you see that as a threat?

I don't see it as a threat. It's not specific to bitcoin and other cryptocurrencies. Any type of value exchange medium for small or medium transactions are subject to abuse. The trade-off is that you have to severely clamp down on the benefits of having digital money in an absolute way, to prevent something happening on the negative side in an absolute way. What I mean by that is that the so-called drug and criminal communities dwarf what's happening in bitcoin. You don't blame the monetary unit for the actions of the criminals.

I agree, although another problem of an unregulated value exchange system is that you get lots of hacking and issues like the Mt. Gox and Bitstamp failures. These things give bitcoin a bad name. Do you see a structure to give consumers more assurance that it is safe to use?

Let's talk about Mt. Gox and the episode of Bitstamp. Regulation cannot be a panacea for *caveat emptor* ("buyer beware"). Regulation cannot be a panacea for everything. It rarely works in a way that a government intends it to, anyway. Look at the United States, where Lehman Brothers and MF Global were both regulated entities and meant to be safe. They weren't. So in terms of protecting consumers, that is just what the government regulators put forward for the justification of massive regulation in the bitcoin arena. We are now seeing major areas of bitcoin taking up best practice, though. If you look at the recent Bitstamp episode, that actually resulted in adoption of new multisig technologies for bitcoin and cryptocurrency exchanges. So the solution for Bitstamp generated a more robust and stronger exchange system, which happened outside the action of any government regulation.

Alongside that you are seeing firms like BitGo, which was the multisig company, and companies like Xapo, Coinbase and more adopting their own private insurance to provide customer security and peace of mind for any funds that they choose to leave there. So the market is stepping up, through best practices and through providing these solutions. The main take away from Mt. Gox, which happened over a year ago, is that it demonstrated the exact opposite of "too big to fail" capitalism. It's always curious to me that some of the critics of Mt. Gox would prefer a world where tax payers always step in and bail everybody out. That's not the world we need to be moving towards, so that Mt. Gox being allowed to fail on its own accord should be taken as a positive sign that the system is working.

It's interesting that traditional value stores have started to pick up on bitcoin since it failed. A lot of institutions that have licenses and government regulation are starting to try to incorporate cryptocurrency and blockchain technology in what they do. That feels like a movement towards the institutionalisation of cryptocurrencies. Do you think that will happen, or would that be the opposite of the wishes of the community that created this capability?

Well, the wishes of the community don't really matter here, and the institutionalisation of bitcoin will be jurisdiction by jurisdiction. Going back to your other point though, the exchange environment has matured significantly over the 12 months since Mt. Gox, and that's a beneficial sign. Not only are they aware of this, but the service providers are a lot more robust. Some of them are taking steps on their own in anticipation of future regulation, but to present a more mature offering. Users of these services have also worked out that it's not right to use firms like Mt. Gox as a bank vault, which they should have never been using as such in the first place. So bitcoin gives you a way to control your own assets and not be required to leave everything on balance. It's down to your own guidelines and comes back to what I said, *caveat emptor*, whether its regulated or unregulated.

On the institutionalisation of bitcoin, you will start to see that happen. I don't think this is a negative and, as mentioned, it will be jurisdiction by jurisdiction. Trading liquidity, increasing volume and depth of the market will lead to institutionalisation. It is unavoidable that we will get to a phase where we see bitcoin derivatives-type instruments, which we are already starting to see evolve in certain markets. It will be just like any other commodity that goes through stages and develops. We are just seeing this on a faster trajectory with bitcoin, which seems like it is moving a lot more quickly. We will get there.

I can see it happening. That's why you see innovators like Fidor Bank and Circle creating cryptocurrency consumer guarantees and assurances, similar to traditional regulated banking licenses, but in the new model world rather than the old model world. Is this a correct view?

It is a correct view. We are also starting to see it on an international level. You will have the small, local regional players, but you will start to see the ones that are large having a global footprint, which will only be beneficial, because a global footprint for a cryptocurrency-type operation really sets the stage for entry into the remittance market. When you have a global player that covers multiple countries, you've pretty much displaced the functionality of someone like Western Union.

That's where things get very interesting. For example, Ripple is working with Wells Fargo and other banks to have their technology capabilities incorporated, but using cryptocurrencies other than bitcoin. Will we see a different cryptocurrency arrive? Is bitcoin the one?

There are already over 300 cryptocurrencies in circulation. Bitcoin has the majority share, at almost 99 percent. Bitcoin is the dominant player. Ripple is making a lot of progress with financial institutions, as they are making this area their main focus of attention. I don't see systems like Ripple as being truly decentralised, however. They have distributed deployment, but the currency unit itself is entirely pre-mined by the founders of the currency. That means it is not decentralised, as there are people who work out where to deploy that initial currency unit. The Ripple currency XRP is what they use as a glue to hold everything together; the test as to whether something is truly decentralised is: who will be the financial winner with Ripple's success? Ripple has lots of venture capitalists participating in it, and investors in XRP. Those people will be the winners. Because of that Ripple doesn't take them away from a single point of failure. Their implementation with lots of financial institutions, and what they are trying to do with various asset webs and connections, is very appealing to banks, as it makes it subject to oversight and regulation. At some point, when you traverse everything in that world however, there is still a single point of failure. Regulators like to have that single point, because then they can regulate it. Bitcoin doesn't give them any type of single point to focus on. That's why it is democratized value.

So if Ripple is not the solution, how will banks manage cryptocurrencies into their operations?
This is actually a very interesting area. I am starting to focus on it a lot more in my work as, in some ways, it's the flip side of Ripple and alternative cryptocurrencies that want to do their own, independent blockchains. What we are starting to see evolve are banks beginning to leverage the existing Bitcoin blockchains, rather than trying to recreate something that will be a second or third tier chain. The reason this is interesting is that it's already there to be exploited. The fact is that banks just have to figure out a way to connect to the Bitcoin network, which gives them the same type of liquidity and ability to do the large amount transactions they currently have on SWIFT.

An interesting company that illustrates this development well came out of the SWIFT innotribe challenge last year. This is a company called epiphyte, based in London, and with offices in New York. They created an interface for commercial banks on both sides to be able to leverage and utilise the Bitcoin network, in lieu of using Fedwire or CHAPS or SWIFT, who are liquidity providers. The banks never end up touching the cryptocurrency. This solves the challenges of correspondent banking for large global banks, which have to tie up a lot of capital in counterparty cover. Equally, there are other parts of the world where banks do not want to leave a lot of money with their correspondent banks, due to the counterparty risk. If they can leverage something like the Bitcoin blockchain, then this will have a significant impact on the future of correspondent banking worldwide.

That's one of the reasons I believe bitcoin as a cryptocurrency has more relevancy at the wholesale level, replacing both Hawala and correspondent banking structures at the same time.

So, if I summarise what we have covered so far, you believe we will have a jurisdiction-based system that regulates usage at a national level but, because it's incorporated by banks into wholesale bank structures, it massively reduces costs. Is that how this plays out?

Yes. It's important to look at jurisdictions, as jurisdictions do have the ability to regulate the in-and-out functionality of their own currencies into cryptocurrencies. When you talk about a country having bitcoin regulation, what they are really regulating is their own currencies exchanged into and out of the cryptocurrency. That's what you're seeing at bitcoin exchanges and banks, and will be one primary level of regulation.

Beyond that, you will have a whole parallel world, which will exist person-to-person. In some ways that world is more interesting than person-to-business uses of cryptocurrencies, as in a person-to-person environment, similar to using Skype or using encrypted email, you find new ways of doing things. In this case, you have an independent financial messaging system, which has allowed us to create a large, global value exchange network. That secondary level of exchanges, person-to-person or otherwise, with a cryptocurrency like bitcoin, is outside the control of regulators. That's not even an area where the regulators have a remit; but it is what they will have to focus upon when cryptocurrencies are converted into and out of their own national currency.

So what will be the protection mechanism in the person-to-person exchange? Will free agents manage the system?

Well, ultimately this will rely on the Bitcoin blockchain, which is secured by the power of the overall mining participants. This represents the largest distributed and secure computing project in the world. In aggregate it exceeds the top 500 or 600 super computers combined.

And here, I want to make a point about the price of bitcoin, as this comes up a lot. I don't think watching the price is that important. It's more important to look at the number of projects and developers working on building user-friendly solutions. It is more important to focus upon the installed base of bitcoin wallets.

The bitcoin price should reflect a price level that is sufficient to protect the aggregate value of transactions that are arriving over the blockchain. If you extrapolate that forward and say that a lot more economic activity is occurring on the Bitcoin blockchain, then the security reaches a level that is consummate with the value riding across that decentralised value transfer network. As a result of this, that will tend to slowly increase the natural price of bitcoin. That's the only way to guarantee that the transactions riding across the network will be secure. Then people will be willing to pay for that additional security in increased transaction fees.

It's a feedback loop, as you won't have those transactions occurring if the miners aren't rewarded through a higher bitcoin price. You won't have the higher bitcoin price if the transactions aren't occurring in the first place. So it's very much a feedback loop in a two-way structure. That's why I don't put a lot of effort or thinking into the alternative cryptocurrencies, as they tend to be a distraction for building the strongest leading network that we need for migrating economic activity and commerce.

Final question. If you were a betting man and you were betting on what will happen in the future, where would you put your money… or don't you use money anymore?

I do still have to use money in some cases and also credit cards but, if I look at it from a bitcoin investment point of view, I would bet on investing in the actual currency and using that as a proxy for the sector, rather than choosing individual companies. I think it's unique and rare that we have an opportunity in the investment world to choose a currency as a way to invest into an entire sector. It is a proxy for the sector. If there was a way to invest into healthcare through a healthcare currency, you have that now for investing in bitcoin as a cryptocurrency for the digital value exchange sector.

In terms of your portfolio, I look at this in the same way as gold. If people are comfortable in having 10–15 percent of their overall net worth in something like gold and precious metals, then equally they should be comfortable in having 10–15 percent in bitcoin. It's investing in assets and commodities on a portfolio percentage basis. I think this whole transition that you describe as the ValueWeb will be complete when we start calling gold an analogue version of bitcoin.

JEFFREY ROBINSON, Author of *BitCon: The Naked Truth About Bitcoin*

Jeffrey Robinson is a native New Yorker and a bestselling author of 30 books. He is a recognised expert on organised crime, fraud and money laundering, and has been labelled by the British Bankers' Association as "the world's most important financial crime journalist". After my recent coverage of bitcoin, the blockchain and cryptocurrencies, he got in touch to provide an alternative view of this world. As his most recent book was a year-long investigation into the other side of bitcoin—BitCon: The Naked Truth About Bitcoin—the conversation proved fascinating.

What is your background with bitcoin and how did you discover some bitcoin activities were rather suspicious?

A few years ago, someone told me that bitcoins were good for money laundering. And after books like *The Laundrymen*, *The Merger*, *The Sink* and *The Takedown*, serious books about dirty money, I was interested. So, I looked into it and eventually came to the conclusion, as I say in *BitCon: The Naked Truth About Bitcoin*, that it is, in fact, not good for money laundering. The system moves it but doesn't inherently disguise the origins of illegal funds or help them reappear as legally obtained funds. However, bitcoin is great for capital flight, terror finance, tax evasion, extortion and criminal finance. But, for money laundering, it basically sucks.

Still, I wanted to know more, so I went to one of these bitcoin meetings—one of these big convention-type things that they hold all the time. I was awestruck at the general level of naïve stupidity. These were pre-pubescent kids. It felt like a bad high school reunion. Everyone was keenly intent on convincing me that the dollar is dead; that bitcoin was about to take over the world; that all the central bankers should be thrown in jail.

I said to myself: "If this is what the Bitcoin movement is all about, it has no chance whatsoever." But, over lunch at that meeting, I spoke with one of the few grown-ups in the room about the technology. It dawned on me that maybe there is something here when it comes to the transferring of assets.

The way I see it, and the way he saw it, too, with greater development of asset transfer, there will be greater emphasis on valuing those assets in dollars and pounds and euros. That means the pretend currency will become increasingly useless and eventually disappear.

By the way, I call it a "pretend currency" because it doesn't satisfy any of the three main criteria for modern currency. Furthermore, it is traded like a pretend commodity on what I have come to believe is a pump-and-dump market; where very few people control the market and the gullible lose money. Only the few people who control the market make money.

The more I got into this the more evident it seemed to me that, if you could separate out the lunatics, the delusionals, the pump-and-dump schemes, the pretend currency and all of that, and get to the core blockchain, you might actually have something interesting. It was with that in mind that I went and spent a year running around Planet Bitcoin, talking to a lot of people and asking the kinds of questions that I didn't see anybody else asking.

I find it intriguing that, in your book *BitCon*, you quite clearly lay out the idea that the currency has no future. And yet, when you talk to the fundamentalists in the Bitcoin community, they believe you can't have a blockchain without bitcoin. The two are integrally linked. Do you agree with that view?

No, not at all. This is the old argument of "the Catholic Church is the only church, and everything else is heresy". It simply isn't true. Preston Byrne in Eris is working on a blockchain that has nothing at all to do with bitcoin.

Ripple has nothing to do with bitcoin. People don't want to know about bitcoin because it is surrounded by so much hype, spin, misinformation and outright fantasy, and it's too clumsy. On the other hand, if you have a bank or a group of banks that could operate a centralised or closed blockchain just among themselves, for the transfer of assets back and forth, that could work. This bank or group of banks could, say, send money from the US to London and back and forth, and if it was just these banks working on these settlements, you wouldn't need bitcoin. You wouldn't need the miners, as you don't need any mining. It's a closed ledger that the banks control, and the banks are essentially inventing their own blockchain.

Of course, that's seen as heresy by the bitcoin faithful. But look at the concept of decentralisation. It's a political ideology. "I don't want the government involved." That makes it non-commercial. How about if the banks don't want to turn over their money for the ten minutes that it takes the miners to verify each transaction, which means they temporarily lose control of the money. A couple of months ago, transactions were taking an hour-and-a-half or almost two hours. No bank is going to give up control of $100 million for two hours, especially when you consider that much of it will be verified by miners in China. It's not going to happen. The decentralisation political ideology does not conform to what the banks want. They want a commercial solution. What they're looking for is a centralised, or closed, blockchain.

Now, the faithful will say, "You can't have a centralised blockchain, it's just a database." Well, decentralised blockchains are just a database. There are efficiencies and inefficiencies in that database, so you take the great efficiency of the decentralised blockchain, you centralise it, close it, and you can say bye-bye bitcoin, because no one needs it.

I can see both sides of the argument in some ways and right now we are seeing a lot of the banks on Wall Street starting to play. For example, UBS recently announced that they're incorporating laboratories to develop blockchain technologies to reduce cost.
That's right, but they don't say they're getting into bitcoin, the pretend currency.

No?

You see this is part of a hype and spin and why we need to separate the pretend currency from the blockchain. Every time someone speaks of the technological advancements, the bitcoin faithful immediately equate it to a success for the pretend currency. But it's not. As a matter of fact, there are no bitcoin pretend-currency successes. I can't find even one of them. You talk about the VCs in Silicon Valley and London and Canada, especially the big ones who have invested upwards of a half a billion dollars. The investment is not in bitcoin the pretend currency; it's in the concept of blockchain technology.

I think Marc Andreessen gave the game away when I contacted him when writing *BitCon*. He said, "My only interest is in finding practical solutions to real problems." When you think about that, he's developing businesses that will ride off the back of the blockchain. What he needs to do is sell it to somebody. So, if it's a financial thing, he's going to have to sell it to a bank or a finance house. If that bank or finance house says, "We have no interest in this pretend currency, we want it in dollars and pounds", he'll abandon bitcoin in a heartbeat. He has no loyalty to the pretend currency, none whatsoever. No one does. Except speculators and the guys trying to flog it to greater fools. In fact, Andreessen told me how he hardly has any of it. He doesn't own much of it.

Yes. If you look at Marc Andreessen in particular, you can see his VC fund Andreessen Horowitz investing heavily in the technology developments, such as Ripple, rather than the currency.

That's right. That is their only interest. You've got $500 million approximately invested in this technology. None of them have seen real returns yet. How sustainable is that if it goes on for another two or three years? It's not. These guys are only interested in seeing two, three, five or ten times their return on money and, if they're not making it, they're going to pull out and put their money into someplace else. That's how venture capitalists stay alive.

I really blame the media for a lot of this. I don't blame the bitcoin media, because there is no bitcoin media. They are simply regurgitating PR releases. CoinDesk is not journalism. I'm sorry, but it isn't. However, the mainstream media—CNN, BBC, the Wall Street Journal, the New York Times, Forbes and the like—aren't asking the right questions. They are blinded and enamoured by the idea of bitcoin. They keep rehashing this "bitcoin is the currency of the future" crap and never look beyond it to say, "hold on a minute, this stuff can't stand close scrutiny".

For example, Dish Network, Dell, Expedia and others supposedly "accept" bitcoin, at least according to the press reports. The truth is that they don't accept it. They simply allow you to pay in bitcoin. And those payments go through Coinbase or BitPay. This is because Dish, Dell, Expedia and the others don't want anything to do with bitcoin. Allowing a customer to pay with bitcoins is not an endorsement of bitcoin, it's a marketing ploy.

Microsoft is not endorsing bitcoin. Bill Gates said recently something about how cryptocurrency may be the future of finance. So, immediately the media screams, "Bill Gates endorses bitcoin!" No, he doesn't. Apparently Bill Gates doesn't even have any bitcoins. That's the kind of hype and spin and misinformation that really drives me nuts. It's a failure of journalism. As an old school journalist, I find that extremely worrying.

In your book you've dug through a lot of the headlines, where claims are being made about bitcoin that actually aren't true.
They're categorically untrue. I'll give you a really good example. Take my pal Patrick Byrne, the CEO and chairman of Overstock. About a year ago, he was saying he had no interest in cryptocurrencies or in bitcoin. Well, somebody convinced him that there were pockets of bitcoin all over the place that couldn't be spent anywhere. So he said, let's go after those pockets of bitcoin and sell them garden furniture. This was a marketing ploy. He announced, "Overstock will accept bitcoins." The press loved it. But Overstock wasn't "accepting" bitcoins, because every sale had to go through Coinbase. What's more, Patrick was smart enough to have negotiated with Coinbase that he wouldn't have to pay a commission on the currency conversion. So "accepting" bitcoin didn't cost him anything. The very first day he racked up $133,000 worth of bitcoin-driven sales. It looked like he was supporting the bitcoin community, so the bitcoin community supported him. Within three months, however, his bitcoin-driven sales were down to $7,000 a day. Why? Because the people who had pockets of bitcoin and no place to spend them, had spent them. And

they didn't buy back in. They saw no reason to buy any more bitcoins simply to use them to purchase pillowcases and garden furniture priced in dollars at Overstock. That's significant. Think about it. How is there any logical reason for anybody to take dollars to buy bitcoins to pay for things priced in dollars? It adds no value and, in fact, creates extra expense. So, his sales dropped down to $7,000 a day. He then announced that he would accept bitcoin worldwide and his sales went up to $8,000 a day. But they have since fallen again. He has even said publicly, there is no international interest in bitcoin. None.

Shortly after admitting worldwide disinterest, he filed a report with the SEC which received no media attention whatsoever. He'd decided to hold on to 10 percent of all his bitcoin sales. It means that Coinbase now converts 90 percent and sends him the remaining 10 percent. So he's holding onto $700 a day worth of bitcoin business, which he says he is giving to his staff as bonuses. (By the way, the staff apparently insisted they put a bitcoin ATM in the lobby of the building in Utah so they could cash out right away.) Now, with $7,000 a day of bitcoin-driven sales, he's saving his three percent Visa and Mastercard fees. That's $210. Okay, $210 a day times 365 adds up. Except, he told the SEC that, in order to integrate the 10 percent he holds, he must integrate $700 a day into his bookkeeping for tax purposes. That's not so easy, because bitcoin is considered property by the tax people, which means there are both capital gains and capital loss calculations on each bitcoin. So far, he told the SEC, for the privilege of keeping a few bitcoins on his books, it has cost him $400,000. Next, Patrick said in that SEC filing, he would probably have to spend another $400,000 to make his bookkeeping fully compatible. So, he's spending $800,000 to save $210 a day. It will take him almost ten years to get his money back. Explain to me how this is a good idea, how this is sustainable, how this makes any sense at all.

The Bitcoin community claim they have created money without government, if they live within the Bitcoin system. What's your reaction to this claim?
But you cannot live within the Bitcoin system. It's impossible. Sure, you can buy bitcoins with your dollars and fool some people into thinking you're living on bitcoins. But you're not. To manage it, you need a circular

flow of income, and with bitcoins, there is none. Every time you purchase something with bitcoins, as soon as the sellers of the goods and services turn it over to Coinbase or BitPay to convert it back to dollars or pounds, each purchase becomes a sale of bitcoins. That way, no one's holding this stuff.

Equally, when you look at the real statistics, you find that a lot of the numbers the Bitcion faithful claim as usage, are outright phony. The faithful say there are 110,000 transactions a day, but only about a thousand of those transactions are for the buying and selling of goods and services. The rest are miners moving bitcoins between different wallets and addresses, and gambling. On top of that, there is what's called "the change factor", which means each transaction gets counted twice. Next, the faithful say, there are eight million wallets. What they don't tell you is that almost all of them are either empty or near empty. In truth, Coinometrics at Cambridge says that fewer than 250,000 wallets hold one bitcoin or more. That's not 250,000 people, that's wallets, and most people have multiple wallets. Based on that, I am correct when I say, there are more people who are members of the Kuwait Airways frequent flier club than there are people on the planet holding bitcoins.

The faithful also say there are 80,000–100,000 businesses around the world that "accept" bitcoin. But they don't "accept" it. Most of them never see any bitcoins and the few that do, mostly, don't hold any. I called some of these businesses and asked, "Since you put a bitcoin button on your site, what's happened?" They said, "It's a pain in the ass. We'd much rather have somebody just give us cash, because what we have to do as soon as we get the bitcoins is sell them. We don't want them."

Of the very few businesses I found that actually keep bitcoins, the one I liked the best is a guy who sells rodeo tickets in Texas. He said to me, "I put the bitcoin button on my site hoping that I'd get one or two, which I would save so that when I hit a million dollars of coins, I could retire. But I also play the lottery and that never comes in." I asked, "How many purchases have you actually had with bitcoins?" He said, "None."

The facts are the facts. No one is using this stuff. To that I add this undeniable fact: as a global economic phenomenon, bitcoin is a non-event. The pretend currency is not working. Where people are saying bitcoin has a future, ask them to point to a bitcoin success. Nobody is saying, "Look at this, here is a huge success," because there aren't any. Instead, they point to the future. They say: "Just wait and see how bitcoin will end poverty by becoming a bank for the great unbanked."

Huh? You and I both live in countries where there are unbanked people, but they're unbanked for various reasons. In some cases it's cultural. There are ethnic communities that don't want banks and that operate only in cash. There are also people who cannot afford banking and have to use payday lenders and cheque cashiers, or things like that. But I cannot find a single case where bitcoin has actually saved any of those people, and this is in the developed world. Not one. In the United States, where there are 70 or 80 million unbanked, there is now a move by Bank of America and Walmart to go after these people and to get them credit, to bring them into the banking system. How do you expect three delusional teenagers on bicycles, wearing t-shirts that say, *In thin air we trust*, to compete with Bank of America and Walmart? It's not going to happen.

Also, in the States and in Britain and throughout the developed world, WiFi and smartphones are cheap and readily available. But the unbanked are still unbanked. Now look at the developing world where WiFi is expensive, where smartphones are not plentiful and where people have traditional, cultural, religious and political distrust of all sorts of things coming from the West. How are you going to sell these people on an invisible currency they can't possibly use? They're simply not going to buy into this.

On the other hand, a bank in Kenya and Vodafone, whom they know, are saying to them: "Look at M-PESA. You can put that on your phone and move money." They have sales and marketing forces. They understand the traditional, culture, religious and political mindset. Those three guys on their bicycle with the t-shirts are never ever going to compete with that.

I still haven't worked out your view on the idea that there's a good technology here, which is going to be useful for banks such as Ripple, which has centralised capabilities.
Or Eris. It's the blockchain that is useful, and the blockchain needn't have anything to do with bitcoin.

Versus the Bitcoin guys, who keep coming back at me and saying, "But it's out there, it's in the wild. We've got it, we don't care about you."

Except no one's using it. Preston Byrne in Eris had a great quote the other day that I re-tweeted, because I think it's the best quote ever about bitcoin: "A paradigm shift is not a paradigm shift if no one is using it." That sums it up. The faithful always talk about bitcoin being disruptive. What they ignore, at their peril, is the fact that the disrupted will always be heard from.

So you see this as a pretend currency, but it actually has a real technology, and your outlook for the future would be: this is a really useful thing?

No. Bitcoin is a pretend currency traded like a pretend commodity and pushed and pumped by snake-oil salesmen who have a self-interest in finding greater fools to buy it from them. Look at the Winklevoss twins and their Bitcoin ETF. These guys are grasping at straws to find greater fools to buy their bitcoins from them. And they're not alone. The problem with the Bitcoin technology is that it is surrounded by the need to recruit the gullible in order to keep the game alive.

What about the way in which bitcoin is used as a community currency, for crowdfunding for example?

Like the Elmer Gantrys of the old south, some of these evangelists are preaching: "Look at crowdsourcing and crowdfunding, and this will save you all." Andreas Antonopoulos testified before the Canadian Senate last fall, telling the committee on banking how wonderful Bitcoin was. I testified in January and spent most of my time debunking everything he said, explaining to the senators: "This guy is pulling the wool over your eyes." One of his misleading contentions was how bitcoin crowdsourcing was changing things for small businesses. The idea that you could have people from around the world collectively giving you two bitcoins so that you could do whatever business you needed to do with two borrowed bitcoins. Again, the media just accepts this stuff, and they accepted his explanation. So I spoke to people who are borrowing crowd-sourced bitcoins, and spoke to people who are lending this stuff, and asked, "How does it work?" One guy in South America said to me, "It works great. I borrowed 1.1 bitcoin and I only paid two percent interest." I said, "Gee, that isn't bad. What was the term of the loan?" He said, "Fifteen days." I said, "Hold on a minute. You paid two percent interest for 15 days? Tony Soprano charges two percent for 15 days. That's 48 percent a year. If you put it on your credit card, you can get it for 19 percent a year. You're paying extortionate usury." I then looked closely at the leading bitcoin crowdsourcing site, and they're listing loans at 204 percent interest, and 305 percent interest—and I even found one at 2,037 percent interest.

Short and simple, this is loan sharking. And there are laws against this. It is even possibly criminal for sites to aide and abet these loans. And it is definitely bad for business. What's more, if you're sitting in Britain and you crowdsource a guy in South America and he doesn't pay you back, how do you collect on your loan? But, Antonopoulos sat in front of those Canadian senators and, with a straight face, told them: "It's a wonderful thing." It took me to say: "Look at the numbers, they don't lie. He's full of crap." That's what gets me about this. All of the spin and the misinformation and the hype, and the mainstream media is not doing its job debunking this. They should be looking more closely, because bitcoin cannot stand close scrutiny. Because, frankly, when it comes to bitcoin, what you see is never what you get.

In *BitCon*, you write about Mt. Gox and the guy who ran it, Mark Kerpeles, being such a geek that he wasn't actually sustainable in his own world, let alone running billions of dollars of other people's money.

Karpeles was a train wreck waiting to happen. And he was in Japan, which meant if you wanted to get your money back, you had to go there. Now, here's Coinbase in the United States, run by a bunch of Americans. If something goes wrong, they're easier to get. But how will you know until it happens, because they don't publish their books? They've just gotten a $75 million fill-up. Why? Because, I would suggest, they were in trouble and needed more money. There is a processor in Slovenia, run by two geeks. Are you telling me that you're going to trust your money to anyone in Slovenia? This is crazy. There are no consumer protections. There's absolutely no guarantees in any of this. And people say it's wonderful. But it isn't wonderful. It's a minefield that's fraught with problems, and it will come unglued because it simply cannot continue.

It's not helped by the criminality that surrounds bitcoin. Not just Mt. Gox, but Ross Ulbricht—aka Dread Pirate Roberts—and his Silk Road conviction. Or Charlie Shrem, one of the original bitcoin stars, now doing time in federal prison for illegal activities with bitcoin. Or the fact that the champion of bitcoin, the Bitcoin Foundation, was near-bankrupt through alleged mismanagement and sheer stupidity.

As soon as the guys at Eris or Etherium or Ripple or any of the many other labs working on bitcoin-less blockchains get it right—by which I mean that they create a blockchain that deals in dollars and pounds and other currencies—that's the end of bitcoin. It's dead. That is when all the bitcoin processors in the United States or Slovenia will find themselves in an economic death-spiral because there won't be enough action to sustain them. I'm not even convinced there's enough action to sustain them for much longer, now. As soon as one of the VCs announces: "I just figured out a way we don't need bitcoin", it's over. We've seen it before. Fads always disappear. Pet Rocks. Goo-Goo Dolls. The guy who invented pogs died the other day. His legacy is pogs. Satoshi's legacy will be the concept of the blockchain.

But what about the whole idea that it will become a centralised technology? In fact, I don't know if you saw it, but the Fed and IBM announced the other day that they're working together on creating a dollar-based cryptocurrency that will be authorised, regulated and centralised. Is that the way it's going to go?

That's right. That's the future. Centralised. Closed. As soon as they work out payment systems in dollars, sterling and euros, bitcoin goes down in history like 8-track, semi-automatic transmissions and Pet.Com. The idea that everyone is going to use this pretend currency because it's an alternative way of beating the central banks is ludicrous. The faithful say: "Why would you believe in a central banker when you can believe in mathematics?" The answer is because mathematics alone and the algorithm alone, can't run an economy. You need the central banker to run the economy. But, they say, central bankers inflate everything so that the value of your money is miniscule. They argue, if you'd put $100 under your mattress in 1913, today it would be worth $3. So what? I don't know anybody who's got 1913 dollars under their mattress. And anybody who puts money under a mattress is a fool, because money invested can keep up, and often, beats inflation.

Inflation is built into the system specifically to avoid deflation. If you have a closed commodity economy, like bitcoin or like gold, the deflation you end up with is ten times worse than inflation. The bitcoin faithful want all the benefits of the gold standard without any of the problems attached to the gold standard. Look around. There isn't a single country left on Earth that's on the gold standard. And for good reason. The bitcoin faithful simply don't understand the world economy. They don't understand money. All they understand is their own self-interest. As one kid said to me: "When bitcoins hit $1 million dollars a coin, I'm going to be a multi-millionaire. I'm going to get rich." Yeah, good luck.

You seem rather anti-bitcoin.

I'm passionate about this stuff because it's easy to see through it, and because nobody is asking the right questions. I see people come on CNBC and Fox Business, talking about the joys of bitcoin, and none of the journalists are doing their jobs by saying, "You're full of crap". They're buying into this stuff and, when it all goes wrong, they will be the first to say, "We knew. We told you so." There was a guy on CNBC that I openly challenged, who has a bitcoin credit card. He said: "You put bitcoins on your credit card and you can pay for anything with bitcoins. You go to Selfridges, John Lewis, a petrol station, and you pay in bitcoin. Isn't that terrific?" No. It's a con. It requires you to buy bitcoins with pounds or euros or dollars first, which is not only completely illogical but a really stupid thing to do. Why bother? Where's the benefit? Just pay in pounds, euros or dollars. Why put bitcoins in the middle? Why add the cost when you're getting no added value? Same thing with the bitcoin ATMs which, by the way, are mostly going broke. Bitcoin ATMs are proving to be non-profitable because (a) nobody's using them, (b) the rent is too high, and (c) the charges are too high. They set their own exchange rate and they add a fee on top of it. There's no reason to use them. The whole concept of bitcoin the pretend currency is illogical. Yes, you can fool some of the people some of the time, but you can't fool all of the people all the time. Bitcoin the pretend currency will die on that.

So it's like "The Emperor's New Clothes"? Eventually you see there's nothing there?

That's right. It's become a cult. It's become a religion. And I'm the heretic because I stand up and say, "This is crazy." So they come after me. There are whole Reddit forums talking about the fact that I don't understand anything. Vehemence, vengeance and juvenile temper tantrums show you the kinds of people who are involved in this, and you quickly understand that they can't possibly sustain this because they truly are delusional. The rational ones are the VCs who are putting real money onto the blockchain to find practical business solutions to real problems. And none of those practical business solutions will involve bitcoin the currency. None of them. Because bitcoin is a solution to a problem that doesn't exist.

And if I'm talking to you in about ten years' time, do you think we'll be looking back and saying, "Look at all these bitcoin fraudsters who have now disappeared, but didn't they give us a great technology?"

But they're not giving us a great technology. They're pumping bitcoin, the pretend currency, which has nothing to do with the technology. Again, they're self-interested. One of these clowns went on the record as saying, "Bitcoin has gone so viral, it is viral cubed." The man needs to keep taking his meds because he's just not in touch with reality. More recently, he's claimed that bitcoin's future is assured because the average life of a fiat currency is 27 years. In the next breath he recalled that Sterling has been around since the 17th century. Only people who want to believe the earth is flat buy into such absurdities. But then, without those flat-earthers, the pretend currency would become worthless. The point is that the blockchain will revolutionise things, but it won't be the bitcoin blockchain. And it won't take ten years. Five years from now, you and I will talk about bitcoin the way we talk about Edsel.

DAVE BIRCH, Digital Money and Identity Guru

Dave Birch is a Director of Consult Hyperion, the technical and strategic consultancy that specialises in electronic transactions. He provides consultancy support to clients around the world, including all of the leading payment brands, major telecommunications providers, government bodies and international organisations, including the Bill & Melinda Gates Foundation. Described at the Oxford Internet Institute as "one of Britain's most acute observers of the internet and social networks", in The Telegraph *as "one of the world's leading experts on digital money", in* The Independent *as a "grade-A geek" and by the Centre for the Study of Financial Innovation as "one of the most user-friendly of the UK's uber-techies", Dave is well-known for his thoughtful leadership blogging, podcasts and events for Consult Hyperion's* Tomorrow's Transactions *series.*

As a man clued up on everything to do with digital money, digital currencies and digital identity, what are the main things that you see happening at the moment?

Well, I would say tokenization, and HCE (Host Card Emulation) is really big for us at the moment. So, there's a lot of effort going into the kind of revitalisation of mobile. And a lot of people who are saying that this is the year that mobile payments finally break through are probably right, if that's anything to go by. So that's very hot.

We have a lot of identity work, which we've been talking about for a long time, but it's interesting to see how the banks are beginning to take identity seriously and start to form their identity strategies.

Coming up out of left field, you've got the whole blockchain thing which, and I know I'll get criticized for this, is quite different from Bitcoin.

For us, we also have a lot of work in transit at the moment. Transit is a very strong area for us because we had the good fortune to be chosen to be consultants by Transport for London a few years ago, to help them migrate to open loop. So, you can use your bank cards on the tube now, you don't need an Oyster Card anymore. And, actually, that's led us into a lot of work. There's a lot of transit authorities around the world that really want to revamp their ticketing and payment systems. These are the main areas of focus we're dealing with at the moment.

Let's delve deeper into some of these ideas. Tokenization and HCE, for example. Can you just explain a bit more about these?
Well, tokenization is the core of the proposition from people like Apple Pay. So, the idea is that instead of storing credit card numbers in your phone, you store an alias to the credit card number. You store a token. And if somebody steals that token, it's of no use to them. They don't know what card that token belongs to. There's a few things going on there because the banks, and various other people of course, have to make quite big investments in this to make it work.

So, one of the interesting things at the moment is in thinking: "If we're going to make a big investment to support Apple Pay, Google, Samsung, whatever, with the tokenization platforms, what else can we use them for? And how can we build them to be most cost-effective in the long term?" And that's actually interesting work because it's very new, and nobody knows how all of this is going to pan out. There's also this whole issue of using tokens for non-payment applications as well.

Tokens such as what, in terms of non-payment?
Well, for example, suppose you have a gambling site and I want to prove to you that I live in the UK and I'm over 18. My bank could give me a

token that I can't use for payments, but I can use for that. I just pass that token on to you, and my personal details are kept safe, secure and private by the bank. I just give you a token that says: "Here are things you need to know about me." I don't want to drop down too many levels of technical boring detail, but because there is a migration to APIs (Application Program Interfaces) underlying all of this, that's an important area as there is pressure on the banks to get their API frameworks together. This pressure is because there are timescales around this. For example, in the UK, it's the Treasury Framework. You've also got the European Framework. You've got the work that's going on in the EPC (European Payments Council) and all that kind of stuff. There's a lot of pressure to get these API frameworks in place and identity management, identity services, are potentially quite a big part of those API platforms.

In some ways it all come together with identity because, as you just mentioned, I could use a token to prove my age. Equally, couldn't you use the blockchain to register devices as part of your identity?
It will be very interesting to look at this kind of swirling intersection of the blockchain, the Internet of Things, and identity. There's something going on in that space, which could be absolutely huge and, if banks play their cards right, they could potentially have an anchoring role in securing this identity layer for all of these things. That's definitely an area to focus on. Of course, it's very early days. People are inventing new kinds of blockchains all the time, and thinking up new ways of using them in new applications. It's very febrile at the moment.

So, if you were looking at how all of that is coming together, what do think would come out of this?
Well, I think there's a plausible hypothesis. For example, do you remember a couple of years ago, SWIFT had that idea for the Digital Asset Grid and it never really got too much traction. The core idea of it wasn't that bad. In fact, it was quite good. The idea was that the bank would lock up your identity and keep your data safe and secure, and protect you in this outside world. I think there's something to that idea, I really do.

Now, if you think about the massive expansion in the identities that are going to need to be managed, from your car to your toothbrush and everything in-between, what is going to underpin the identity that is safe and trusted? Because banks have to comply with KYC (Know Your Client), AML (Anti-Money Laundering), CTF (Counter-Terrorism Funding), they already know who you are. They've already checked your documents. I think, with a decent strategy and, just as importantly, decent APIs, banks can stand to play a pretty interesting part in that, and it's certainly a way of keeping banks as part of the transactional infrastructure around that.

So, in your opening you mentioned tokenization, HCE, blockchain and identity. They're all really intermingled and the question is, what part will banks play in the new digital asset grid?
Yes, I think that's a good way of thinking about it. I see it when you're challenging people saying, "Well, what is a digital bank?" I wonder if there's a formulation, that states, "Well, a digital bank is a bank which is formed around managing your identity rather than managing your money," if you see what I mean. In the old economy, you only have one identity, as you only needed somewhere safe to put your money. We all understood what banks did in that world.

But in the digital world, you can store money anywhere. The bank has no privileged position. You might have some of your money in a mutual fund, some of it in Zopa, some of it in Funding Circle, maybe a small amount in the bank. But in that digital world, your identity becomes the crucial asset, and this is why it makes more sense for the bank to focus on protecting that. I think you can see an emerging narrative around those things.

Yes. As you look at the re-architecting of the traditional banking structure, what role do you think SWIFT, VISA, MasterCard and the like will play?
That's a tough one. You go to conferences and people stand up and say, "The blockchain is going to eradicate SWIFT and bank tokenization is going to eradicate VISA." That hinges on the people who run SWIFT and

VISA being idiots who cannot see these new technological developments. I can tell you that's not true, because the people at places like VISA, AmEx, MasterCard and Discover are very smart people, and they can read the paper just as well as I can, so they can see this stuff coming.

Now, it's reasonable to say "Well, yes, but it's really hard to disrupt yourself. When you're the incumbent, it's very hard to do that." But yes, people are developing all sorts of new strategies that they can accelerate through partnerships and subsidiaries and just buying people. So I would say it's a bit simplistic to say that these new technologies are going to bypass the incumbents, because that assumes the incumbents don't do anything, and I can't see that happening.

I was arguing with some bitcoin guy the other day. He said, "Well, you know, it's the banks, man. The banks are trying to keep bitcoin down because they don't want to be able to transfer money cheaply from place to place." I responded: "You're kidding me, right?" The bank I'm working for right now finds that about a third of its costs are payments. If you can find a way of moving money around more cheaply, banks will be one of the first and biggest users of it. They're going to use these new technologies to disrupt, as well.

So, yes, there are threats, of course, but the people you think of as the legacy incumbents, they're going to use these new technologies too, right?

Yes, I agree that they don't have their heads in the sand. Although one of the things that's quite intriguing is when you look at Ripple, for example, then that does take out a stack of what traditionally has been managed by SWIFT, because it's looking at the counterparty banking trust mechanisms. So what comes into play is that SWIFT, VISA, and MasterCard won't be the control mechanisms of everything they used to be. They'll probably be more aggregating lots of different pieces for the banking system.

Yes, although they might do a little bit more than that because they might reinvent themselves as well. You say: "Okay, conceptually, Ripple could take out a lot of the costs which are currently associated with SWIFT."

That's true but, on the other hand, SWIFT could use Ripple to take those costs out of itself and offer a cheaper service. You can then imagine that there are structural reasons why banks would prefer to deal with SWIFT rather than Ripple. So, if SWIFT could use Ripple and cut costs, then everyone's happy. VISA and MasterCard is a more interesting situation, because they have the opportunity to use the new technologies to make a radical change, as they are also under a lot of cost pressures, right?

So if it turns out that you can send money from place to place using bitcoin for one percent, and it's going to cost two percent with VISA or MasterCard, then surely VISA or MasterCard will just come up with bitcoin-based propositions. After all, I would still rather use Visa or MasterCard, because of all the rules and regulations and rights and charge-backs, and all the other stuff that goes with it, to turn the payment mechanism into an actual infrastructure for retailers and merchants.

Bitcoin does polarise people, as typified by the interviews with Jon Matonis and Jeffrey Robinson. Jon Matonis is saying "Bitcoin is the future and it will create a money without government, and it's already out there in the open source land." Jeffrey is saying "That's ridiculous because you need this regulated and under the control of central banks." Where do you sit?

Yes. I guess I'm slightly negative on the "bitcoin as money" thing. The people that are really pro-bitcoin like the fact that it's not under government control, it's anonymous, and see those things as positives. I'm not sure. I think they're actually negatives. I don't know if you want money that's anonymous, for example. Do you really want to live in a world like that? That means the rich and privileged can act with absolute impunity, with nobody ever knowing what they're doing, doesn't it? That doesn't sound right to me. So to the bitcoin guys, it's a negative that you have central banks and governments involved, but I think it probably isn't. Of course, I want them to operate more efficiently and more effectively and do good things for all of us, but it's not transparently obvious that bypassing them is the best way to do that.

A final thought, which I don't think we've articulated clearly enough, is on the future of digital identity, because that's been a focus of yours for a long time. How do you think it's going to play out in the future?

Well, it's kind of exciting for me now, because some of those concepts that we've been kicking around for a long time are now becoming elements of business strategy, and that's really fun. But the big picture that you're alluding to is whether it is going to be banks that actually do this, or are they going to be bypassed? And people always think about Facebook and Amazon providing identifiers to sign on, and there could be other people out there who could do this as well.

But if the idea is that digital identity essentially becomes a platform that's crucial to the future of business, the future economy and future transactions, then it becomes really important who controls that, who structures it and who sets its parameters. There are very good reasons for thinking banks are in a good position to do that, but there are also plenty of good reasons for thinking Amazon or Apple could do it, or the government could do it, or telcos. Nevertheless, I think that if the banks get their act together and did it properly, they'd be in pole position.

But the banks would always bring it back to the trust factor, based on the fact they're licensed by governments, whereas telcos and technology companies are not.

Yes, and that's not a negligible factor. That's not something to be dismissed.

So, in the long-term, what you're saying is there are contenders to take over digital identities, but banks, if they play their cards right—particularly their bank license card—will win.

I think that's a reasonable way of putting it, Chris, yes. I think that there is a huge caveat about if they do it right but, let's not be negative, I think there are some real positives there.

I think you and I have seen enough over the years of people saying banks will be disintermediated to know that it hasn't really happened yet. It may, but banks are pretty good at responding to this stuff.

Yes. And it's not likely they're going to disappear tomorrow, so they have time to work on that.

Have we missed anything, Dave?

No, I think that's a really good way of finishing up to summarize the conversation. Banks are in pole position. But, to use a very clumsy metaphor, have they got the right engine, the right tires and the right driver?

GOTTFRIED LEIBBRANDT, CEO, SWIFT

Gottfried Leibbrandt became CEO of SWIFT in July 2012. He joined SWIFT in 2005 to focus on the development of the SWIFT2010 strategy. Upon completion of the strategy, he was appointed Head of Standards, and then in 2007 he was promoted to Head of Marketing. Gottfried was a key architect behind the SWIFT2015 strategy, which is now nearing its successful completion. Prior to joining SWIFT, Gottfried worked at McKinsey & Company for 18 years.

About SWIFT

SWIFT is the Society for Worldwide Interbank Financial Telecommunication, a member-owned cooperative through which the financial world conducts its business operations with speed, certainty and confidence. More than 10,800 banking organisations, securities institutions and corporate customers in over 200 countries use SWIFT every day to exchange millions of standardised financial messages.

How do you see value exchange on the internet changing the game for banks and for infrastructures like SWIFT?

Let's take a step back so that I can give you my overall perspective. I always like to make a distinction between cryptocurrencies and blockchain technology. I've been involved with cryptocurrencies since quite early on. I found the mathematics behind it fascinating and delved into the blockchain mechanics, which is a very intriguing idea. I've used bitcoin, and I have to say, as a user, it is a fantastic user experience. It really is nifty that with a push of a button you can send real value to somebody else. I urge everybody I speak about it to actually download a wallet and do it, because that helps you understand what it's about.

Now having said that, I am not sure I believe in the notion of currencies that are not backed by governments. Money is very closely related to taxation and governments. I can see bitcoin as a phenomenon for low-end transactions, exchanging low values. But I have a hard time seeing something like bitcoin replacing large-value transactions, or being used as a store of value on a big scale. The whole outstanding value of bitcoin is just a couple of billion dollars and the daily volume, if I'm not mistaken, is in the order of $50–100 million.

The volumes that are going through the global financial system are about 100,000 times that number. That's the order of magnitude of what happens today, and I'm not sure I can see that being replaced by bitcoin on a meaningful scale. That's not to say that it won't be there in its niche.

Another important thing to realise is that people claim it's frictionless, but it's not. If you have a look at the mining costs being paid out to bitcoin miners right now, it's about one percent of the total transaction volume. That's not negligible. It may become less as the transaction volume grows, but it will never be zero. Therefore I have yet to be convinced that bitcoin is completely frictionless.

Having said that, I think the whole notion of a distributed ledger of doing things peer-to-peer without something in the centre is fascinating, and that's absolutely something we are looking at. Now does that mean that I think banks will be completely bypassed? There I'm less convinced. Back in 2000, I remember everybody saying, "Well, banks will become dinosaurs and will be taken over by pure-play internet banks, telephone banks and new startups."

If you look back at what happened 15 years ago, all of the technology has been absorbed by banks. They have not stood still. They have developed mobile banking. They have developed phone banks. They have developed e-banking solutions. Actually, the only real pure-play that I can think of that has made it is PayPal, which admittedly is a good success. The banks have survived, and banks have undergone quite an impressive transformation of going from a branch-based system to an internet-based system.

That's not to say that it will happen again the same way with mobile and blockchain. I think the challenge is for banks to keep up with this. They have a few things in their favour.

One of them is infrastructure. Infrastructures benefit from network effects, and that tends to be persistent and difficult to displace. It's not that easy to build new infrastructures or replace existing ones, unless the existing infrastructures have failings. As such, it can be better to work with them, than to try and build your own. My favourite example is Apple Pay. Apple Pay did the smart thing and leveraged the credit card technology and networks that were out there. Yes, Apple will capture part of the value created, so there's some transfer of value. But the banks and their infrastructures are still playing a large role in this new set-up. So infrastructures such as SWIFT have a few things in their favour.

The other thing banks have in their favour is that they know how to deal with high value exchange—with credit and market risk, capitalization, and the frameworks, as well as the regulation that goes around it. There is much discussion that blockchain/shared ledger, and in particular smart contracts, could offer real DVP (delivery versus payment) and thus take some of this risk out of the system—but that remains to be proven. Meanwhile, in high-value transaction systems, as in large securities transactions or large foreign exchange transactions, you do need to worry about default risk and about collateral and the capital against it. Regulators certainly do worry about it.

So I'm not so sure that banks are going to be completely cut out of the loop, as long as they play it smartly. We could look at another interesting example: peer-to-peer lending. Peer-to-peer lending is a very interesting phenomenon. The default risk sits squarely with the lenders, not with the intermediary. It's different from a bank deposit, which the bank protects against defaults. The worry here is that defaults tend to go through cycles. For a while, it goes very well and you get high returns. We will have to see what happens in a downturn when defaults go up and lenders may panic.

Clearly there is an opportunity here for banks. Maybe they can use the peer-to peer technology themselves and combine it with insuring peer-to-peer lenders against all or some of these defaults. So again, I think banks will change the way they operate rather than become extinct. There's a big potential for banks to absorb the technology and put better value to their consumers.

I want to come back to your opening discussion of bitcoin. The libertarian vision is of a world of money without government and regulation. You dismiss that, but the libertarians say you cannot regulate the exchange of value on the internet, because the internet is global. Do you believe that will change?
I think that's complete baloney. People said you couldn't tax things on the internet, because the internet is global. I think governments have made pretty good progress in taxing internet commerce. You can tax it in the country of the receiver or in the country of the sender of the goods—or both. People have found ways to deal with that, so to say, "You can't regulate things on the internet", I just don't buy that. I firmly believe that where there is value exchange, it will be regulated and it will be taxed. That's a whole framework we've had in place for thousands of years, and I don't see that being turned on its head by this technology. I think everybody realizes that regulation and taxation is needed.

And the whole idea of money without governments? It's interesting to look back in history, where successful examples of money not backed or controlled by governments are very scarce. There's a very compelling case to be made that money has always been very closely linked to governments and taxation. So no, I cannot believe in the libertarian view.

Maybe one more point on the libertarian view and the argument financial markets are best left alone with light or no regulation. We went through massive deregulation in the late 1990s and early 2000s, and then witnessed the global financial crisis.

What about blockchain technology creating a friction between the old financial networks and the new ones? We have SWIFT, Visa and

MasterCard that were built by banks for the pre-internet age, and now we have Ripple, Apple Pay, Klarna and other things that are creating this new friction, because they've been built for the new age. Do you see the old structures, like SWIFT, being challenged by these new capabilities, or will you evolve with them?

Yes, certainly I see all of us being challenged. Absolutely. I think these things have the potential to fundamentally change how we do things with money and banks have to worry about how to absorb and leverage it. That applies to SWIFT as well. I think the right way to look at it is, again, how Apple Pay was conceived, which is a combination of the old and the new. I hope the same is true for SWIFT. What we do for our member banks is allow them to exchange value between themselves and, if there are newer technologies, there are two options: either we leverage that to provide even better value to our banks, or there's no need for us anymore. And if there is no need for us anymore, then we should stop what we are doing and return the money to our owners. But I firmly believe we can leverage these new technologies to provide even better value. We're looking at the blockchain technology, keeping a very close eye on it. If there is a way to improve the service we provide to the banks with that new technology, then we will use it. We are absolutely on it.

Does that mean, in five to ten years, most of SWIFT's architecture will move onto the blockchain?

I'm not there yet. I haven't got my head around it enough to see how that move will play out. I think there's also another interesting angle to this, as it's not just the technology layer. What we do is message exchange between banks. If you look at the cost of a cross-border transaction for a consumer, a very small fraction of that is SWIFT. A SWIFT message costs about $0.04. A cross-border transaction can cost anywhere in the order of $5 to $50, depending on which bank you use. So yes, we're taking a look at these technologies—but I think there's also room for the banks to look at the whole correspondent banking value chain, and see if there are ways to do that more efficiently. Is there a way to change the business layers of correspondent banking with this technology, and thereby reduce the cost and the friction to the consumer? That is something we are working with the banks to explore.

If we're looking at where you see the priorities of the banks now, how do they see technology changing things? For example, Know Your Client (KYC) processes are getting very interesting.

Yes, they are. Before you can start creating direct relationships or direct exchange between banks that do not have a commercial relationship with each other, they need to build trust; how will they do that? In cross-border banking today, the banks have longstanding relationships with each other. If you start to bypass that, as Ripple does, then you need to worry about KYC between the banks. Do I know what bank I'm dealing with and what transactions I'm getting into, etc.? I'm not saying it's unsolvable, but it is a problem that needs to be addressed.

KYC is one of the challenges, but there are others. For example, how to provide value on a mobile platform and be visible to consumers. There are some interesting challenges there. I believe that regulations like Europe's PSD2, which provides third parties with direct access to bank accounts. It allows other people to turn the bank into a utility that's invisible to the consumer. This is not new, though. We had the same discussion fifteen years ago when Tesco Bank launched and used one of the big banks as their back office. That same dynamic is going to be played out again.

How can banks continue to provide value in that new environment? I would submit that there are many ways for banks to do this. One is leveraging data. There's a whole discussion about Google now knowing a lot of data about people but, if you think about it, banks have an incredible amount of data about people, too. The question is: can they use that to the advantage of both themselves and the consumer? Can they do that in a way that the consumer accepts, from a data privacy perspective?

Everyone keeps talking about Google, Amazon and Facebook being the big threats to banks, but I don't agree. I think it's much more that banks are a threat to themselves if they don't move fast enough to take on board the challenges of data analytics and the need for change.

To be fair to banks, I think they are actually dealing with those demands for change. Most banks now do data analytics. They have that expertise or are developing it. Most of them "get it".

A big challenge is data privacy regulation. What are you allowed to do with that data? We have seen some high profile experiments by banks backfire. For example, in the Netherlands, where the banks proposed to use anonymised debit card transaction data for marketing purposes, allowing consumer goods companies to mine that data for marketing purposes. There was a big media backlash and they ended up cancelling the idea. It would be very interesting to explore the line between when data can be used in a way that consumers accept and see the value of, and when data usage constitutes such an invasion of privacy that consumers will not support it.

We have talked a lot about the consumer side of things, but there's quite a lot happening in the corporate world too, in terms of technology changing bank-to-corporate relationships. Is there anything you see there that is noteworthy?

Yes, I think a couple of things. One is that you see an increased acceptance of multibanking and of platforms that allow corporate treasurers to access multiple banks in a single way. We've been active in that field as SWIFT, with single sign-on and a single messaging standard to provide a single interface to the banks with corporate connectivity. I think you see renewed discussions about trade, where the old documentation-based world of trade is stable. Open account has been growing, and people are finding ways to combine the best of these two approaches with, for example, the BPO (bank payment obligation).

You will see continued growth of direct information exchange between corporates, with systems that enable direct information exchange and increased automation of supply chains. That's a rapidly changing field. Corporates are changing the way they exchange information with each other, and that creates challenges for banks being disintermediated and opportunities for banks in terms of providing finances to smooth these trade and exchanges.

If you look at the last decade of change you've seen with SWIFT, maybe you could summarize what those changes have been and what will be the big changes in the next ten years?

Let me see what's changed. The last ten years have seen three big ones. First, the global financial crisis. It's very hard to deny the impact of that one. The second big change is regulation. Governments are using the system as a political tool for collecting tax, claiming sovereignty over taxation data, clamping down on tax avoidance and tax evasion and limiting both terrorist financing and money laundering. All of that comes to mind. The third big trend is technology, and I'll put all the cyber activity in that one as well.

If I look forward, then technology can only be moving to impact banking and SWIFT more over the next ten years than it has in the past ten. The whole discussion is a huge challenge for banks. Disruptive technologies, cyber activities, how to protect data and how to protect assets in that new world.

A second big challenge is the geopolitical shift, and I think the move to Asia will continue. That is not to be underestimated. The whole discussion about reserve currencies will continue and there will be new financial centres and new financial flows.

CASE STUDIES

THE FINTECH START-UPS

CHRIS LARSEN, CEO and cofounder, Ripple Labs

Chris Larsen is CEO and Co-founder of Ripple Labs, creators of Ripple, an open-source, distributed payment protocol. Mr. Larsen also cofounded and served as CEO of Prosper, a peer-to-peer lending marketplace, and E-LOAN, a publicly traded online lender. During his tenure at E-LOAN, he pioneered the open access to credit scores movement by making E-LOAN the first company to show consumers their FICO scores.

A lot of people have not heard of Ripple. Can you give us some background?

Sure. We've all experienced the inefficiencies of payments—I can physically travel to Europe faster than my payment settles from the US to Europe using a wire service. The delays and costs inherent in today's infrastructure restrict the expansion of businesses, international trade, economic growth and ultimately financial inclusion.

Think of the internet's revolution. By providing common, neutral, global infrastructure for free and instant information exchange, the internet opened access to, and dramatically increased participation in, global knowledge and information sharing. It spawned entire new, previously unimaginable industries. Services like eBay, Twitter, and Uber have changed the world, but wouldn't have been possible without the internet.

The same concept applies to payments. Payment systems were created before the internet existed, built country-by-country as closed loops. Payments needs a common, neutral, global infrastructure for free and instant value exchange. It's the dawn of the Internet of Value. Ripple is a decentralised payments technology that enables free and instant payments in any currency, anywhere in the world. It is an infrastructure that sews together and modernizes today's payment systems so money can move on the web, just like information does today.

But then some people might struggle with this, thinking, why do I need Ripple when we've got Bitcoin?

Ripple was born out of Bitcoin's incredible revolution. Bitcoin solved the double-spend problem, creating, for the first time in history, a digital asset and decentralised ledger with no central operator. This breakthrough means people can send this new currency (bitcoins) to anyone else in the world in minutes and at no cost. But Bitcoin is only efficient as a payment system if everyone in the world adopts bitcoin as the one and only currency, and in that scenario, Bitcoin replaces today's systems—from ACH to SWIFT to Visa, banks, PayPal, etc.

By design, Ripple is optimized to serve as an improved, IP-based infrastructure for today's payment systems. Amongst distributed payments technologies, Ripple uniquely works with any currency (dollars, euros, yen, etc), and it settles transactions, including cross-currency transactions, in five seconds.

So, whereas bitcoin depends on consumers and merchants adopting the currency and exclusively using the blockchain for payments, Ripple is meant for financial institutions to integrate into their core systems to dramatically increase the speed and lower the cost of payments. Financial institutions and networks using Ripple never have to touch digital currency; they continue to use the fiat currencies they deal in today.

So if I summarise: there is the Bitcoin-blockchain technology. This technology is fantastic, but it also allows a bit of a Wild West to exist, as it's out there and open sourced. The community use it as "money without government", which is not what the government wants, so you have made the technology appropriate more for corporations and banks to use in a structured way.

Bitcoin was designed with a different objective than Ripple. For bitcoin, the goal was to create a decentralised currency and ledger, independent from any government or central operator. For Ripple, the goal was to create a decentralised ledger that could work with and improve the foundation of today's payments systems.

Government regulators, central banks, financial institutions, and corporates aren't interested in experimenting with digital currency or upending the banking and payments industry. They are interested in improving and modernizing the industry. They're open to the benefits of lowering costs and risks in the system, end-to-end transaction transparency, and the possibility of exponential growth in volume—all of which Ripple enables.

Ripple is settlement technology that plugs into banks' existing core systems, including compliance, messaging, and other systems. For example, Earthport is fusing Ripple with its robust compliance framework to offer bank clients a trusted, secure, real-time payments option.

Lastly, because payments on Ripple settle instantly and point-to-point, banks, regulators and law enforcement have complete visibility into transactions as needed, which reduces costs for everyone involved.

Yes, I have seen a few references to some of the folks that you are working with, such as new companies like Fidor Bank and Earthport. Equally you are working with some of the big guys (the banks you know and love to hate). How is that progressing?

We've had a great response from the market—from community or regional banks to the top global banks and payment networks. The value proposition is clear to them: enable real-time payments, lower the costs of liquidity and compliance. Sibos last year was a turning point for Ripple, where the common question we heard was, "How do we get started?"

We've announced integrations with Fidor Bank (in Germany), CBW Bank (in Kansas), Cross River Bank (in New Jersey) and Earthport. We're working on dozens more integrations behind the scenes in private pilots.

It's a pivotal time for our company. We have exciting opportunities in the pipeline and we're focused on executing them. We just brought on Brad Garlinghouse as our COO (previously of Yahoo!, AOL, Hightail) to dig our heels in and focus on delivering to the market.

I guess that the core motivation for banks to use Ripple is that it takes out a lot of the handovers between the likes of CHAPS, SWIFT and Fedwire, and does it for free. Is that right?
Ripple doesn't replace local rails and standards (like SWIFT). Rather, it connects them. Today, every bank in the world relies on correspondent banking for cross-border payments. Every link in the correspondent banking chain creates costs in the form of fees, risk and time delays. There are only five or six global money centre banks that provide liquidity for cross-border payments, so foreign exchange rates aren't competitive.

On Ripple, banks can transact directly with each other, instantly and for free. By way of example, Ripple enables a bank like Fidor in Germany to provide Europe–US real-time payments to its customers at a fraction of the cost, by working directly with a bank like Cross River Bank. In that scenario, Ripple connects SEPA to ACH and works with SWIFT's messaging layer— so another bank in the US or a bank in Europe could actually use Cross River Bank or Fidor Bank as its "correspondent" to get more competitive rates and delivery speed, which is a new business opportunity for banks outside of the top five.

It always amuses me when banks talk about cryptocurrencies, such as Ripple, since their first question is always: "Is this approved by the regulators? Does the Fed support this approach?"
Yes, and for good reason! Banks using Ripple aren't touching cryptocurrencies. They continue to deal in fiat currencies. And, Ripple works in synchronization with their existing compliance systems.

Regulators in the U.S., Europe, the UK and abroad have been proactive about learning about these technologies. They're interested in the potential for improving compliance practices, lowering costs, increasing the speed of payments, and enabling interoperability for global systems. Real-time payments isn't just a consumer feature. The speed of payments has huge implications for the cost of liquidity, and as a result, economic expansion. History has shown us (take FPS in the UK, for example) that if you increase speed and lower costs, volume explodes.

Do you see Ripple currency being a big game player 5–10 years from now, or is that not the focus?
Our focus is really on creating utility for Ripple as a payments technology. I think in 5–10 years people will use Ripple for domestic and international payments without knowing it, just like how I use ACH daily but I don't need to think about it.

As more and more banks adopt Ripple and they push more and more cross-border volume through Ripple, market makers will need efficient ways to trade less liquid currencies. XRP is a useful tool for market making when a currency trade takes multiple "hops" (for example, Nepalese Rupee to Indian Rupee to Euros to Kenyan Shilling). Because it has no counterparty, XRP is always a one "hop" trade (Nepalese Rupee to XRP to Kenyan Shilling). So then, XRP as a utility for trading creates its demand.

One of the biggest issues in capital markets right now is collateral management, and the efficient use of capital and liquidity. I guess what you are saying is that Ripple directly addresses that challenge of the efficient use of capital?
Yes, that's exactly right. Liquidity management is a big cost to banks today that's intrinsic to the correspondent banking system. Capital outlays for cross-border payments restricts working capital. Imagine if banks don't have to make those outlays and they can instantly and directly transact with the institutions they chose to work with. That's the reality of Ripple today.

NIKLAS ADALBERTH, Co-Founder, Deputy CEO and Board Member, Klarna

Niklas Adalberth is Klarna's third founding member. He has a Masters in Economics from the Stockholm School of Economics and experience in being an entrepreneur within the IT sector.

About Klarna

Klarna was founded in Stockholm in 2005 with the idea to simplify buying. Today, Klarna is one of Europe's fastest growing companies and, after joining forces with SOFORT in 2014 to form Klarna Group, claims to be the leading European online payment provider. Klarna Group has over 1,200 employees and is active in 18 markets, serving 35 million consumers and working with 50,000 merchants.

To begin with, perhaps you can tell me how you and your colleagues came up with the idea of Klarna.

Sure. When we started this company, the entire idea was around safety. In Sweden, where we started, people were reluctant to use their credit card online because they didn't like the idea that their card number would be out on the internet. They were also sceptical as to whether they would actually get the products they ordered. They would be worried they might receive a blue shirt instead of a red shirt, or a size 43 shoe instead of the size 41 they ordered, for example.

In other words, the internet and e-commerce in Sweden and the Nordics was being hindered by this lack of safety. People didn't trust the card networks online basically, and that is where the idea came around for Klarna. We wanted to work out how to make consumers feel safe shopping online.

Early on we figured out that the only answer would be to create a company that acts as a middleman, taking on the full risk for the merchant and for the consumer of paying and delivering online goods and services. That's the basic idea of Klarna. We pay the merchant, no matter what happens, and the consumer can pay us up to 14 days later, once they have received and are happy with the goods.

The key to being successful in this was to construct an algorithm to calculate the risks involved. This is core to our model as to whether we should accept an order or not, as we must know the risk of the consumer not paying. We also knew that we could only take on this risk if we made scale out of this, as you need thousands of transactions if you are to allow one to fail.

We also had one other big advantage, and that was that we had no previous banking or payment expertise. My expertise or experience came from flipping burgers at Burger King. That's all the knowledge I had when we started this business. This was a good thing, because it made us rethink everything. For example, we knew immediately that we could not base this on the normal card scheme standards, as these had been designed from the 1970s or earlier. They do not work on the internet, and that was why we rebuilt everything and questioned everything, as we wanted to launch a company built for the internet that could make the best customer experience there is.

So initially, Klarna was all about being a payment method. It meant that you could go to an e-commerce site as a consumer, select whatever you want, and then when you come to the checkout have the option to click on "Buy Now, Pay In Fourteen Days". When you did select that payment method, instead of Visa or MasterCard, you just entered your name, address and date of birth. That was all the information we needed. Based on that limited information we were able to take that data, perform the risk assessment and give a "yes" or "no" answer within a second. If the answer was "yes", then the merchant was paid there and then, no matter what happened. This meant they could be confident in shipping the goods right away to the customer, who would pay up to 14 days later.

This worked because Sweden is a very open society and so you can get data, such as someone's exact income, using your name, address and date of birth. The information even tells us your income based upon earnings and income from capital. All of this data is made publicly available in Sweden, and hence this kind of risk assessment is actually quite easy. As a result, we were able to start without significant losses per transaction, and this is how Klarna began.

I'm guessing from the experience of the founders, that you were just frustrated with the problem and wanted to solve it. Did you all have a technology background?

We did not. We were starting a FinTech business with no technical expertise, no financial expertise and no money. That was quite a tough start, but we were able to raise money and we were able to take in the technical expertise in exchange for equity.

And what was the real kick-starter to the business?

We were just frustrated that we, the founders, didn't dare to shop online. We also discovered it was complex making a purchase online. You had to register an account; remember a username and password; answer questions like "What's your mother's maiden name?"; and all of these were very annoying steps you needed to do in order to proceed with your purchase. If you were to compare that to the physical world, it would be super strange to arrive at the checkout and then suddenly have the cashier asking you all of these questions. You would just leave without buying.

So we started developing the idea of Klarna and when we launched this product, we got a great reaction. Typically, the feedback was something like: "Guys, you know what? This payment method is not only the safest because I don't need to pay until I get my stuff, but it's also the fastest because I don't need to take out my credit card and start filling out the details. It's even easier, as I don't have to enter all these numbers on this very small smartphone. I can just enter my zip code, and instantly you guys approve the transaction. Why don't you guys do this for the entire checkout, to make the entire checkout easier?"

And that's when we discovered the Klarna Checkout, which is a product that we have launched in the UK and are about to launch in the US. It works well. For example, in Sweden, we've been able to convert more than 50 percent of all our transactions into this new payment solution. The way it works is that, when you come into the checkout, you only need to enter your email address and zip code, and that's it. It's the only thing you need to do before pressing the "Buy Now" button or "Place Order" button. You come to the confirmation page instantly, and the order is approved. You also have the option, on that confirmation page, to decide if you want to change the payment method but, if you don't, you can just close down your smartphone and you will get your goods. You can then decide when you want to pay, up to 14 days later. That's the essence of Klarna—what we've really done is separated the buying from the paying, where the paying is often the more complex part.

Heavy-weight players like Google and PayPal are focused on the same issue, and yet they didn't solve it. Why have you been successful where they haven't?

Because they base it on Visa and MasterCard, the old traditional card scheme standards that go 50 years back in time. When you read about all of these fantastic start-ups on TechCrunch or whatever, and you look into them more closely, you will see the same. They're all based on the old card schemes. So you could ask: how innovative are these new companies in reality? Sure, if you look at Stripe for example, I think they're very good in terms of providing credit card solutions in an easier way for the merchant. They simplify the sign-up of a merchant that wants to sell online. That's good. If you look at Square, same thing. But it's all still based on old systems or old standards, and you still need to pull out that credit card.

I was going to ask you about Stripe, because they're going to go head-to-head against you. Is that a concern?

Not really. All competition is good, and I think that they've created a really good sign-up process, but we provide something completely different. We provide a separation from buying and paying. We make it super easy to checkout for the consumer.

In terms of Klarna's growth, you're developing across Europe right now. What challenges have you found there?

So we've separated the buying from paying. The buying should be super easy and the paying should also be super easy, but every country is different and has different views and needs. In fact, many markets have payments that are very localised. In Germany for example, the consumer could actually settle in the end with the Visa or MasterCard, or they might do it through a direct transfer to the bank, or through the domestic Elektronisches Lastschriftverfahren (ELV) system, which is very popular in Germany and works like a direct debit.

Now we know that we cannot force consumers to use our option only, so all those options are still there. We don't force the consumer to go through a cumbersome process before they are accepted and before the merchant gets the order completed. The challenge then is to make all of this local. We need to have all of these local payment methods supported in every geography where we operate, to provide a great experience because, in each market, it's very different.

In the UK for example, there is now Zapp and Paym. If Zapp takes off, as is likely, then it should be included in the Klarna Checkout as a way of settling in the end. The same with Apple Pay, Google Pay, Alipay or whatever method people prefer in the end, when they are ready to make the actual purchase. That puts a lot of pressure on us to continually develop and incorporate all of these options, and that is why we employ more than 350 people in our engineering department.

We are constantly developing and constantly making it more and more localised. On top of this, as with any payments company, we also have all the KYC requirements that are slightly different, depending upon which markets you operate in. These legal requirements need to be a hundred percent compliant with all of the different regulations in the different markets and, once again, that creates a lot of work for us to still make it very easy and also a hundred percent compliant.

When I talk about the Klarna model, some people say to me: "How can they solve the credit risk if you don't have the data?" You mentioned you had access to all this data in Sweden but, in some countries, they don't have data.

That would be trickier for sure and, once again, I think that if we had started this business in the UK, where you don't have as much data, maybe we would never have succeeded. The thing that we have discovered over each expansion—just taking this business idea to Norway, for example—is that people said: "Oh, you will never be able to do this in Norway because we don't have this Social Security Number that everyone uses, so you can't identify the customer as easily. Also, you don't have access to income data, so how will you be able to assess the risk?"

What we did is recognise that we had to work with less data, but we were still quite data-rich. We were able to get the losses down to lower than any other bank, because we discovered that behavioural data is very, very powerful. Behavioural data means that we take in the data and analyse the risk from that data. If you shop at three o'clock in the morning, we see that as higher risk than if you shop at three o'clock in the afternoon. Our risk models recognise that a transaction is higher risk in the middle of the night than during the day.

Other examples are that we also take in the line item data so that, if you buy a book about champagne, we see that as lower risk than a book about beer. We take that data into our models. We also take in, for example, if you write in upper case or lower case. If you write with capital letters, we see that as higher risk than if you write with normal letters. So all of these criteria are almost the same, whether we are approving a transaction in the UK, Spain or in Sweden.

In addition to this, we have a lot of external data. We are plugged into over 25 external data providers, depending on what geography they cover. All of this—the data and our algorithms—helps us to assess the risk.

326 VALUE WEB

I was told that all I need to do to use Klarna is just give my ZIP code or post code and that's it. Is it really as simple as that?
Klarna Checkout is very dynamic, flexible and interactive, making it super easy for you regardless of who you are, what market you are in, or what transaction it is. For example, in Sweden, the e-mail and zip code could be enough data for us, if it is for a lower transaction amount. This is because we recognize the IP address and the zip code, and can check that they are geographically aligned. That is enough if you are buying a low-risk item. It all comes back to that very easy experience, especially if you're a returning customer. It may be different for a first time user, where we may need slightly more data, especially if you're buying something more expensive. Let's say that you're a completely new customer and you want to buy two iPads at the same time at three o'clock in the morning. Let's say you want to do this through a hotmail.com email address. Of course, with those risks, we would then ask you a few more questions. It might even be that we want you to enter credit card details in advance.

But what's important here is that only one percent of the transactions are risky or will cause a loss. We don't want to punish the other 99 percent of the population for that one percent. Banks, because they only focus upon risk, force us to enter all these cumbersome details because they distrust a 100 percent of buyers, rather than the one percent. We do the opposite. We give 85 percent of customers a very nice experience, because we think the risk is actually quite low. As long as the transaction makes sense; the IP address makes sense; you write with normal letters in lower case; it's a daytime purchase; it's a low cost item; and so on. As long as all of these variables are right then, for 85 percent of transactions, we deliver a fantastic purchasing experience. The remaining 15 percent that we're not sure of, then we start asking more questions in the checkout process, but it's still super easy and very dynamic.

Ultimately, it's all about a much nicer experience for the majority of people.

A lot of new FinTech companies are addressing issues that the banks don't deal with and, when I talk about Klarna, you are honey for the

merchant bees, if I can put it that way. This is because the merchants are looking at conversion, they want more business, but the banks are prohibitive because of their risk mitigation and they make it difficult. You've solved the issue both for the merchant and the consumers.

Absolutely. And if you look at the normal credit card payment, which players are involved in making that transaction possible? Well, first you have the technical standards, which is either Visa or MasterCard, who have their way of working for what they need for data to make the transaction. Then you have the issuing bank. They are the ones that have the consumer risk. Then you have the acquirers, who take the merchant risk and approve the merchant—the online shop, in this case. The issuers and acquirers are usually very traditional and, most of the time, come from very old systems with banks that were using mainframe computers from the 1970s. Then you have the gateway, which is yet another player in this transaction.

That is four different players involved in a payment. In order to make all of these different players work together, to make them innovate and change, is difficult. To get all of these different players in the payment system to work together requires a lot of coordination, a lot of time, a lot of agreement. That's why we see most of the payment schemes being based on old components that are slow to change.

That is why we have rediscovered the process, and are doing all of these four things in one payment system. We are our own issuer. We do our own underwriting for the consumer. That is our system. We do our own acquiring. We are the acquiring player in this transaction. We hold our own brand, our own technical standards and we own our own gateway. If you do all of these four things in one player, one company, one innovation and one technical platform, then you can innovate like no one else. It is far easier to innovate if you control the whole transaction, rather than just a fourth of the transaction.

Where do you see yourselves going as a business?

We believe that there is a need all over the world to make payments much, much easier. There is a strong need for a one-click system that covers the risk that you will actually receive what you order, and that you don't need to send the money in advance if you don't want to. We think there is a strong need for that all over the world, and we think that the e-commerce boom has now really started. If we can simplify the entire process around the checkout into one click, I think there's a great need for Klarna all over the world.

CARLOS SANCHEZ, founder of ipagoo

Carlos Sanchez has a wealth of experience in banking, where he has held board and executive positions in various organisations. He worked at Dexia Group, where he was appointed Head of Operations of Dexia Private Bank France, France Country head of the Fund Services division, then CEO of the newly created Dexia Investor Services Bank France. In 2006 he joined RBC Dexia in Milan as CEO. Returning from Italy, Carlos joined Goldman Sachs in London as Executive Director, acting as Financial Advisor for the European corporate market in investments. Carlos holds both an MSc in Telematics and an Engineering Degree from the ETSI of Telecommunications of the University of Vigo, Spain, and a MBA from IMD, in Lausanne, Switzerland.

About ipagoo

ipagoo was founded by banking professionals and IT experts who have experienced first-hand the obstacles that banking fragmentation represents for mobility and recognise the need for better banking. The company is focused on Europe, and believes that Europe, with its large internal market, is a perfect place for businesses to grow and develop.

Perhaps you can give us some background on exactly what you are developing at ipagoo?

OK, let me give you the history of ipagoo and what it actually is. ipagoo is owned by Orwell Group, a small financial services group based in London. We were set up five years ago by a wealth manager. I am in charge of everything that is financial services, and one of the co-founders.

Going back in time to my first job, I worked in commercial wealth management. One of my clients was a family-owned business in Europe. For me, it was one of the first times I was actually facing real entrepreneurs and I realised that they struggled to set up and maintain multiple banking relations in Europe for their international trading activity. Whilst we were having these meetings with them to talk about investment management, succession planning, corporate finance and many other things, they spent a lot of the time complaining about the relationships they had with banks. So we identified that banking fragmentation in Europe in itself was one of the trading barriers for the European Union. The frustration was enormous. I could relate to my own experience, I have had to open bank accounts with different banks in each one of the six European countries where I have lived. Why do we have to do that, and why do we have to maintain so many banking relations? We have to become treasurers in our own right, and that's not to mention the inconvenience. So we started to find out why we had to do this, and why there is this problem.

Whilst we need current accounts and payments as a basic service, banks want our deposits to feed their balance sheet—they want that to be stable. Banks look at cash management, which includes payments, current accounts and so on—as an appeal product; for them, it is a necessary evil to attract money to the balance sheet, so that they can carry on creditor activities. These two functions of the bank, cash and credit, are together as a legal entity in every bank, the restrictions applied to the credit function are also applied to the cash management function—as such, we have a fragmented banking industry in Europe. If we break the bank in two—which is actually what regulation is intending to do—we create a new generation of banking, thanks to the appearance of a new banking entity, exclusive to cash management. Not bound to a single country, this entity can now spread geographically over a number of countries. We created ipagoo to prove that this was possible. A new kind of bank that covers the whole of Europe, so our clients can hold a single relationship with as many bank accounts as they want.

So is ipagoo actually a bank, or is it a payment processor?
Technically ipagoo is an authorised electronic money institution. However, the term "bank" is not defined legally or regulatory anywhere, so what is a bank? The regulation is bad for picking names for the different licences you can have. So what we traditionally call a bank is in fact a credit institution. But it is not defined anywhere. Previously, the origin of the credit institution, savings and credit, was everything those entities were doing, but they have now evolved into payment providers, too. That we do not give credit or make investments places us in the category of a new kind of bank, a new generation of bank devoted to cash management.

I guess you can only exist thanks to the opening of the payments markets through regulations in Europe?
Absolutely—the payments directive is an economic regulation that aims to open up the market and to foster competition. Shaking up the traditional banking industry that is archaic and not evolving by its own will. Regulation is an enabler, in this case—it is what is driving this new competition in Europe.

So in terms of ipagoo plans, is the company open for business? And how is the growth plan looking?
We are not open for business yet. The system is live—we have a number of clients, which are mainly friends, family and ourselves for the purpose of testing. We are doing something that no one has done before, a single entity connecting at launch with four different countries. This is extremely complex. I know traditional banks very well, I set up two in the past to connect one country, which took almost two years—we are connecting four countries at the same time. It's a huge achievement, and we are almost there. The payment system works, but we are still finishing services and having problems with delays with some of the banks in Europe, who are taking their time to update the payments routing tables. This makes the activation of new entities slow. Some haven't updated tables in the last six months and this shows how they perceive the market. They are very slow. As you can imagine, the internet DNS server is updated every six months or every year,

which many banks are doing. We are connecting the last modules for the service. We think we will be able to open up to the public by the end of the year, which will be in record time, as its less than two years since we started to develop the platform.

In terms of the structure of ipagoo, will it mainly be technology orientated with pure access through online services, or it will be more than that?

Initially it will be online and mobile, but not exclusively. At ipagoo, we are developing a network of agents to support the access to accounts through cash. So when you have to cash cheques for example, we can do it through specific network arrangements, and sometimes within a network of retail banks established in the country. Eventually, we will develop a concept of light ipagoo brand branch stores. Also, one of the consequences of ipagoo's cash management focus is that we will offer many services you won't expect, and that will be a novelty. We need to give client's support, to show clients how to make the most out of these services. Like conditional payments, budget tools, cash pooling, multi-user relationships, alerts and notifications, etc.

A lot of the commercial bankers I talk to believe that corporates won't change or switch their accounts—but who are you targeting that is unhappy and will do so? What's the profile of the customer?

First of all, we have to address the reason why people aren't switching banks. Currently the retail banking or cash-banking world is completely commoditised, you wont find something that will fit your niche. A different logo but the same service. Incentive to change doesn't really exist. With ipagoo, the advantage is so important that that barrier disappears, the breakthrough is in convenience and adaptability. Think of the first time the iPhone was presented by Steve Jobs—we all wondered whether we would use it? But now look at what we can do with it; however, we had to try it first, as we had no reference point to know what to expect. The same thing will happen with ipagoo—its services and capabilities need to be experienced to understand what it is now possible. Our initial target is to focus on businesses and individuals with an international outlook. There are between 25–30 million EU nationals living in a country other than their country of origin. There are also 2.5 million Europeans changing country each year. There are 2.4 million businesses that have a presence in more than one country. Banking fragmentation obliges all those individuals and businesses to open new accounts every year. It is not just about switching, it's about starting a new relationship. We cover their needs regardless of the country they are in.

In terms of looking at what's available today, there are also companies like Klarna, Zopa and Funding Circle. Do you see yourselves in the same campus as these FinTech start-ups, or are you in another category?

We are in a different category. Funding circle is a good example, as they are addressing a specific need, so they are very good at providing credit to specific companies in a specific way. They represent a niche, specialised player. They represent the disintegration of banking services that you mention in your book. Traditional retail banks pretend to be big supermarkets of everything within a single brand. But they cannot be good at everything, its impossible. Banks still pretend to be good at everything. This model is dead and Funding Circle and other niche players are proof of that. However, the problem for the end customer is that now he is facing hundreds, if not thousands, of new providers, so consumers need an aggregator. The natural aggregation layer is cash management. Whether you are going to receive or invest money from Funding Circle, you need a current account. We are the cash management bank for Europe, underneath which anyone of those new, specialised providers can access clients to be funded or offered credit to. We will work in open architecture—ipagoo is going to start connecting with third-party providers or investment banks that offer AAA cash funds and others. Even if you live in the UK, you can actually do business with a German bank you have never heard of before. We become the distribution channel, in the same way that eBay have merchants that only exist in eBay. We think that in the future some banks will evolve to distribute exclusively through us, where they can reach 500 million people in Europe rather than be constrained to the country where they are today.

If you are looking 10 years on, do you think that banking will be radically different because of people like yourself coming into the marketplace? Obviously you will say yes, but what do you think will change?

Entities such a ipagoo are going to provoke the disappearance of some banks who exist as they enjoy a quasi monopoly or an oligopoly in the geography where they are. Once you bring competition in from the outside in the way that we will do, the mere existence of multiple tiny banks has nothing to offer. They will have to merge and evolve in some way. Consumers have given up expecting something good from banks. Thanks to technology and innovation, we can demonstrate to the market that it is possible to expect something good from banking as well, as you expect from other industries.

If you looked at the way in which regulations are coming through, you've got trusted third party access and PSD2 coming in. That's going to open up the markets even more—so do you think there will be an explosion of new competitors, and is there any "low hanging fruit" that banks should worry about in terms of where they will see an attack?

Third party payments are potentially going to bring a lot of disruption. There are some preconditions for that to happen, however, such as viable consumer protection and clear allocation of responsibilities, and also technical preconditions, such as standardized interfaces. I see a lot of potential for change, even large traditional banks are all starting to accept the fact that they change or they will be replaced. Change will happen whether we want it or not. Banking is lagging behind how other industries have changed. Much more specialized and flexible for the end user, the PSD2 is seeking to allow a full unbundling of payment services.

Is there anything else we haven't covered that you wanted to mention?

Yes, I think there is something else to mention regarding ipagoo. ipagoo is what we describe as very disruptive—it really breaks the system-banking model. Each bank is a factory of products through the balance sheet and distribution channel through the cash management—in that it remains in a single country. So for example, any large banking group like HSBC or Barclays have a collection of banks, one in each country. So, what is the strategy for any bank in Europe in terms of growth? Some of them have no strategy, especially as they don't have the deep pockets required to go out and buy other banks or organically opening new subsidiaries—but even these two models we know don't work very well. So ipagoo is disruptive in the sense that it allows a traditional bank in Europe, with a single balance sheet in a single country, to become European and serve 500 million people. Within banking, ipagoo represents that innovation. Banks become efficient. You reduce your distribution costs much more. That is fundamentally different from today's model of fragmented balance sheets and difficult to manage. What I am saying is that no bank will resist the need to do this. The digitilisation of the banking industry as it has been preached so far has nothing to do with being innovative—banks are simply trying to reduce the cost of distribution by reducing the cost and access to the client. Digitalisation is one thing—changing your model to achieve tremendous efficiency and flexibility that unleashes innovation in such an advanced way is another.

GILES ANDREWS, Co-Founder and CEO, Zopa

Giles Andrews spent the first ten years of his career in the motor industry, pursuing his interest in all things automotive. This included co-founding Caverdale in 1992, a start-up taken to a £250m turnover motor retailer and sold in 1997. After an MBA at INSEAD he set up his own consultancy business, whose clients included Tesco and Tesco Personal Finance. In 2004, Giles co-founded Zopa, a social lending website that connects people who want to borrow money with people who want to lend it. As CFO, he raised a total of $33m from European and US investors. UK Managing Director since July 2007 and CEO since January 2009, Giles has led the company through a period of dramatic growth that has seen it established as a real threat to the banks.

About Zopa

Zopa is the UK's leading peer-to-peer lending service and can claim to be the first peer-to-peer lender. Since being founded in 2005 by chief executive Giles Andrews with members of the management team of former internet bank Egg, Zopa has helped lend more than £1 billion in peer-to-peer loans. Over 51,000 people are lending between £10 and £1 million to credit-worthy borrowers. The company has been voted "Most Trusted Personal Loan Provider" in the Moneywise Customer Awards for the past six years in a row.

How did Zopa start?

Well firstly, it wasn't my idea. I joined a team of three people who had an idea, about four slides of PowerPoint. They weren't quite sure where to take the idea and how to get it financed. I joined them to help out on that side of things, and enjoyed it so much that I stayed.

And that was when?

The idea was hatched in 2004. I would say in the first quarter of 2004. I joined the team in spring, and we went on to raise money in the summer of 2004 and closed the first round of funding in the autumn of 2004. The business was launched in March 2005.

And this was the very first peer-to-peer lender on the planet.

Absolutely. Yes.

And has now been copied in most countries around the world.

People all over the world. All and sundry.

In the 11 years since you started, what has changed?

The basic idea hasn't changed, which was to provide better value to consumers by being a more efficient connection for people who have money to connect with people who wanted money, and to do it in a fairer manner that didn't involve a bank. This meant not taking deposits, but connecting people's money through a marketplace solution.

The original vision was for all that to be done at an individual level by individual lenders. Now that idea has moved through a pretty subtle morph, as there are now some businesses supplying capital. Institutions supply capital and, more recently, banks and the UK government supplied capital. In our case, we only lend to consumers, but now there are also other lending models, too. For example, retail consumers funding businesses through Funding Circle. Even so, the basic idea of connecting people with money to people who want it hasn't changed.

The idea of that happening in a marketplace, not involving a bank, or bank balance sheets, means not requiring the regulations and the associated regulatory capital requirements of deposit-taking and, crucially in my mind, without any maturity transformation taking place. Therefore, it is not only creating a more efficient system in the marketplace, but also a more stable one, where both sides understand and agree the duration of a loan contract. It avoids the situation where people are borrowing short and lending long, which brought down the financial world in 2008 in the global financial crisis.

As I said, the basic idea has not changed. It's remarkably consistent. Every market is different in terms of how regulators deal with the idea, though. Regulators in different markets all around the world require subtly different interpretations of the basic business model. In some cases they require different licenses and different permissions and, in some cases, banks have to be involved. For example, in the US, securities are created and sold for the loans, and that has to be done via banks. In Germany, a banking license is needed. Even so, by and large, around most of the world, the idea is pretty much as it was created by us.

You saw a real uptick in business after the crisis hit in 2008 and as the bank credit markets dried up. Has that demand been sustained?
Yes it has. That was an inflection point in our growth. How causal the crisis was is difficult to tell, as it happened when we were three years old with an increasing track record. We had prioritised delivering a great credit performance. That meant that when the crisis hit we were just coming of age, gaining some maturity and showing great results—but, no question, the crisis helped us get to where we are today.

Had the crisis occurred when we were younger, without so much of a track record, we probably wouldn't have benefitted so much. It wasn't just the crisis, but the timing of the crisis, that was helpful. As with many genuinely new businesses, consumer adoption can be a bit slower than optimistic entrepreneurs may hope for; but, similarly, accelerating growth is sometimes more traumatic than you might hope for as well, it can be difficult to keep up with.

I remember when we first met, the concept of peer-to-peer lending was actually quite alien.

It was interesting as, completely by accident, our early adopter customer base contained many IT professionals. The way I rationalize this is that if you show an IT professional a solution to a known problem that involves the clever use of IT, then their due diligence on the business involves checking the IT works. When it came to the really thorny stuff like, "Do these people know how to lend money and get it back?" these IT professionals seemed to take this more on trust. In fact, they were, with hindsight, a fantastic early adopter user base, and most of them are still with us.

How has the demographics of the customer base changed?

Surprisingly, in the first year or two, the average borrower was from a higher demographic than the average lender. This was probably due to our overly stringent credit risk requirements. Back then, you basically had to be rich and have no need for a loan whatsoever to be given one by us.

Interestingly, lenders were from a lower demographic. They were generally younger and lending quite small amounts of money. They typically weren't terribly wealthy and, as the business matured, that has changed gradually.

Today, our average lenders are ten years older than our average borrower. Our lenders are typically in their early 50s, and that's getting older all the time. This means they are now often wealthier and more conservative.

These folks are attracted to us because we started getting written about in *The Daily Telegraph* rather than *Wired*. So, over time, the customer base and view has changed a lot, which has been helpful.

Can you give me a few numbers in terms of the volume of lending and borrowing?

We have been lending £45 million a month and expect that to be £50 million this month.

That indicates that your lending seems to be doubling year-on-year?

Yes. We've doubled most years since 2008, and certainly are on track to double our volumes again this year.

If you look at that in the context of the mainstream banking marketplace for credit, it's still peanuts though, isn't it?
Well, we've got about two percent market share now. I remember when we started and were presenting our business plans, we said, "It's a very big market, we only need one percent of it," and the venture capitalist looks down over their glasses and says, "Yes, the first one percent is always the hardest one to get." We achieved about one percent last year of the UK unsecured consumer loans market and are now on track to do about two percent this year.

It's doubling year-on-year.
Yes. This means it gets to be significant pretty quickly and certainly now, there's no reason why we shouldn't get into double-digit market share at some point very soon. It will level up at some point, but not in the immediate future.

Do you see this as taking market share from the banks, or is this creating an alternative marketplace?
I think it's substitutional. I don't think we're growing the market for consumer finance. I think we are taking share from banks on the basis that we have the better product. It's typically about providing the best value, but customers are not choosing us because we're always cheaper. We have won customer service awards for the last six years in a row with influential consumer finance publications like *Moneywise*, *Moneyfacts* and more.

This is because we began by trying to not only create a great offer, but a great service, too. We went on service; we went on value; and we went on some other product benefits as well, such as the fact that you can repay your loan at any point and leave with no charge.

Therefore, we created new product features that also would attract. The idea with all of this was to set us apart from the banks. The fact that we had a slightly funny-sounding name, and it was new.

Then there was the PPI (Payments Protection Insurance) scandal, which clearly helped us.

But even despite our features and benefits, and even despite all of that bad bank history and headlines, most people are still, on balance, more likely to go with someone they've heard of. In other words, we still have to fight hard to win business, as the average lender and borrower will still go to the brand they know first.

That is where we have had a pretty big nut to crack, in terms of growing awareness of what we do. We need to have more awareness to achieve the level of conversion from marketing and from Best Buy tables and awards for service.

Another notable factor is that your loan default rates are lower than the banks. Is that because of the software, analytics, risk management or something else?

I think now it's down to superior analytics and risk management, but initially I think it was because we were more conservative than banks. So our losses in the early years from loan defaults were zero, which is clearly too low. It meant that we were turning down a lot of business that we should have been writing. Since the crisis we've continued to outperform banks, but we have seen some credit loss, which is a good thing. It's a good thing as long as we manage the risk effectively. During the first years, we were too stringent and we learned lessons from being very conservative. It's always better to learn by starting from a conservative base. It's easier to add more risk than to take it away. You learn a lot from conservative behaviour, because you can do retrospective analysis of the customers you declined. You can look at the past data and find cells of people who didn't look great to you when you made your decision, but who actually turned out to be fine. By doing this, you can then improve your models and your algorithms to reflect that. In other words, we were building a credit model in exactly the opposite way to a payday lender strategy, which is to learn from the people they shouldn't have lent to.

We learned from this that we had been lending incredibly conservatively. We didn't lend to people who subsequently went on to get a loan and pay it back. We then asked: "How can we try to lend to those people, as well as the people we lent to before?" It's just a slow process. You have to wait a couple of years to find out who the people you declined were, who then went on to pay back and behave well, because you can't judge them quickly. You can't judge them on their first six or twelve months behaviour, for example. You have to wait a couple of years. Contrast this with the payday lending credit model. Payday lenders can lend indiscriminately at first. They are lending small amounts of their own money, and learn more rapidly based on very quick repayment cycles, but we couldn't do that because it isn't our money and the repayment cycles are much slower. We lend somebody else's money. But, if you take longer, you can work intelligently to build better credit models.

But couldn't you just use FICO, Experian, Equifax and credit rating agencies to assess risk?

We don't really take a huge amount of notice of their scores. Scores are useful to people who don't have their own data, and are directionally accurate, but we have found that having our own data is more valuable. We still buy raw data from the credit bureau and use this in constructing our own scores.

Less experienced lenders tend to buy a score, and that's all they do. I'm not belittling that as a product, but we've moved it on a stage. We buy raw data from several bureau, which costs more money, and then overlay that with our own data. This means we have far more accurate models for lending.

If you're doubling your volume of lending year-on-year, have you also had to double the number of staff?

The staffing hasn't gone in the same way, no. We've tended to grow staff numbers more in steps, rather than directly in tandem with growth. We operated consistently with somewhere between 25 and 40 people during the start-up period, during which we probably quadrupled our business. So business growth and growth in staff numbers were not consistent. Staff growth was slower.

This year, we're up at about a hundred people, and so over the last ten years we have more than doubled staff. Now we're investing in a team that could probably deliver three or four times the business that we're currently writing, which will already be twice what it was last year. So we've invested ahead of the curve, if you like. A lot of that investment is in areas like technology.

A hundred people with a £500 million portfolio of lending sounds fairly efficient when compared with a bank.

Yes, and I think that will continue. In fact, our operational cost advantage should harden rather than soften over time. In terms of general numbers though, we will do £550 million of lending in 2015. In fact, the loan book will probably end up nearer £600 million. In 2016, we're forecasting a billion pounds of lending, and the portfolio should end up around £1.3 billion by the end of 2016, or something like that.

In terms of technology, do you process everything in-house, or do you use any external software houses and suppliers?

We use a mixture of services that are hosted remotely, particularly the hardware, so it's a mixture of in-house software development and external hosting. We have invested in hardware from time to time for certain areas of application processing, and we host certain parts of the applications on our own systems remotely. We probably won't do this forever, but we do now.

Why do you need some things on your own service?

That's a very good question. There are some people who think that security is easier if it's on your own hardware and they have concerns about regulation. There are some very good cloud-based solutions out there that we could use, and other players do use, but they aren't typically new businesses getting regulated for the first time.

I find it interesting that peer-to-peer lending has been so successful but, if you look at peer-to-peer insurances or crowdfunding mortgages, they don't seem so successful. Do you have a view as to why that might be?

Well, the kind of lending we do is a great marriage for a marketplace platform, because it is relatively short- to medium-term. This means that there is an easily understood return for lenders without maturity transformation. The matching of those loans to somebody who wants to make a return on their cash is quite easy. A mortgage is a harder match because of the extra duration involved, and what could happen to interest rates and so on. In this country at least, consumers are signed up for their mortgages for 25 years. Lenders might sign up for that in the States but that's not the nature of the market here yet, as it requires a different level of sophistication from the providers of the capital. But it absolutely doesn't mean it won't happen.

Life insurance companies and institutional investors are buying mortgage-backed securities today, issued in loan securitizations. The investment cycle for that marketplace has to go through lots and lots of middlemen and so it's not too far-fetched to imagine them going straight to the originators and cutting out a lot of middlemen. I think that will happen, and we might have played a part in making it happen, but it's a more complicated business. Also, unsecured lending is all done on a loan contract. Our contract doesn't involve taking security and conveyancing, and having to perform legal searches and due diligence. None of that is unsolvable, but it is more difficult. That's another reason why mortgages are more difficult.

Currencies are difficult because genuinely matching two people peer-to-peer who need money at the same time is tough. The trade has to happen in real time, whereas lending uses money that is much more fungible. Exchanging my dollars to euros is not so easy, I need to send out euros for them. My dollars are not the same as someone else's in that sense, because some other person with dollars might want pounds for them. It's just not a fungible item in the same way. A currency transaction has to be matched like an immaculate conception that occurs exactly at the same time, whereas our matching of lenders doesn't have to be an immaculate conception because the transactions can be separated.

Insurance is ripe for disruption, because I think the insurance industry is even more antediluvian than the banking industry. Their technology problems are as great as banks, if not greater, and therefore the opportunity for a new start-up to do one bit of insurance and understand the risk of that insurance well is definitely a market ripe for change.

Maybe consumers also don't feel the same need, maybe consumers don't feel as ripped off by insurance companies, as the transactions lack transparency. The rate the bank will lend money to you over four years is pretty transparent, but the rates for insurances are not.

The lack of a peer-to-peer insurer may be due to trust, as you're buying a promise to cover my risk if an incident occurs, and maybe the consumer wouldn't trust an untested name and business model.

Maybe. There is trust involved in loans and savings, but it's clearer, as you're getting a rate and can see the term. You're right in the insurance world, it's different. I'm buying a promise, not a product, and maybe that's harder to trust.

Final question. Goldman Sachs came out with a report saying seven percent of bank profits will move to peer-to-peer lenders and crowdfunders over the next five years. Their response is that they've launched a peer-to-peer lender. If you're doubling market share each year, won't all banks do this?

Goldman Sachs has launched a direct lender, and it's not peer-to-peer at all. I mean it's a bank. It's just them saying they can effectively be a lender, but they can take some lessons from these peer-to-peer or marketplace lenders. We take the capital and deploy it directly, but what they're doing is no different from any other bank. Why are they going to lend money any better than we can? I'm not sure they can. And the regulatory requirements are also no different to any other bank, because they are lending depositors' money.

But the core question is, at some point, banks will want to squeeze you out or buy you out.

They might or they may just have to give up a bit of their business. They're more likely to just go out and hire McKinsey, though. I suspect the CFO of the bank will just order some very smart consultants to unpick the earnings from its personal lending operations. Do you think any bank has actually made money from consumer lending in the last 30 years? I don't think so. Even before that £30 billion cost of the PPI payouts. Even ignoring the PPI bill, they tend to lose money through credit losses in bad times of the cycle, and then they tend to out-compete each other furiously at good times in the cycle. I'm not sure that consumer lending is a bit of banking that they do that well.

Now, how many bits of banking can they afford to give up on? This is a different question. In any conversation with bank board members, they would all fight to keep the main current account, as they see that as a gateway product. They believe they can then make money by selling lots of other products through that account. Let them continue to think that way.

RON SUBER, President, Prosper Marketplace

Ron Suber is President of Prosper, one of America's first and largest peer-to-peer lenders. As President of Prosper Marketplace, Ron is responsible for developing and executing the business development strategy to attract borrowers to the site, as well as ensure a balance between institutional and retail investors on the Prosper platform. He brings more than 20 years' experience in sales, marketing and business development across the hedge fund, broker dealer and registered investment advisor industries. Before joining Prosper, Ron was Managing Director at Wells Fargo Securities.

About Prosper

Prosper is an online marketplace for consumer credit, connecting people who want to borrow money with people who want to invest money. Between 2009 and 2015, more than $2.5 billion in personal loans originated through the Prosper platform.

Who is the typical user of Prosper?

Prosper is an online marketplace for credit that offers access to consumer loans. We focus on three types of borrowers. The first is the person who wants to consolidate high-interest debt with a loan that offers a competitively priced fixed-rate and a fixed-term. The second type of borrower is someone who needs money for a large purchase. This could include things like a medical procedure, a home improvement project, purchasing a car, or funding a special occasion or travel. We also have people who are entrepreneurs who want to borrow on their personal credit for the purpose of their business. For all of these borrowers, Prosper offers access to fixed-rate, fixed-term loans that have no pre-payment penalty. On the other side, there are the investors—both individual and institutional—who want to help fund loan requests. We connect these three types of borrowers with these two types of investors.

I believe you are far more focused upon connecting institutional lenders and investors to borrowers, rather than being a pure peer-to-peer lender?

We are one of only two platforms in the US that offer individual investors access to marketplace lending. This group of investors has always been a core part of the Prosper platform, and we're looking for new ways to expand access and distribution. The UK has been a leader in this area, and we've learned from what has happened in that market. Many institutions buy loans from Prosper and then make them available to retail people in exchange traded, closed-end funds and in pool vehicles and in securitizations. We're very focused on expanding access to retail investors in the US with similar types of opportunities.

Are we seeing a fundamental change to the model of credit, or are we just seeing an evolution to an alternative model of credit?

I think we're seeing a multi-generational change in the way that Gen X and Gen Y are doing everything, from the way they book travel and listen to music, to the way they pay for things and move money, to the way they do banking, wealth management, borrow and invest. This creates a wave of opportunity that is far bigger than people think. A lot of times people just think these marketplaces are only doing debt consolidation, but that is just part of the total addressable market—it is much bigger than anyone believed. That's really evident in the numbers. Just take a look at Prosper for a moment. In the first quarter of 2015, Prosper facilitated $595 million dollars in loans through its platform, and in the second quarter we did $912 million.

And that's loans and margin lost to the traditional banking industry.
It is important people understand that Prosper works very closely with banks. The cash from our investors is held at our bank partners, there are banks that are equity investors in the company, there are banks buying loans, there are also banks securitizing loans through Prosper; and all loans on the platform are issued by banks. It's not accurate to say that Prosper doesn't work with banks. We are very complementary in many ways.

There's a view that the US model has forced new lenders to work with the banking community—or have you actively sought out the banking community to work with?
It's somewhere in between. There is a collision happening between Wall Street, Silicon Valley and the banks. We're telling our story about the benefits to investors and the benefits to borrowers, and how the rating agencies will now rate the loans. As a result, banks are now interested in working with us in various ways, including the big banks who are buying loans from Prosper and securitizing them with a single A rating from the credit rating agencies, as we saw with the Citigroup securitization that included $377 million in loans originated through Prosper in July 2015.

How do you see the lending marketplace structuring itself over time? Do you see a particular model emerging?
We're connecting people who want to invest their money, and get their money back with a return. That's debt crowdfunding. This is very different to equity crowdfunding, which is investing in projects or companies rather than lending. In debt crowdfunding, long term, I'd imagine a day when there is a portal where people all over the world could go on to a site and invest money. I also envisage a portal where borrowers and investors from around the world can go and meet. This is the beginning of innovation in these markets, and there is big growth in front of us. I'm more excited to be in this industry today than I've ever been.

So you see a few global, peer-to-peer funding platforms in the future?
I really do. As data becomes more readily available and funding and

capabilities of the leading platforms can process that data and create access to terms and loans for different people in different areas, it is possible. I also think investors around the world are all looking for the same thing. For example, I just got back from travels around the world, including China and Italy, telling the Prosper story. There is no place in the world that investors aren't looking for yields of short duration that reports interest daily and pays monthly, and that's exactly what we're doing here. There are also many benefits to the borrower around speed and convenience. People who apply for a loan through Prosper can be at home 24 hours a day and have a great experience. They don't have to put on a suit and visit the bank and hope that a loan officer would give them a loan, like my father did. Online marketplaces for credit are far more efficient for investors and borrowers, to meet and do business together.

In terms of access to data, that's what is being addressed by companies like Klarna, who assess risk based on your zip code. However, in a lot of the emerging markets you don't have access to that form of data enrichment.
What Klarna is doing is awesome. There's a lot of data out there, and they're leading the market. What's most important is what the platforms do with the data once they get it. In Asia, there are the "BATS", which includes Baidu, Alibaba, Tencent and some of the alternative lending sites. There's so much data that the marketplace in Asia can utilize to help them do credit. So it's not just getting all this traditional and alternative data, but what we can do with machine learning and some of the other big data analytic systems and new developments out there. This is really just the beginning.

How do you see Prosper changing over the coming years?
There will be economic change, employment change, interest rate change and more. There will also be an explosion of new platforms for finance, and each of these platforms is going to have to adjust and integrate over time. That's something that is going to tell a lot about the strengths of the different marketplaces: how are adjustments in rates, terms and credit made as the economy changes?

What will other P2P lenders be doing as you gear up for these changes?
I think we will end up like all industries, where there will be two or three leaders. If you look at drinks you have Coke and Pepsi; with credit cards you have MasterCard or Visa; or, in the US, you have AT&T and Verizon in the cellular business. In each industry, you have two or three leaders and then you have a mid-group and a smaller group, and I think that's what's ahead for us in marketplace lending. The leaders are being established now and they will pull away from the pack. You'll see tremendous growth of Prosper Marketplace and Lending Club here in the US, and then you'll see leaders converge on each other on the different continents.

And then each of the players starts to merge and acquire?
Sure. It will start with mergers and acquisitions within the continents and then across the continents. Funding Circle is an example where they started in the UK and then came to the US with an acquisition. You will see more of that over time. Some of the firms in Asia may be forced to look to acquire in other parts of the world, but that will take time, as they have a market that is much larger. For example, 500 million people of the 1.4 billion people of China are truly underbanked or poorly banked, given they don't have the equivalent of credit unions and regional banks. So the population of China loves what peer-to-peer offers, giving them a place to borrow and invest.

So in five to ten years we have a global, peer-to-peer credit marketplace that's taken the consumer credit and small business market away from the banking community. Will the banking community then be primarily a source of funding for these peer-to-peer marketplaces?
You're going to see banks and online marketplaces partner to give consumers access to the type of personal loans that Prosper offers. The bank introduces the customer to the product and then the marketplace does what it does best: assisting banks with underwriting, credit scores and customer service. Then the banks fund that loan. Banks often outsource key things, whether that's credit cards or ATM networks, and this may be another thing that banks learn to deal with as an outsourced function.

Do the banks understand this?

Some do, but we have a lot of work to do. I spend a lot of my time doing what we call *E, A & U*, which is *Education, Awareness and Understanding*. I've visited many banks in this country and they are starting to become more aware of what we are doing. They are seeing the volume of loans we're facilitating, the great customer service we're offering and the accurate evaluations that we're able to provide, as a financial technology company.

And I guess Lending Club's IPO helped (Lending Club went public in December 2015 with an $8 billion IPO)?

Lending Club's IPO was great for branding and awareness. I am a huge fan of what they're doing, I think they're great operators and they're great leaders of this industry. We are definitely a one–two in the marketplace here, and that gap is closing very rapidly.

I saw that PayPal recently announced it would lend to merchants based on digital footprints of volume and value processed through the PayPal network. Do you see many new models coming out like this, using data analytics to offer alternative ways of doing things compared to your own model?

It's even bigger than that. I think you're going to see many of the large tech companies get interested in FinTech. They are all able to take their networks and their large user base, and connect parties for anything from payments to loans. It's just a matter of time.

CASE STUDIES

THE BANK
START-UPS

MARK MULLEN, CEO of Atom Bank

Mark Mullen is the CEO and Co-Founder of Atom Bank and former CEO of First Direct. Atom Bank is a major new digital bank due to launch in the UK.

How did Atom Bank come about and how do you envision the launch of the bank?

It is fair to say that Atom Bank is Anthony Thomson's brainchild, in the sense that Anthony wanted to launch a new bank after leaving Metro Bank. He began having serious conversations with me in March 2013, and we started to discuss what sort of bank we could create. It was not just about whether there was a space for a new competitor in the industry, but what sort of bank we would develop.

We very quickly agreed that a "digital first" bank was a model worth building, considering all the changes we had seen in the industry, so we started to work more closely together around this vision. Anthony then went and found additional expertise and team members, so then we knew we had plenty of opportunity to change the market and increase competition, since the change of pace has been slow so far. In fact, it is strange to see such slow change when you have these incredible stresses and drivers for change, both technologically and behaviourally. The lack of change in the face of clear demand and opportunity now creates the focal points for the team as we move towards the launch of Atom Bank.

I recognise that you are looking to launch a radically different digital bank, but what exactly does this mean?

I think it's important to look at the entire business model.

Existing big banks can go and spend millions of dollars on building out their digital platform—and they will. But when it comes to being radically different, they simply cannot. To be radical you need to have a blank sheet of paper and build something from scratch. Then, every decision you make can be aligned to your vision, and can be aligned to the competitive advantages that you're trying to create. Whereas if you are in a big, established bank, every decision you make is compromised by the need for it to connect to whatever is already on the table—by way of legacy, existing customers, or existing products and services.

So, at a very simple level, we can be radically different because we don't have to create a single product we don't believe in. An existing bank has to make sure all existing products can be distributed by all channels, whether they are new or not. That is a fundamental difference between "radical new", as opposed to evolutionary or even revolutionary.

A radical approach in how we use this one-off opportunity to be new allows us to challenge and examine every single decision, every aspect of our supply chain and our business model. It allows us to potentially focus on a different set of customers. We don't have to be for everyone. It allows us to narrow the range of focus. In particular, it means that we are not trying to live up to a reputation, as we don't have one.

There are a few radical digital banks out there, like Simple and Moven. How do you see your vision playing out against those guys, for example?

Well, I have tremendous interest in and admiration for them, but these are front ends to banking, rather than banks. We had a discussion about whether it was necessary for us to build both the back end and the front end and, on balance, we decided to build the complete service, from product through customer service to delivery. We would own the entire supply chain. That's a much bigger ask, as we need to be an authorised financial institution—it's not just a technological play.

We believe we need to do this, as we are not then hostage to the agenda of the owners of the balance sheet or a service provider. We are not attached to something that has its own reputation and its own legacy issues. But clearly the downside is that you have a lot of work to do, and it becomes a lot more complex to build the entire enterprise. Having said that, there is plenty of room for different models.

What's really interesting about a Simple or Moven, and something I really believe in, is that they're not just technology players. Rather, they are new brands. It's very difficult for a long-established brand to get its customers to reconsider who it is and what it stands for. Whereas if you launch a new brand, you get that opportunity to establish a set of credentials from scratch.

I'm really quite surprised in many respects that a lot of bigger players in the UK have not looked at this potential avenue for growth. I suppose, given the context of the banking crisis, it may be understandable. Even so, these new firms are interesting for me not just as technology players, but also because of their brand play. Equally, these firms are different from Atom. They are not building the entire bank. They are building a piece of it, or a layer. We are not doing that. We are building the whole thing.

On the other side, I discovered recently there are other digital start-ups in the UK, such as Starling Bank (see following interview with Starling CEO Anne Boden). Do you see yourself as a player running alongside a bank like that, or is your vision different?

I don't know, to be absolutely honest. I don't know what the vision of Starling Bank is. I think it was called "Bank Possible" until fairly recently. I think Starling is a relatively new announcement and, as is always the case in this sector, you hear rumours about what someone is doing or might be doing, and they may or may not be true. Therefore, to be absolutely frank, I don't know what the scope of Starling Bank is or their vision.

In any case, we run our own race and we have a pretty clear idea of what we stand for, who we are and what we are building, and that's our all-consuming task. We aren't worrying about what other people are doing yet. We haven't got the head space for it. I also think there is plenty of opportunity for new players in the industry. I genuinely believe that. I think the base case assumption that a bank has to be big is no longer as true as it was, and potentially it's quite unattractive for customers, and may be even unattractive for regulators and taxpayers, as it comes with a lot of downsides.

I know from our previous conversations that your vision is different. For example, you aren't going to offer a typical bank call centre. You do have one, but it's just there for technical issues rather than financial questions. Is that correct?

Yes. If we haven't delivered a digital app that can help you with answers to not just basic questions but pretty sophisticated questions, then why did we bother building a digital bank? I absolutely believe in digital, and not just as an alternative channel. I've always believed in at as a fundamentally superior way of delivering banking services. The data doesn't lie. The UK's most satisfied customers in the banking sector are customers who use digital channels to consume banking services. That's not a recent phenomenon, as you can trace this back 15 years or more.

The irony is that the less you see and speak to your customers, the more satisfied they are with you. I know this is a paradox, but they feel better informed and more in control of their money as they are the ones making the decisions. I don't think it's an accident that some of the oldest digital platforms are in the investment markets, for example. These platforms have proven to have longevity, when other aspects of the personal selling environment have declined in popularity and, indeed, represent higher risks to the distributors.

So, in that context, if you are building that sort of model, you still want to provide a support service for people, and you want to make that available and convenient. However, the primary role of that support service is to help answer technical questions. It is to answer the "How do I do this?" questions, as opposed to performing the transaction for the customer. I think our customers are more than capable of doing the latter themselves but, if there is a problem with the app, we will be on hand to help.

Will you be offering the typical banking services, such as deposit accounts, credit cards, etc?

We want to be a proper, full-service competitor for both personal and business banking. There are a lot of new entrants—and some not so new—to the market that are essentially niche players. They are perfectly respectable and admirable enterprises. For us though, we want to go after the current account market and offer something new and fresh. So yes, we will certainly include what you might describe as the fundamental banking services and bank accounts.

Again, taking your experience with First Direct, you have got that knowledge of how to deal with customers remotely without branches. I am guessing you will still have the usual access to ATMs through the LINK network and all those sort of things?

We are looking at it and have a lot of dialogue with people on how our customers can get access to such services, and what they expect from the orthodox banking channel. For example, as long as cash is still a big part of our society, we will offer debit cards and access to the ATM network. We are having a big debate over cheques, though. We are not big fans of them, and we would rather not incur the cost of a solution that is many years out of date. There are some practicalities where you have to move towards customers' needs, however, and not compromise how they come to you. These are real debates at Atom right now.

One of your interesting moves is to base the head office in Durham. Is there a specific reason why you chose there?

There are a whole bunch of reasons, not the least of which is that Anthony is originally from Newcastle. I have worked in Leeds for many years, and I know it is possible to build and run a world-class business in the banking category outside London.

There is a lot to be said for being outside London, not least because it's an expensive place to base a business. If you don't need to be in London, it doesn't make sense to place a business where the ground rents and employment costs are so high, and where the markets are so massively competitive.

Durham is appealing as the real estate is less expensive; but cheap land gets you nowhere when you're building a high-end company. Importantly, there are fabulous universities; a huge population catchment area; and the city is well connected by trains to north and south. Equally, there is actually not that much in the way of alternative financial institutions, so we are offering an alternative employment proposition in the local market. That's quite an attractive thing to do.

Bear in mind that we are also a digital bank and, as a consequence, there is no need for us to put the bank in an expensive place, as ultimately the customer would have to pay for it. This is why it made no sense to base ourselves in an expensive location, but in one with the most talent availability and growth opportunities.

Looking ahead, are there some milestones we should be looking out for?

When can we get the first Atom bank account opened? It's difficult to give dates Chris, as I don't want to commit to them. We want to have completed the launch end-to-end within one year of opening our doors, so there is an awful lot to do. We don't intend to open with all products and services from day one, and are more conscious about the need to get it right than the need to do it all. Our aim is to build our reputation on high quality, and we can be small and grow well through that approach. The alternative is to try to be big early and encounter problems, and so we know which way we would rather go. Overall, the implementation will take about a year, but we certainly want to start that journey in the second half of 2015. Those are the plans.

I know one of the biggest challenges is getting the banking license, but equally you have an experienced team and might be able to fast-track that cycle, since you have all done this before?

Yes, to an extent. One of the nice things about the process is that we're doing our own work. We haven't outsourced or contracted work to any consultancy. Our bank is designed by our team. We have written our own documents and applications to the regulators. We have taken in subject matter experts to help out in specific parts of it but, ultimately, it has been blueprinted and designed from the ground-up by us. A lot of this comes down to with whom you surround yourself with, and we've got some hugely talented people. It's funny, as I was talking to the team during the briefing this morning and I kind of said, "You're not looking over your shoulders saying someone else did it". Whatever happens at Atom will happen because we did it. Consequently if it's good, we get to pat ourselves on the back. If it's bad, there's no one else to blame. I am confident we have got the right talent and I am sure I speak for everyone that works there when I say: how many opportunities will you get to build a bank from the blueprint plans on a clean sheet of paper through to the reality?

It is also important to have the funding to make these things happen. What sort of people are involved in backing Atom Bank?
As you probably know we have Neil Woodford's fund, Jon Boulton, and Jim O'Neill, the noted economist who coined the term "BRICS" and was previously with Goldman Sachs. Anthemis and Polar are also involved, alongside our 20 or so original angel investors, so it is an interesting mix of City institutions, fairly big names and influential backers from the North East. It creates a clear link to the City and to where we are based. That has been very helpful in building the bank locally, as well as building the broader story of the bank in the City. It is also reassuring when people choose to back you. It is a vote of confidence. That adds momentum to a team, especially when these investors are pretty shrewd, renowned and respected investors.

If you are outlining the vision of what you would like to see at Atom Bank five years from now, do you have an idea of what that will be?
I want it to be a major brand with a fabulous reputation. I don't need it to be huge, just special, well respected, successful, reliable and sustainable. If I wanted anything, it would to be recognised as a special brand doing something quite remarkable in its industry. If I had all my wishes, it would be respected and recognised outside the banking industry, too. Then it becomes a brand, not just a bank. That's what I really want.

Who will be the typical customer of the bank?

That used to be a relatively straightforward question to answer if you looked at any innovation adoption curve. You could pretty much say, if you were going to invest in new technology, you could go to the professional services sector such as teachers, accountants and so on. Or go to new students and graduates. If you look at the adoption across the age spectrum, you see that there are massive differences in every age demographic. What we have concluded, therefore, is that there is a mindset about digital adoption, and certainly a relationship between financial literacy and digital literacy. So, if you follow the orthodox thinking within the industry, you are probably looking at people who switch banks in their late 20s or early 30s, but we want to appeal to a broad generation. So, I may be wrong on this, but I think our primary appeal will be to a median age around 25 or 26. These people are not bound to the industry that I grew up in, and they are absolutely using technology on an increasing basis to manage their life and money.

ANNE BODEN, CEO of Starling Bank

Starling Bank is the name of a new challenger bank being set up in London. The bank's early days show how challenging the process of creating a new bank can be. Nevertheless, there is grand ambition to shake up the banking establishment, as outlined in this interview with founder and CEO Anne Boden.

A lot of people haven't heard of Starling Bank. Can you give us an introduction and background to what you are doing, and the plans for the bank?

We're creating the first "smart bank" in the UK. A bank that focuses on making money easy for people, so that they can answer the important questions like "Can I really afford this?", send and spend money with friends, and avoid nasty surprises and ridiculous charges. It's the next generation of banking focused on customers rather than products.

In terms of background, I started my career in Lloyds Banks in the early 1980s, and the sad thing is that not a lot has really changed since then. The big banks have added some channels, and we've moved from branch to phone to internet to mobile, but the product, the model, hasn't changed.

At the moment digital banking is just like branch-based banking on a screen. You're provided with what comes down to a self service terminal, which is a bit like playing radio on a TV, or putting sales brochures on the internet... it kind of works, but we can do so much better.

We're looking to make that leap. To create a truly smart bank that applies modern technology directly to solving customer problems, with a simple, easy-to-use interface.

How will Starling Bank be different?
Retailing has been radically changed by Amazon, Broadcast TV by Netflix, music by the likes of Spotify, social media by Facebook, but banking is still stuck in the last century, because the big banks are stuck with hundreds of old systems, their legacy IT.

We all know that the vast majority of the banks today are based on technology built in the 1960s and 1970s, enhanced from the 1980s onwards. These systems have just had more and more channels and propositions layered on, but the core structure hasn't changed, and that's the problem that they all have.

We're not building a traditional bank, we're not taking an off-the-shelf banking package and adding a prettier interface, biometrics, and video chat. We're building services for digitally savvy customers that make their lives easier.

So yes, we're starting from the customer needs and wants, rather than starting from a specific product or a package. And that's a big difference. It doesn't constrain your thinking in old ways. It changes the game.

And the results are night and day. It's the difference between looking up where you want to go, planning when you want to leave and phoning a taxi firm, versus pressing one button to book on Uber as you stand on the street. It's banking turned upside down. Customer driven and technology enabled— the bank for the digital age. That's what we are really aiming to become.

I am intrigued to know the vision of your bank model. Other banks are using multiple distribution systems from branches through call centres. Will that be part of your model? Or are you a pure digital play on mobile, tablet and other devices of choice?
Our soon-to-be customers drive all of our decisions, and from the interviews we do a few times a week we've confirmed that the smartphone generation don't want to go to a branch to deal with their everyday banking. They want

to watch TV, pay a bill, check how they are doing, and be told if anything out of the ordinary happens. Otherwise they want banks to stay out of the way, so that they can get on with their lives.

So we won't have branches, but we will deliver the best proposition on a mobile device. A smart bank that does an amazing job and stays out of the way.

You've mentioned the models of Amazon and Facebook, and the idea that you will be using Facebook. How will that work?
Successful internet platforms have a lot to teach banks. From being able to sign up in a couple of minutes, to really elegant flows, and that continual push to improve, test, and develop ever better services. Banks obviously have regulatory constraints, and the need to deliver a rock solid, secure service, but the lessons are still there.

In that respect we will be more like Amazon or Facebook than a traditional bank. But in terms of using and connecting with Facebook or any of the big internet platforms, it's an interesting question. We're testing a variety of ideas on how customers might want to connect with us and with their friends. Most of are sceptical of any bank connecting with their social networks… rightly so, when you look at the current reputation of the big banks. But we are a very different kind of bank, and there are some interesting areas where it might work.

Will you be a full-service bank from day one?
To begin with, we will be only offering a current account with a bit of saving and borrowing. We're focused on helping customers with their everyday banking needs. But the world is changing. As I think I mentioned earlier, the old model of the big banks capturing a customer and then trying to sell them lots of different products through lots of channels is going away. There will be lots of new entrants taking pieces of the pie, and there will be a lot of disaggregation. We will soon see a very different model.

How far have you got with your plans?
We've put together a world-class team to deliver this proposition. It's an

amazing mix of banking experts and start-up talent. We've got people from the big banks, GoCardless, Hailo, the US, Spain, and further afield. When you're doing something this big with a real vision, the right people find you. We have offices in Farringdon, London. We are well into the banking license application process, and we're really taking off. The support from everyone is just amazing.

There are some other banks that are challenging the model, like Moven and Simple in the States and Atom Bank in the UK, which is also launching soon. Do you see yourselves as similar to those, or are there any radical differences?

Simple and Moven blazed a trail. They were in that first generation of banking improvements, great veneers, bolted onto other people's banking licenses, or traditional banking packages. They really showed what's possible, and we've got a lot of respect for what they did.

We're a group of people very experienced at running banks, together with a group of people obsessed with making a difference to customers, together with a group of world class engineers, and we're creating a service, a platform built from the ground up for one purpose.

We're the next generation. There is no veneer, no join. Just the most advanced, real-time contextual banking system ever created with the purpose of helping customers.

As far as Atom is concerned, they say very little in public, so I don't really know a lot. I believe they are offering a product range on packaged software. Competition is good and the market is big enough for more non-traditional, multi-product banking models such as Atom and ourselves.

What technologies are you talking about here? Will you be offering wearables and such like?

The important thing here is to deliver what customers want. What we are creating is a bank that moves at the pace of consumers. In a traditional bank, an idea is created and a year or so later, it is implemented. The world is moving faster and faster, so things could be very different this time next year. We don't know what is going to happen with the

Internet of Things, but we will be able to respond quickly if such a market develops.

The important thing is that we focus on what we do well, which is to provide the best service for a product, and making sure we can plug into the other services. We aim to be quick: quick to respond in a timeframe that our customers expect from other industries, and in a way that we have never been able to achieve in the banking industry before.

Do you have a vision of where you will be in 2020?

I am highly ambitious and our sights are aimed at changing banking across the world. There is a new generation of smart banks coming and we're leading the way in the UK. The world of financial services will be radically different in 2020, there will be many niches, many players, and models we haven't even seen yet.

The banks and companies that succeed will be those that can adapt the fastest to all of these changes, while staying completely focused on delivering truly great services for their customers. People ask me what our secret feature is. Is there something that I can't tell them about? And I tell them that it isn't about secret features. It's about fantastic execution and rapid adaptation. It's about taking care of people and helping them take care of themselves, by making money easy.

RENÉ FRIJTERS, Founder and CEO of Knab Bank

René Frijters is Founder and CEO of Knab. Knab is a bank built with customers and takes the financial situation and the interests of its customers as the starting point. He vows to be completely transparent with fees, and describes Knab as "socially conscious", encouraging customers to allocate part of their savings to selected charities. Before Knab was founded, he was CEO of the Alex Investment Bank for 12 years. In Aegon's latest results summary, there are some interesting comments. Knab, Aegon's online bank in the Netherlands, has been recognized as having the best new investment concept for its simple, convenient and accessible investing. Knab's innovations have now attracted more than 50,000 customers, following a strong increase in 2014. Gross deposits tripled to one billion euros. This was mainly the result of the continued strong performance of Knab, Aegon's online bank. Knab accounted for 0.6 billion euros of gross deposits in the fourth quarter, up from 42 million euros in the same quarter of 2013.

Can you give me some background on Knab and who is behind it?

Knab was founded in September 2012. The initiative was started in mid 2009 by Rachelle van der Linden, Marcel Kalse and me. Rachelle has a marketing background. Marcel and myself were heavily involved in Alex Vermogensbank, a stockbrokerage that we had set up in 1999. Alex Vermogensbank was sold in 2007 for 380 million Euros to Binck Bank. I was co-founder of Alex and Marcel head of business development.

For setting up Knab we needed a banking license and a lot of funding, not only for the necessary investments but also for the required capital. Because of this we contacted several financial institutions to see if they wanted to support our idea. Aegon Bank (part of Aegon Insurance) was enthusiastic about our vision and became a hundred percent shareholder at the end of 2010, the moment we started building the bank.

What is the bank trying to achieve and how did you see the market opportunity before you launched?
The reason why we started the bank is threefold.

First, we wanted to give customers a better insight into their financial situation, because increasingly they are becoming more and more responsible for their financial future. For example, governments are reducing tax-facilities to build up pensions, to deduct interest on your mortgage, etc and companies are moving away from defined benefit to defined contribution systems, so pension risks are transferred to the employees themselves.

Second, we wanted to build a bank which really acts in the interest of its customers, instead of only talking about customer-centricity while the company tries to earn as much money as possible without telling the customer at the same time.

Third, we wanted to give customers real attention. Preferred and private banking concepts completely fail in the Dutch market. Only a very small group of customers really get the attention and the pro-active advice they require from their bank.

Has that view of the market changed at all since you launched?
Not really. Because of the economical crisis, we see more and more laws coming in, which strengthens the need to get better insight into your financial situation yourself. Banks try to be more customer-centric, but they change very slowly for various reasons (impact on P&L, legacy, reorganisations, compliance).

Why is the bank called Knab?
The name "Knab" says everything about our intention. Knab is "bank"

The Bank Start-ups 369

spelled backwards. We try to work in exactly the opposite way to the established banks. We put the customer—which, in Dutch, is *"K"lant*— first, and the "B"onus last, as in we don't pay bonuses.

And do you offer all the usual bank services, such as deposit accounts, debit and credit cards, chequebooks, loans, mortgages, and so on?

Yes, we do. At the moment we offer a current account, a savings account, term deposits, a credit card, two investment products (Execution Only and Asset Management) and a lot of services and tools. In fact, we offer our customers a PFM platform together with a bank. So our tools and services are even more important than our products.

You talk about Banking-as-a-Service—could you explain that a little more?

Traditional banks live from product push. They talk about customer-centricity, but their focus is on selling as many products as possible. We don't believe in this model and really try to stand on the customers' side, by offering them all kind of services to improve their financial insight and situation. Let me give you three examples.

Personal (highest) Interest Service.

With this service we monitor the interest savings rates of the customer's accounts at other banks, and warn the customer when a change has taken place. Even when a competitor of Knab offers a higher interest rate than Knab, we send the customer an alert to make him/her aware.

Smart Cash Management Service.

With this service we automatically transfer money from the current account to the savings account when the amount on the current account exceeds a customized threshold. And we do the opposite when an overdraft occurs on the current account. At traditional banks customers pay 14 percent on the overdraft, while they get one percent on their savings at the same time. We see this as a kind of robbing of customers and refuse to do it.

Smart Alerting.
Based on all the data we have, we send our customers alerts to call their attention to potential financial gains and risks. We have built about a hundred of these alerts, and they are only being sent to customers if it's relevant according to his or her profile. This also comes with an "subscription-like" payment model. A customer subscribes to one of our services (basic, plus, premium or business) and then gets a bank that is on his/her side.

You also talk about Knab as a Digital Bank—how do you define a Digital Bank?

Knab is a hundred percent digital. We don't have any branches and will not have them in the future (except for, perhaps, a flagship store in Amsterdam). Customers can do all their activities via internet and mobile apps. They can reach our customer service desk via phone, (video) chat and social media (FB and Twitter). Signing of legal contracts can be done using your bankcard—the same applies for changing your address, you card limits, etc.

What about customer onboarding, how you deal with KYC and all that?

The onboarding process is a hundred percent automated. Customers can open a current account with us within five minutes. The only thing that they have to do is transfer money from an existing account at another bank, with exactly the same name, to Knab, to identify themselves. We do all kinds of checks and balances (EVA-check, world compliance check, etc) in the background, fully automated.

Is the bank using any form of social media outreach and, if yes, how?

We have introduced Knab Live. Knab Live is our community platform where customers can give feedback about our services and bring up their ideas. It's a hundred percent open and transparent. We also organise a monthly Knab Open session at our office. Each customer is welcome and we use these events to co-create our products and services together with our customers. And, of course, we interact with our (potential) customers via social media.

You are a Dutch-based bank, and many Dutch folks seem more digital than elsewhere. Would you agree, and what's the typical sort of customer you are attracting?

In Holland we have a very good infrastructure and 95 percent of the people are online. Most of our customers are between 35 and 55 years old, but in comparison to the Dutch population, we are more dominant in the age group between 20 and 35. Our customers are well-educated and most of them have more than double the average Dutch income.

I note that you've achieved quite a high take-up of new customers compared to other banks. Is that through heavy promotion, advertising, or are you offering special deals on interest or other account opening incentives?

It's a combination of factors.

First, banking is about trust and we see that, after two years, people believe we are here to stay.

Second, after a difficult start with only one proposition (premium), we introduced in November 2013 a Spotify-like type of proposition. Customers can start saving with us without paying a subscription fee and grow within our bank (Basic, Plus, Premium).

Third we have changed our ATL-campaign from a more "brand advertising" type of campaign to a more "proposition" type of campaign, where we communicate concrete advantages (two-times interest, fixed subscription fee, etc).

Fourth, we started a multi-channel distribution strategy: partnerships/ channels, comparison sites (referrals), independent advisors, Aegon customers.

We started doing "fact-based marketing". So, we measure every step a customer makes, do A/B testing on our site, etc.

Finally, we offer one of the top three interest rates in the savings market.

All these things helped us to grow our business, with more than 40,000 customers in 2014.

From a marketing perspective, does the bank have any brand values, and what are they?

The brand values of Knab are:

a.   We build the bank together with our customers.

b.   We share our tools and knowledge to help our customers to get better insight in their financial situation, so they can get the most out of their money.

c.   We offer outstanding service, 7 days a week, 16 hours a day.

d.   We are a hundred percent transparent.

e.   We always keep innovating to make maximum use of new technological possibilities.

Specifically, are you providing a service that is different to other banks and, if so, how?

Yes, and maybe this a one of the biggest differentiators. Although we are a digital bank, we believe that customer service is one of the most important things to become successful and to create ambassadors. The employees who have contact with our customers are all selected based on the right "DNA". Can they really listen to the customer and are they able "to stand in the customers shoes" when they talk to them. Are they able to "over deliver" and "surprise" customers. That's the way we like it and so, why shouldn't customers like to be treated this way?

We have a Net Promoter Score (NPS) of +26 and customer service is an important part of this value (Dutch financial institutions have a negative value of -20 on average). It's impossible for traditional players to reach this level. They have a product- and procedure-based service instead of a customer-based service.

Looking ahead, how do you see the longer-term vision for the bank?

We really need to focus on personal finance and on customer experience. These will be the differentiating areas for the future, because products will become more and more commodities. We will enlarge our products and service offering and add on services like P2P-financing, mortgages, and, perhaps, bitcoins. The last one isn't possible today because of rules and regulations set by Dutch Central Bank.

Finally, what would you like the bank to be best known for?
We like to be known as the most customer-driven bank.

CRAIG DONALDSON, CEO of Metro Bank

As CEO of Metro Bank, Craig Donaldson is responsible for providing executive leadership to the bank's rapidly expanding team. He is chartered with guiding the bank's evolution from fresh, new entrant in retail banking to trusted financial services partner to millions of UK customers. From helping define Metro Bank's brand values, to hiring its inaugural employees and ensuring that the bank's staff deliver daily customer satisfaction, Craig has been instrumental to Metro Bank from day one. Craig's prior roles included managing director of retail products at RBS, as well as senior roles with Barclays and HBOS. He has a degree in management and technology from the University of Bradford.

You've been on this rollercoaster ride with Metro Bank since the start. Perhaps you could give us a perspective on the origins of the bank and how you got to where you are today?

The origins of the bank are based on convenience. Banks have forgotten how to deliver service to customers in the right way, and in the way they want them. So our founders, Vernon Hill and Anthony Thompson, discussed the situation of banking in Britain and Anthony convinced Vernon to come to the UK. Vernon's model is all about building for convenience and providing superior service across every channel. Our customers are empowered to bank with us, however, wherever and whenever they want to. Yes, we have stores, and we are rapidly growing our footprint, which will continue, as with the development of all our channels.

The stores are open seven days a week, 362 days a year, from 8am to 8pm, and we have great internet banking services and telephony. Our local contact centre is open 24–7, with two lines: one if you want to talk to a person, and one if you want to talk to a computer. It is all about service and convenience and giving the customer a choice. Our job is to allow the customers to be in control. That's why our stores are tangible.

We were the first bank able to produce contactless chip and PIN cards within minutes in store for new and existing accounts, which meant we were able to give customers a different experience. If you think about our personal mobile app, we give customers the opportunity to temporarily block and unblock their cards—something no other bank lets you do. For customers, that's been a fantastic delivery service, as often they've just mislaid their card. To me, technology is not about digital channels. It is about how you interact with customers through every channel.

Our service convenience comes from a proven model built in America through Vernon's previous bank, Commerce Bank. We now leverage that model through every channel in the UK. This is how we interact and are able to deliver unparalleled levels of service to our customers.

When Metro Bank opened with a store-based model, it had some unusual features about welcoming dogs, and having coin convertors in the foyers. A lot of people might think these are just gimmicks. Does it have any substance?

Absolutely. For example, take the idea that we give out lollipops to children or water bowls and treats for dogs. This is because we want to be there for our customers. We want you to bring your children into the store, and make it easy for you to do so as we know parents have very busy lives, and for them to be able to bank whenever they want, makes life that little bit easier. We want you to bring your dog into the store, and make it easy for you to do so. It is why, for the last three years, we are the only bank to have won a gold award from Mumsnet for being family friendly, and that is for both our customers and our colleagues. So is it a gimmick to have lollipops and toilets in all of our stores? Is it a gimmick to have baby changing facilities? Well again, Mumsnet have given us their award for innovation for those things. So to me, that's not a gimmick. We've also won the Kennel Club, Open For Business With Dogs Award for the last three years in a row, as they recognise who we are and what we do for all of our customers. We keep winning these well-publicised awards and, as a result, we win a lot of business and customers through those little things that matter. So no, we don't think these are gimmicks—we are telling customers we are open for business, want to serve them and it works.

I know you have been growing aggressively. Last time we spoke, I think you had just over 20 stores and were opening around 14,000 accounts a month. What are the numbers today?

We are now at 32 stores and will be at 41 by the end of this year. Our aim is to open almost one a month as we go through 2015. We are opening around 18,000 accounts per month now, as we open more stores. Such growth allows us to build proper relationships with our customers and businesses. We deliver service and convenience, and as a result, our customers tend to stay with us. I would rather win a customer because of what we offer through service in stores, than because we have an offer that gives £100 for an account opening and then they leave as someone else offers £150. Our contract with our customers is really clear and I think that's a better model for the long term.

Before you existed, First Direct topped the awards for customer service and satisfaction. Is that your benchmark? Is that who you mark yourself against?

No. Our benchmark is John Lewis. To me, John Lewis is streets ahead when you look at all their services. We did a piece of work where we benchmarked ourselves against Apple, John Lewis, Disney, Richer Sounds, Pret, and Lush. We do our own benchmarking against those that offer the best service and convenience through all channels—not other banks.

In that context, if I look at the new challenger banks, they tend to talk digital only. How integral is the store in this offering?

Being part of the community is where we want to be—we know that customers want to be able to go into store if they need to. However, we also want to offer the best in digital, mobile and internet banking, but having the high street presence to connect locally with the community is very important to us. To me, I want to be offering the very best in every channel, not just to a select few because it is cheaper for me as a bank. Service and convenience is all about giving customers choice, and what customers want is the ability to choose which channels they want to interact with their bank, and not the other way round.

If you look at John Lewis, they have click-and-collect services. I can buy goods from them on my iPad for delivery; or I can buy it in one of their stores; or I could collect it at 2pm the next day in store or even from my local Waitrose when I am doing my shopping; or I could take it there and then. That's brilliant service, as it provides options, and banking needs to provide that style of service—when, where and how is what we need to remember.

I don't think you need 2,000 stores to be able to provide a successful service, but I don't understand why customers would compromise when banks could deliver the same great digital offering with a store option in their community as well.

On a storefront, people such as Brett King are saying that the cost overhead of stores is too high and adds unnecessary costs for the customer. Equally, customers don't want stores, especially millennial customers who don't feel they need to see anyone face-to-face and get advice. I guess you would disagree?

I think it is important that the customer is given the choice as to how they wish to interact with the bank—they are the customer! But there are times when people really do want face-to-face service, no matter what. Have you ever lost a card? Do you want to wait until it's posted out to you in seven days' time or do you want to pop in and wait three minutes whilst it is being printed for you in store? I think people would come into a store for that. Do you want to count your coins at home, or do you want to go to Sainsbury's and Tesco's and pay an 8 percent fee for that? Or do you want to use our coin counters for free?

If you look at our account openings in the first half of last year, 77 percent of our customers had their accounts opened in 15 minutes, from first keystroke to last keystroke. That is a full account opening with Know Your Customer and delivery of a personalised card and chequebook. That is 15 minutes from the first keystroke to the last keystroke. No other bank can do that.

I don't know where you keep your valuables, but for a lot of small businesses, they want to keep it locked away in a big safe. We offer safety deposit boxes in our in-store vaults. It is a tangible offering which most high street banks no longer offer their customers unless they are private banking customers.

We work with our communities to build relationships not only with personal banking customers but with local businesses, too. We had over 11,000 school children come into our stores as part of the national curriculum, so they could be educated on personal finance through our Metro Money Zone program. We have worked at over 2,000 community events close to our stores to help local communities. To me, being part of the community is massively important and we can only truly do that with our stores.

If stores are the focus, what is the role of digital capabilities? I remember you mentioned to me using Twitter, for example. What does that mean?

We don't market through Twitter, but we can answer customer as well as potential customer queries through Twitter. Our social media team is bigger than our marketing team, because we want to be able to work with customers at a time that works for them. My view is that the banks aren't trusted generally in the UK, so what's the point in banks spending millions of pounds on advertising, so they can tell people what they don't believe? It's an old fashioned way of thinking. My view is that customers want answers when they want them and, for many, social media is where they expect to get answers these days, so you've got to be there. Then it is choice so that, if they want to be able to get a new card instantly, they can walk into a store and get it. Some may want to be able to check something out on their phone and use the app, others want to make a call.

If you're only a digital bank you can only offer digital services. By offering a multi-channel service the customers can be in control across all of their needs, and my job is to support them in doing that. I think the stores are a massive part of that. Two thousand stores is too many, but 250–300 stores is the perfect number, if you truly are going to part of a community. I don't know how you do that if you are just digital.

Looking at the digital side of things, I am a big exponent of reinventing core systems. Your core system is only five years old but I get the sense that you're slightly different.

We are very much where banks want to be, and probably trailblazed as a bank by building Software-as-a-Service (SaaS) in banking. We use Temenos core banking software on what we call "pay as you grow", and therefore you keep your cost base appropriate to the size of your organisation. That was massively important to us.

The thing that is often missed is that so much of what we do is a straight through process—we fulfil all things at the point of sale, in-store.

When you walk into the stores we can open your account end-to-end in 15–30 minutes. That's print your card; give you a chequebook; set up your internet banking; and download the mobile app. If you are at another bank, they need to send you multiple pieces of paper in the post. They send it to you and it take days or weeks to process. We do it all straight through process at the point of sale. So our cost base is where the customer is and not in huge back offices.

Equally, one of the big challenges for digital banks is KYC.

Absolutely. Eighty percent of our customer account openings are straight through process. We are really very, very good at how we open accounts. This means customers who try to be naughty can be caught at point of sale. Our machine checks every passport and document at the point of sale. We can stop third party frauds straight away.

Also, the way we have built our systems, they are much simpler to use. We can really hire for attitude and train for skill. Our biggest advocates are our colleagues, who sell our brand to their families, friends and their businesses because they believe in what we are doing.

That is not forgetting that we are also an SME bank. We do retail and business banking for small and medium sized businesses, and I have many small businesses that use our coin counting services, for example. We have a dry cleaner who needs cash management services, and who wants to be able to get coins and notes out. There are a lot of the SMEs out there that have cash needs and, to fulfil those cash needs, you need a store environment. I think the SME market is the most underserved.

I want to take a view on the future. Vernon's ambition was to have 200 branches by 2020 and to get to an IPO within a decade. How on track is this?

In January last year we went out and raised a further £370 million of equity to fund our growth, so we do not need to raise any more money at the moment. We have now had six quarters of reducing losses and that will continue every quarter as we grow into profitability. As for an IPO, we are definitely considering it in 2016 but that is a decision for later this year, early next year. As for being on track, we are probably 18 months ahead of where we hoped to be.

As for additional stores, my view is that by 2020 we will have around 130–150 stores, as we are investing a lot more into digital channels. As we grow, we can make a decision on where we grow, rather than carrying all the legacies, and so we can grow appropriately with technology.

In terms of the landscape five years from now, will these new start-ups and challengers still be on your radar, or will your radar be focused on the incumbent banks?

I genuinely hope there are new challengers. The more diversity we have in the banking ecosystem, the better the UK will be. One of my concerns is that we don't need more of the same monoline offerings appearing, like savings with mortgages. We need people coming to market offering different things to attract different people. By 2020 I would like to see well-performing challenger banks bringing differential offerings to the market, not just a bunch of imitations.

ROBERTO FERRARI, General Manager of CheBanca!

Roberto Ferrari is the General Manager of CheBanca! and Board Member of Mediobanca Innovation Services, the IT and operations service company of Mediobanca Group in Milan. Since doing a degree in Economics and Business Administration, he has spent time in very large enterprises, such as Procter&Gamble in Rome, where he led sales development of franchising network and product marketing. In 2006 he entered Mediobanca Group as Marketing & Partnership VP in Compass, the consumer finance and payments company of the financial group, where he was in charge of marketing, product and business development.

What does innovation mean at such an exciting historic moment?
Everyone is talking about innovation these days. The hardest thing is to manage the technology in order to provide new, simple solutions to clients. Innovation is a means, not an end. As Leonardo da Vinci said, "Simplicity is the highest level of sophistication." Never forget that. One can claim to have truly changed the market when one's innovative solutions are adopted by the masses of clients, thus modifying the dynamics of the system itself. So, it takes a lot of intuition, speed, vision and a sense of priorities. It must be the customer experience that one wants to develop.

What does innovation mean for the banking and finance sector?

It is a huge challenge because the sector is hyper-regulated, and in Italy even more so. But, at the same time, it is an adventure because the sector truly lives on schemes, services models, and infrastructures that are decades old, and inadequate for digitalisation. Therefore, it may be more difficult when compared to other markets that have already been transformed (music, publishing, and travel come to mind) but this does not mean that it is any less intriguing. It is necessary to have more strength and decision-making in challenging the status quo and not be stopped by the first objection that "this can't be done". If one tries hard enough there is always a way to change things. Always.

CheBanca! is a start-up: what goal did it start with?

We can define CheBanca! as a FinTech bank, a new bank. It began in 2008, precisely when Italy was reaching its historic record for the number of bank teller windows (!). It had another vision, to change the model of bank retailing in Italy and to position itself where the market would be heading. It is a native multichannel bank, focused increasingly more on its digital affluent. It acts strategically as a funding arm of our shareholder Mediobanca, guaranteeing the parent company direct access to collecting. But it does so in a disruptive manner in respect to the market, challenging from the inside the various status quo and consolidated business models. We have done it with physical retailing, with customer service and products, and we are doing it with payments and investment advisory. It may be a long path but with a very clear vision. We have over 500,000 clients and we have 13 billion in overall collections, even having passed through the darkest phase of the country's economic and financial crisis. For years, now, we have been the best online bank for customer satisfaction. I'd say that's quite a success. But we won't stop here.

Thinking in general of the start-up ecosystem, is it a resource or a threat for traditional banking?

Start-ups are the lifeblood of every sector. Challenging the market, bringing innovation, forcing incumbents to move, nourishing the competition and, thus, in the final analysis, favouring the improvement of the ecosystem. If someone sees them as a threat they are making a mistake. Those who wall themselves in are destined for extinction, it is just a question of time. We work with FinTech start-ups, we develop services. It is very good for us. And we help them grow and get stronger.

What is the most explosive idea that you have seen in recent months?
The one that most impressed me is IMPS, a real-time mobile payments project in India. Just during the month of December in 2014, it registered over 9.5 million real-time transactions, mainly via mobile—not necessarily smartphones—surpassing by a good five times its results from the preceding year. It has a user park of over 70 million digital account holders. A boom, and it is just the beginning. To sum it up, it managed to apply the success of a scheme like that of M-PESA to a population of over 1.2 billion individuals. This is something that is truly breaking the mould and changing the game. True innovation is measured by the number of people whose lives it can truly improve. We tend to look towards the West, primarily the US, but I have the impression that innovation in the world of banking and finance will increasingly come from the south and east. There are many other examples in Africa, China, Australia, Korea…

And the external actors, like Facebook and Apple, who are making space in their sectors: what role will they have?
They will have the role of challenger, very strong because based on economies of scale and on client bases that are unattainable for any bank in the world. But I don't think they will become banks in the true sense of the word. It is much more probable that they will concentrate on the most mass market and easiest to manage parts internationally, like with payments. It will not be easy to get out of the US. It will be a long path, just like it was for PayPal. I wouldn't underestimate Amazon and Google. The first one already manages payments globally, the second has such a mass that it can do what it wants. There will surely be great disruptions from them as well. The wave is long, it started with PayPal, which was born in 1998.

Bitcoin is having yet another delicate moment: are we at the end of its trajectory or in a transformation phase? What future do you see?

Bitcoin is the second attempt at creating a real-time, global, digital currency outside of the control schemes of the central banks. With this, other virtual currencies were created just about everywhere. In my opinion, though, bitcoin is still not a true currency and suffers from the same mechanisms that brought about its success one year ago: too much volatility and zero regulations. A year ago, it registered a positive value and, so, everyone was enthusiastic. Now, it seems like a failure—because bitcoin is perceived speculatively, as an investment, and not as an exchange value. The history of money teaches that exchange rates and values cannot be too volatile. This is the limitation of bitcoin, though I don't think it's impossible to resolve. But, above and beyond its future, whether it will be successful or not—and this will definitely take years and years—bitcoin is a sign that the current banking and transaction system on a global scale must confront digitalisation. Currently, it is too old, too obsolete. A different transnational system is necessary, that functions like the digital economy: real-time on a global level, and, inevitably, with some form of transparent governance. Because, without trust, a currency does not exist. This is its true message.

MATTHIAS KRÖNER, CEO of Fidor Bank

Matthias Kröner is CEO and founder of Fidor Bank, Germany. He has been CEO since 2006. He is responsible for investor relations, corporate communications, strategic development and communities. Fidor is an internet bank, its primary account combines elements of a traditional bank account with internet payments and innovative banking services. Fidor was the first bank to integrate Ripple's payment protocol, allowing its customers to instantly send money in any currency in any amount.

How is Fidor bank doing?

We launched the bank just over five years ago and, looking back, it really has been quite challenging, but also very exciting. It is amazing what you can create within the financial services industry in the past few years with technology, and that fascinates and motivates me extremely.

Regarding 2014, I think we have had a really tremendous year. A really positive outcome with a steep increase in our customers and our user base. All of our KPIs are moving north, and are proof that customer-centric banking is something that people need and want. In comparison to "normal digital concepts" we may have grown faster, but we did not and could not, as we are a bank that is restricted to the [MK1] regulatory capital requirements that are needed to support such growth. In a nutshell, one can say that we are forced to grow profitably and you can only do that as long as you have the capital. That, of course, is not always easy, but in a world of double-digit-valued, powerpoint concepts, this is a well appreciated alternative.

The next steps involve further overseas growth. We announced a while back that we will be a borderless banking partner, simply because we live in an increasingly globalized society, and by the nature of the web, in a borderless environment.

On the other side, it is not a matter of where you locate a company, it's a matter of where you scale it. We have to keep a continuous and close eye on "meta developments" that are happening, and simply cannot ignore them. These are political developments, as in the Ukraine crisis; and economical developments, as in the ongoing European crisis; and social developments, as in the adoption and willingness of people to take on board digital-based innovations.

Now we walk the talk and execute our first steps. We opened a public beta in the UK and we are preparing to launch in the US.

My daily life is already very international. Just take yesterday as an example. In the morning we had a meeting with our MDs for Germany, UK and the US, dealing with the future developments of our customer-centric offers. Then, around lunchtime, we had a discussion with potential partners talking about the Eastern European distribution of the Fidor operating system. In the afternoon, we hosted an honourable guest from the Middle East, discussing several options with us, and at night I was coordinating my next trip to Singapore and New York.

In a recent article I saw that Fidor finds it hard to get a payment partner in the UK. Is that truly the case?

Well, Chris, I am happy you are asking me, because in particular the headline of the online version of that article was absolutely giving a wrong impression of the real developments. But yes, one has to admit, that onboarding to local UK payment-rails is not an easy task, even for a fully EU-licensed and regulated bank; but we have great partners we talk to and I am extremely confident that we will have a solution in the time we planned it.

On the other side, that particular headline caused a very positive reaction, in that we had a series of organisations and people come back to us, asking whether that article was correct and offering their support to us. That was outstanding and was another reason why I love the internet.

What about your launch in Russia, Matthias? I guess, in retrospect, that was bad timing?

Well, yes, obviously that is one of those meta-developments with the issues in the Ukraine that, had we known, we might have planned it in another sequence and priority. Being optimistic though I, first and foremost, still regard it to be a success because, technically, we did make a connection within nine months from our Fidor operating system to the local core banking of our partner, which is simply great.

Second, in the light of this crisis and with all of the sanctions, we had a meeting in Q1 about how to move on and, despite the impression that everything is collapsing in Russia, we are still optimistic to find ways of how to go to market and leverage on the technological developments.

One has to see that, in this case, we do not talk about the risk of a bricks-and-mortar banking approach. We talk about the go to market of a digital approach, and this enables us to be very flexible. Whether that will happen with Fidor brand or not is open; nevertheless, it will be Fidor technology.

And I find it interesting that you are coming into the UK direct and the US through a bank partnership. I guess the model of Fidor is evolving from one that is being a true bank to maybe a software house, or am I mistaken?

Well, in our eyes it is extremely necessary to be a software house if you want to work successfully as a bank within the next five years or, on the flip side, a bank that is not a FinTech company will face tough times. So, in our interpretation, there is no difference.

Talking about technology, we have Fidor TecS, our software house. This, I can say, is one huge differentiator as we eat our own dog food. This means that Fidor bank's customer-centric offer can be seen as the showcase of what you can do with the Fidor operating system.

Coming back to our UK and European approach, we have a German banking license, which is passportable to the rest of the EU. This the

German banking license is a "full service banking license". This means that we can take deposits, grant loans, execute payments and much more, anywhere in Europe. Europe is therefore our home turf, in relation to the banking license and to the technological issues. What we want to do, we can do on our own, and no partner is needed. Step by step we will onboard European customers and service them out of our Berlin-based customer experience company.

In the US and in all other regions, the situation is different because we have no banking license there. As a consequence, we have to think about whether to apply for a banking license in a specific region we are targeting, or to team up with somebody that already has a banking license. For time-to-market reasons number two is definitely the better option, not only in the US, but also in other parts of the world. So we are particularly happy that we have found an entrepreneurial US banking partner with whom we can execute our vision with a mutual understanding and culture.

Why the US market after Europe?
Because we've been asked to come to the US. There have been a number of different parties approaching us, making us think about a go-to-market in the US. You do not imagine how supportive social media is in this? That was one motivation. The other one is pretty easy as, once you show up in the UK, Americans can read your website. In fact, at that point, if somebody likes what we do, there is a huge danger of being copied instantly. That's one of the brutal developments of the network, and so this needs to be anticipated and you proactively have to react on such a potential development.

You claim to bank anything the customer sees of value, from World of Warcraft Gold to bitcoins. How is that thinking evolving?
Well, to be precise: we claim to be open—in a cultural and technical way—for any digital asset category. These could be the ones mentioned, or any other form of digital asset. That means we have the objective to handle and integrate assets that customers regard to be of digital "purchasing-value" or, in other words, a very general description of a currency. But in our eyes this could be more than a traditional currency, such as the Euro.

That is our difference from regular and normal banks. In our mind, even air miles could be an asset class. Data itself is an asset class. Points, coins or whatever that exist in our digital environment can be an asset class, and whatever is accepted to acquire a service or goods is one, too. At the end of the day, this is a very philosophical question that we discuss actively with our community. In that discussion, we also had a comment whether "time" could be a currency and how a bank account could handle that. All that is super exciting and extremely interesting and leads us into blockchain related issues, such as Ripple.

Besides those future-oriented conceptual discussions, we already today have created a multi-asset current account. For example, the Fidor Smart Account offers the ability to trade, send and store precious metals and foreign currencies.

You briefly mentioned Ripple and blockchain. Are those integral to the backbone of what Fidor offers, or are they experiments you are playing with?

It's definitely too early to integrate a blockchain technology into the core of our operating systems, but I am forcing discussions within Fidor to consider how a blockchain technology could affect us and what our position is with that development. This includes a deep look at the risks involved, as well as the opportunities of such a development that is still is in its infancy.

I always use your Facebook *likes* story in my presentations, as it's such a great story about how to build conversation and relevance at low cost. The figures I've been using is that you spend about €100,000 on marketing and on-board a full customer with KYC for around €16.7, which are amazing figures. Is that holding true?

Without sharing too many company secrets, I will not disagree on the figure regarding the cost per new retail customer. The figure for German SME customers is slightly higher. Regarding the €100,000, we have to differentiate that a little in that, talking about brand-related communications, I could say the cost is even zero.

Wow—so how do people find Fidor through Facebook? Or are they finding you through the news and word-of-mouth recommendation?

It is a mix. I think it's a mix of word-of-mouth and social media, blogs, PR and affiliation, embedded in an authentically open concept, and lived by people who stand for what they are doing and what they are offering to their customers.

Are customers switching their main accounts across to Fidor?

Oh absolutely, increasingly. We did a survey most recently in January asking this question. Forty percent said that they were using us as their primary banking association, which I find an extremely impressive figure.

One of the banks I deal with said Fidor is only building customers very slowly, compared to competing with an incumbent with millions of customers. I guess you would have a comment about that?

Yes, I am aware of that point. Well, as said in the beginning, it is a little bit of an ambivalent situation: as an entrepreneurial concept we are forced to grow and we believe in growth as one part of our value-creation. As a regulated entity, we are well advanced to fulfil our capital adequacy ratios. In the combination of those two points, we are growing profitably and generate an impressive customer life-time value. To improve that situation we are currently analysing the market and evaluating our options to increase our regulatory capital with exactly that objective: to fuel and increase our growth.

One of the really intriguing things is that we talk a lot about millennials and the young generation being the natural focus for a digital bank like Fidor, but some say they're not actually the ones that we should focus upon, as they are not financially confident or have not had a mortgage or a job before. The people that are more mature and financially confident may be in their 30s and are the natural digital customer. What demographic indicators help you identify your customers?

It's absolutely proving this thesis. Around 60 percent of our customers are 30–50 year-olds but, if I would make up the range from 40 to 60 year olds, it would still be above 50 percent of the customer base. This is totally proving this thesis. Nevertheless, we do differentiate through social media channels and the customers who come through those channels. One example is that we know that Facebook users are 10 years younger than, for instance, our YouTube audiences.

So looking to the future and the long-term vision of Fidor, do you see the bank growing into a universal, global bank?
As I said in the beginning, we think that a web-based concept is a cross-border concept. We live in a digital society which is doing business not only in a regional context, but having friends all over the planet and going on holidays across all continents, and so on. And we have to understand, that the place of origin of a concept is not necessarily the place of scale. This does not mean that we would leave Germany. That is not what I am saying. I am saying that, from a risk-management perspective, we have to operate in different markets, creating a portfolio that allows us to grow as efficiently as possible.

In the meantime, I hear you are also launching a cryptocurrency bank?
Well, that's a little too much you have heard there. The fact is that we discussed that vision with selected market participants by running a workshop in Berlin in December 2014. That was an extremely interesting and intense event. We had 250 applications for the workshop. We invited 30 market participants and 40 came from all over the planet.

Our wish was that somebody would step up and say that he or she is taking the lead for such a project, but that did not happen. On the other side we have to focus on our geographical expansion, so the vision of a dedicated cryptocurrency bank has to wait a little, simply because we need to be focused.

GUILHERME (GUGA) STOCCO, CEO of Banco Original

A pure digital bank in Brazil, Banco Original was launched by the largest meat-processing firm in the world, J&F. Guga Stocco was brought into the business to shape the bank's vision and shake up the market.

About Banco Original

Banco Original is the first 100 percent digital bank in Brazil, and as such has innovation at its core. Born with state-of-the-art systems infrastructure and no legacy, the bank offers a customer-centred experience for all the services of a traditional bank with transparency and simplicity. Its Open Banking® platform allows FinTech companies to access APIs and datasets, to easily explore the Brazilian market.

Can you tell me a little about your background and how you came to work for the bank?

Sure. I was working for an internet company called Buscapé, which is one of the largest internet firms in Brazil. Buscapé is an online, price comparison website in Brazil and, after several acquisitions, they hired me from Microsoft to run their acquisitions business professionally. I ended up acquiring more than 15 companies between 2011 and 2014. So I was involved with acquisitions and building products. It was a great learning experience to develop a product, then work with the production process itself, and then later do the marketing of it. During this period I was involved with all these new theories of business in a lean start-up. We're involved in new design thinking, new design businesses, new users experiences and more.

I was involved with the theory but I was also doing the practice in a very fast way, and with my team soon developed our own methodology. That's when I was able to envision whether to build, buy or partner. We needed to grow and we were competing with big guys like Google. This means you need to ask: can we build it? If yes, let's do it. If we cannot build, can we acquire a company to do this? If we cannot acquire, then you have to partner. This is a simple "A–B–C" of what building the business means.

In Buscapé's case, everything was done to try to block Google. We did not want Google to get into our market because we were really trying to win in the price comparison "fight arena", and all the commerce needed to do that. What we did was pretty successful, because we became the biggest internet company in Brazil.

After four to five years of doing this, I decided to leave the company to open a venture capital fund, together with one of the founders of Buscapé and with Kees Koolen, who was one of the founders of booking.com.

So Kees became the main linchpin of our fund and we started acquiring some companies here in Brazil. I'm still with the fund, acquiring and selling some companies on the internet, and then in the middle of all of this, the bank called me.

This is part of J&F, who owns one of the largest meat-processing firms in the world. They called me and said: "Hey, we want to open a new digital bank in Brazil." I told him: "I cannot go there because I have the fund, but explain to me a little bit more because I'm quite intrigued to understand what is a digital bank here in Brazil." They explained to me what they wanted to do, and then I looked and said: "That's not quite a digital bank. That's kind of a traditional bank with digital channels. A digital bank's something different, in my opinion." I then showed them what Tencent was doing with WeChat, and how WeChat became a banking service through their messaging platform. I started showing examples of other things from all over the digital world, such as what Starbucks is doing with mobile payments. Then, I told them about all of the new FinTech companies starting up.

It was soon clear that they wanted me to join the bank and I said: "No, I can't. I have the fund, I cannot leave it." Then I had a meeting with Henrique Meirelles, the CEO of the bank and the former Central Bank President of Brazil and he said, "Do whatever you want, but tomorrow you are here", and it's pretty difficult to say no to a guy like him. He's one of the finance masters in Brazil and very well respected, so I said: "OK, let's go and see what happens."

And how is it going?
When I first joined, I began giving lectures to everybody at the bank to explain my vision, how digital works and where we needed to get to. The executive team then said to me: "If you want to stay here at the bank, what do you need?" and I said: "I need to create my own department." As a result, we created the Digital Vision Innovation and Strategy Department to address the challenges at the bank, and to use all the knowledge I gained from 15 years working and making acquisitions on the internet.

I created this department that focuses upon all aspects of innovation because, when we speak about innovation, we're not just speaking about technology. Many of the greatest innovations are not technology innovations. They are business innovations. It's very important to understand that you have a business piece in the middle of all that technology that changes everything. Technology alone is only a tool for you to get there, but the strategy has to be different.

So I created this department and, within the department, I also created the Build, Buy and Partner team. It's a multidisciplinary team, which I call the "Two Pizza Team". I call it the Two Pizza Team because, if you have a team who's going to build some products, their size should be no more than the number of people you can feed with two pizzas. If you need more than two pizzas, it means that the team is too big and you will lose the momentum.

This Two Pizza Team is multidisciplinary and behaves exactly like a start-up within the bank. If you go to a start-up, you have a tech guy, a design guy, the marketing guy and so on. This is like the FinTech companies and like Instagram, Facebook, WhatsApp, and all those guys became like a "Pizza Team". This term was created by Jeff Bezos at Amazon and is working very well in the digital world.

We have this multidisciplinary team focused upon back-end and front-end design, the user experience with growth hacking in mind. Few people know what a growth hacker is, but a growth hacker is the marketer of the future. He's the guy who does marketing without spending money on marketing; he builds the community instead. They have a lot of different skills.

I created this team, the first of its kind within the bank, and then we started working upon our corporate venture, and recognized that we needed to acquire some FinTech companies for the business development side.

The first thing we did was to build a matrix to understand what a bank is, from beginning to end. We looked at all the pieces of the bank, and particularly for the user. We developed this matrix to understand what bank we currently had and what aspects of the bank we didn't have. When you launch a bank, you need to know how it's going to be competitive. This is a key question, because when you launch a big innovation, a new digital bank, you need to know how the competitors will respond. They're firstly going to try to copy us. This means that the only way for us to compete was with innovation. We could not create one innovation, but we had to be innovating every month. If they started copying, no problem. They could copy a few times, but if they keep copying, they would become a follower, not a leader. That was our objective: to make all the banks followers, and for us to gain this competitive advantage.

If they could not copy us then they were going to do something else, and the most likely response would have been to go to the media and try to destroy us. We also needed to be prepared for that and the best way to prepare was through innovation and leadership.

This is all part of the reason why we needed to be fast. We needed to prototype and deploy fast. We needed to fail fast and fail cheap, and make sure that we do not see failure as failure. Failure was learning. If it was fast and cheap, it was good, as we were learning and going to the next stage.

So having that in mind, we started building some products that were not related to the bank. They were related to banking but not bank products.

We were going to go live with these products, and we were also going to acquire companies who were building products that were relevant. This way, we were gaining customers and users and bringing these customers to the bank. The key was to decide when was the right time to do that.

But you're still at the bank?
People don't need banks but people need banking, and that's where we focus upon how we're going to do that. I'm following what the other guys are doing, but not the banks. I'm following what WeChat is doing in China. They just launched WeBank, because they were pretty successful in their banking activities inside WeChat. WhatsApp and Facebook are going to follow what WeChat is doing. Google is doing something similar, as well as Apple and PayPal. Samsung recently acquired Loop Payments, and they're heading the same way.

The key thing to understand here is that the side payment is the beginning for the internet companies to do banking. That is why I'm really looking at what they're doing and trying to replicate a big part of their strategy in a different way.

In other words, how as a brand-new innovation department, can we be successful in banking without knowing anything about banking? This is important because the real focus is upon the users, how the user needs to do things online, and how the user works. We look to the user so that we can understand, for example, the difference in needs between doing banking on a computer versus a mobile. That's quite an easy answer, but one that most banks do not understand because they do not think this way. You only need to look at the graph and understand how people are using the internet: they're now on the mobile internet, not on the computer, because they're not going to have computers. They're going to use computers at work, but in their homes they use tablets or cell phones.

When you are commuting, you don't use your computer, but instead you use your mobile. The mobile can now make transfers and, as you have the camera there, you can pay the bills. It's much easier to do banking on the phone than to do banking on the computer. That's why I'm 100 percent focused on mobile and looking to companies and products that are very successful in mobile, in terms of user experience. Then we replicate that in banking.

Are there any other things feeding into your business model, like gamification?

Yes absolutely. For example, just look at a company like Foldit. This company develops science games. They've developed a game that connects different proteins and the impact different protein connections make to our bodies. One of the big problems is that you have these proteins changing every time and scientists had spent ten years trying to understand how these proteins work. Foldit's created a game where you can combine the proteins; when they launched the game, all the gamers started playing, and they solved the problem that the scientists had spent ten years trying to solve in just three weeks.

The games are more intelligent than science? No, but with a strategy like that you put the right people with the right skills in the right place with the right tools. If you do that you can be much faster and stronger.

For some problems that I'm tackling here I'm still using some of the young guys like gamers, because to engage people I need to do gamification. Who are the best people to do some gamification strategies for us? Our gamers, of course.

In a similar way, when we look at social networking, how are we going to be Googled in a social network? Who is going to use social networks on our behalf? So we use young guys who have used social networks since they were born to be our social network designers. As with Foldit, I just need to put the right people in the right place and then we can have this kind of disruption. Similar to Foldit, we can solve problems in weeks that used to take years to solve.

In the end, we really need to be very open-minded to figure out how the problem works, and that's something that I'm doing. I'm lucky that the bank has allowed me to do that. Sometimes they don't understand what I'm doing, but they say "Okay, do it, let's see what happens. If you make us more competitive and bring us more business as a result, then good for us."

I believe you are using data analytics and bringing in social data, combining it with financial data and using that to assist in getting better deals for the customer.

Yes, that's very important, because the data is there. Why not use it? Why are you not going to use it? I might not get access to social data or feel that it would give me access to too much information about the user. We know exactly what the user wants, so let me give you an example. We're creating a new technology to allow our users to place all of their personal financial objectives inside the bank. That's extremely powerful. Imagine if I have 10,000 people who have given me access to their personal financial aspirations. That's so powerful, but most of the financial people don't understand how powerful it is. Let me show one example:

Imagine if we have 10,000 people and that 3,000 want to buy a car. Now I have access to this financial information and I know that they want to buy a car, so I can act on that. I can go and negotiate a deal for them with a car dealer. If I'm going to buy 3,000 cars, I can get a massive discount. Then I can run the credit score on these guys and, the next time that you open our app, we can offer you the possibility to pay just $500 per month to get this brand new car—it can be preapproved. It is this kind of action that you can take if you can use a lot of social data. You can use that to understand how things behave.

Is this part of what you mentioned as a "concierge"?

On the concierge, if I go onto your Facebook profile and know all the content that you like, then I know the places that you like already and I can personalize things for you. I gave you this example with the car that we're selling as well as financing. In this example, I'm able to understand what you need and I'm going to source it, and save money on your behalf and then offer a very easy user tool so that you can just click and buy on your phone at any time. When I'm combining all of that, I have a powerful thing.

So, social data is important for your bank?

Absolutely. Another example: I want to know if you are really you. If I go to your LinkedIn profile and you have a profile that is only one year old, then I can check facts you provide. If you say: "I've worked five years in a certain company" and you don't have any contacts in that company, then maybe you are not who you say you are. On the other hand, if you've had your LinkedIn profile for ten years and you said that you've worked for five years in a certain company, and you have 300 contacts from that company, and you say that you are the director of that company, then probably you are. It's going to be very hard for you to commit a fraud because, to create that fraud, you need to think ten years in advance. This is why we believe social data is important, and we're going to use that as one of the ways of onboarding customers. When we have all of that, that's pretty powerful and why not use it?

Why don't other banks do this?
I can tell you why the banks do not use this data, it is because the banks are managed by bankers. People that have stayed there for 10–20 years manage them and they just don't know this technology, because they don't use this technology on a daily basis. I can tell you that you need to have a different mix of people. Again, you need to create multidisciplinary teams and you need to be very open-minded for the people to start building products and solving problems. You need to open up your organisation to use everything that's new, and it's going to be very hard for the banks to do that. That brings us to a different thing, that is, culture.

The first step for banks to compete in this new era is that they need to change their culture, and that's extremely hard. Changing culture means changing how people behave, how the bank behaves for their employees and how they (the employees) behave for their clients. It's a very difficult thing to do. The ones who do that well are going to succeed, even if they don't have the right technology in place. If they have the right behaviour, they're going to succeed.

Do you think traditional banks will survive this digital mobile future change?
When people say "Are banks going to die?" the answer is "Yes". The traditional bank is going to die. If its users are all going to use the mobile first

and the bank has not changed, it will die. Some of the banks are adapting and making big bets to succeed in the future. For example, BBVA acquired Simple. Some banks are building a new bank. A completely new digital mobile bank, with a different name. They are then migrating all their clients to this new bank and in the end, as soon as they migrate everybody there, the old bank is going to be turned off with all of its legacy and everything.

You are not going to be able to compete if you have legacy left behind you, because the people who don't have legacy are going to be faster than you. This means that the big banks have 3–5 years to change completely. Forget the way that you're doing things today, create the new things and get in the game philosophically.

This means that the banks that will fail, who will disappear, are the banks that will fail to confront the change. You need to embrace the change—and that's because people who used to do banking, who used to go to the branch, believe that customers will stay in the branch, or keep using the old ways to do banking. That's how they used to do things but, in ten years, they're going to do banking on the mobile, and banking on the mobile means extreme simplicity. It should be extremely simple and direct. You should solve 99 percent of the problems using technology and social data. You use these tools to truly understand the user's needs digitally, and that's a different company. You need different people to develop software. You need different people to solve the problems. You need different strategies. It's a different way to do marketing, as you need to be delivering deep data analytics in seconds, not on a daily basis. You need to be real-time because things change all the time, and they're changing in real-time according to the user's access. This means the bank is no longer in the branch but it is software in the cloud, as that is the only way you can change whatever you want to change at any time you want in seconds.

You need to be testing all the time. You launch your product, you understand if that works, and then you scale that product. Then it becomes a lot of work and then we change that again, and then we scale that again to become a different product. This means the new competitive battle is to be very agile and very fast. So the new banks are different companies. They need different skills. Can the existing banks create this?

Another thing is that when you try to create these digital skills in the same culture, it's going to be very hard because you need to be two banks at the same time. Old bank and new bank.

WeBank in China is not a mobile-first bank. It's a mobile-only bank. If they have $10 million to invest they're going to invest millions to solve problems on the cell phone. They don't even have a website because they want to address the people who are going to be doing banking in the future, not the people who are doing banking today. So they want to create the bank of the future, and the bank of the future is going to be a mobile-only bank. The web is going to be a secondary thing, something that you need to have, but is more related to business, trading and other kinds of things.

CASE STUDIES

THE PHILANTHROPIST

KOSTANTIN (KOSTA) PERIC, The Bill & Melinda Gates Foundation

Kosta Peric is Deputy Director, Financial Services for the Poor, at the Bill & Melinda Gates Foundation, where he leads the digital payments team. From governance through business models to technology, from ideas through architecture to development, he oversees the strategy and grants to deliver secure, reliable and affordable digital payment solutions. Previously, he was the co-founder and leader of Innotribe, the SWIFT initiative to enable collaborative innovation in the financial industry. At SWIFT, he was also the chief architect of SWIFTNet, the backbone worldwide secure network currently connecting 8,000 banks and 1,000 corporations. Kosta summarises his experiences as a technologist, and his interests lie at the point of fusion between technology, finance and innovation. He is also the author of The Castle And The Sandbox, *a book on how to innovate in conservative companies using open innovation.*

About the Bill & Melinda Gates Foundation

Guided by the belief that every life has equal value, the Bill & Melinda Gates Foundation works to help all people lead healthy, productive lives. In developing countries, it focuses on improving people's health and giving them the chance to lift themselves out of hunger and extreme poverty. In the United States, it seeks to ensure that all people—especially those with the fewest resources—have access to the opportunities they need to succeed in school and life.

What is the Bill and Melinda Gates Foundation doing with mobile money and its objective of raising people out of poverty by 2030?
Our vision is that every life has equal value. The Foundation is then active in many ways to realise that vision in health, family planning, agriculture and other markets. One of the facts we found, from quite a lot of substantial academic and experimental research, is that using cash is a key inhibiting factor.

When I say "poor people", I'm really looking at extreme poverty that is currently being defined by the World Bank as people who have, on average, less than $2 of income per day. Remember, that's an average, with many living well below even this level of poverty. As a matter of fact, these people live quite complicated lives from a financial perspective, with many sources of irregular revenues coming from jobs, oftentimes several jobs. Equally, if you think about agriculture, there is of course the irregularity of crops and harvests, with some years of crop failure and famine.

So dealing with cash in these circumstances actually proves to be an aggravating factor from several perspectives. Of course, there is the risk perspective of simply having cash. Secondly, there is the risk of being exposed to a lot of corruption that goes with the distribution of cash. Third, absorbing financial shocks, which is all about financial instruments being available, such as payments, as well as the capacity to save money. We need to help people to manage money in order to have the capacity to finance projects, to pay school tuitions, for children to pay for utilities, and also unforeseen shocks that inevitably come. Good shocks, such as marriage, or challenging shocks, such as death in the family, and so on.

We will all gain from an economy that benefits everyone. That is why we have embarked on this ambitious program that is about financial inclusion and, from our perspective, is really all about digital financial inclusion. This is because the one thing that these people have in abundance, in terms of technology, are mobile phones. Contrary to banks, whose ATMs and branches are nowhere near the people we look at in terms of geographical locations, the mobile phone technology antenna and supporting infrastructure of agents is actually quite close to these people. This is why it is a very natural step to actually use this technology, and that's how the mobile money concept comes into the picture as a key instrument.

The last thing to mention is that mobile money is also helpful for another of our Foundation's strategies. For example, we have found that a lot of our polio, health, agriculture and maternal health strategies rely on workers in the countries who have to be paid, and mobile money is a very helpful enabler for that.

How many people are we talking about who are living on less than $2 a day?

The latest number, which was just updated recently by the World Bank's global database called Findex, is two billion people who live on less than $2 per day, and who are currently without bank accounts. This number actually decreased from 2.5 billion in 2011, which has been a great indicator that the overall focus on financial inclusion is having positive results.

You mentioned remote areas are not served by banks, but can be served by the mobile networks. How will the mobile network bring these people into financial inclusion?

That's where we start discussing some of the technological aspects of how this can work. The most talked about system is M-PESA in Kenya, which is an initiative of a mobile network operator who basically provided a way for people to associate electronic wallets to their mobile phone number. It's an evolution of the airtime concept, because airtime represents value. When you have airtime, you can call on the mobile wallet from the mobile phone. So the mobile wallet is actually an evolution of that concept, where you can offer stored value associated with the SIM card on the phone or, most often, by the provider as value.

Once you have that, then it becomes relatively easy to start talking about sending money from one phone number to another phone number, which is also what M-PESA has done. That transfer can be fast, instantaneous and real-time. It is relatively affordable for the users, because the technology involved is very streamlined and efficient.

Another important point is the onboarding of people to that system; because you need to subscribe people to mobile wallets and then enable them to digitize cash. In other words, to put cash on their account wallet and to take money out of the system as well, which is a natural evolution of the agents that the mobile network operators (MNOs) have to sell airtime. So the agent concept evolves, and they become not only resellers of airtime but also handlers who can bring people on board so that they can cash in and cash out. They add a fee, of course, but now the money is onboarded to a digitized network.

M-PESA is a notable example, but there are others. In fact, one of the fastest growing mobile money implementations is bKash in Bangladesh, who now have over 15 million users, and that is growing fast in terms of transactions and value transferred.

bKash operates on the same concept as M-PESA, being able to send and receive money very easily. The idea is that, in the same way that you send a text message, you can send and receive money. So that's good progress, but we don't see that as the ultimate success. For example, exactly as it was with mobile phones at the very beginning, where it was very difficult to call across network providers, it's the same now when you have an M-PESA wallet.

There are ways around that, and the ideal way to solve this problem is to actually have several providers. In our vision, a single player will never cover the entire geography and customer segments, so inter-operability is also very important. This is not only better because you reach more of the population, but also because it provides for more competitive offerings, which is good because the end user price of all of this is very important. The other aspect that's very important is not only the subscription to mobile money services, but also the capacity to use the money to purchase things.

The Foundation has a focus to bring on more providers and to bring more merchants on board. This is because if the only thing that we achieve is simply that we can cash in, send money and cash out on the other side, then we are just another competitor to Western Union. Our ultimate measure of success is not that. The measure of success is that the money keeps on being digital and keeps on moving, rather than being cashed out. That means you need to have an interoperable environment. That means you have to connect merchants to the network, so that all the users can do much more with it and keep the money inside the system.

And when you talk about such a vision, then of course this becomes almost like a national good, creating a national infrastructure for payments that is parallel to the traditional banking system that's connected to it. This brings up the issue of regulation because, as the system grows transactions, then it must obey certain characteristics and comply to regulations, anti-money laundering, anti-terrorism, Know Your Client (KYC) and more.

The challenge is how to implement, how to deploy such a system, in a way that remains very streamlined so that it can be super-scalable and also very cost effective. When you look at existing traditional financial systems, none of that is actually the case. So this digital financial system needs to have some of the same characteristics, but with a much faster, cheaper technological base.

You mentioned M-PESA, but it is difficult to repeat because it had two distinct unusual features. One was the agency network, which was already in place, and the other is government endorsement and support. How do you overcome those factors in countries that don't have government support or an agency network?

Yes. Indeed, these two things are very important, and were present in some way, shape or form for M-PESA. If we look at a country like Nigeria, for example, none of these things actually exist. There is no specific regulation allowing mobile money and there is a multitude of small players with very little reach individually. This is where, again, if you look at this as a national infrastructure for payments, then this argument of essentially a shared utility or a shared infrastructure makes a lot of sense.

For example, in order to make the system accepted by the regulators, it needs to have things such as a strong, anti money-laundering structure embedded, but if you start asking each and every provider of mobile money services to implement that themselves, then two things will immediately happen. First, the overall cost of the system will dramatically increase; and second, the system will be only as reliable as the weakest of the components or the providers.

What we suggest therefore is that, in countries which start from further away such as Nigeria, there is a very strong argument to provide a shared infrastructure that does certain things all at once from the beginning, on behalf of the community of providers. These things would include fraud management and KYC, as typical examples of such things. These things can be quite tricky to implement and manage. This means that doing it once on behalf of the whole community, and having the regulator look at only one system, makes it a lot easier.

The same argument can be made for agents. In Nigeria, there is a multitude of small providers and they each try to cultivate their own agency networks; but, in fact, what's happening underground is they are poaching agents from each other, and as a result the agent network as a whole is not increasing. So in Nigeria, if you put all of these agent networks together, there's about 15,000 of them. Most are located in the big cities while, in fact, Nigeria needs around 100,000 agents, mostly located outside of the big cities. That's where this notion of seeing the agent network as a shared good, or shared utility among providers, starts making a lot of sense.

To answer your question, it's really about looking at this as a national good that will crack the problem of the costs and reach, rather than trying to simply regulate it and then let everyone have a go, because then we will not reach the objective.

You also mentioned KYC again. What are the challenges in performing KYC in a mobile money environment?

This is an area of huge business and technology innovation that I can see because the poor people that we want to connect often don't have fixed addresses, and it's very rare that they would have all the requirements of the identity schemes that would onboard them to a traditional system. So tiered KYC schemes and identity schemes that rely on digital, such as e-Aadhaar in India, is a whole new, very rich domain of innovation.

Yes, I've read quite a lot about the biometric identity card program in India and, to a large extent, that is the biggest challenge: to actually make sure the people are who they say they are.

That's right. And a way to do that, at huge scales, when we're talking about billions of people, is with biometrics and with new innovative schemes such as the Aadhaar numbering schemes. It's all hugely important as well, and it's an integral part of what we do. It's not at all related to payments, but it's really the basic infrastructure to get people onboard.

What is the Foundation actually doing to make this happen?
We do several things to make this happen. The first is that we always enter into key partnerships with the central banks in the countries where we work because mobile money is money, and therefore has to be regulated. If the central bank doesn't allow for it, then it does not work. This was the case in India, where mobile money circumvented the central bank and was restricted to very specific use cases in very specific domains. We have established a very strong partnership with the central banks in the eight countries we work in (India, Indonesia, Pakistan, Bangladesh, Nigeria, Kenya, Uganda and Tanzania).

The second thing is that we establish partnerships with the private sector players, such as banks, mobile network operators and FinTech infrastructure or service providers. The Foundation does not implement the digital platforms for mobile money systems. That's not our job. Our job is to foster the creation of this system by the private sector players on the ground, either local or regional or global. What we do then is we de-risk the beginning of this implementation with philanthropy capital.

If you look at mobile money systems, digital money systems, it's a question of scale. This is not about charity. It's about making a sustainable business of serving the people but, as we know, the transaction sizes are so small that, in order to make a profit, you need to have a huge scale from the system. You need a huge number of payments to be digital, so that profits can be made through this huge scale. To get to that scale is difficult, because the business might not be material for the providers. They may say: "This is great, but if I need to invest for three years to break even, I just won't do it. I don't have a case for that." This is where we can play a role by providing philanthropy capital.

When I say philanthropy capital, it means that we invest our own philanthropic money with no expectation on any return for our investment.

Our aim is to simply de-risk this for the private sector so that they will engage in this activity, and that ultimately they will see the value and be self-sustainable.

We also work with infrastructure and the large funders, such as the African Development Bank, so it is not all philanthropic capital, as that's infrastructure development capital. It is loans, but they have a huge financing power and so we can also bring these players to the table.

In summary, we will all benefit from an economy that includes everyone. We call this the Level One Project: creating the national infrastructure for digital payments that will achieve this vision. You can read more about it at http://leveloneproject.org.

One of the things needed to make this happen is a cheaper form of value exchange. Is that bitcoin?

No. Our goal is that the payment infrastructure supports the national currency. The majority of the users have to purchase things, to pay schools, to send money and this means that we need to use the national currency. Of course, bitcoin as a currency can be useful in some specific cases, like international remittances. But the major use cases of mobile money will be with the national currency.

What we then need to do is to make the processing and the transactioning with the national currency very affordable. One way to do that, which we have explored in depth, is the use of distributed ledgers and blockchain technologies which, of course, underlie bitcoin.

When we mean affordable, it's really the technology-related processing of transfers that has to be super efficient in terms of costs, as well as the streamlining of the business intermediaries and partnerships to make that happen.

Let us take one example showing the way we would like to see the system work. It's that user-to-user payment transactions are instantaneous and settled immediately, even if they are on different providers. That's objective number one. The consequence of this is that if these users are served by different providers then, of course, the providers have to settle between themselves. That settlement currently takes place once a day in the traditional banking system. This is where the blockchain concept of a distributed ledger can make inter-provider settlements happen much faster than intraday, simply because the way the technology works makes that possible. In this process, there is a reduction of intermediaries and reduction of time, and this will also have very positive consequences by settling several times a day. The outcome is that you actually drastically reduce the risk of one of the providers being unable to settle and reduce the capital requirements needed from them.

So the in-depth operation of the system can benefit greatly from new technologies, and that's why we also see digital payment platforms as separate from, but connected to, traditional banking systems.

In the newsletter for the Foundation that went out in 2015, there is an ambition to raise all people out of extreme poverty, globally, by 2030. Originally, I thought that the ambition was to wipe out poverty by 2035. Has the ambition been modfied, or is it adapting?

No. I think it really depends on what you're looking at. The document you mention is the annual letter of the Bill and Melinda Gates Foundation, our co-chairs, where they expressed their views on this. In parallel with that, there are a number of initiatives at the global level with the United Nations, the World Bank and the so-called Millennium Development Goals (MDGs). These are all the commitments that countries make to reduce poverty in many sectors, and that could be different timescales for these initiatives.

APPENDIX:
THE LARGEST
FINTECH
UNICORNS

1. Lufax—Chinese peer-to-peer lender

Value: $10 billion (£6.3 billion).

What it does: Chinese peer-to-peer loans and financing platform, one of the countries largest. As well as operating online, the company has around a hundred shops in 80 cities.

Why it's hot: Lufax has financed 20,000 loans worth a collective $2.5 billion (£1.6 billion) since launch.

HQ: Shanghai.

Founded: 2011.

Raised: $485 million (£309 million).

2. Square—smartphone card readers, small business loans, and online payments

Value: $6 billion (£3.8 billion).

What it does: Originally focusing on smartphone debit and credit card readers, the company now has various different payment processing offerings and Square Capital, a small business financing operation.

Why it's hot: The company is run by Twitter co-founder Jack Dorsey. Sequoia Capital, Goldman Sachs, and Citi are all investors and the company has major partnerships with Starbucks and Whole Foods.

HQ: San Francisco.

Founded: 2009.

Raised: $590.5 million (£376.9 million).

3. Markit—financial information and data provider

Value: $5.1 billion (£3.2 billion).

What it does: Financial information and data. The company began as a credit derivative pricing platform, which exploded in popularity in the run up to the sub-prime mortgage crisis.

Why it's hot: The company IPO'd on the NASDAQ last year, with stock shooting up over 50 percent on debut. Shareholders include RBS, Goldman Sachs and J.P. Morgan.

HQ: London.

Founded: 2003.

Raised: Public.

4. Stripe—online payment processing

Value: $5 billion (£3.1 billion).

What it does: Online payment processing, letting both businesses and companies accept payment over the internet.

Why it's hot: Fitbit, Pinterest, Twitter, Salesforce.com, Lyft, The Guardian, Kickstarter, and Reddit are some of the notable companies that use it.

HQ: San Francisco.

Founded: 2010.

Raised: $190 million (£121 million).

5. Lending Club—America's biggest peer-to-peer consumer loans platform

Value: $4.7 billion (£3 billion).

What it does: A consumer peer-to-peer loans platform, America's biggest.

Why it's hot: To date it has funded $11.1 billion (£7 billion) worth of loans, with $1.9 billion (£1.2 billion) of that in the last quarter. The company had one of the largest tech IPOs of 2014, raising $900 million (£574.5 million).

HQ: San Francisco.

Founded: 2007.

Raised: Public.

6. Zenefits—free HR software for small businesses

Value: $4.5 billion (£2.8 billion).

What it does: Payroll, HR, health insurance, and compliance management software for small businesses. It offers its platform for free and makes money by charging health insurers a broker fee.

Why it's hot: Revenue grew from $1 million (£640,000) to $20 million (£12.7 million) between 2013 and 2014, leading TechCrunch to call Zenefits one of the fastest growing software companies of all-time.

HQ: San Francisco.

Founded: 2013.

Raised: $583.6 million (£372.5 million).

7. Credit Karma—free credit scores

Value: $3.5 billion (£2.2 billion).

What it does: Provides free online credit reports, offsetting the cost of paying for them with targeted advertising of financial products.

Why it's hot: The company has 35 million users and Google Capital is an investor.

HQ: San Francisco.

Founded: 2007.

Raised: $368 million (£234.9 million).

8. Powa Technologies—makes mobile payment products

Value: $2.7 billion (£1.7 billion).

What it does: Mobile payment technologies both for online and in person purchases.

Why it's hot: The company closed a massive $76 million (£48.5 million) Series A funding round in 2013 and works with retailers such as Adidas, Reebok, Universal Music, L'Oreal, and Carrefour.

HQ: London.

Founded: 2007.

Raised: $176.7 million (£112.8 million).

9. Klarna—online payment processing

Value: $2.25 billion (£1.4 billion).

What it does: User-friendly payment systems for mobile and web.

Why it's hot: In 2014, it processed $9 billion (£5.7 billion) worth of transactions and it deals with 30 percent of all online payments in its native Sweden. Sequoia Capital, the Silicon Valley fund that backed PayPal, is an investor.

HQ: Stockholm.

Founded: 2005.

Raised: $282 million (£180 million).

10. CommonBond—a peer-to-peer student loans marketplace

Value: $2 billion (£1.2 billion).

What it does: Peer-to-peer student loan financing marketplace.

Why it's hot: The company is on track to do $500 million (£319 million) worth of loans by the end of the year and in June began securitizing loans. Former Citigroup CEO Vikram Pandit is an investor.

HQ: New York.

Founded: 2011.

Raised: $253 million (£161.5 million).

11. One97—online platform for shopping online

Value: $2 billion (£1.2 billion).

What it does: Runs Paytm, an online platform that lets people pay bills and shop online. It's India's largest mobile marketplace.

Why it's hot: Paytm has 50 million registered wallets and handles 800,000 orders a day. Uber is a partner.

HQ: New Delhi.

Founded: 2000.

Raised: $585 million (£373.4 million).

12. Prosper—a peer-to-peer lending platform for consumers

Value: $1.9 billion (£1.2 billion).

What it does: A peer-to-peer lending marketplace for consumers.

Why it's hot: Almost $5 billion (£2.5 billion) has been lent over the platform. Backers include former Google CEO Eric Schmidt, famed Silicon Valley VC fund Sequoia Capital, and Credit Suisse.

HQ: San Francisco.

Founded: 2005.

Raised: $354.9 million (£226.5 million).

13. Zuora—software that lets companies take subscriptions

Value: $1.5 billion (£960 million).

What it does: Provides software that lets companies easily take subscriptions.

Why it's hot: Everyone from the Financial Times to cloud storage company Box, Dell, DocuSign, and ZenDesk use the service.

HQ: San Francisco.
Founded: 2007.
Raised: $242.5 million (£154.8 million).

14. FinancialForce.com—sells cloud-based accounting apps

Value: $1.5 billion (£960 million).
What it does: Makes cloud-based financial service apps, covering accounting, billing, revenue recognition, supply chain management, and more.
Why its hot: Numerous big enterprise companies use it, including Hewlett Packard and Lexmark.
HQ: San Francisco.
Founded: 2009.
Raised: $186.3 million (£118.9 million).

15. Oscar Health—online health insurance

Value: $1.5 billion (£960 million).
What it does: Digital health insurance for the post Obamacare era.
Why it's hot: The company took just 16 months to break the $1 billion valuation mark; backers include PayPal co-founder Peter Thiel, Goldman Sachs, and Li Ka-shing, Asia's richest man.
HQ: New York.
Founded: 2013.
Raised: $295 million (£188.3 million).

16. Adyen—an online payment processor

Value: $1.5 billion (£960 million).
What it does: Payment platform that accepts multiple forms and methods of transaction.
Why it's hot: Facebook, Airbnb, Uber, SoundCloud, and Netflix are all customers.
HQ: Amsterdam.
Founded: 2006.
Raised: $266 million (£169.8 million).

17. Xero—makes cloud-based accountancy software for small businesses

Value: $1.4 billion (£890 million).

What it does: Cloud-based accounting software for small businesses.

Why it's hot: PayPal co-founder Peter Thiel was an early investor. CEO Rob Drury announced the company had 500,000 paying subscribers at the start of 2015.

HQ: Wellington, New Zealand.

Founded: 2006.

Raised: Publicly traded.

18. iZettle—makes card readers for smartphones

Value: $1.4 billion (£890 million).

What it does: Makes card readers for smartphones to let independent traders and small businesses accept payments.

Why it's hot: A "couple of hundred thousand" iZettle terminals are in use across Europe, according to CEO Jacob de Geer, and 46 percent of card readers in Sweden are iZettles.

HQ: Stockholm.

Founded: 2010.

Raised: $114.3 million (£72.9 million).

19. SoFi—a marketplace for student loan refinancing

Value: $1.3 billion (£830 million).

What it does: Peer-to-peer student loan refinancing, mortgages, and other types of personal loans.

Why it's hot: It has financed $3 billion (£1.9 billion) of loans to date and is rumoured to be planning an IPO in the next year.

HQ: San Francisco.

Founded: 2011.

Raised: $766.2 million (£489 million).

20. Housing.com—online Indian real estate platform

Value: $1.3 billion (£830 million).

What it does: Indian online real estate platform that also provides home loans.

Why it's hot: Japanese technology giant SoftBank is the company's largest backer, recognising the potential of the property market in a country with 1.2 billion people.

HQ: Mumbai.

Founded: 2012.

Raised: $139.5 million (£89 million).

21. Qufenqi—lets Chinese consumers buy electronics in instalments

Value: $1.3 billion (£830 million).

What it does: An online Chinese electronics retailer that allows buyers to pay in monthly instalments.

Why it's hot: It's raised a huge amount of money in little over a year and is targeting China's fast-growing aspirational classes. Like a lot of Chinese companies, it hasn't disclosed much more than funding, but investors clearly see big growth potential.

HQ: Beijing.

Founded: 2014.

Raised: $225 million (£143.6 million).

22. Funding Circle—a peer-to-peer loan platform for small businesses

Value: $1 billion (£640 million).

What it does: Peer-to-peer marketplace for business loans.

Why it's hot: It has funded £775 million ($1.2 billion) worth of loans since launch and is currently growing its business in America.

HQ: London.

Founded: 2009.

Raised: $273.2 million (£174.4 million).

23. Jimubox—a Chinese peer-to-peer loan provider

Value: $1 billion (£640 million).

What it does: Online peer-to-peer loans for small businesses and consumers.

Why it's hot: The company is part of a wave of so-called "internet finance" companies that have sprung up across China in the last few years and is experiencing explosive growth.

HQ: Beijing.

Founded: 2013.

Raised: $131.2 million (£83.7 million).

24. TransferWise—an international money transfer service

Value: $1 billion (£640 million).

What it does: Online international money transfer with cheaper fees than banks.

Why it's hot: The company has transferred £3 billion ($4.7 billion) since launch and is now doing £500 million ($783 million) a month. Sir Richard Branson and Silicon Valley VC fund Andreessen Horowitz are both investors.

HQ: London.

Founded: 2010.

Raised: $90.4 million (£57.7 million).

25. Mozido—a mobile payment and wallet provider

Value: $1 billion (£640 million).

What it does: White-label mobile payment, shopping, and marketing products. Lets small businesses send out offers to customers and collect loyalty points.

Why it's hot: The company is targeting emerging markets like Mexico, Southeast Asia, and Africa, where a generation of consumers are skipping banking and moving straight to mobile money. Former Google CEO Eric Schmidt is an investor through his early-stage fund TomorrowVentures.

HQ: New York.

Founded: 2005.

Raised: $307.2 million (£196.2 million).

ABOUT THE AUTHOR

Chris Skinner is best known as an independent commentator on the financial markets through his blog, the Finanser.com, as well as being the author of the bestselling book *Digital Bank* and Chair of the European networking forum, the Financial Services Club. He has been voted one of the most influential people in banking by *The Financial Brand* (as well as one of the best blogs), a FinTech Titan (Next Bank), one of the FinTech Leaders you need to follow *(City AM, Deluxe* and *Jax Finance)*, one of the world's top experts on banking according to Klout, as well as one of the Top 40 most influential people in financial technology by the *Wall Street Journal's Financial News*.

Mr. Skinner is the author of a range of books about the financial markets, covering all aspects of innovation and regulation:

Also published by Marshall Cavendish:
Digital Bank, May 2014

Published by John Wiley & Co:
The Future of Investing in Europe's Markets after MiFID, August 2007
The Future of Banking in a Globalised World, October 2007
The Future of Finance after SEPA, May 2008

Published by Searching Finance:
Money for Nothing and your Cheques for Free, September 2010
Socialising the Antisocial Bank, September 2010
It's Banking Jim, But Not As We Know It, September 2010
Not Every Bank is Goldman Sachs, September 2010
The Extraordinary Madness of Banks, September 2010
The Extreme Folly of Governments, November 2011
The City of London: How it Developed into the World's Leading Financial Centre, January 2012
Are Bankers Good or Bad for Society? January 2012
Banking Rebooted (with John Bertrand), August 2014

Definition of terms

Throughout this book I regularly refer to ValueWeb, blockchain, FinTech, digital bank, mobile internet and terms that may be misunderstood or unknown to some readers. I am often asked, for example, to define the phrase "digital bank", the title of my last book. Therefore, for quick reference, I'm explaining the key terms below.

ValueWeb

ValueWeb is a term I've been using to describe the Internet of Value, or Web 3.0. It is the new generation of the internet that succeeds the World Wide Web and social network. The reason why it has its own moniker is because it is a clear step up from the last generation of the internet. The last generation was about linking people, peer-to-peer, but this generation is about linking people and machines, the Internet of Things. You cannot have a new generation of internet without an easy way to exchange goods, services, *shares*, *likes*, *favourites*, money and currencies, unless the bottom-line infrastructure is based upon something that is real-time and almost free. That means making a reconstruction of everything related to value exchange and value stores—the banking, insurance, capital, asset, fund, investment markets and more—to be fit for a real-time and near free global connection. That reconstruction is based upon two swathes of technology developments working in combination. The technologies are mobile telecommunications and the mobile internet combined with bitcoin cryptocurrencies and its shared ledger system, called the blockchain. These technologies are being used by FinTech start-up companies to rethink value tokens, value exchange and value stores. It is a massive change in world structures and is creating the ValueWeb, or Web 3.0.

Mobile

Mobile is a critical technology, underpinning the ValueWeb. It takes two forms: mobile connections and mobile internet connections. The former is based on first-generation telephones that use SMS text messaging to transfer value. This is hugely transformational for the unbanked or under-developed economies, where large swathes of the population are in poverty. The latter mobile is based upon smartphones being able to use the internet as well as telecommunications connectivity. These are generally the iPhone, Samsung and Android users in developed economies, and are seeing an equally transformational process, as they no longer need branch-based services but can manage all the things they value in apps.

Bitcoin

Bitcoin is an electronic currency system that allows payments to be made directly from person to person without using a financial institution (as you would with a credit or debit card transaction) or another third party (like PayPal). Bitcoin functions on a peer-to-peer computer network rather than through a third party, and is open-source and self-governing. This means that no one is in charge of Bitcoin or, rather, Bitcoin runs itself. The convention is to refer to the technology and network as "Bitcoin" with a capital "B", while referring to the currency itself as "bitcoin".

Blockchain

The blockchain is a general ledger system that records transactions on the internet and is accessible to everyone on the network. That means all of your value exchanges can be seen publicly. No one knows who made the transaction, but the fact there is an electronic shared ledger ensures transactions cannot be made twice. This is why the blockchain is critical, as the entire network relies upon it for trust. All confirmed transactions are included in the blockchain. The integrity and the chronological order of the blockchain are enforced with cryptography, and this is why this technology is spreading, particularly for contractual exchanges. For example, you can use the blockchain to record practically any contractual exchange, from wedding vows to a house sale.

FinTech

FinTech is a new market that integrates finance and technology. It is more than this, however, as it is the backbone of the ValueWeb. Therefore FinTech redefines everything, from how we think of and exchange value, to the tokens we use and how to store value. Many FinTech firms are focusing upon the parts of this process and, as we build this new market, we see a whole new industry being generated. This is because FinTech has become a hybrid of the traditional processes of finance—working capital, supply chain, payments processing, deposit accounts, life assurance and so on—and a replacement of those traditional structures with a new technology-based process that incorporates the mobile internet, cryptocurrencies, gamification and social networking.

Digital Bank
A digital bank is designed for the digital distribution of data through the globalised network of the internet; a traditional bank is designed for the physical distribution of paper in the localised network of the branch.